The Miracle of
Castel di Sangro

Also by Joe McGinniss

The Selling of The President 1968

The Dream Team

Heroes

Going to Extremes

Fatal Vision

Blind Faith

Cruel Doubt

The Last Brother

The Miracle of
Castel di Sangro

JOE McGINNISS

LITTLE, BROWN AND COMPANY
Boston · New York · London

FIRST EDITION

Library of Congress Cataloging-in-Publication Data
McGinniss, Joe.
    The miracle of Castel di Sangro / by Joe McGinniss.
       p.   cm.
   ISBN 0-316-55736-6 (hc)
    1. Castel di Sangro (Soccer team) – History. 2. Soccer – Italy.
3. McGinniss, Joe – Journeys – Italy.   4. Italy – Description and
travel. I. Title.
GV943.6.C35M35   1999
796.33′0945 – dc21   98-51151

10 9 8 7 6 5 4 3 2 1

MV-NY

Printed in the United States of America

For Nancy

And for Dylan, Sebastien, and Lauren

Trentino-
Alto Adige
Friuli-Venezia
Giulia

Valle
d'Aosta
Lombardia
Veneto

Milano ○
(Milan)
Brescia ■
Verona ■
Padova ■
(Padua)
Venezia ■
(Venice)

Torino ■
(Turin)
Cremona ■

Piemonte
Emilia-
Romagna
Bologna ○

Genova ■
(Genoa)

Liguria
Empoli ■
Lucca ■
Firenze ○
(Florence)
Ravenna ■
Cesena ■
Le
Marche

N
↑

Corsica
(France)

Toscana
Umbria
Civitanova ○

Lazio
Pescara ■
Chieti ○
Abruzzo

Roma ○
(Rome)
Castel di Sangro
Molise
Foggia ■

Campania
Bari ■

Napoli ○
(Naples)
Basilicata
Puglia

Salerno ■
Lecce ■

Adriatic Sea

Sardegna

Tyrrhenian Sea

Cosenza ■

Calabria

Ionian Sea

Palermo ■
Reggio di
Calabria ■

Mediterranean Sea

Sicilia

0   100 miles
0   150 km

■ 1996–1997 *Serie B* town/city   Map provided by Fodor's Travel Publications, Inc.

Years have gone by and I've finally learned to accept myself for who I am: a beggar for good football. I go about the world, hand outstretched, and in the stadiums I plead: "A pretty move, for the love of God."

And when good football happens, I give thanks for the miracle and I don't give a damn which team or country performs it.

– Eduardo Galeano

The Miracle of
Castel di Sangro

CASTEL DI SANGRO PLAYERS

FORWARDS (Attaccanti)

Gionatha Spinesi   Andrea Pistella
Giacomo Galli   Daniele Russo
Danilo Di Vincenzo   Luca Albieri

MIDFIELDERS (Centrocampisti)

Left	*Center*	*Center*	*Right*
Claudio Bonomi	Guido Di Fabio	Robert Alberti	Tonino Martino
	Paolo Michelini	Domenico Cristiano	Daniele Franceschini

DEFENDERS (Difensori)

Left	*Center*	*Center*	*Right*
Pierluigi Prete	Luca D'Angelo	Davide Cei	Pietro Fusco
Fabio Rimedio		Antonello Altamura	Filippo Biondi

GOALKEEPER (Portiere)

Massino Lotti
Roberto De Juliis
Pietro Spinosa

Prologue

In 1994 I traveled to Italy in pursuit of a fresh passion. During the first week of December, I was riding a train from Padua to Rome, where four days later my new friend Alexi Lalas would play soccer.

Lalas was the tall, bearded redhead who had been a star of the 1994 United States team in the World Cup of soccer, a tournament that, like the Olympics, is held once every four years in a different country and had taken place that summer in America. So well had Lalas played that he'd attracted attention from the club representing Padua in the Italian *Serie A*, the best soccer league in Italy and the world. He'd signed a contract with Padua and moved to Italy in August. Three months later I had followed, hoping Lalas might let me spend some time with him so that I could learn more about this game that had quite recently become my obsession.

Both Alexi and his girlfriend, Jill McNeal, had been more than hospitable, devoting extravagant amounts of time to me. But now it was December, and after watching Lalas play this one last match, it would be time for me to go home.

I had just taken my seat on the train to Rome when a man spotted me reading a copy of *La Gazzetta dello Sport*. (I'd found that reading it in public was an infallible way to meet Italians. Its pink pages made it unmistakable, while the fact that I clearly did not look Italian invariably engendered a curiosity that overcame reserve.)

So the man, who was perhaps in his late thirties, with a medium build and brown hair, was wearing a business suit and conservative necktie, and spoke impressively good English, asked if I was British. No. Dutch? No. Norwegian? No. Not German, surely? No, actually I'm American.

I might as well have thrown a glass of cold water in his face. *"No!"* he cried. *"Non è possibile!"* No American could be reading *La Gazzetta dello Sport,* because it was well known the world over that Americans did not care about soccer.

Naturally, we got into a conversation. He was an army air corps paratroop commander who had just been to Padua to face court-martial on charges of embezzlement. He was based in Grosseto, on the Tyrrhenian coast, southwest of Siena. Only one hour earlier he'd been found not guilty and was understandably relieved. But already that paled next to his having met an American who actually liked soccer.

And who not only liked it, but who, even then, knew a fair amount about it, especially the Italian variety. Less than three months earlier, my wife, Nancy, and I had been to our first match at the San Siro in Milan – the La Scala among the world's soccer stadia – but even before that, we'd followed the Italian team closely enough during the World Cup so that I was able to dazzle this paratrooper with what, coming from an American, seemed a dizzying array of names and arcane facts (though any eight-year-old in Italy could have re-cited them in his sleep).

Before his posting to Grosseto, he'd been an aide to the Italian NATO commander in Portugal. (It was in preparation for that job that he'd become so fluent in English.) He was now engaged to the woman who had finished fourth in the Miss Portugal contest of 1992, he proudly told me, but prior to meeting me the most amazing moment of his life had been when he'd gone to a Christmas party at the U.S. embassy in Lisbon and had had to use the bathroom and when he'd reached for the toilet paper, the roller played "The Star-Spangled Banner." Forever after he had thought of America as a magical land because not only did it have Disney World and Hollywood and Las Vegas, but it supplied its embassies with toilet paper that played the national anthem.

And I, apparently, seemed equally fantastic. He said, No, no, I must not go directly to Rome. There were still four days before the match. I must come with him to the town of Orbetello, where he now lived, south of Grosseto, so he could display to his friends and colleagues this American who knew about soccer.

Thus, when we changed trains in Bologna, he went directly to a pay phone and called my hotel in Rome to cancel my reservation, and then called about eight people in Grosseto and Orbetello to tell them this science-fiction story about meeting me and that he would actually bring me to meet them! – and also to say he'd been found not guilty and would not have to go to prison for twenty years.

I should say that everything was amplified considerably by the fact that I was carrying an A.C. Milan traveling bag and that this man – whom I have always thought of as the Major, although he quickly had told me his name – was a *tifoso,* or rabid fan, of A.C. Milan, the club that had won the *Serie A* championship for the past three years in a row.

Moreover, that very day A.C. Milan was in Tokyo playing against Velez Sarsfeld of Argentina in what was, and is, billed as the world championship of clubs: a single match in which the winner of the previous season's European Champions Cup plays against its South American equivalent.

In reality, if the European representative is Italian, as it usually is, it's a huge bother for the players, who have to fly to Tokyo and back during the middle of the week, while still maintaining a full *Serie A* schedule, but the prize money is rich enough that for club management it's a very lucrative cherry, easily picked.

Within Italy, however, this Toyota Cup, as it's called, is considered more a curiosity than a match that induces passion and hysteria . . . except, as I quickly learned, in the Major. For him, *nothing* A.C. Milan did, had done, or had ever had done to them was taken lightly.

As it happened, I'd watched the first half of the match before leaving my hotel for the train, so I knew the score at that point was 0–0. But the match would be shown again in prime time for those particularly disadvantaged Italians, such as the Major, who were being court-martialed or for some other reason had been unable to take a weekday morning off work in order to watch a soccer match from Japan (as well as for the millions who, assuming a Milan win, would want to see it again).

I mentioned to the Major that I'd just seen the first half before boarding the train, and that – "NO!" he screamed. "No, no, no, no, no! You must not say nothing that occur because tonight in Orbetello, in my apartment, we will watch this together, and I must not know nothing!"

But surely, I said, somewhere on our journey we are going to learn the final score, however inadvertently, for this is Italy and people will be speaking of the match on the trains and at the station when we change again (which we would have to do in Florence).

"No, no, no, no, no! This must not 'appen! It is a weekday, is December, the train are not full, and you and I, we sit by ourself and never stop the conversing so in accident we do not 'ear the score. And in Firenze station I plug my ears and walk behind you with my eyes in the ground, so you can look ahead to be sure that no news of the match is display."

Which he did, tearing pieces from my *Gazzetta* and shoving them into his ears, which did not seem the most comfortable or even effective way of plugging them, but already I understood a little of the mania that soccer produces, and had in fact already been affected by it, or else I wouldn't have been there, so I knew enough to let him plug his ears in any way he chose.

When we got off the train in Florence, he walked along behind me like a blind man, one hand gripping my shoulder, with pieces of pink newspaper sticking out of his ears. And nobody gave us a second look: this six-foot-three American leading an Italian gentleman in a business suit and necktie with pink newspaper sticking out of his ears, into the main terminal of the station. It is not merely a cliché that the people of Florence are not easily flustered.

The express trains did not go to Orbetello, so eventually, as late-afternoon darkness fell, the Major and I found ourselves on what must have been as local a rail line as existed in all of Italy. The combination of the heat in the shabby coach and the cold outside steamed up the windows, which the Major took to be an almost God-sent blessing because it meant that as he spoke about great moments in the history of A.C. Milan (which he did, fervently and ceaselessly), he could now illustrate his lecture by diagramming famous plays on the fogged-up window of the train.

We rode and we rode and we rode, and he drew lines on the window with his finger and kept saying to me, " 'Ave a look! 'Ave a look!" but then got so excited by his x's and o's that he lapsed into Italian, which at that point I could neither speak nor understand. Finally, at 7:30 P.M., we reached Orbetello.

We'd never had lunch, what with changing trains and all, and I was desperate to eat. But the videotaped replay of the match was scheduled for an 8:30 broadcast, and the Major said we did not have time for a respectable dinner before then, and besides, a restaurant would be the most dangerous place to go in terms of not learning the score. As soon as the match was over, however, he promised me a magnificent meal in the finest restaurant in all of Orbetello (of which there must have been about three altogether). At this point, however, we had to proceed directly to his apartment.

He'd parked his car at the station, and it was only a ten-minute drive. The apartment was a perfectly typical and featureless sort of middle-class residence in which an unmarried Italian man might live. By the time we'd washed up, it was 8 P.M. and the Major began to pace nervously in front of his television set while I looked at about 5,000 pictures of the woman who had finished fourth in the Miss Portugal contest of 1992 and who was indeed good to look at, but maybe not 5,000 times. It occurred to me at about this point to ask the Major why we were not watching the match in a restaurant with his comrades in arms, sworn to silence, for always in Italy the viewing of an important match is a significant social experience.

Because, the Major told me, this was *A.C. Milan.* And when A.C. Milan played, he watched alone, or only in the company of someone such as myself who would know enough to keep his mouth shut during the match and not disrupt the Major's concentration.

The match began. As the Major watched, in utter silence, totally fixated on the screen, he began to perspire. Within fifteen minutes – though absolutely nothing of consequence had happened – sweat was pouring from his forehead, and large stains had begun to spread darkly from the underarm area of the blue shirt into which he'd changed. Half an hour into the match, his entire shirt was as soaked as if he himself had been playing.

At halftime, he stared at me with a look of utter misery on his face: forty-five minutes had elapsed and still Milan had not scored against these Argentines! He said he needed to lie down. When he returned, only seconds before the second half began, I noticed that he'd toweled off his face and changed his shirt.

He took his seat, which was about three feet from the screen, on a frail, straightbacked wooden chair. (I was sitting in a comfortable armchair, about ten feet away, and slightly off to one side.) Six minutes into the second half, the Milan defender Costacurta fouled a Velez player in the penalty area, and the Argentine team converted the penalty kick to take a 1–0 lead. Because it was totally dark in his living room except for the glow of the screen, I could not see this, but for the first and only time in my life I could actually feel someone turn pale. And the foul had been so obvious that he could not even curse the referee!

Six minutes later the same Costacurta (a member of the Italian national team, then and now, incidentally) attempted to kick the ball back to Rossi, the goalkeeper, but did so with such inappropriate casualness that an onrushing Velez Sarsfeld player, to whose presence Costacurta had seemed totally oblivious, got to it first and put it quickly into the net: 2–0 in favor of Velez Sarsfeld.

And that was the score at the end.

At the final whistle, the Major leaned forward in his chair and turned off the set. Then he took the straightbacked wooden chair and turned it so that when he sat again, he was facing me directly, from about five feet away.

"In the spring," he said, "the floods 'ave come in Torino. They wipe out every thing for me. My 'ouse, where I was born and grow up, she is gone. Destroyed with the floods. And my mother, she 'ave then suffer the emotional collapse so bad, I must go there and put this lady in the . . . *manicomio* . . . in English is . . . okay, 'ospital for the people with no mind anymore. The crazies. So all I 'ave the floods take."

He looked over his shoulder at the television set. Then he looked back at me. "And now this," he said. "And now this."

He took a deep breath. "I am sorry, but I cannot take you for the dinner. But Orbetello, she is small, no trouble for you to find the restaurant. Now, 'owever, it is necessary that I be with myself. I am sorry. I take a walk. I take a long walk with myself. You 'ave a good meal. You 'ave a good sleep. Tomorrow maybe is better. We will see."

"I'm really sorry," I said. "About the floods. And about tonight."

"Thank you. But in truth is for me to be sorry. Because a man does not put his troubles on his friends. And already you are my friend. I should 'ave just find out the score in Bologna."

Then he walked out the door. And he didn't come back. I waited for him all day Saturday and again stayed in his apartment on Saturday night. I did not know whom to call or what to do in order to see if he was all right, and I could not speak the Italian necessary to find out, and Orbetello was not a town where English was spoken.

And so, on Sunday morning, as I had to, I boarded the lone train for Rome, leaving behind a note thanking the Major for his hospitality and saying I hoped he was all right and that we would be able to stay in touch with each other.

The next day I had to return to America, and I never heard from him again. Although I wrote to the military authorities in Grosseto and later in Rome, giving his name, and to the town officials of Orbetello, and even to officials in Turin, I never was able to find out what had happened to him.

By June I began to fear the worst, and still do. The Major might have survived the weekend, but given his suffering in the aftermath of the floods, I doubt he could have made it through a season in which A.C. Milan not only failed to win the championship but fell ignominiously to fourth place.

Part I

1

The day before I went back to Italy, I got a fax from a man named Giuseppe. The news it contained was not good.

> As I've promised, I take you the details of your arrive. It is not easy to go from Rome to Castel di Sangro: we are in a montain zone (800 m on sea level; much than 200 km from Rome) and you'll take the train to arrive.
>
> If you are at 7:35 A.M. on Fiumicino Airport in Rome, you'll be able to take a taxi to go to Termini Railway Station to take the 11:50 train from Rome to SULMONA. The arrive is on 15:06 P.M. Sulmona is at 150 km from Castel di Sangro and I'll be at Sulmona station. Excuse me, but I'm very busy in this days before the first match of the championship for some manifestation about Castel di Sangro and it is very impossible for me to be at Rome as I want. . . . But we are mointain people and, don't worry, we are used to combact against difficulties. As Lilliput people in a Gigant World.

So Giuseppe would not meet my plane after all. I flew to Rome anyway, of course. But as soon as I wheeled my luggage cart through customs, and the horde of cab drivers descended upon me, I picked the first one.

"How much to Sulmona?"

"Five 'undred thousand."

"Four," I said.

He motioned with his thumb. "Follow me." And so I was off to the Abruzzo, well in advance of the 11:50 from Rome.

Italy is composed of twenty regions. Some are legendary, others extremely popular with foreign tourists, and still more, though not as well known to outsiders, prized by the Italians themselves. And then there is the Abruzzo.

Frommer's 1996 guide to Italy describes it as "one of the poorest and least visited regions" in the country. "Arid and sunscorched . . . prone to frequent earthquakes, the Abruzzo is . . . impoverished and visually stark." It is a region, says another guidebook, "in which there is little of interest to see and even less to do."

This reputation was not acquired overnight. Nathaniel Hawthorne visited in the nineteenth century and wrote even then that the region was "without enough of life and juiciness to be any longer susceptible of decay. An earthquake would afford it the only chance of ruin, beyond its present ruin."

And that was *in* season. The English poet Swinburne, for reasons never adequately explained, attempted to penetrate the Abruzzo's mountainous defenses in the winter of 1879 but was driven back by "as outrageous a blast of snow as any I've ever faced." He returned to Rome and did not try again.

As for the inhabitants, the English travel essayist Norman Douglas wrote in the early years of this century that "their life is one of miserable, revolting destitution." And Frommer's pointed out more recently that "many of its people have emigrated to more prosperous regions," leaving behind only "clannish local families," described in another book as "atavistic and introspective."

"This is still a land," author Tim Jepson has written, "that could provide settings for a dozen fairy tales, with its wolves and bears and sturdy country folk. . . . Villages on snow-dusted hills are wreathed in mist amid the wild mountains, deep valleys and dark forests; and ancient are crafts practiced for their own uses, not for the tourists."

But I was no tourist. For better or worse, I had business in the Abruzzo. My destination was the remote town of Castel di Sangro, which some contend means "castle of blood" in the local dialect.

The town is shielded from outsiders by what one reference book describes as an "inaccessibility extreme even by the standards of the Abruzzo." It is located almost 3,000 feet above sea level. Winter lasts from October to May, and in all seasons bestial winds gust down upon it from higher mountains above.

On one side, Castel di Sangro is bordered by the Abruzzo National Park, which still contains wolves and brown bears, as well as more than thirty species of reptile. On the other side lies the immense and silent Valle della Femmina Morta, or "valley of the dead woman." Strangers to the region who ask how such a name came to attach itself to such a vast and empty expanse reportedly receive only shrugs or the shaking of heads in response.

Beyond the valley rises La Maiella, an enormous limestone massif cut by deep and treacherous canyons and containing more than fifty peaks, the highest of which, Monte Amaro, or "the bitter mountain," reaches an altitude of almost 10,000 feet. Again, the origin of the name has been lost in the mists of time and legend.

"This is a landscape," warns yet another guidebook, "that should be approached with caution." Or, in the alternative, not approached at all. Yet so deep in the grip of mania was I that I was not only approaching but preparing to plunge into its core: alone, knowing no one, speaking not a word of Italian, yet committed to staying for more than nine months.

My arrival came on a warm Saturday in early September of 1996. The driver dropped me at the deserted Sulmona train station just before noon. All seemed tranquil and pleasant. Leaving my mass of luggage in the somewhat drowsy custody of a ticket agent, I walked a few hundred yards into the center of the city (population: 25,000), ate a moderate lunch, and returned to the station. I napped intermittently for an hour or two, lying on the platform next to the tracks, my head resting on a duffel bag and dappled sunlight falling on me through late-summer leaves.

In midafternoon I heard a train whistle in the distance. *My* train! The 11:50 from Rome. I looked at my watch: 3 P.M. Right on time. Leaving my luggage again, I walked to the front of the station, looking for someone who might be Giuseppe, hoping that some new "manifestation" had not prevented him from coming to Sulmona.

Just then, a small, battered automobile entered the parking lot at high speed and jerked to a halt. Out bounded a man who appeared to be in his mid-twenties, with dark hair and an alert look in his eyes.

"Giuseppe?" I called.

He looked at me and recognized immediately that I must be the *scrittore americano*. But he looked puzzled. "Joe?" he said, looking from me to his watch.

"Yes, yes, all my bags are just around the other side."

"But the train. She is not arrive."

"No, no, but I get ride. Not important. Here, I'll drag the bags around front."

Giuseppe seemed perplexed but did not pursue it. If a man pursued everything that did not make sense, he'd never get anything done.

As soon as the bags were safely stowed – the last two rising from my lap to the top of my head as I scrunched into the front seat of his tiny car – we were off to Castel di Sangro, or so I thought. Giuseppe drove at what felt to me like a recklessly high speed, but I'd soon learn it was well below the norm. I couldn't tell whether not being able to see the road through my suitcases made it better or worse.

Before I could even attempt conversation, I heard a shrill chirping next to me and Giuseppe pulled a cellular phone out of his pocket and began speaking even faster than he drove. As soon as that call was concluded, he made one of his own, looking intently at the buttons, not at the road, as he tapped them in rapid succession. He spoke for only ten seconds, then signed off with a quick burst of *ciao*s. But immediately he made another call. Then he received two more. He made one, then received three in a row. I was trying to keep score. Another two calls incoming, three outgoing. Giuseppe 5, Incoming 9. *"Ciao,"* he would say toward the end of each. *"Ciao . . . ciao, ciao, ciao . . . ciao ciao ciao . . . ciaociaociaociaociao."*

As I would soon learn, one of the fiercest everyday competitions among Italians who speak to one another by cellular phone is to see who can cram the most *ciao*s into the close of a conversation. To win an undisputed victory, you must not only have muttered the word more times than your conversational opponent but also have gotten in the last *ciao* of all, clicking your OFF button even as you utter the word.

Eventually, he slipped the phone back into his pocket, looked at me, and said, "Excuse." Clearly, the time for our conversation had arrived. Giuseppe gazed at me earnestly. This meant, of course, that his eyes were not watching the road, which, though I myself could not see it through my luggage, seemed – from the motion of the car and the straining of its feeble engine – to have begun the ascent of a mountain.

"You can see?" I said, pointing toward his front windshield.

He looked puzzled, glanced in that direction, then looked back at me. "*Sì . . . sì, sì, sì.*"

"No. I mean, 'see.' "

He laughed gleefully. *"No . . . sì. No . . . sì.* What you meaning, *'no, sì?'* Yes, no in *inglese, no?"*

"Sì," I said. "I mean, yes."

He glanced briefly back toward the road, turned the steering wheel a bit, then looked back at me. "I no understand too much the English, no? I have not speak this. Is easier to have write, yes? Not for the speak."

"Sì," I said. *"No.* But Castel di Sangro. Much far?"

"Castel di Sangro?" He pronounced the name with an incredulity that suggested he'd never before heard it in his life.

"*Sì.* We go Castel di Sangro, yes? I mean, *sì?"*

"No, no, no, no, no. I take you for arrive Roccaraso."

"Where?"

"Roccaraso. But you no worry. Not far."

"But I'm going to Castel di Sangro."

Giuseppe shook his head. "Not possible," he said. "No arrange."

"What do you mean?"

"Castel di Sangro no hotel. Roccaraso many. For much *schee.* You like the *schee?"*

"Schee?"

"When very much the snowing. *Schee.* Like Tomba."

"Oh, *ski!* I understand. Well, no. Not really. I no *schee.* But, Giuseppe, what about Castel di Sangro?"

"No problem. I say you – you no worry. You Best Western Roccaraso. You sleep. At later I call with you. Very busy this days. But Best Western okay, okay? No problem. You no worry."

Then he got another half a dozen phone calls – his *ciao ciao ciao ciao ciao* firing like the pistons of his engine – and eventually pulled off the road and into a parking lot. Looking out my side window, I could see, sure enough, a Best Western motel.

Stumbling out of the car with suitcases falling all around me, I could see that we were on a strip of road lined with motels, which were separated, it seemed, only by sporting-goods stores that had pairs of skis and colorful ski parkas in the windows.

"Don't worry. No problem. Don't worry," Giuseppe said. "Much events for me now. You have sleeping. I calls later. No problem."

"What time, Giuseppe?" I pointed at my watch. "At what time will you call?"

He tossed both hands upward and exhaled sharply. I was meant to understand, I think, that my question was impossible to answer. How could he know when he would call when he had much events and was very busy this days? "Don't worry," he said. "No problem."

"Okay, Giuseppe. No problem. And . . . thanks for the ride. I mean, *grazie*."

"*Prego*. See, write is more easy than talk, no?"

"Yes. I mean, *sì*. But, Giuseppe, I have a room here?"

"*Sì, sì,* I tell you no problem."

"Okay. Good. No problem. But, Giuseppe – where *is* Castel di Sangro?"

"You don't worry. She not far. *Ciao, ciao*."

"Okay. *Ciao*."

"*Ciao, ciao, ciao*."

"*Ciao, ciao, ciao,* Giuseppe."

"*Sì. Ciao ciao ciao ciao ciao*." Then he rolled up his car window and drove off, already making a new call on his cell phone.

2

I retain clear memories of what my life was like before. In many ways, I suppose it was better. My children respected me. My wife and I shared numerous interests. I had friends. I enjoyed music. I read books. That I would grow suddenly obsessed with "football" (the term used throughout the world to describe the sport that is called "soccer" in America) seemed no more likely than my becoming an astronaut.

And there was nothing gradual about the onset. I simply woke up one morning in late spring of 1994 suddenly overwhelmed by enthusiasm over the fact that the United States that summer would host the World Cup, a competition held every four years to determine the world's champion of soccer. That I had never seen a single match in all my life did not seem relevant in the least.

Desperately craving information in that pre-Internet age, I made forays to obscure bookstores far afield, returning on good days with volumes that contained not only statistical summaries of all World Cup matches played since the tournament was first held in 1930 but also descriptions and analyses of the twenty-four national teams that would be competing in America. I began blurting out names like Frank De Boer, Gheorghe Hagi, and Gabriel Batistuta, and statements such as "Did you realize that this is the first time Norway has qualified since 1938?"

My doctor, who was also a friend, watched a preliminary match in my company and at its conclusion only half jokingly attributed my condition to a ministroke, one that – while leaving all motor functions intact – had apparently disabled that portion of the brain that normally protects Americans against any appreciation of soccer or even interest in the sport.

In retrospect, I can see that a less alarming explanation might have been that for a variety of reasons of no great relevance to this story, I was psychically ripe for a consuming passion that had no connection to any of my previous experience. In any case, it matters not. As Kierkegaard once observed: "The absurd is not one of the factors which can be discriminated within the proper compass of the understanding."

Less than two weeks later the World Cup began. From the tournament's first day I was drawn irresistibly to my television set, watching matches both live and taped at all hours. And the manic nature of my new enthusiasm was evident from the start.

Germany, the defending champions, opened the tournament with a match against Bolivia. In the second half Bolivia sent on a wild-eyed, long-haired substitute named Etcheverry, who within sixty seconds was ejected for what the referee deemed an excessively violent tackle of a German.

I grew irate. *"What?!"* I screamed at my television set. "That's *unbelievable!* He can't be sent off for *that!*" It was as if I had been born and raised in La Paz, such was my anger (the irrationality of which was compounded by the fact that at that point I had only the most passing acquaintance with soccer's rules, and thus no basis whatsoever for questioning the referee's judgment – much less at the top of my lungs).

Worse, between matches I would babble incessantly to family and friends about such heretofore unknown (to me) eminences as Stoichkov of Bulgaria, Dahlin of Sweden, Bergkamp of Holland, Bebeto of Brazil, Omam-Biyick of Cameroon, and even a chap named Saeed Owairan of Saudi Arabia. *"Did you see that goal against the Belgians?!"*

The United States was competing, but I must confess that patriotism played no part in my obsession. I was as enthralled by the draw between Spain and South Korea as by America's shocking upset of Colombia. And when I learned on short notice that tickets were available for a June 25 match at Foxboro Stadium, outside Boston, three hours from my western Massachusetts home, it mattered little that the two teams playing would be Nigeria and Argentina.

Nor, despite my coming to admire the Nigerians immensely, was I overly disturbed, at day's end, by the fact that Argentina had won. What forever changed the world as I had known it was not the outcome but the sheer spectacle and grandeur of the event: the passion, both in the stands and on the field; the color, the flair, the intensity; as well as the grace, athleticism, and subtlety involved in the playing of the match itself.

Until then, I'd been able to satisfy my craving simply by watching matches on television. But that first taste of the real thing swept me into a new dimension. To use a sexual metaphor (for which I might apologize, except that throughout the world – outside of America and, I suppose, Canada – it is recognized that man's two most powerful passions are those excited by sex and soccer) the difference between watching on television and being there proved the same in regard to soccer as with sex.

Circumstances restricted me to only one more live match, in Foxboro, on July 5. Again one team was Nigeria, which had survived the tournament's round-robin first phase despite its loss to Argentina. This time, however, the opponent was Italy, which, despite being one of the pretournament favorites, had played so poorly in the first round that only by the thinnest of statistical margins had it even qualified for the single-elimination phase, in which the sixteen remaining countries would compete.

Nor, for almost all of that insufferably hot and humid afternoon in Foxboro, did Italy seem even slightly improved. Indeed, my second live match was looking as if it would become one of the more significant upsets in soccer history. With only two minutes remaining, Nigeria led, 1-0. The 55,000 spectators – all that Foxboro Stadium could hold – had screamed themselves hoarse, had been swept along the entire gamut of human emotion, and, as the end neared, were as emotionally exhausted as were the players physically.

But just when it appeared certain that no one on either side could possibly have anything left to give, physically or emotionally, a slight and graceful Italian named Roberto Baggio, employing a deft, controlled flick of his right foot, scored a goal. This same Baggio scored again in overtime, and Italy won.

A Buddhist who stood only five foot seven, weighed only 145

pounds, and wore his hair in a ponytail, the twenty-seven-year-old Baggio had salvaged the pride of his nation.

I was enthralled. Now my obsession had a focal point. Baggio brought to the game a degree of elegance, a grace, and an aura of magic that I'd not before seen displayed in any sport.

Four days later, in the quarterfinal against Spain, Baggio did it again, scoring with only two minutes remaining to give Italy a 2–1 win. And then at the Meadowlands in New Jersey on July 13, he scored two astonishing goals within four minutes to assure Italy of a 2–1 triumph over rugged Bulgaria.

Baggio had scored five goals in three of the most important matches he'd ever played. (And this in a sport in which the leading scorer in any given league around the world would average approximately .75 goals per match.) Baggio's had been a performance that ranked with the greatest of individual World Cup achievements since the tournament was first held in 1932.

Unfortunately, late in the Bulgaria match he injured a hamstring muscle so severely that at the end he left the field in tears, certain that he would not be able to play in the final, when Italy would face Brazil in the Rose Bowl four days later.

And, indeed, he was not fit to play. But with so much at stake, he took the field anyway, though no competent sports physician (or coach) should have permitted him to do so. He hobbled gamely through ninety minutes of scoreless play against Brazil, and then through the thirty minutes of overtime, which also ended without a goal having been scored.

The match, and world championship, now would have to be decided by penalty kicks. Five players from each team would try to kick the ball into the opponent's goal (which was twenty-four feet wide and eight feet high) from a distance of twelve yards, with only the opponent's goalkeeper allowed to try to block the shot.

Of the first four players from each side to kick, three Brazilians but only two Italians were successful. Baggio was the fifth and last Italian to try. He missed also, and Brazil was world champion. The picture of him standing alone in the center of the Rose Bowl afterward, head bowed, one hand held to his tear-filled eyes, struck me as so wrenching and poignant that for days afterward I could scarcely eat or speak. And I wasn't even Italian!

In mid-September, two months before my stay in Italy with Alexi Lalas, Nancy and I went to Switzerland in the hope that some Alpine hiking might clear my head. But one afternoon we arrived at a small village on the shore of Lake Lucerne and, from a distance of at least fifty yards, I spotted a copy of *La Gazzetta dello Sport* at a newsstand.

La Gazzetta is the best of the three Italian daily papers devoted almost entirely to news and rumors of the world of *il calcio,* which is what the Italians call soccer (literal meaning: the kick). It is printed on shocking-pink paper with jet-black headlines that shriek in oversize type in order to rouse a reader's emotions to fever pitch before he even knows whether it's anger or joy he's supposed to be feeling, which is perfectly in keeping with the operatic hysteria the sport carries into every nook and cranny of Italian life.

And on that tranquil Saturday afternoon on Lake Lucerne, its effect upon me was electric. With one quick glance at the front page, I learned that A.C. Milan was playing a home match the next day against powerful Lazio of Rome. After that, I needed only five minutes of scanning timetables to know that it could be done.

If we got up at 5:30 A.M., I explained to Nancy, and caught the first ferry to Lucerne and then connected to the fast train to Zurich, and then switched to the train that went to Zurich airport, we could make a 12:30 P.M. flight that would have us at the Milan airport by 2 P.M., from which we could take a taxi to the Milan stadium, the San Siro, in time for the 4 P.M. match. Afterward, we could take a cab back to the airport, catch the last flight from Milan to Zurich that night, and be back high in the Alps the next day.

And that's what happened. We reached the San Siro – a multi-tiered temple of adoration to the role of *calcio* in Italian society – a full hour before the match began. And, disbelieving, we experienced true mass hysteria for the first time in our lives. Wave upon wave of urgent, driving, throbbing passion, exemplified by the bursting red flares, billowing pink smoke, and deafening chants from the 70,000 Milan fans by whom we were surrounded, washed over us and crashed against the stadium's concrete decks.

This match did not involve the national team. That group was essentially an all-star squad brought together for the relatively infrequent competitions among countries. With the World Cup over, the

Italian national team's members had returned to their respective club teams to begin the nine-month Italian league season.

Nor was this in any way like watching a World Cup match in America, where courteous deference to the preferences of one's neighbor had seemed the reigning ethic. This was *war!* And Lazio was the enemy, notwithstanding that three members of the Lazio squad had played for the national team only two months earlier and had been supported with the same fervor with which they were now scorned.

The thousand or so Lazio fans who had somehow acquired tickets and come up from Rome were guarded by at least that many police; hemmed in on all sides in one far corner so that none of the flare-throwing, chanting *milanisti* could get at them to do them harm.

For it must be acknowledged that not only did Italians learn to *play* soccer better than the people of almost any other country in the world, they also infused the game with a raw, untamable passion which – as we were witness to at the San Siro – manifested itself on a weekly basis to a degree that was roughly equivalent to the sum total of that produced by *all* the sporting events, rock concerts, political protest movements, born-again Christian revival meetings, civil rights demonstrations, antiwar rallies, and any and all other public displays of emotion ever to have taken place in America.

The intensity hit its first peak just moments before the 4 P.M. starting time as A.C. Milan, in their distinctive red-and-black-striped shirts, took the field. The second and third – each twice as high as the one before – were attained through the brilliance of a dreadlocked Dutchman of Sumatran heritage, one Ruud Gullit, who scored two glorious goals for Milan; the second – which gave Milan a 2-1 victory – coming only seconds before the end of the match.

Dancing joyously around the thronged parking lot afterward, in the company of thousands of Italians of all ages who'd obviously been *milanisti* since birth, or at least since the day of their baptism (it being customary in many Italian families not only to name the baby during the baptismal ceremony but also to decree which *calcio* team he will root for all his life), Nancy and I bumped into an especially exuberant cabdriver who, once he deduced that we were *Americans,* come all the way to Milan just for the match, insisted on driving us to the airport free of charge.

And in that first pure rush of uncut *estasi del calcio,* or *calcio-*

induced ecstasy, we did not foresee the dark side: that my obsession would only worsen, to the point where this recreational pursuit would become the force that dominated my life and would inevitably send me tumbling far down from the pinnacle of joy that magical afternoon at the San Siro represented, and onto the distant windswept plains of Castel di Sangro.

3

The phone rang. One hour later? Two? I didn't know.

"Hello?"

"Hello, Joe." It was a female voice I did not recognize. Speaking English.

"This is Barbara." She spoke with a very slight Italian accent.

"Yes?"

"So. I am in the lobby. Would you like me to wait for you here?"

Through the many layers of sleeplessness, jet lag, and weirdness, I tried to find something to latch on to but could not.

"Well, sure. Wait for me there. But why? I mean, who are you?"

"Oh, you don't remember? In your fax you said you hope that *La Società* would find an interpreter for you."

"Ah, yes, *sì, sì, sì, sì, sì.* You'll have to excuse me. I was sleeping." I did remember. *La Società* was the organization that owned and operated Castel di Sangro Calcio – the town soccer team – and Signor Gabriele Gravina was its president. In one of my faxes, either to him or to Giuseppe, the club's brand-new "assistant for external relations," I had asked whether it would be possible to hire a local resident to work as my interpreter, at least at the start. Apparently it had been. And now she was waiting in the lobby, although at the moment I could think of nothing that needed interpretation, except possibly my jumbled dreams.

"I am so sorry," she said. "If this is not convenient, we can meet at a later time. But Giuseppe suggested that I call you. Because President Gravina has invited you to dinner at the pizzeria at nine P.M., and I thought that before we went there, I could give you a brief tour of Castel di Sangro."

"Yes, of course. Or at least you could show me where it is."

"Oh, don't you worry," she said, laughing. "It is not far."

I met her in the lobby. Through my still reddened and puffy eyes I saw an attractive and smartly dressed woman of perhaps forty. She greeted me with a warm smile and firm handshake. I must have seemed a bit bewildered because she immediately asked, "Is something wrong?"

I shook my head. "Oh, no, no. It's just – well, I don't know. I wasn't expecting you. I mean, someone like you. Look, excuse me . . . right now everything's still a little out of focus."

She smiled again. "Ah," she said. "You were not expecting someone poised and well educated and decently dressed and who speaks English with only a slight accent?"

"Exactly. I thought you'd be, well . . . maybe atavistic and introspective."

"Atavistic, no," she said. "But at times I can be introspective."

"Do you come from a clannish local family?"

"Yes, I think you could say so."

"But do you live a life of miserable, revolting destitution?"

"Not since college. And excuse me, but is this my job interview?"

"Oh, no, please. Don't misunderstand. It's just, I'm still groggy from the flight, you know, and I haven't even gotten to Castel di Sangro yet and already all my stereotypes are falling apart."

She laughed. "Well, I am sorry to participate in such a traumatic process, but I grew up in Castel di Sangro, then went away to university, then lived overseas for many years, in England, in Tunisia, and I have even spent time in America, and two years ago I came back because my mother is older and not feeling well and from Castel di Sangro with my fax machine and my knowledge of language and my automobile, I am able to work full-time as a translator of medical texts and journal articles for several different English and American pharmaceutical companies with large offices in Rome, spending maybe three working days per week in Castel di Sangro and two in Rome."

"Wow."

"No, not so 'wow.' It is just the best life I can make for myself at the present. But to put your mind and your stereotypes at ease, there are not many like me in Castel di Sangro. It would not be immodest, I think, to say that in the whole town I have the best qualifications for speaking and translating into English. So if you arrive with your picture of us in the Abruzzo living in dank hovels with the women stoop-shouldered and wearing dark shawls and staring silently with suspicious eyes and toothless mouths, it is incomplete and somewhat outdated and very exaggerated but not entirely inaccurate."

"I hope I did not give offense."

"Of course not. I am not offended by a stereotype. It is no worse than the newspapers calling us Lilliputians and saying that now, because of the miracle, all of our lives have turned to fairy tales. If my life is now a fairy tale, I would like at the least to have Prince Charming and maybe also the pot of gold at the end of the rainbow. But so far these have not materialized."

"But the miracle?" I said. "The miracle did happen, didn't it?"

"Oh, yes. The miracle happened. For three months it is the only thing anyone can talk about. Myself, I think in the end it may prove a bad thing, leading to false hopes and worse disappointments, but I am in a very small minority. For almost everyone the miracle has brought the first smile to the face for many years. It has brought hope. It has brought faith. It has brought self-respect. And now it has brought something else."

"Which is?"

"You. The American. And now you, too, will be part of the fairy tale: the mysterious stranger from afar. We hope he brings us more good luck, but we can't be sure."

"And if not?" I asked.

She shrugged. *"Non si sa mai,"* she said. "One never knows."

As we drove to Castel di Sangro, which turned out to be only twelve kilometers down the road, the early-evening light was gauzy and soft – the way my head felt – and broad vistas extended from either side of the road to even higher, snowcapped mountains in the distance.

"It's beautiful," I said.

"Bellissimo," Barbara agreed. "Unfortunately, the town itself is not

so much so. In the war, first the Germans occupied and the Americans bombed from the air. Then, when the Germans left, they bombed from the ground all that remained. So we have only one church that is old. All else is built since the war. And built not for charm but for profit. But here: you can see for yourself."

Barbara turned off the road we'd been on and followed a smaller, narrower street that swung to the left and was suddenly lined on both sides with small shops. "We are a small town," Barbara said, "but for many miles around we are the only town. So the people from the *comuni* and villages, which are even smaller, come here to shop. Also, people who ski" – she gave the word its English pronunciation effortlessly – "sometimes they come from Roccaraso to buy things. And on weekends and holidays, some come from Napoli in order to find clean streets and clean air for a day. So there is just enough for our small shops to survive. Very few of us are rich, but nobody starves.

"But where our soul was when I was a girl here now seems empty. The landscape, the mountains, they are beautiful. But they are outside us. For too many, I am afraid, life is like these shops you see. Better than nothing, but scarcely worth taking note of. In a big sense, even though it is more than fifty years ago, we never have recovered from the war. So many of our people fled, so few came back. And they came back to find only rubble. And from the rubble we have built only this. We should have twenty-five thousand in this town, but we have only five."

"But maybe the miracle will change all that."

"Yes, this is what Gabriele – Signor Gravina – keeps saying. But for me, I do not see how. Because even a miracle, you know, is not forever."

She parked in what was obviously the center of town. It was as nondescript as she had said. (Over time, I would find that almost everything was as Barbara said. I would find also that when she did not know, she did not say, which alone would have made her unique, and not only in Castel di Sangro.) The town was not ugly – no sharp stick in the eye, like so many Italian towns through which I'd pass during the next nine months – but it was inarguably drab.

But that did not matter to me. I had not come to buy postcards.

What pleased me was the scale of it: manageable and small. One could survive here without a car. A good pair of shoes, a warm coat for cold weather, an outergarment for protection against rain, and it seemed that one could walk to any possible destination within the town.

The sidewalks, in fact, were filled with walkers spilling out into the street. "This is the time of the *passeggiata*," Barbara said. "Everywhere in Italy, in early evening, almost everyone turns out for a walk. No destination. No purpose. Just to walk slowly and to look and to talk occasionally with one's friends. Maybe to shop, but that is usually an afterthought, not the purpose. The charm of the *passeggiata* is that it has no purpose beyond itself."

"But when do they practice the ancient crafts for their own uses?"

"Excuse me?"

"Oh, never mind. Just something else I read in a book."

"There is no book that tells the truth of the Abruzzo. For here we have many truths, and also – oh, look, across the street, there is Signor Rezza!"

I gazed at a throng of people.

"The short man. With the long coat and the big cigar. He is the owner of Castel di Sangro Calcio. Gabriele Gravina, the president, is married to his niece. And those tall men on either side of him? They are his bodyguards."

"Wait a minute. The owner of the *calcio* team needs bodyguards?"

"He *has* bodyguards. I did not say 'needs.' "

"But why does he have them? And who is he?"

"You have not heard his name? Oh, but you will. He is *la presenza occulta,* the hidden presence, behind everything. Not only the miracle but everything in Castel di Sangro."

"But what does he do?"

"Signor Rezza? It is not what he does. It is what he *can* do. And also how much money he has."

"How did he get so much money?"

"I would not know," Barbara said evenly. "It is not my business to ask a man why he is rich. He is a businessman. Maybe he has worked very hard."

"Okay, but just tell me why he's – whatever you said – occult."

"For many reasons Signor Rezza does not wish publicity. He

wants to create the appearance that he is far removed from *La Società*. Because the miracle is a simple, happy story for the newspapers and for television, and maybe Signor Rezza is not so simple."

"You said a businessman. What sort of business?"

"Many sorts. But first was the construction business. In Napoli. And you do not need to offer a comment in response."

She smiled again. Then we joined the hundreds of others in the *passeggiata*.

Five minutes later I spotted a sign on a square concrete building that dwarfed its surroundings, at least in unattractiveness. The sign said *albergo*. Even I knew that this meant "hotel."

"Barbara. Look, right there. At the end of the block. A hotel. I thought there were no hotels in Castel di Sangro."

Barbara stopped walking. She folded her arms. She looked at the building. She sighed. Then she looked at me. "Signor Gravina," she said, "knew of course that this was here, but he preferred to arrange the Best Western. For your comfort."

"Well, I appreciate that. And I will certainly thank him. But I simply can't be twelve kilometers out of town."

"If you insist, we will step inside and you can look. But I must tell you. Our government, you know, ranks all the hotels in the country. Five stars, four stars, and so on down."

"Yes, yes. So how many for this one?"

"Zero."

It was a grim cube of concrete, painted a dull rust color that might be called crumbled brick. It was the "Hotel" Coradetti, and the proprietor was a man who did not smile. He seemed, in fact, annoyed when Barbara explained that I wished to book a room for at least a week or two while I looked for a more permanent place to live. Finally, he nodded and muttered a few words. Barbara smiled at me, but I could tell she didn't mean it. The room would cost forty dollars a night and I would have to pay cash in advance for two weeks.

"No credit cards?" I asked her.

She rolled her eyes.

So I agreed and began to count out the money as Barbara told the proprietor I would move in on Monday. I asked Barbara if there would be a telephone in my room. She said no without even bothering to ask. But she made some inquiry regarding a phone, which caused the proprietor to shake his heavy head and mutter a few more words.

"He says the only phone is this one here behind the desk, but you will not be permitted to use it."

"Ah, how convenient."

"Now you see," Barbara said, "why Signor Gravina did not wish this to be your first impression of Castel di Sangro."

"Yes, Barbara, but location. In my business, like the restaurant business, location is everything."

"I wonder," she said, "if you will still say that in three weeks."

Outside, as darkness fell, the *passeggiata* drew to a close. The narrow streets quickly emptied, shops closed, lights went out, and within five minutes it seemed as if it might have been 3 A.M.

"Where did everybody go?"

"Home. The life at night here is not like that of Rome."

"And us?"

"We go to Marcella's. Signor Gravina will be already there."

"Uh-oh. I hope it's not rude to keep him waiting."

"He is not *waiting*. Gabriele is not a man who waits. He will be surrounded by many people. He is, after all, the president of *La Società*, which has just accomplished a miracle, and this is the night before the first match of the new season."

We walked down an alley that led from what appeared to be the main street of Castel di Sangro. At the end of the alley, we turned right. There was a small parking area, jammed with cars parked so close together that it seemed none of them would ever get out. On one side the Sangro River, which seemed more like a stream, flowed slowly. On the other side was Marcella's.

Earlier, Barbara had referred to Marcella's as a pizzeria, but it seemed a full-scale restaurant. It also provided a further answer to my earlier question about where all the people had gone. Anyone who was not home must have been here, for the single dining room was noisy, hot, smoke filled, and so crowded that I didn't think Barbara and I would be able to walk across it, much less find seats.

But she glided through the throng like the native she was, and I followed, muttering, *"Scusi,"* whenever I bumped into or stepped on someone, which was about with every step I took. Remarkably, we made it to the far end, closest to the kitchen. On one side of us was a corner where pizza ovens were working at capacity. On the other side was a small bar, from behind which a young man filled pitchers with beer from a tap. Wine bottles lined a wall alongside. Through swinging doors that led from the kitchen, perspiring and breathless young men and women bore trays and plates filled with food. There must been been 500 people in a space designed to hold no more than 100, and all seemed to be simultaneously smoking cigarettes, eating, drinking, and speaking as loudly as they could.

A wave of jet lag washed over me, and I felt my hold on reality starting to slip. Then I felt Barbara pulling my arm. We'd been standing next to a single long table that dominated the back of the room. From somewhere, two empty chairs were produced. Barbara motioned for me to sit.

As I did, a whole pizza appeared in front of me, as if by magic. An instant later, someone filled a glass with red wine and placed next to it an empty glass and full bottle of mineral water.

"–duce you to Signor Gravina." That was Barbara's voice, at my right ear. I turned in her direction and found myself facing a trim and handsome middle-aged man wearing a suede jacket and blue jeans. He was smoking, speaking into a cell phone, sipping from a wine glass, talking to a woman next to him, and taking a bite of pizza all at once. Somehow, he managed to smile at me and to raise a hand in greeting.

I smiled and waved back. Then in my left ear I heard a warm female voice and turned in that direction to see a short blond woman standing over me. She was wearing an apron and grinning at me, and she reached out to take my hands in hers. Her mouth was moving so fast that I could tell she was saying many things to me, but in the noise I could barely hear her voice, much less have any hope of understanding.

"Marcella," Barbara said. "She says she welcomes you here as if you were her son."

I looked back up at her. "Thank you," I said loudly. "Thank you!" She nodded, smiling. "Tell her thank you," I said to Barbara.

"No, you say it yourself. You must start sometime. Very simple. *'Grazie. Molto grazie.'* "

I tried it.

The woman named Marcella beamed. *"Ah, prego!"* she said, and leaned forward and hugged me. Then she said something to Barbara that made her laugh.

"What was that?"

"She says now that she sees you, of course you are too old to be her son, so maybe she should welcome you like her father."

"Wait a minute! I'm not *that* old. And she's not that young."

Barbara apparently translated this, because a moment later Marcella threw back her head and laughed delightedly. Then she leaned forward and hugged me again, and said, *"Mangia! Mangia!"*

"Tomorrow she can meet you more formally," Barbara said. "Now she would like you to eat. But first, excuse me, I think Gabriele may be free."

So we turned back to the head of the table. Signor Gravina was indeed free, or at least as close to it as he apparently would be on this evening. Still smoking and speaking into his cell phone, he reached out a hand and shook mine, nodding at me. Then he placed his hand over the mouthpiece of the cell phone and spoke quickly to Barbara. Then he nodded at me again, took a quick sip of wine, and still speaking into the cell phone, stood to embrace a man who'd just walked up to greet him.

Barbara stood immediately and said, "All right. Now we can leave."

"You mean that was it?"

"That was what?"

"That was my introduction to Signor Gravina?"

"Well, yes, for tonight, because you can see he is very busy. But he just told me that tomorrow he will come to get you personally at ten o'clock in the morning at the Best Western. I, too, will be there. In the car there will be time for conversation."

"Good, good. But wait. In the car to where? And what do you mean 'leave'? We just got here. And there's all this food."

"That is the problem. You cannot eat it."

"But I'm starving."

"I will explain. Oh, all right, take one or two slices of pizza and you can eat them in the car. But now we should go, for tomorrow will be a very important day." Barbara turned immediately and began to make her way back to the front door.

And so, with another clumsy wave in the direction of Signor Gravina, who did not seem to notice, and awkward smiles in the direction of the people among whom I'd been briefly seated but had not met, I stood and tripped my way back out of Marcella's, saying, *"Scusi . . . scusi . . . scusi,"* all the way.

Once outside, I said *scusi* one more time – this time to Barbara – and added, "I think besides being tired, I'm really confused."

"Of course," she said. "This was an unexpected development. And I must say, even I am very surprised. And for you it is a very, very great honor."

"What is?"

"I will explain in the car," she said. And we were quickly on our way back to the Best Western.

"Tomorrow," Barbara said, "because of its historic significance, Signor Rezza – not simply Signor Gravina – wishes to celebrate by having a special lunch for his family and close friends at his personal club in Pescara, and Gabriele just told me that *you* are invited."

"Why, that's wonderful. How gracious of him."

"Yes," Barbara said. "It is a high compliment. If there are five thousand people in Castel di Sangro, probably four thousand nine hundred and ninety have never once shared a meal with Signor Rezza."

"I'm truly honored."

"More important than honored," Barbara said, "is to be hungry. Signor Rezza, you see, becomes very displeased – very, *very* displeased – if he sees that someone at his table has not finished everything on the plate."

I laughed.

"This is no joke," Barbara said. "You will risk giving great offense to Signor Rezza if you do not finish everything you are served. And to do so at such an occasion as the luncheon tomorrow – well, it simply must not occur."

"You are serious."

"Very much so."

We had reached the Best Western, and Barbara pulled into the parking lot.

"When I was a little kid," I said, "I used to hide my peas and string beans under the dining room rug."

Barbara smiled but shook her head strongly. "Do not attempt any tricks tomorrow. Signor Rezza is always watching. Or if not him, one of his bodyguards. Good night."

4

In the first months after World War II, a young priest named Don Arbete was entrusted with the task of rebuilding a rudimentary society in Castel di Sangro, as grieving families slowly made their way back to the ruins of what had been their town from the exile that the war had imposed upon them.

The priest began in the only way he knew: with children eager to kick and a "ball" composed of dirty socks held together with twine. By the fall he was so proud of his charges that he issued a challenge to a neighboring, though somewhat less devastated, village. It was accepted, and early one October morning in 1945 – the roads still impassable because of the bombing, but one short spur of railroad line undamaged – he loaded his shoeless *ragazzi* and their ball of socks onto a flatcar, and hand-pumped the ten kilometers to the grassless and rock-strewn *campo* where the opposition waited: arrogant in the extreme because they had not only shoes but an actual prewar, if somewhat deflated, football for use in the match.

These disadvantages notwithstanding, the lads of Castel di Sangro escaped with a victory – and "escape" is the operative word – running barefoot for their lives toward the flatcar, Don Arbete's black cassock flapping about his legs as he sprinted alongside them. Thanks largely to a herculean team effort aboard the flatcar (and a slight downgrade at the start), they managed to flee successfully from their irate pursuers, returning to their ravaged village with a tale of triumph so unlikely that had not the priest himself vouched for it, many would never have believed it.

Over the years the ball of socks was replaced by a regulation soccer ball, but the heroics of that first postwar Castel di Sangro "squad" set the tone for the villagers' approach to the sport. The population was low, but standards were high.

A town team was officially formed in 1953, and in the decades that followed Castel di Sangro acquired a reputation (at least within the southern Abruzzo) for being a hard-nosed squad that played with unusual tenacity. The team enjoyed a fair degree of success in local amateur and semiprofessional ranks.

These ranks – not so incidentally, in terms of the later miracle – were clearly distinguishable from one another. Because of its unique position at the fulcrum of communal life, soccer in Italy developed a structure and hierarchy as complex, extensive, and rigidly adhered to as that of either the Vatican or the Mafia. There are levels upon levels upon levels, and within each level there are layers upon layers upon layers. One might envision the structure as a pyramid, although, especially toward the bottom, the smooth geometric shape tends to buckle a bit and the sort of existential untidiness so common to other facets of Italian life holds sway.

At the tip of the pyramid are the eighteen teams that play each year in the *Serie A*. Here, one perennially finds A.C. Milan, Inter Milan, Juventus, Roma, Lazio, and Fiorentina, as well as a dozen other clubs that have climbed, at least temporarily, the slippery slope that leads to this highest level.

To win the *Serie A* championship is to have won the World Series, the Super Bowl, and the NBA championship all rolled together. *Lo scudetto,* as it is called, is the *only* sporting championship that matters in Italy, and it matters more – far more – than any American can easily comprehend.

In addition to the glory, there is money: tens of millions of dollars. Some is the reward for having won the championship, but much more comes from the champion club's access the following season to the European international competition known as the Champions Cup. This is a most lucrative and prestigious season-long tournament contested among clubs, as opposed to the national teams of various countries. The sale of worldwide television rights (some of these matches can even be seen in America!) has made the Champions

Cup competition the golden egg, if not the goose itself, for which every club in Europe mightily strives.

There are also two other international club competitions for teams that, while strong, did not win their country's league championship. From these, too, great riches and much prestige can be garnered.

Were such bonuses not enough to ensure fierce competition throughout the *Serie A* season (which stretches from September through May), a stick, as well as a carrot, is employed. To wit: the bottom four finishers each season are "relegated," or demoted, to the next level down, *Serie B*. Likewise, the top four *Serie B* clubs are promoted to *Serie A*.

To get even a slight sense of the fear induced by the prospect of relegation, one might imagine the New York Yankees, for example, finishing last in their division and being told that as a result they would not play in the American League the next season but in the minor International League. And that only by winning there could they gain readmittance to the majors. Imagine the empty seats that would result from an announcement that it would not be the Boston Red Sox coming to town for the weekend, but Pawtucket.

Of course, it is possible to fall out the bottom of *Serie B*, too. Each year, as the top four finishers in that twenty-team league advance to *A,* the bottom four drop into the no-longer fully national division *C1*. Here, the thirty-six teams are split into two divisions, a northern and southern (largely to cut down on transportation costs, which take an increasing toll on club finances the further a squad slips from filled seats in large stadia and the glamor and glory of international competition).

Below *C1* there lies the netherworld of *C2*, whose fifty-four teams are split into three regional divisions. Professional soccer in Italy, therefore, consists of 128 teams, with perhaps an average of twenty players on each, meaning that about 2,500 men earn their living playing the game, receiving salaries that might range from $20,000 in *C2* up to the many millions paid to the stars of *Serie A*.

But even from *C2* the structure continues downward. Thus, below *C2* is the *Campionato Nazionale Dilettanti,* or national amateur league, which is divided into nine regional *gironi,* or circles (as in Dante's circles of hell), each consisting of eighteen teams. Despite its name, even in this league the players receive some compensation, adding 112 semipro clubs to the 128 that are professional.

And even at this depth stagnation is avoided by having the bottom three finishers from each of the *C2* divisions relegated to the *Dilettanti,* while the winner of each amateur *girone* gets a crack at *C2*. Meanwhile, the bottom four clubs from each *Dilettanti* sector are reassigned to the almost unimaginably lowly *Campionati di Eccellenza Regionale,* or championship for the "excellent teams of the region," an appellation that skirts the edge of euphemism.

Yet even from there the downward spiral continues, through *Campionato Promozione* and finally to the land of no names, where the hierarchy becomes simply *Prima Categoria, Seconda Categoria,* and, at the very, very bottom, *Terza Categoria,* or third category, a level below which there are no teams but simply out-of-shape factory workers kicking a ball around on Sunday mornings instead of going to church.

Castel di Sangro started on the bottom: *Terza Categoria.* This was an appropriate level for an *abruzzese* squad of locals from a town of five thousand still rebuilding from the war.

Among the newer residents was a burly young southerner named Pietro Rezza, who had ridden into town on a donkey one day and started immediately to build housing for a town that needed it. Rezza also soon married the daughter of one of the wealthiest families to have returned to Castel di Sangro after the war.

Assured by his marriage to access to capital, Rezza began to build farther afield, ranging south, toward and eventually into the city of Napoli, where newcomers who sought to make large sums of money were not welcomed warmly by *la Camorra,* the Neapolitan cousin to Sicily's *Mafia,* and where the phrase "construction business" was used to describe a variety of enterprises that – were disputes to arise among those involved – tended to put men below ground (or at the bottom of Napoli's harbor) even faster than they provided new housing above it.

Rezza, however – and if one asks about the details, one is quickly advised not to – not only stayed above ground but grew wealthy enough to build for himself an estate of *Jurassic Park* style and proportion high above the *cittadina* (small town) of Castel di Sangro. He also purchased equally lavish vacation homes near the sea, in Pescara, and in Lugano, Switzerland, where many high-ranking members of organized-crime syndicates were buying or building personal retreats.

Meanwhile, thirty years after it had been founded, the soccer team of Signor Rezza's adopted hometown of Castel di Sangro earned promotion from *Terza* to *Seconda Categoria,* which at the time was probably *the* major event in the town's scant postwar history. Unfortunately, the team and the town were flat broke. To play in *Seconda Categoria* would require not much money – a small fee to the *Categoria* central office for its operating budget, a few thousand lire to give to each player after a win, a bit of new equipment, and enough cash on hand to reimburse for fuel costs those players who drove their cars to away matches.

Yet the difference between "not much money" and all the money in the world is virtually nonexistent if you have none. Thus, it appeared for some weeks during the summer of 1982 that the Castel di Sangro squad might actually have to decline its promotion because it could not afford to accept. Half the players didn't even have two socks that matched. Yet in their own small way, they'd accomplished something: earning the right to climb one stone higher on the massive if patchwork *calcio* pyramid, built from the hundreds of local leagues that stretched from the Alps almost to the coast of North Africa.

Signor Rezza, who'd not evinced any prior interest in *il calcio,* quickly solved the problem by buying the team. He was, at the time, sixty-two years old, childless, and separated from his wife, who lived in her own apartment in Castel di Sangro. Some town residents considered his act civic minded. Others noted that the sloppy financial practices of low-level soccer franchises in Italy provided a convenient way for a man so inclined to move at least small sums of money about to avoid the payment of taxes.

Signor Rezza had two nieces. One married an oral surgeon, who gave not a whit about *calcio.* The other, Maria Teresa, married the debonair Gabriele Gravina, who, like Rezza himself, had come north from the region of Puglia and had also come of age with large if somewhat undefined ambitions for himself.

After his marriage, Gravina began to work closely with Signor Rezza, both in the construction business and in related enterprises. The Castel di Sangro soccer team fell into the category of a "related enterprise." Rezza put Gravina in charge of the club and promptly forgot all about it.

In its first year in *Seconda Categoria* Castel di Sangro finished second. The following year, they finished first, thereby earning promotion to *Prima Categoria*. Even at this low level, it was not possible to field a competitive team made up only of men born and raised in Castel di Sangro. Thus, while still not offering salaries, the canny Gravina arranged jobs and in-season living quarters for a few players of higher quality, inducing them to play for the squad.

Their ranks thus bolstered, Castel di Sangro quickly achieved *Promozione* status, a level at which most teams represented cities with populations of at least 20,000, and some far larger than that.

And so it continued throughout the 1980s, with Castel di Sangro steadily climbing and never slipping back. More and more players arrived from farther and farther away until finally in 1989, to nationwide (if minor) astonishment, the team broke through to *Serie C2* and true professionalism.

Serie C2, however, was more than just another step up. It was a quantum leap into an entirely new and unstable orbit. There would be no waltzing through *C2* the way they'd come up through the amateur and semiprofessional ranks. The first two years were a struggle to simply stay afloat: to avoid relegation back to nonprofessional status. From 1991 onward, however, Gravina's keen eye for useful talent at bargain prices produced consecutive finishes of fifth and fourth place. But then, as often happens in the hypertensive world of *il calcio,* the manager left at the end of the season and his replacement turned out not to be to Gravina's liking.

One-third of the way through the 1993–94 season, in fact, Castel di Sangro was last in their division, their professional phase seemingly headed for a quick and ignominious end. Just after Christmas Gravina fired the man who displeased him, and handed the frozen reins to an unemployed former manager named Osvaldo Jaconi, a man from the northern region of Lake Como, whose résumé hung like a millstone from his thick ex-player's neck.

Jaconi lived about three hours up the Adriatic Coast in the *C2* city of Civitanova. Professionally, *il calcio* was all he'd ever known. After fifteen years as a player, mostly in the lower divisions and memorable chiefly to himself, he'd retired at the age of thirty-four and had embarked upon a managerial career.

Over the next decade, in pursuit of this calling, he had roamed the country, from the northern lakes to the sweltering village of

Lentini, deep in the interior of southern Sicily. He was hired and fired at levels from *C1* down to the semiprofessional, but in all enjoyed only sporadic success.

Jaconi was married and the father of two teenage daughters. He also was single-minded, egotistical, authoritarian, stubborn, and physically powerful, with a voice best measured in foghorn decibels, and had an inexhaustible appetite for work.

He could be cheerful, even merry, and among friends he displayed genuine warmth. On the job, however, he was not a man who enjoyed listening to the opinions of others. Years later he would proclaim proudly that he knew only one word of English: "bulldozer." And pointing to his massive chest, he would say, "I bulldozer." This was, as self-assessments go, remarkably accurate, and encapsulated almost all of Jaconi's professional strengths and weaknesses.

When Gravina hired him, he was one month short of his forty-sixth birthday, and for the first time since he'd become a professional player at the age of nineteen, he'd been out of work for six months. Many a manager would have taken one look at Castel di Sangro and said no thanks, and many another would have said no without having bothered to take the look. But Jaconi was desperate and said yes.

He enjoyed immediate success. His strong-arm (some said, bullying) methods lifted the team from the bottom of the pack to seventh place by the end of the season. The following year, he astonished everyone by leading Castel di Sangro through the six-year *C2* logjam and winning promotion to *C1*.

It may be difficult to grasp the extent of the difference between *C2*, central division, and *C1*, south, but it is vast. Although *C2* is professional, it is just barely so. A majority of its clubs come from cities and towns so obscure that even many Italians have a hard time finding them on a map. Ternana, Fermana, Giorgione, Sandonà, Forlì, Tolentino, Imola: this was backwater, workaday, minor-league Italy. Tourism was not a major source of income.

It was astonishing, nonetheless, that Castel di Sangro, from so deep in the Abruzzo and with its population of only 5,000, had risen to this level and had managed to last for seven years. But that they were about to go *higher* – to go to *C1* – was, like the distance between galaxies, beyond one's power to imagine.

In the 1995–96 season in *Serie C1, girone B,* Castel di Sangro would face opponents such as Ascoli, which had played in *Serie A* for fourteen seasons, as recently as 1990. And Lecce, the distant metropolis to the south with a population of more than 100,000 and a team that had played in *Serie A* only *two* years before.

The geographic range alone was daunting. From Lecce, located in the heel of Italy's boot, the southern division of *C1* ranged as far north as Siena, in Tuscany. From Castel di Sangro, no opponent would be within easy reach. Renting a team bus would be required, and money to fill the fuel tank of the bus. There would have to be meals and overnight hotel rooms for the players. Signor Rezza, it was rumored, was not entirely pleased. He'd never intended to *lose* money on his soccer team, but with a home stadium that seated only 4,000 (and even that was 80 percent of the town's population), it would not be easy to profit from success.

Not that success could be expected in *C1*. Gravina – pinching pennies so hard, his forefingers and thumbs turned black and blue – refused to augment the squad in any way. The townspeople, however, had developed an almost childlike faith in the presumed magical powers of Jaconi. Maybe he did it with smoke and mirrors, maybe through sheer force of will (his players fearing his anger so much that they were too frightened to lose), or maybe he was simply, as some said, *l'uomo della provvidenza,* a gift from God. In any event, he got results, and he did it entirely with men who possessed no special aptitude for the game.

For the adventure of *Serie C1,* Jaconi would have to make do with what he had. It was the *abruzzese* way. There were a few in the town who believed he might be able to save the team from immediate relegation back to *C2,* but no one foresaw what actually happened: Castel di Sangro finished the season in second place. There is no point in even asking how this was done, for it was the first phase of the miracle, and the miraculous, by definition, defies any attempt at explanation.

Lecce, the first-place finisher, would advance automatically to *Serie B,* but new regulations required that a playoff be held among the teams that finished second through fifth to determine which other club would be promoted.

In the first round of the playoff, Castel di Sangro played a home-and-home series against fifth-place Gualdo, a team from the city of Macerata in the region of Marche, just to the north of the Abruzzo.

In Gualdo on Sunday, June 16, 1996, Castel di Sangro gave up a goal with only six minutes left in the match and lost, 1-0. A week later in Castel di Sangro, with only fifteen *seconds* remaining and the score 0-0 – which would mean defeat for Castel di Sangro – Jaconi made a bizarre substitution. He sent onto the field a defender who had played in only seven matches all season and who had never scored a goal. Seven seconds after entering the match, the defender scored.

Later, when asked how he could possibly have chosen that particular substitute at that particular moment, Jaconi simply shrugged his broad shoulders, cast his eyes skyward, held out to either side the upraised palms of his hands, and said, *"Chissà!"* Who knows? The home-and-home series ended tied at 1-1, but Castel di Sangro, being the team that had finished higher in the regular-season standings, advanced to the final.

This was to take place on June 22, in the neutral city of Foggia, about 150 miles southeast of Castel di Sangro: a single match to determine which team from *Serie C1, girone B,* would join Lecce the following season in the seemingly mythical realm of *Serie B.* The opponent would be Ascoli, from a provincial capital within the Marche, a city with ten times the population of Castel di Sangro, and a team that had defeated Castel di Sangro in both matches played during the regular season.

At this point, the townspeople found themselves in a state of agitation not experienced since the start of World War II, or, for some, not since the great earthquake of 1915, which had killed about half the town. But for the first time, the excitement was linked with hope instead of fear.

Gravina announced that he would provide a chartered bus for any town residents who wished to make the journey to Foggia to cheer for the team. He had been thinking one bus, maybe two. But as soon as they realized he was serious, the simple folk of Castel di Sangro began to line up outside the offices of *La Società* in order to assure themselves a place on the bus. The line quickly grew: first to hundreds, then to thousands.

Horrified, the club president looked out his window and saw almost the entire population of the town, singing, cheering, laughing, but also begging, *demanding* a seat on the bus. In the end, Gravina had to pay for more than thirty chartered buses – virtually wiping out the team's profit for the season and sending Signor Rezza into the deepest of funks.

Little need be said about the match. Conditions on the field resembled those in a greenhouse, the heat and humidity of a sultry summer day in southern Italy combining to sap the strength of players from both sides – players who already were virtually paralyzed by the fear that arose from knowing that a single error could prove fatal to the dreams of thousands.

The ninety-minute match ended with the score 0–0. The score remained 0–0 well into the thirty-minute overtime period, which would be followed, if necessary, by a penalty-kick shootout similar to that in the World Cup final between Italy and Brazil.

Under the rules of soccer, each team is permitted only three substitutions, and once substituted, a player is not permitted to return. As the scorching afternoon waned and the players wilted, Jaconi made first one substitution, then a second.

Throughout the entire ninety minutes, however, and then throughout virtually all of the thirty that followed, he held back his third substitute. This greatly perplexed the Castel di Sangro fans, for it was clear that of the village team's eleven players, only the goalkeeper, who had not had to run at full speed, fighting off fierce and frequently violent opponents with every stride, amid such stifling and exhausting conditions, remained capable of further exertion.

Still, Jaconi waited. And then, in the 119th minute, this man of magic made his move. And what an incomprehensible move it was! For the player he waved to the sidelines was not one of his depleted and dehydrated defenders, midfielders, or forwards, but Roberto De Juliis, the highly capable and – on this day at least – absolutely unblemished twenty-four-year-old goalkeeper.

Trotting onto the field in his stead was the thirty-four-year-old reserve keeper, Pietro Spinosa, who had not played a minute all season long. Spinosa, though he'd put in ten seasons as a professional, had never risen above the level of *C2,* and his last match even at that level had come two years earlier.

Yet here he was, suddenly: the Castel di Sangro goalkeeper for the decisive penalty-kick phase. Young De Juliis left the field in tears, oblivious to the standing ovation he received.

During the play of a match, penalty kicks are occasionally awarded by a referee who thinks he has detected a significant foul committed within the penalty area, a rectangle that extends eighteen yards laterally beyond either goalpost and eighteen yards forward onto the field of play.

But a round of postmatch penalty kicks is also used to break ties in games that must produce a winner. Five players from each side (who must be chosen from among those on the field at the end of regulation time) alternate in taking kicks, and the team that makes the most, wins. (If the penalty score is tied after the five designated players from each team have shot, the kicks continue on a sudden-death basis.)

Of penalty kicks awarded during the course of a match, about eight of ten are taken successfully, so unlikely is a skilled player to miss the goal from such short range and so unlikely is the goalkeeper to block such a shot.

But as the 1994 World Cup final showed, when penalty kicks are used to determine a winner after 120 exhausting minutes have failed to do so, the percentage of successful kicks can be considerably lower, and here a skilled goalkeeper can be of immeasurable value.

So what *was* Jaconi thinking? Experience over youth? The hope that a surprise might prove unsettling to Ascoli? A quiver of nervousness in young De Juliis that only the preternaturally observant Jaconi could detect? Or instead, as the villagers later came to believe, a moment of divine inspiration? *Chissà!* Who knows?

One by one, the players took their kicks. At the end of the fifth round the tally was even, four from each side having scored and each goalkeeper having blocked one shot.

The match had now reached the stage of sudden death. Castel di Sangro kicked and scored. Ascoli kicked and scored. All even after six. Castel di Sangro kicked and scored. Then a player named Milana shot for Ascoli, and he shot superbly: a hard drive, well to Spinosa's right but still clearly inside the upright of the goal. The penalties would move on to an eighth round.

But *no!*

For the blessed Spinosa, propelled by every canny instinct he'd developed over the years, and showing the catlike quickness of a man ten years younger, sprang to his right at the instant the ball was kicked and, with both arms extended and his body stretched to its full horizontal length, managed to get just the tip of a glove on the ball, which was coming at him from only twelve yards away at almost sixty miles per hour, and deflected it inches wide of the goalmouth.

This was the moment at which critical mass was achieved. This was the instant that would become known overnight as the Miracle of Castel di Sangro.

Tiny and obscure and isolated Castel di Sangro was going to *Serie B!* A miracle? *Assolutamente!* Indeed, for the Italian press, not even that one word would any longer suffice: *"Di miracolo in miracolo!"* – Miracle of miracles! – declared one paper.

Castel di Sangro, from the much-derided Abruzzo – but also from the land of Lilliput! – was going to *Serie B,* where the following season it would compete across the length and breadth of Italy against the teams of such metropolises as Turin, Genoa, Padua, Palermo, Verona, Bari, and Venice.

It was beyond comprehension, beyond the wildest forays of the most fervid imagination. And the minute I read about it – in June of 1996, in *Guerin Sportivo,* an Italian soccer magazine to which I subscribed, I knew I would have to go to Castel di Sangro, to write about the miracle and about whatever might happen next.

"The way some people talk about soccer," a manager of the Liverpool team once said, "you'd think it was a matter of life and death. They don't understand. It is far more important than that."

This much, at least, I understood.

5

Sunday morning was cool, yet filled with brilliant sunshine. It was the kind of day that makes a man feel like buying a new pair of skis, but I resisted. I also resisted any thoughts of breakfast. I was even afraid to drink water.

And not for the first time, I was puzzled. I'd looked at a map and had seen that the city of Pescara, where Barbara had said we'd be going for lunch with Signor Rezza, was well over 100 kilometers (60 miles) distant from Castel di Sangro. It was, in fact, located on the shore of the Adriatic Sea. That seemed an awfully long way to go just for lunch, especially when as soon as the meal was over, we presumably would have to race back into the mountains to be in Castel di Sangro in time for the 4 P.M. match.

It was 10 A.M. when Signor Gravina arrived at the Best Western, his tires sending up flurries of gravel as he swung into the driveway at about sixty miles per hour. He was driving a dark blue Lancia, wearing even darker sunglasses, smoking a cigarette, and talking on his cell phone. Again he wore a suede jacket and blue jeans. Seeing the president of the club for the first time in the clear light of day, I was even more struck by his rangy good looks – something on the order of Kirk Douglas. His wife, Signor Rezza's niece, sat next to him, a short and rather plump woman with a very sweet smile. Barbara was in the backseat.

The Gravinas, she told me, had two teenage sons, but they would not be coming to lunch because there was not enough room in the car. Gabriele had insisted on driving me to Pescara, instead of his sons, as one means of displaying the warmth with which he welcomed me to Castel di Sangro. Of course, driving me meant driving Barbara also, because neither Gabriele nor his wife spoke any English.

After explaining this, Barbara nudged me and pointed toward the front of the car, indicating that I should express my gratitude to Signor Gravina.

I leaned forward. *"Grazie mille, signore. Lei è molto gentile."* A thousand thanks, sir. You are very kind. I'd been up since 6 A.M. memorizing this phrase and repeating it out loud to myself. I was hoping that along with *"mangio! mangio!"* (I'm eating! I'm eating!) it would be enough to get me through the day.

"Niente," Signor Gravina said with a dismissive wave of the hand that was not holding the cell phone. It is nothing. He had not actually looked at me since I'd gotten into the car, but now his wife turned and smiled. I smiled back. The phone beeped. Gravina began speaking in a low tone, his lips brushing the mouthpiece, as if he did not wish to be overheard. He had nothing to fear from me on that score.

"Because the ride to Pescara is somewhat long," Barbara said, a new formality having crept into her syntax in the presence of *il presidente,* although he couldn't understand a word she was saying, "Signor Gravina has requested that I accompany you in order to facilitate conversation."

"Right, but I can't talk to him while he's on the phone," I said.

"No, but you could comment to Signora Gravina on the beauty of the region and on the fineness of the weather. You also could inform her, as you informed me yesterday, of your schedule. That you must go back to America in three weeks but that you will return here as quickly as possible and stay until Christmas and then remain with the team until the end of the season, next June."

"Scusi." I leaned forward and tapped Signora Gravina on the shoulder. She turned again, startled by the physical contact.

"This is beautiful!" I said, waving my hand in what I hoped was an all-inclusive gesture. "And the weather? Hey, couldn't be better!" I smiled. "In three weeks I have to go home, just some odds and ends, but then I'll come back and stay until Christmas." I smiled brightly.

Barbara said a very few words in Italian, presumably translating my spontaneous remarks. Then a burst of rapid-fire Italian came from over Gravina's right shoulder, directed apparently toward the backseat.

Barbara listened attentively. "Ah," she said. "Signor Gravina wishes to know if your accommodations last night were satisfactory."

"Oh, yes. Absolutely. But you'd better tell him that I'm moving to that Coradetti dive tomorrow."

Barbara did, which precipitated a series of short conversational bursts back and forth. At the end, she said to me, "Signor Gravina regrets that you have done this, because the Coradetti, in his point of view, is not suitable for a man of your station. This was why he booked your room at the Best Western in the first place."

"Yeah, but Barbara, *explain* to him, please. About how I have to be downtown, near everything. Especially the stadium. I looked on a map and I think the Coradetti is only about three or four blocks from the stadium."

But Barbara shook her head. "On this most special morning it would not be appropriate to mention the stadium."

"What? Why in the world not?"

"It is what you would call, I think, a sore point."

"Barbara, we're going to be *sitting* in the stadium at four o'clock this afternoon. That is, if we get back from lunch on time."

"I would have thought," Barbara said, "that someone who comes all the way from America to write a book about our miracle might have done a bit of research in advance."

"I was in a hurry to get here. But what's that supposed to mean, anyway?"

"This is not the time for us to have that conversation, not here in Signor Gravina's car, as he is most graciously driving us to the luncheon being given by Signor Rezza."

Hearing his own name and that of Rezza mentioned in the same sentence, Gravina turned more fully toward the backseat.

"Grazie mille, signore. Lei è molto gentile," I said.

All the while, I should mention, Gravina was driving the Lancia down a two-lane road at a speed approaching 200 kilometers per hour, which is about 120 mph. I was the only one wearing a seat belt.

"There is no stadium," Barbara said.

"What? What did you say?"

"I think you will need to learn how to say, 'What?' in Italian. You might try, *'Che?!'*"

"Okay, okay, but what – I mean, *che* did you just say? About no stadium?"

"Well, yes, there *is* a stadium. But it cannot be used. The regulations of *Serie B* require that all stadiums be able to seat at least ten thousand people, and our old stadium had room only for four thousand, so much construction work is being done. Unfortunately, this work has not been completed. For today, therefore, the match will not take place in Castel di Sangro, but in Chieti, where Gabriele has quite cleverly procured the use of a stadium and which is a city quite near Pescara. For this reason, Signor Rezza has chosen to eat lunch at a restaurant in Pescara."

"I find this hard to believe. First, there's no hotel, and now you're telling me there's no *stadium?*"

"Many in Castel di Sangro find it hard to believe also," Barbara said. "It is not a comfortable situation."

"But how can it be? They've had all summer to add six thousand seats, if that's what they needed to do. How come it didn't get done?"

"This is a question asked frequently, as I say. There is a great deal of confusion, which of course gives rise to speculation, much of which, no doubt, is uninformed. For example, money for the construction was to have come from the region and from the province. Gabriele declares that this money did not arrive. Others suggest that it did arrive but maybe was diverted elsewhere. Signor Rezza and Gabriele, you know, have many business interests in addition to Castel di Sangro Calcio."

"Are you saying they *stole* the money that was supposed to go for the stadium?"

"Of course not. I would never make such an accusation against either Signor Rezza or Gabriele. I am only relating the theories of others for background purposes."

"But why can't Rezza use some of his own millions to add the six thousand seats? And you said Rezza was a big construction guy in Napoli? One phone call and a guy like that has his six thousand seats in overnight! No *stadium?* That's the most ridiculous thing I've ever heard of in my life."

"Please!" Barbara said. "When you raise your voice in that fashion, and especially when you mention the name of Signor Rezza, it is disconcerting for our host and hostess in the front seat."

"What, you don't want me to say their names because you don't want them to know we're talking about them? I mean, *che?*"

"*Che?*" Barbara said.

"Yes, at the start of what I just said I said, 'What,' and I should have said, '*Che.*' I mean, at the start of *che* I just said."

"No, it is not so simple, this use of *che*. Please. Forget I even mentioned it. When we have a formal lesson, I will explain. Also please recognize that while it comes as a shock to you, the problem of the stadium is all too well known in Castel di Sangro and throughout the Abruzzo. In our present company and in the company of our host at lunch, it would be most inappropriate for you to raise this topic."

Then Barbara put a cheerful lilt back in her voice and smiled broadly and spoke nonstop to the Gravinas. Both Signor and Signora Gravina nodded in response, then smiled at me, then faced front again as Gravina accelerated rapidly, lit a cigarette, and made another call on his cell phone.

"Okay," I said. "What the *che* did you tell them?"

"I said merely that you were wishing to emphasize to me how important it was to be sure that Signor Gravina and Signor Rezza recognized the full extent of your gratitude for the extraordinary hospitality they are showing you. I also said that it is a regional attribute of people from certain parts of America that when they are very pleased, they use a tone of voice that can be mistaken for indignant."

"Wow. I'll bet you didn't learn that in any classroom."

"What is that?"

"How to bullshit. But if you're telling me the truth, you're doing a hell of a job."

"Please," Barbara said, blushing ever so slightly as she smiled.

I leaned forward once again. "*Grazie mille,*" I said again.

Gravina nodded briefly. His wife smiled.

"*Mangio! Mangio!*" I added. They stared.

"What did you just say?" Barbara asked.

"Nothing important, Barbara. I'm just practicing."

The temperature in Pescara was at least thirty degrees warmer than it had been outside the Best Western. I guessed that maybe ten degrees resulted from it being noon and no longer 10 A.M., but that the other twenty could be attributed to the difference in altitude: from Castel di Sangro's 3,000 feet to sea level. In early September this was not significant, but as I thought ahead to the long, cold, windy winter, I had my first moment of true appreciation for Swinburne.

Leaving *autostrade* behind, Gravina maneuvered expertly through a maze of back roads and one-way streets to arrive at the lush and tranquil Sea River Club.

"Why does it have an English name?" I asked Barbara as we entered the restaurant.

"They think that makes it seem more prestigious. Many Italians foolishly believe that using English terms is a sign of sophistication."

"Does Signor Rezza speak English?"

Her lips tightened as she suppressed a smile. "Signor Rezza does not even speak Italian. Signor Rezza looks and Signor Rezza gestures and Signor Rezza gets what he wants."

In that moment, Rezza's eyes fell upon me. Actually, the old man's eyes do not so much "fall" upon one as *jump* at the object of his attention. He was smoking a cigar that was at least nine inches long. He himself could not have been more than five foot six and was slightly stooped and had a large round belly. But no images of Santa Claus formed in my mind. Rezza's bristly gray hair was cropped short as that of a prison guard, his face was more square than round, and his lips formed a line as thin and steely as a garrote.

On either side of him stood the men who presumably were his bodyguards. One, in his twenties, must have weighed 300 pounds, with none of it fat. He was wearing a short-sleeved shirt, and I could see that his forearms were of about the same circumference as my thighs. The other man, much older, was cadaverously thin, slightly stooped, and wore, paradoxically, sunglasses as well as a dark brown trench coat.

"The older one doesn't look like much of a bodyguard," I whispered to Barbara. "In fact, he looks like he needs one."

"Yes," she said. "But he's retired *carabiniere*. The tough-guy police. And he's the one with the gun."

Barbara took three steps forward. The bodyguards parted, permitting her to kiss Signor Rezza on both cheeks and then to gesture in my direction. The guy with the forearms never took his eyes off me. Probably the other one didn't either, but with the dark glasses I couldn't tell.

If Rezza himself nodded to me, it was done with head movement of less than an inch. More likely, it had not been done at all. Certainly, his expression did not change. His mouth did not open. His gaze did not soften. Cigar in hand, he just stood there.

"Please tell Signor Rezza," I said to Barbara, "that I am very honored to be included in such special company on such an auspicious occasion and that I wish him and his team the greatest success possible, not only for today but for the entire forthcoming season. Also, you might mention that I'm glad we are eating at a restaurant called the Sea River Club, not because of the English name, but because I am especially fond of fish, and it's hard to get good fresh fish where I live in America, being so many miles from the sea. Also, that —"

I was interrupted by a grunt. From Rezza. He was looking at me with, if possible, an even less inviting expression on his face.

"He wants you to stop talking," Barbara said. "He does not like men who talk too much. He likes men who know how to eat and who know how to keep silent."

"When did he say all that? He just grunted."

"I have known Signor Rezza for many years," Barbara told me. "I can interpret his grunts."

Then she turned to Rezza, uttered about six rapid words, smiled broadly, and led me away.

"So," she said, seeming relieved. "Now the formalities are over."

"What did you say to him?"

"Only to please excuse you; that you were simply nervous about the match."

"What you said, though. It sounded different. It was very quick, but it was different."

"Yes, I was not speaking in Italian. I spoke to Signor Rezza in dialect."

"Dialect?"

"The *abruzzese* dialect. It is what he understands best. The dialects of Puglia and the Abruzzo are what he's always spoken. Italian was taught only in the schools, and Signor Rezza has had very little schooling."

"In the traditional sense," I said.

Barbara smiled. "Yes. In the traditional sense."

• • •

Fortunately, the group was large enough to be divided among several big tables, and I was at the table headed by Gravina, which enabled me not to speak to him during the lunch, rather than not to speak to Signor Rezza. Of course, I did not speak to Signor Rezza either.

What I did was eat. I ate every morsel of every course served to me, and there were at least eight of them. I did not drop so much as a fishbone on the rug. The fish and seafood – ranging from Adriatic oysters to Adriatic lobsters, and including at least half a dozen types of fish I'd never encountered before – were the best I'd ever been served. They were accompanied by three different white wines and followed by champagne.

At the end, Signor Rezza lit a new cigar and stood. His bodyguards jumped from their places. Signor Rezza looked at his watch. Immediately, the older bodyguard nodded to the younger, who broke into a half trot as he left the dining room for the parking lot to bring around Signor Rezza's car.

Throughout the room, conversations stopped in mid-sentence. Everyone stood. Nodding and grunting in the direction of the hovering maître d', Signor Rezza began a slow, penguinlike walk from the room, the smoke from his fresh cigar rising like that from a brushfire. Behind him, people scrambled to follow as closely as possible without it appearing that this was what they were trying to do.

Gravina mumbled rapidly into his cell phone as he walked. He'd not once removed his sunglasses, so it was only from the twitching around his mouth that one got the impression that as the hour of the match drew near, he was suddenly nervous enough to eat his newest cigarette instead of smoking it.

It was 3:30 P.M. and Castel di Sangro's historic, even miraculous debut in *Serie B* would kick off in only half an hour – unfortunately, nowhere near Castel di Sangro.

6

If the city of Chieti (population: 50,000), a few miles inland from Pescara, had attractive aspects, they escaped me during our rush to its stadium, a charmless hunk of concrete that seated the requisite 10,000.

The afternoon was glorious. As 4 P.M. approached, the sun remained hot and strong in a clear blue sky. The grassy field that spread out before us was impeccably green. Yet – something new in my experience – the stadium was only half full.

Having seen only World Cup and *Serie A* matches before, it had not occurred to me that seats in a soccer stadium might be left unoccupied. But here, outside our immediate VIP section, vast benches of concrete devoid of spectators stretched to the goal lines and beyond.

Only at each curved end of the stadium were there signs of life: to the left, Castel di Sangro fans waved red-and-yellow flags and set off red flares while, to the right, a far smaller band of Calabrians who'd come up from the south to root for the opening-day opponents, Cosenza, unfurled their blue-and-white banners and set off blue flares.

"Where is everybody?" I asked Barbara, who was seated one row behind me. "At the beach?"

"Many are. That is where I would be if I had not agreed to be here."

"But this is historic."

"Yes, and there probably *are* three thousand people here from

Castel di Sangro, which is sixty percent of the population. If sixty percent of the population of Torino had come to this match, that would be more than half a million. You must always remember how very, very small we really are."

Just then the teams took the field, giving me my first look at the miracle workers with whom I'd be spending the next nine months.

Throughout Europe and South America, soccer jerseys do not bear the team name but instead, in return for the highest payment that can be negotiated, the name of the team's principal sponsor. I was already aware of this. A.C. Milan jerseys said OPEL, for example, and those of Juventus carried the Sony logo.

Still, it came as a bit of a shock to see that the eleven Castel di Sangro players who trotted on to the pitch for their historic debut in *Serie B* wore jerseys that said SOVIET JEANS.

I turned to Barbara. *"Soviet Jeans?"*

She laughed. "It must look strange to an American. But this is a manufacturer of leisurewear from Napoli."

"But there isn't even a Soviet *Union* anymore!"

"Yes, and that is why the name is trendy."

"Trendy where? This brand name isn't exactly Calvin Klein."

"No, but as Castel di Sangro becomes ever more famous, people will learn of Soviet Jeans. Besides, one must do the best one can. The big brands want the famous teams."

"So, how about the jeans? Are they any good?"

"Well, *I* wouldn't wear them," she said.

More to the point, of course, was whether the Castel di Sangro team was any good. I had not yet been able to pose this question to anyone who might be knowledgeable, but inevitably the answer would do more than anything else to determine the shape and feel of the nine months to come.

If the club was hopelessly overmatched in *Serie B* and received a sound drubbing every week, my experience with them – while not uninteresting – would be of a different quality than if they somehow contrived to make a legitimate try for *la salvezza,* that beatific state reached at the end of the season by an exhausted and desperate club that narrowly escapes relegation.

For Castel di Sangro, success in the coming season would be synonymous with only one thing: survival. Their goal was nothing more grand than to get to the end of the thirty-eight-match marathon in a position no worse than sixteenth out of twenty, which would permit them to live to fight another year in *Serie B*.

From an American perspective, to say that a team was starting a season hoping to finish in sixteenth place would be laughable. Yet so logical and unbending was the system of promotion and relegation in Italy that there was nothing amusing about it.

The few newspapers and *calcio* magazines I'd had a chance to look at so far seemed unanimous in their opinion that *la salvezza* would lie far beyond the means of Castel di Sangro, however heartwarming *il miracolo* might have been.

Serie B, it was implied, was a no-nonsense, blue-collar league, barren soil in which no fairy tales took root. So close to the glory and glamor of *A* and yet so far, it was far more a boulevard of broken dreams than a haven for dreamers. A club did not survive at this level on managerial legerdemain, nor even on *il cuore* and *la grinta* – heart and pluck – combined. It was in *Serie B* that talent came to the fore, and that sort of talent did not come cheap.

As a promotion bonus, Castel di Sangro had received upwards of 5 million dollars from the *Federazione* that governs *calcio,* yet Gravina had been quoted in *La Gazzetta dello Sport* as saying, "We are only a poor team from a small village in the Abruzzo and we cannot pay to obtain the finest players." He apparently intended to scrape by with essentially the same team that had won the promotion, which was also, in large part, the squad that had won promotion from *C2* the year before. Whatever they lacked in talent, Gravina said, Castel di Sangro would make up for through *la potenza della speranza,* the power of hope.

Cosenza, which had finished twelfth the previous season and represented a poverty-stricken Calabrian city with a population of 100,000, promised to test the true strength of this somewhat ephemeral power. It was a squad without stars but with a mix of presumably cynical veterans and tough if only moderately talented youngsters, who already were grasping the hard fact that where they were right now might well be as far as they were going.

We, meanwhile (and by "we" I mean Castel di Sangro, for as soon as the squad took the field, I felt all traces of objectivity and detachment vanish: for better or worse, this was *my* team now, in a way no other in any sport had ever been), were not even at our *C1* best.

I'd learned from the morning papers that the goalkeeper, De

Juliis, who despite having made way for Spinosa in Foggia, had apparently shown great skill all through the previous season, was suspended for this match because of an accumulation of minor rule infractions carried over from the previous season. Also suspended was a thirty-two-year-old midfielder named Michelini, who'd been with the team for nine consecutive seasons, starting at the *Dilettanti* level.

In addition, kept out by injuries were a first-team defender named Fusco, as well as a player reputed to be the club's best, twenty-four-year-old midfielder Claudio Bonomi, who'd played in all but one match the year before. For some weeks to come, we also would be without injured forward Giacomo Galli, whose nine goals had led the team in *C1*.

Gravina had reinforced the power of hope only meagerly. He'd made one expensive acquisition: a thirty-year-old attacker named Pistella, purchased from the *Serie B* team Lucchese, which represented the Tuscan city of Lucca. For far less he had acquired another forward, Danilo Di Vincenzo, who had been voted Player of the Year the previous season in *C2;* a young defender named Luca D'Angelo, from right here in Chieti; and an aging midfielder named Di Fabio, whose last *Serie B* experience was five years behind him.

As an afterthought, only two weeks earlier, Gravina had apparently decided that the now-fabled Pietro Spinosa should be allowed to retire with his miraculous aura intact. Thus, as a backup goalkeeper for De Juliis he had obtained one Massimo Lotti, twenty-seven years old, who'd played the past three seasons with an undistinguished *C2* club located not far from Napoli.

Lotti was clearly intended for emergency use only – De Juliis was the number one man. Unfortunately, due to the brief suspension of De Juliis, our first emergency was occurring today, in our very first match in *Serie B*.

Then, with no ado whatsoever, the referee dropped the ball in the middle of the field and Castel di Sangro – and I – began life in *Serie B*.

There are eleven players on a soccer team, of whom only the goalkeeper is permitted to touch the ball with his hands while it is in play. The object of the game, which lasts for ninety minutes (divided into two halves of forty-five minutes each), is to put the ball into the opponent's goal more times than they put it into yours. Many Americans tend to laugh at how difficult this is, sneering at the large number of 0-0 and 1-0 matches rather than marveling at the fact that a goal can ever be scored.

Once my defense mechanisms against the glories of the sport had broken down, among the first of its elements to enchant me was the degree to which skilled players could execute all the basic maneuvers of a basketball player – dribbling, passing accurately, and shooting on target – using only their feet. Also while running nonstop (for there are no time-outs in soccer) over an area considerably larger than an American football field for a total of an hour and a half, all the while at the mercy of defenders who, unlike in basketball, were permitted to make frequent and often violent bodily contact.

At the very highest level – that of Baggio, for example – there is introduced into these physical executions an element of the sublime, or even mystical: "actions that refuse to submit to existing logic and knowledge of the possibilities of foot and ball," as expressed by the Dutch writer Oosterwijk.

Sublimity, however, as I would soon learn, was not a quality on frequent display in *Serie B*. Indeed, my first great revelation in connection with Castel di Sangro came as I watched the lusterless early minutes of the match: none of the elements that had combined to produce my obsession in the first place was anywhere to be found in Chieti.

As compensation, I experienced a wild rush of partisanship that left me feeling as if I'd just crunched down on an ampule of adrenaline. From the first moment, all I could do was to scream and groan and cheer and curse (in English, but that would not last long) as Castel di Sangro either moved forward or, more frequently, fell back on defense in apparent disarray.

I didn't want artistry, I didn't want bursts of spectacular skill, I didn't want transcendent moments: *I just wanted us to beat Cosenza!* And I hadn't even met the players yet.

Eventually, a bit of my excitement began to show. To be precise, it was in the nineteenth minute. Di Vincenzo, who was starting alongside Pistella on attack (in place of the injured Galli), was fouled by a Cosenza defender in the specially marked penalty area and thus was awarded a penalty kick. He made it with ease, thus scoring his and Castel di Sangro's first goal ever in *Serie B*.

I screamed as I jumped up and down hysterically and, in my excitement, began punching and squeezing simultaneously the left arm of Gravina, the president of Castel di Sangro Calcio. He sat perfectly still and stared at me coldly.

"Gabriele! Gabriele!" I shouted. *"We scored a fucking goal! We are winning!"* I turned back toward the field and shook my fist in the air. *"Bravvvoooo, Di Vincenzo!"*

Still, Gravina said nothing, leaving me an opportunity to consider that my reaction might have been inappropriate. Possibly, no matter what happened on the field, a guest should not start punching the team president in the arm. And so, as the halftime whistle blew, I took the opportunity to say to Gravina, *"Scusi. Grazie mille. Lei è molto gentile."* He said nothing. He simply lit a cigarette, stood up, and walked away.

The *intervallo* was brief – only fifteen minutes, with no extraneous entertainment designed to amuse and distract the spectators. At a good soccer match, you need *oxygen* at halftime, not superfluous dog-and-pony acts.

As the second half began, it was obvious that during the *intervallo* Cosenza realized just what an embarrassment it would be to lose to Castel di Sangro. From the first moment, they attacked, displaying the poise, focus, and confidence that one would have expected of an experienced *Serie B* team from the start.

And it soon became evident that Castel di Sangro might have been only masquerading as a team worthy of *Serie B*. Seeming to fear this, and in an attempt to protect his – *our* – unexpected one-goal lead, manager Jaconi sent the squad into a totally defensive formation.

In this alignment, we battled tenaciously in the midfield for a time, but eventually Cosenza began to penetrate, firing accurate shots on goal from every distance and direction.

Jumping up and down in rage and fear, racing back and forth in front of the *panchina,* or sideline bench, on which the substitutes sat, Jaconi, who from my vantage point looked like a cinder block wearing a necktie, seemed to be trying to create a barrier around our goal with only the sound of his voice. Increasingly, the question seemed to be not if but when Cosenza would score and, after that, how often.

Yet this did not take the new goalkeeper Lotti into account. As second-half minute piled upon minute and the sun gradually made its way westward, this afterthought, this backup *portiere* (goalkeeper) from *C2* seemed to grow larger and larger, until his presence in the goalmouth dwarfed everyone else on the field. He was playing not as if he were a new arrival in Castel di Sangro but as though he were a veteran of the national team.

Time after time, Cosenza overran or passed through or around the scrambling but tiring Castel di Sangro defenders, yet Lotti, standing six foot two and looking for all the world as if he were enjoying a relaxing afternoon in the park, repelled every thrust. He blocked corner kicks, free kicks, one-on-one breakaways, sixty-five-mile-per-hour blasts from twenty yards out – anything and everything he had to, even as Cosenza's frantic barrage became incessant.

Exactly at the ninety-minute mark, the *arbitro* (referee), whose powers in soccer are limitless, awarded Cosenza yet another corner kick. This is a direct free kick taken from one of the two corners of the field closest to the defensive goal. An attacking team earns the right to take such a kick if the defending team was last to touch a ball that crossed its own goal line – though, of course, without having entered the goal.

Like other free kicks – which can be awarded by the *arbitro* anywhere on the field if he deems a defensive player to have committed a foul – corner kicks can be devilishly difficult to defend.

For one thing, no defender is permitted to stand within ten yards of the player taking the kick. For another, almost the entire offense masses in the defensive penalty area, creating the substantial possibility that one of them might – with head or foot – deflect the kicked ball into the goal.

The rules generally protect the goalkeeper from deliberate physical attack by an opponent. On corner kicks, however, as the ball curls toward the goal at high speed and as six or eight players leap for it at once, this right of the keeper to be protected from harm slips into a decidedly gray area, and it is a brave and skilled man indeed who will outjump half a dozen onrushing opponents in order to pluck the ball from midair and hold it safely.

After already having demonstrated so much else, Lotti showed himself, on this ninetieth-minute corner kick, to be both brave and skilled beyond anyone's reasonable expectation. His spectacular save preserved our fragile lead.

Then, for four more minutes of extra time (the *arbitro* allotting this, at his sole discretion, to compensate for time lost because of injury or other stoppage of play) Cosenza continued to pound away, kicking and kicking, shooting and shooting, and in the process transforming the previously anonymous Lotti from a scrub goalkeeper into a world-class juggler, acrobat, and magician.

Those extra four minutes seemed like forty, but finally the whistle blew. It was over. Castel di Sangro 1, Cosenza 0.

I couldn't help myself. I turned to Gravina and embraced him. *"Bravo, Gabriele!"* I said.

"Grazie," he muttered, then lit another cigarette and stood up.

As for me, I climbed on top of my seat and shouted as loudly as I could: *"Bravo, Lotti! Bravo, Lotti! Bravo, Castel di Sangro!"*

I could see that hundreds of other Castel di Sangro fans – the ones able to afford the more expensive midfield seats and thus not forced to watch from the distant *curva* – were staring at me. As they heard my last *"Bravo!"* and saw my upraised arms, they, too, began to shout and cheer, waving at me and grinning.

My heart filled with joy. Finally, at the age of fifty-three, I had been united with my people.

7

At 10 A.M. Monday, Giuseppe helped me move to the Coradetti. The proprietor, bald and burly, seemed as glum as he'd been on Saturday, despite the Castel di Sangro win.

I would be in room number 8, which was up four flights of stairs. There was, of course, no elevator, this being a no-star hotel. (There also were no other guests, so the proprietor could just as easily have given me a room that was up only one flight of stairs, but the Coradetti's motto seemed to be WHEN YOU DESERVE THE VERY WORST.)

Having handed me the key, the proprietor returned to a small Formica table at which he'd been looking at *Il Corriere dello Sport,* the *calcio* newspaper favored by those in Bologna and points south because it was published in Rome and was therefore presumed (by southerners) to be more reliable than *La Gazzetta dello Sport,* which, being published in Milan, was undoubtedly filled each day with all manner of antisouthern slurs and inaccuracies.

The proprietor mumbled something to Giuseppe.

"Oh, yes," Giuseppe said. "He tell to me to remember you that the 'otel will be close *mercoledì.*"

Already, I knew that *mercoledì* meant Wednesday, but I failed to grasp the larger implications of the remark.

"Closed this Wednesday? Big deal. It doesn't seem very open right now."

"No, no, no," Giuseppe said. "This day she open. Otherwise, we not get in, *sì?* When he be close, like Wen-nes day, you no come in."

"But I'm already in."

"*Sì, sì, certo.* But Wen-nes day, you go out, he maybe not be easy for you come back."

"Do you mean to say that if I go out this Wednesday, I may not be able to get back in?"

"No, no, no," Giuseppe said. "Not be thees Wen-nes day. Ever' Wen-nes day he be close. *Mercoledì. Ogni volta. Chiuso. Ecco fatto!*" He waved an arm in a swift, horizontal motion. He advised me to speak to Barbara for more "specification" of this matter, and then he left, apologizing but saying he had "much busy things" that needed doing now that Castel di Sangro was not only in *Serie B* but tied, however temporarily, for first place.

As I was to learn, young Giuseppe was a man of many hats. Not only was he in charge of "external relations" for *La Società* but he was also the Castel di Sangro Calcio correspondent for *Il Centro,* the daily paper of the Abruzzo, and for *La Gazzetta dello Sport,* and for *Guerin Sportivo,* as well as host of a weekly local television program devoted to the doings of the team.

This meant, essentially, that if it involved the Castel di Sangro soccer team, it hadn't happened unless and until Giuseppe said it had, and he wouldn't unless and until Gravina told him to. In America, this might have been perceived as a conflict of interest, but in America hotels did not close every Wednesday either.

My mass of luggage virtually filled the tiny anteroom that passed for both lobby and bar at the Coradetti. I tried to calculate: 800 pounds times 4 flights of stairs equals 3,200 stair-pounds.

"Eccole!" I said to the proprietor, pointing toward my many pieces of baggage. There they are.

He nodded wordlessly, scarcely looking up from his paper. So I began. At first, I carried up only my two smallest bags, feeling certain that once the proprietor took note of the enormous task confronting me, he'd jump up from the table and with a big, convivial smile, insist not only on helping but on carrying the bags himself, while I, the guest, had a seat in the lobby, a look at the newspaper, and while I was at it, why not a coffee, too?

Such did not turn out to be the case. Half an hour later, exhausted and panting, my shirt soaked with sweat, I stumbled back into the anteroom, slumped into a chair, and pointing toward the small bar on one side, behind which stood an espresso machine and bottles of various sorts of drinks, gasped at the proprietor, *"Una Coca-Cola, per favore?"*

He shook his head quickly from side to side, then resumed his study of *Il Corriere dello Sport*. He was still on the same page, I noted uncharitably, as he'd been on half an hour before.

"No?" I said, disbelieving. "No Coca-Cola? Why not? This isn't Wednesday."

He shook his head again, clearly irritated by this sudden outburst in a foreign tongue.

"Scusi," I said – excuse me – reminding myself that this was not, after all, the Four Seasons in Beverly Hills. *"No Coca-Cola. Okay. Un'acqua minerale, per favore."* Surely, a glass of mineral water would be available.

Now the proprietor actually leaned forward, the first time he'd moved anything but his head.

"Chiuso!"

"Excuse me?"

He pointed toward the bar, which was actually so close to him that if he'd leaned back in his chair, he could have rested his hand on it.

"Chiuso!" he repeated. I was starting to pick up on the fact that this word meant "closed." Then, with a great show of annoyance, he stood, gathered together his newspaper, and walked out of the anteroom and into what I'd already been told were the family quarters – off-limits to guests – from which I could hear a television blaring.

I waited for about thirty seconds, then followed him. If I didn't get something cold to drink within another thirty seconds, my season threatened to be a short one.

He was seated at a table, still gazing: same paper, same page. A portly woman stood at an ironing board. Two hefty children of elementary-school age lay on the floor, glazed eyes gaping unblinkingly at the television.

He looked up. The woman put down her iron and glared at me. The children remained transfixed by the television. I made one of my typical lightning-fast assessments of the situation and instead of inquiring further about the possibility of obtaining a Coca-Cola or mineral water, said simply, *"Scusi,"* and left.

I weaved dizzily up the four flights of stairs to my room. The tap water from the cold faucet ran lukewarm. Indeed, it was exactly the same temperature as the water from the hot faucet: not cold enough to drink, yet not hot enough for a shower. A man of few words, this proprietor, but fiendishly clever.

I gulped down eight or ten glasses anyway and then collapsed on the narrow cot that was my bed until my heartbeat and breathing slowed to something resembling a normal pace. Then I changed into a dry shirt and set out to explore this magical mountain village I'd chosen to call home for the next nine months.

My first stop was the newsstand, three blocks away, in the central square. Because it was Monday, the players had the day off, as they always did the day after a match. I spotted Gravina standing just across the street from the newspaper kiosk. He was still wearing dark glasses, suede jacket, jeans, and leather boots, still smoking a cigarette and still speaking on his cell phone even as he simultaneously carried on a conversation with someone standing directly in front of him. He called to me, and I crossed the street.

"*La potenza della speranza,*" he said by way of greeting. The power of hope. Clearly, this was to be the motto for the year. As he said it, he actually smiled. Relieved that my excesses of the previous afternoon had apparently been forgiven, I continued on to a coffee shop, where in addition to an espresso, I drank six glasses of mineral water.

I had purchased not only *Il Corriere dello Sport* but the local *Il Centro* and, from stubborn loyalty, also *La Gazzetta dello Sport.* All three papers emphasized most strongly the historic nature of the Castel di Sangro triumph (we were now, and might forever be, the team from the smallest town ever to win a match in *Serie B*) and the dramatic revelation that had sprung to life in the person of goalkeeper Massimo Lotti.

In Italy, after every match, each newspaper rates every player's performance numerically, on a scale of one to ten. In practice, one almost never sees ratings lower than 4 or higher than 8, with the majority clustered in the 5.5-6.5 midrange, with 6 translating as "adequate."

Lotti received one 7 and two 7.5s. This would be splendid for anyone under any circumstance but was absolutely dazzling for a substitute goalkeeper making a debut at a higher level. Di Vincenzo, who'd scored the goal on the penalty kick, fell mostly in the 6-6.5 range, again quite creditable for anyone and a bit more than that for another player stepping up from *C2*.

The low men were a defender and midfielder, both of whom were destined for the substitute's bench now that defender Fusco and midfielder Bonomi would return. The expensive new attacker, Pistella, also received poor grades, but it had seemed to me he'd spent the first half merely getting his sea legs, and in the second might as well not have been on the field, so focused had Jaconi become on defense.

But the win had been the important thing. Three points were awarded to a winning team, none to the loser each week. For a draw, each team received one point. And it was these points that were all important, for they determined a team's rank in *la classifica,* or the weekly standings, and at the end of the thirty-eight-match season it was the four teams with the fewest points that would be demoted to *C1*. In any case, the papers were unanimous in proclaiming that *la favola,* or fairy tale, continued. They also had taken note of the arrival of the *famoso scrittore americano,* Alex Guinness.

That afternoon I took my first look at the stadium. Or at what had been and presumably one day again would be the stadium. Somewhere, amid oceans of mud and rubble, stood the remains of the old stadium. But all else was chaos. Bulldozers, cranes, flatbed trucks, cement mixers, steel girders, and huge slabs of concrete that might have been airlifted from Stonehenge were circled together in a pit – as if conferring about their next step.

Whatever that next step might be, it did not seem likely to be taken anytime soon. I thought it certain that no match would be played here in two weeks, or even in two weeks after that, no matter how many assurances to the contrary Gravina was giving to the press.

As things stood, in fact – virtually idle – no match might ever be played here. Although this was a Monday afternoon – and a fine one at that, with strong sun shining and the sky still clear blue – there were only half a dozen lackadaisical men and boys slumping against the heavy equipment, smoking cigarettes, while nearly 100 townspeople – presumably among the many unemployed – gathered outside a locked fence, talking quietly among themselves as they gazed at the inactive site.

. . .

That evening, as soon as the sun set behind the high mountain ridge to the west, a cold wind rose . . . and rose . . . and rose. At the Coradetti, I turned up the heat in my room. Rather, I tried to.

There was an antiquated thermostat and there were radiators, but clearly neither was functioning. No matter what dial I turned or what valve I twisted, nothing happened, except that the wind-chill factor in the room continued to drop. I took note of the two thin blankets on my cot. No, no, this would not do.

I walked down the four flights of stairs to the anteroom, which was, of course, empty. Once again, from behind the swinging doors, I could hear the blare of the television. I could also smell food, and through the crack between the doors see light and – I swear it!– feel heat.

I knocked on the door. The proprietor pushed it outward so fast that it bumped me before I could move out of the way. He was wearing only an undershirt and dark trousers, while I was clad in long underwear, a woolen shirt, and a North Face Steep Tech mountain parka.

He stared at me without speaking.

"Molto freddo," I said, pointing upstairs. Very cold.

He shrugged.

"Il caldo?" I asked. The heat? So this was how you learned a new language: you would either freeze or starve if you did not.

The proprietor shook his heavy head. *"Ottobre."*

I didn't need Barbara, or even Giuseppe, to help me with that one. October. No matter how cold it got, the heat in the Coradetti would not come on until October. Except, of course, in the family quarters. I nodded and trudged back upstairs, resigned to spending the night wrapped in my parka.

I could have all the *speranza* I wanted, but the *potenza* belonged to the proprietor and to him alone.

8

On Tuesday afternoon Osvaldo Jaconi and his players returned to town to begin the work of the season's second week. This would culminate on Sunday, in Foggia, in the same stadium in which the miracle had occurred. This time, however, the site would not be neutral: the opponents would *be* the Foggia team, 2–0 losers on opening day but a squad that had competed in *Serie A* only two years earlier.

The field on which Castel di Sangro trained, adjacent to but separate from the mess that might someday become a new stadium, was uncommonly picturesque. Even as it absorbed the warmth of a mid-September sun, snowcapped mountains rose above it on two sides.

Indeed, while the town's buildings may have lacked the charm of antiquity, its natural setting, with mountains pressing close against it on the west and an even higher range clearly visible to the north, more than compensated. This was a perfect setting for a fairy tale; a landscape that might well beckon the miraculous.

I had gone to the session hoping to meet a few of the players, but primarily to introduce myself to Jaconi and to determine how tolerant of my presence he might be. The last thing I wanted was to disrupt his training routine.

Unfortunately, print journalists and television crews swarmed all over me from the moment I set foot at the edge of the field. The American *was* here. It was true. I was, for one day at least, *una curiosità* – a curiosity – a new element. It was therefore necessary to speak to me even if true communication would not be possible. Giuseppe assured me that it made no difference that I could not understand the questions I was asked or that even if I had understood them, I would not have been able to answer. "No problem," he assured me. "No problem."

So, one after another, the print journalists and TV people took their turns. A few did speak some English, which enabled them to conduct at least a rudimentary interview. Why had I come, they asked. My answer was simple and true: as improbable as it might seem, I was an American obsessed with *il calcio,* and I had come to spend the season in Castel di Sangro to see what life was like in the aftermath of a miracle.

As for the others, I would listen with a polite but blank expression, and when they stopped talking, I would smile and nod and then blurt out, *"La potenza della speranza. Sì, sì, grazie a Lei. Ciao, ciao, ciao, ciao, ciao."*

It proved educational to see the results that night and the next day. In the case of television, my incomprehensible mumblings quickly gave way to an authoritative voice-over, summarizing what were said to be my comments and impressions, as I was seen staring helplessly at the camera.

But it was in the newspapers that the true magic occurred. There, my one or two shards of badly broken Italian were somehow transformed into full paragraphs within quotation marks that seemed not only grammatically flawless but gave evidence of an extensive vocabulary and of a speaking style that appeared to border on the eloquent.

When I commented on this to Giuseppe, he said, "But for sure. Since you cannot speak in our language, they must write what they wish for you to say if you could."

"But they made it up out of nothing."

"*Sì,* but is no problem because is good."

"But they could have stayed in their offices. If they were going to make it up anyway, they didn't even need to speak to me."

At this Giuseppe looked troubled. He shook his head. "No. Is not possible. First you must interview. Then you make up."

Jaconi, whom I immediately sensed was not a patient man, smiled benignly upon me all through that first afternoon. With Giuseppe serving as interpreter, he extended to me, in fact, a warmer welcome than I could have hoped for. He assured me that he considered my presence a gift to his team, not a nuisance to him; that I should feel free to go wherever I wanted, whenever I wanted – as if I were Jaconi himself – and that I should feel free to talk to him or to any of the players at any time, except during the actual training sessions. (Unfortunately, none of the players spoke any English, while his own was limited to "I bulldozer," so until I acquired at least rudimentary Italian, these conversations, of necessity, would be brief.)

But I would be welcome in Jaconi's office, in his apartment (which was only three doors down from the Coradetti), and in the team locker room. In addition, for meals, which the unmarried players ate as a group at Marcella's, he had reserved for me the seat next to him at the head of the table. And while the players were expected to address him as "Mister," a long-standing carryover from the game's introduction into Italy by the English, he and I would be on a first-name basis.

"I, Osvaldo," he said. "You, Joe."

"No, Signor," I replied. "You, bulldozer; I, Joe."

He threw back his head and laughed loudly. Then, clapping me on the shoulder as he waved toward the training field with his other arm, he indicated that I should feel free to wander at will on my own.

Having no assistant except the newly promoted Spinosa – without whose "miracle" save of the penalty kick none of this would have been possible – Jaconi had to do everything himself, from devising tactics to conducting conditioning drills to lugging bags of soccer balls back and forth between the locker room and the field. This might be *Serie B,* only one rung down the ladder, but it seemed a long way from A.C. Milan.

I took to the training field, exchanging waves and smiles and *ciao*s with small groups of players who were doing stretching exercises. My first task clearly would be to match faces with names. There were twenty-one on the squad, and on that first afternoon I was able to recognize only three: Lotti, the substitute goalkeeper who'd played so brilliantly; Galli, because he was on crutches; and Di Vincenzo, who had scored the goal and whose ready grin was unmistakable.

All the players were Italian. Expensive foreign talent was imported almost exclusively by *Serie A* teams, with only a few of the upper echelon of *Serie B,* such as Torino, Genoa, and Bari, making forays into the world of these *stranieri.*

The Castel di Sangro squad members ranged in age from nineteen to thirty-five and in height from five foot six to six foot two. All obviously were physically fit, despite the fact that more than half of them smoked (a habit that Jaconi said he encouraged because he believed that it "relaxed" them). Most seemed cheerful and gregarious.

Almost immediately I sensed that my presence was pretty much taken for granted. That a fifty-three-year-old American had suddenly materialized in their midst, announcing his intention to write a book about them, seemed no more unlikely than much else that had happened since June – or over the past three years, for that matter.

The first to approach me was a tall, sturdy, and almost absurdly handsome man who introduced himself as the team captain. This was Davide Cei, a native of Pisa, who had been at Castel di Sangro for eight years, having taken the whole ride up from *C2.* Now nearing the end of his career, Cei suddenly found himself the linchpin of the defense of a *Serie B* team, surely not something he'd ever envisioned.

"A rising tide lifts all boats" was a phrase I thought I should learn in Italian because it seemed applicable to at least half the Castel di Sangro team. These were *C2* players who individually never would have shown enough promise or flair to have attracted the attention of any club in *C1* – much less *Serie B* – but who together had won that coveted and unlikely status for themselves and for one another.

What became clear to me almost immediately was that they took enormous pride in their accomplishment of having made Castel di Sangro the smallest town in all of Italy ever to have risen to *Serie B* and that they would fight to the death to keep it there.

Cei, of course, did not intimate any of this to me at our first meeting. He merely said – or seemed to be saying, in an Italian whose word-per-second rate I was sure he was slowing for my benefit – that he wanted to welcome me on behalf of the players and to tell me that I should consider myself from the start as *uno di noi,* which even I understood as "one of us," and for which graciousness I tried to thank him appropriately.

He then actually apologized for his and his teammates' inability to speak English (as though they should have spent their summer vacations learning for my benefit!) and, with many gestures, including one toward the wedding ring on his left hand and another that suggested a belly swelling, indicated to me that he would not be taking his meals at Marcella's, but that no doubt we would see each other from time to time while walking around town and that more likely than not he'd be with his wife, who was pregnant.

It is remarkable, really, how much specific information can be conveyed through even the most impermeable of language barriers if the conveyor truly wishes to do so and has the patience and resourcefulness to keep trying, no matter how obtuse the listener might seem. From the start, I considered myself extraordinarily lucky to have stumbled upon a team whose manager and captain were both willing to make this extra and contractually unrequired effort on my behalf.

In time, as I found that virtually all the other players were eager to do the same and – no matter what part of the country they came from or how much or little education they had received – that they did so with an unselfconscious, instinctive graciousness, I came to feel not only that Italy was like no other country on earth in this regard but that this Castel di Sangro squad must be like no other professional *calcio* team in all of Italy.

Over time and with instruction by two talented teachers, I grew able to meet the players more than halfway linguistically, and eventually to amuse them occasionally as I groped my way toward an extremely attenuated understanding of their tongue.

Cei ended our first "chat"– if it could be called that – by calling to a player who was passing nearby. This was Danilo Di Vincenzo, Roman by birth, twenty-eight years old, and the man who'd scored our first goal in *Serie B*. It seemed that Cei wanted to be sure I was properly introduced to such a personage.

Di Vincenzo had remarkably bright eyes and a luminous grin that seemed ready to surface at the slightest provocation. *"Grande Joe,"* he said, dispensing with formalities. *"Tu porti bene."* You bring good luck.

"Speriamo," I replied. Let's hope so.

Unfortunately, my prompt use of one of the few conversational responses I'd so far learned gave Di Vincenzo the erroneous impression that I spoke and understood Italian, and being Roman, he was at least five or six sentences into his next remarks before Cei was able to flag him down to tell him that my riposte had been merely a lucky stab. Nonetheless, I felt an embryonic bond start to form with this high-spirited new *attaccante,* or forward.

Seven years earlier Di Vincenzo had played half a season in *Serie B* – oddly enough, for Cosenza. Having failed to score even a single goal, however, he'd been returned to the lower levels, where his overall career path might have been plotted by a drunk throwing darts at a map: Lodigiani, Civitavecchia, Arezzo, Carrarese, Pavia, Pistoiese, L'Aquila, and Giulianova. Not a journey on which one would encounter many American tourists.

At twenty-eight, he was well past the age when dramatic improvement usually occurs, but in the previous season he'd scored a career-high eighteen goals and had been named Player of the Year in C2. So who could tell? Maybe now Danilo of the sparkling eyes would also find his place in *la favola.*

The player I made a point of seeking out was Lotti. He had blue eyes and curly, sand-colored hair; he stood six foot two, was half my age and obviously fit in a way I had not been for years – or, frankly, ever.

"Piacere," he said, shaking my hand. I knew what that meant. Glad to meet you. I'd spent all morning memorizing phrases.

"Molto bravo domenica," I said, pointing to him. *"Molto bravo."* This, I was hoping, would convey the notion that I thought he'd played a strong match on Sunday. He had, of course, been far more than *bravo,* but at this early stage I was not about to risk a superlative.

"Grazie a Lei," he said, speaking formally to me. He had been born on the Mediterranean coast, south of Rome but north of Naples, so this *tu* and *Lei* business, the informal and formal ways to say "you," was clearly as much a matter of personal style as of geography, whose conventions assume that northerners are more formal than southerners.

I wanted to tell Lotti that I hoped over time we might establish a more easygoing and familiar relationship of the *tu* sort, but I did not know how. He stood, looking at me politely but expectantly, obviously eager to get on with training but not wanting to give offense.

My mind worked frantically. I wanted to tell him even more emphatically that he'd played a spectacular match on Sunday. But how to say that, how to say that? Ah, now I remembered the key phrase.

"Per te," I said, lapsing into the informal mode of saying "for you,"

"it was, it was" – I knew this was English but I couldn't help it – *"un bel pasticcio."* A beautiful match.

Lotti looked at me oddly, tilting his head to one side. *"Sì, davvero?"* he said. *"Perché?"* Yes, really? Why? Too late I realized I had blundered. "Ah, *scusi, scusi, per favore. Bello. Bella. Lei è molto gentile e molto bravo. Bravo! Bravo! Ciao!"*

Then I turned and walked away from the bewildered new goalkeeper, looking for a private place where I could glance at my phrase book to see just see what mistake I had made.

Damn! It had been a big one. I had used the wrong word for "match." I should have said *una bella partita* – a beautiful match. *Un bel pasticcio,* unfortunately, meant "a fine mess."

Only a few hours later, at Marcella's – where, over the next nine months, I would spend more waking hours than in any other location in Italy, including the apartment I would eventually rent – I also blundered with the number one goalkeeper, Roberto De Juliis.

He was twenty-four and from Teramo, a city of 50,000 in the northern Abruzzo. He'd never played professionally for any team except Castel di Sangro and had become the squad's number one (literally, in that the starting goalkeeper wears the jersey with the number 1 on its back) the previous season, playing every minute of every match until making way for Spinosa in the last seconds of the last one.

It had not occurred to me to think about whom I might be dispossessing as I took the proffered empty seat immediately to the left of Jaconi. I soon learned, however, that the seat had belonged to De Juliis, who had moved down one chair to make way for me.

I soon learned also that the seating at the team table at Marcella's could be viewed as latter-day Kremlinology, as one read significance (correctly or not) into who was seated closest to Jaconi and who was seated farthest away. There was no written chart, but the pattern never varied, and it was the "golden boys" that Jaconi valued most highly (often for their personal loyalty more than for their talent) who claimed the coveted seats closest to the master.

Thus, Jaconi was flanked on his left by De Juliis and Giacomo Galli, respectively the number one keeper and top goal scorer from the year before, and on his right by midfielder Tonino Martino and the scrappy Neapolitan defender Pietro Fusco, two close friends who had joined the club together at the start of the 1992 season, even before Jaconi himself. The newcomers filled the seats farther down the table.

The other veterans of the miracle – who were, in many cases, veterans also of many bleak seasons with Castel di Sangro – were married and thus did not eat regularly at Marcella's.

Besides Cei, these included the defenders Prete and Altamura; the midfielders Bonomi, Alberti, and Michelini; and, of course, Spinosa himself, who lived with his wife and young son in an ancient stone house only a corner-kick's distance from the thirteenth-century church that had been spared annihilation in World War II. It was only fitting, it seemed, that the man who'd actually performed the miracle would live so close to the church.

But my arrival disrupted the orderly universe of Marcella's. Had I known at the start what I learned later, I would have thanked Jaconi for the offer of a seat next to him but would have added that I – a newcomer also – should sit at the far end with the others.

Instead, I had seized upon the offer at face value, giving no thought to the psychic static it would cause – not only to De Juliis, who after Lotti's sterling debut was suddenly worried about keeping his number one position, but also among his friends and teammates of years' standing.

That first night I simply took the empty chair as if by birthright, and when De Juliis, to my immediate left, murmured only the most subdued of greetings, I mentally wrote him off as rather churlish.

Boundless is the arrogance of the ignorant! But no one (least of all De Juliis) ever said a word about it, and I'm afraid that nearly two weeks passed before I realized how graceless I had been. Then one night I simply arrived early and took a seat midway down the table. When De Juliis walked in, I motioned toward the chair I had been occupying and said only, *"Per te."* For you. He said, *"Grazie,"* and nodded toward me, and that was the end of that. It was one of my first, though far from last, lessons in innate Italian subtlety – not all of which, I must confess, I absorbed with equal grace and understanding.

Marcella was a short, blond woman of forty-some years. About fifteen years earlier, she, her husband, and three small children had moved to Castel di Sangro from an outlying village. At first, she and her husband had worked as janitors at the school, but soon they opened the pizzeria. Over the past ten years Marcella's had grown into perhaps the only true landmark in Castel di Sangro. This had far less to do with the quality of the food than with the quality of Marcella.

For the past several years she'd contracted with Gravina to provide lunch and dinner to the unmarried players and to Jaconi, whose wife and children remained in Civitanova throughout the season. This meant that the same thirteen or fourteen men would gather twice a day, five days a week, at the same long, rectangular table next to the kitchen, eating the same food and hearing the rasp of Jaconi's voice week after week from September to June. A journalist once wrote of this as dining "seminary style," and were it not for Marcella's song-filled heart, it could have been a bleak and trying experience.

Yet because of Marcella – her spontaneity, her capacity for empathy, her innate warmth – even the married players would bring their wives and children for dinner every week. And Gravina would regularly host large parties for family, business associates, and friends. Laundry was dropped off and picked up at Marcella's. Mail for players was delivered to Marcella's. International cup matches were watched on television at Marcella's. Bets were phoned in (legally) to offshore bookmakers from Marcella's. Romances bloomed, withered, died, and were reborn on her pay phone, not to mention on the dozen or so cell phones that were in use on her premises at any given time, day or night.

With her husband, their two by now grown sons, Christian and Giovanni, their daughter, Rosita (who divided her time between the pizzeria and the university at Perugia, where she was majoring in pharmacology), and their five-year-old son, Gianmarco – quite possibly the most endearing person of any age in all of Italy – Marcella provided far more than food and drink to the team.

She was earth mother to all, radiating warmth and good cheer on even the darkest of days and providing a degree of emotional sustenance throughout the season, without which it might not have been possible to survive intact, given the deprivations imposed by Castel di Sangro. Always loving and fiercely loyal, Marcella was unwilling to even listen to criticism of "her boys," much less engage in it herself.

Ennobled and enlivened by her presence, Marcella's was, in

short, the quintessence of the Castel di Sangro experience. For Jaconi and the single players – and, from the first night, also for me – it was more of a home than where we slept.

Seated among the veterans, I noticed quickly that despite having been dispossessed of his chair, De Juliis enjoyed privileged status. He had, in fact, assumed a number of proprietary duties, chief among which was smelling the cheese.

It seemed a pervasive fear that due to her myriad distractions, Marcella would let her Parmesan-type cheese sit too long in unsealed jars on the salad bar next to the table. Thus, before each meal, taking care not to let his long, curly hair make contact with the contents, De Juliis would carry each jar to the table and smell the cheese that lay inside, a process somewhat akin to a sommelier sniffing the cork of a just-opened bottle of wine.

And there were times when he would shake his head, grimace, and call out for Marcella or one of her sons to remove the offending vessel from his presence and to repair to the kitchen to grate cheese afresh.

The chair to his left was occupied by Giacomo Galli, twenty-five, nicknamed "Boom Boom" by the fans, in honor of the team-leading nine goals he'd scored the previous season, as well as for his ebullient personality. Like Di Vincenzo, Galli was a native of Rome. He possessed an ego strong enough to dwarf the light of the brightest Roman candle and a mouth that kept pace with it in every way. Despite having spent, like Di Vincenzo, several nomadic seasons in *C1* and *C2* without any achievements of note, Galli reeked of self-confidence and assured me on our first meeting that as soon as his ankle was healed, I would see offensive fireworks on a scale I'd never imagined.

Flamboyantly handsome and proud as a peacock in the finest tradition of Rome, Galli suffered from an uncontrollable head twitch, a tic that, when combined with his compulsion to run his hands constantly through his thick brown hair and an inability to either sit still or keep from speaking for longer than about thirty seconds at a time, caused me to suspect that his boyhood school days must have been less than tranquil.

Opposite me sat the two players who – aside from Claudio Bonomi, the fleet midfielder with braces on his teeth who was married to a woman from Castel di Sangro and thus ate only rarely at Marcella's – were probably Jaconi's favorites, something the manager made no effort to disguise.

Despite markedly different personalities, Fusco and Martino had played together for so long (a year with the *C2* squad Lanciano before joining Castel di Sangro together five years earlier) that in the hurly-burly, rapidly changing world of minor-league *calcio,* they were the virtual equivalent of Siamese twins.

Pietro Fusco was a short but muscular twenty-five-year-old defender who'd been born and raised in Napoli, and not in one of the wealthier sections either. A laconic young man with tired eyes that often projected a sense that they'd already seen far more than they should have, he made clear that one would accept him on his terms or not at all, and that even then there was no reason to believe that he would accept you on any terms whatsoever.

Martino could not have been a greater contrast. He had short, curly hair that he dyed blond; he sported a large, gold ring in his left ear; he drank red wine at both lunch and dinner but insisted on diluting it with Sprite. Along with De Juliis and a newly acquired defender, Luca D'Angelo, he was a native Abruzzan, having been born in a small town near Pescara.

Tonino, who never failed to greet me by first yodeling the name of his favorite American sports hero – *KarrrEEEEEEM AaabDDDUL JabbbAAARRRRRR!* – with the finest rolling of a final *r* I ever heard in Italy, was without doubt among the most extroverted, warm-hearted, and gregarious members of a notably open and sociable team, but no one would have termed him an intellectual.

One night, after my language skills had improved considerably, I came upon him puzzling over a new Nintendo game he'd just rented. "A problem, Tonino?" I asked. He looked at me with genuine worry. "Oh, Joe, this one is going to be the most difficult yet. I cannot even understand the instructions!" He handed me the box to show me just what he was up against. I looked at it quickly. Then I handed it back. "Tonino," I said, "these are in Spanish."

And then, of course, there was Jaconi. Within five minutes, I became aware that he had given me the seat to his immediate left not only as a courtesy but so he could more easily and repeatedly expound to me his philosophy of *calcio* and of life, without permitting anything so fragile as a language barrier to interfere.

The first matter to be pronounced upon was garlic. It was strictly prohibited from his table. He believed garlic to be unhealthy in the extreme, and especially to the digestive system of athletes. No garlic itself and no foods flavored with garlic to even the slightest degree would be permitted at any point during the season. I was expected — as a Westerner would be expected to remove his shoes before dining at a Japanese table — to observe this protocol every bit as religiously as did the players.

In addition, hot peppers, while not strictly forbidden, were frowned upon. Jaconi did not like them himself and could see no good that came from consuming them. Marcella did not use them in her cooking, and although a bowl of them, marinating in olive oil, lay available for use at the salad bar, Jaconi let it be known that he would view their consumption as offensive.

The smoking lamp, on the other hand, was always lit. Players could and did smoke before, during, and after meals, as well as at other times throughout the day and night. The notion that such a practice might be deleterious to the health — not to mention to the stamina — of the players was something that Jaconi insisted was nothing more than American-inspired gobbledygook, akin to the preposterous belief that consumption of animal fat in large quantity might be harmful.

On the very first night, Jaconi moved directly to the subject of *il calcio*, which was, after all, the reason why both of us were there. *"No, no, no, no, no!"* He didn't want to hear any nonsense about *la potenza della speranza*. Let Gravina feed that to the press. The truth, sad to say, was very different.

"In Serie B," he said, staring directly into my eyes from a distance of less than three feet, *"la stagione è lunga e dura."* The season is long and hard. He said it once, twice, then a third time. *"La stagione è lunga e dura."* Then he tapped my notebook with the thick fingers of his right hand, and I thought for a moment that he was going to tell me to move to a separate table and to write out the sentence one hundred times before returning for my dinner.

Yes, they had won their first match. But that meant nothing. *Niente!* What was one match of thirty-eight? They'd earned three points. But those might be the only points they'd earn all year. And what then of the fairy tale? What if the miracle had been only a cruel hoax? I had to understand: this was *Serie B!* And they were only Castel di Sangro! Not Torino, not Palermo, not Padova or Genoa or Bari or Brescia or Venezia. Not even Foggia, the team they'd face in their first away match on Sunday. This was not child's play. This was not some lark. Goddamnit, this was *Serie B,* and in his fifteen years as a professional football manager Osvaldo Jaconi had never been here before, and no matter what happened – no matter *what!* – no one was going to be able to accuse him of having underestimated the difficulties involved.

The whole monologue was delivered in Italian. And yet so unmistakable were Jaconi's gestures, so marked his inflections, so great the range of volume of his voice, that even though I recognized only about 10 percent of his words, I had no doubt that I'd absorbed the full meaning.

There was nothing I could yet say in response, but Jaconi was not looking for a response. As I would learn, Jaconi seldom spoke with the intention of eliciting a response. His words were the words that mattered. He was the one who knew, who understood, who controlled. Thus, a response was seldom in order, be it in regard to garlic or to a shift from a 4-5-1 to a 4-4-2 formation.

To argue with him – whether about *calcio,* food, music, automobiles, women, psychology, history, or quantum mechanics – was very much like throwing pebbles at a bulldozer. It might prove entertaining in the short run, and if you threw enough at the same time and they all landed squarely on the window, the driver might turn his head momentarily, but that was all: the bulldozer would continue on its fixed course, changing neither speed nor direction, no matter what the weather, no matter what the terrain, no matter how many bodies jumped or were thrown in its path.

I listened transfixed, and more than a little terrified, and I wasn't even a player. This, of course, was exactly the reaction Jaconi had hoped to provoke. Having seen that he'd succeeded, he leaned back, slapped me on the shoulder, and called to Marcella for a lemon liqueur sipped only on special occasions.

"Benvenuto a Castel di Sangro!" he said. *"A casa mia tu sei sempre il benvenuto. Sarò lieto di poterti essere utile in qualsiasi cosa, e anche i presenti sono invitati a rispondere sempre alle tue domande!"*

This burst of good fellowship required Marcella to bring her son Christian, who spoke discernible if primitive English, out from the kitchen.

"Mister Jaconi," Christian said, "he say to you welcome, no? But more, he say always you welcome in his home. And any helps he can be for you, he want to. And always from you the questions about any-thing, he will be glad to have them and to answer, to help you to learn."

"Christian," I said, "please tell Mister Jaconi that I am more grate-ful for his hospitality than I could say even in English. He is very, very kind and he makes me very, very happy and I wish him and the team very, very much success and I will be very, very much the num-ber one supporter. It is a great honor for me that he should give me this welcome, and someday I will find the right way to repay his ex-traordinary generosity."

Christian was nodding as I spoke but, it seemed to me, ever more doubtfully as my words of gratitude spilled forth.

And before he could even begin to translate, Jaconi spoke again, then laughed loudly and slapped me on the back even harder than before.

"Mister say it be okay, he sees you are bullshitter. Not to bother. He is glad you here. And he say, you save the rest until you learn the bullshits in Italian."

9

The next morning I walked down the Coradetti's four flights of stairs but immediately noticed something different at the bottom. The door to the small room where the front desk was located was closed. Not only that, it was locked.

"Mamma mia," I said to myself. This is Wen-nes day. *Chiuso!* Barbara was working in Rome until Thursday, and I never had gotten around to asking her what Giuseppe and the proprietor had been trying to tell me about *mercoledì,* but now I remembered. Closed.

Well, the Coradetti never really seemed open anyway, and I had no business to conduct at the front desk, so I simply stepped to the glass door that led directly from the bottom of the stairwell to the street.

But the door would not open. It had been locked, and it could not be opened even from the inside. I could not call the front desk to complain, because there was no one at the front desk and I didn't have a phone in my room.

Still, it took me a moment to realize that I was trapped. I stepped to the locked door that led to the anteroom and began pounding on it and shouting. There was no response. I shouted and pounded for ten minutes and heard not a whimper in return.

What if there was a fire? *Mercoledì. Chiuso.* The words took on a new and ominous meaning. I was locked inside this no-star fleabag of an igloo, and that fat son of a bitch proprietor and his sullen family had probably gone off on a *picnic,* for Christ's sake, and I wouldn't be able to get out of here until tomorrow! Oh, how I wished I had already learned some decent curses in Italian. Instead, I unleashed a long, loud string of English obscenities.

This had an effect. My ranting did not disturb the silence that lay beyond the anteroom door, but the noise filtered through the glass door to the street and attracted the attention of several teenagers walking past, on their way to morning classes at the Castel di Sangro high school.

"Aiuto!" I shouted to them, somehow remembering that this was the Italian word for "help!" And I pounded on the glass door. *"Fuori! Fuori!"* I shouted, recalling that this was the word that meant, "out."

But the sons of bitches – and daughters of bitches, as well, for there were two or three girls in the group – just started laughing. What, they think the American comes all the way to Castel di Sangro to practice bilingual stand-up comedy?

"Io sono il famoso scrittore americano, goddamnit!" I shouted. Then I remembered that I had with me the English-Italian dictionary I carried everywhere.

"Wait a minute! Wait a minute!" I shouted to the kids, holding up a finger. Fortunately, they seemed to be enjoying the show and not in any hurry to get to school.

I paged frantically through the book, looking for the word for "imprisoned." Son of a bitch! It was a tough one: *im-pri-gio-na-re.* And that was only the infinitive. Here, I clearly needed the reflexive. *Mamma mia,* why hadn't I learned this language before I'd come? Nonetheless, I took a stab. Anything was better than having the kids lose interest and walk away.

"Sono imprigionato in questo albergo!" I shouted, hoping that it meant "I am imprisoned in this hotel" or something close to it. Then I rattled the door handle to demonstrate.

But these damned kids were loving it! I could hear their laughter roll right through the glass, which, if I'd had a suitable implement, I would have broken in a moment.

Well, might as well close with a flourish. I got down on one knee and held out my hands, imploring.

"Aiuto! Aiuto! Per piacere!"

Still they just stood there laughing.

I looked back at my dictionary, which was still opened to the page containing "imprison." This time my eyes fell upon a word that might truly prompt action. I stood quickly to my full height and tried to make a show of real anger.

"*Aiuto! Subito!*" I shouted, looking the tallest of the girls straight in the eye and pointing right at her. "*Oppure ti ingravido!*" Help right away! Or else I'll impregnate you! If that didn't bring the proprietor, maybe it would bring the police. At that point, I didn't really care.

The rest of the group laughed at the tall girl, and even she began to smile. Then they moved on, and apparently in the right direction, because no more than five minutes later I heard footsteps from the anteroom and the door swung open to reveal, in what I would have sworn were silk pajamas if that would not have been quite so far out of character, the proprietor.

At first I thought he might hit me. Instead, he merely glared with maximum ferocity and thrust into my hand a tiny key, not more than an inch and a half long and scarcely as thick as a razor blade. Then he waved a hairy hand toward the glass door that led to the street.

Approaching it and leaning forward, I saw a slight incision just below the handle. A keyhole perhaps? *Mannaggia,* yes! Damn, I was in business! The tiny key slid into it, I turned my hand slowly about one inch to the right, and heard a click. The door handle now moved freely, and the glass door itself swung open.

Barefoot, the proprietor now lumbered past me, into the street, which was clearly not someplace he wanted to be seen in silk pajamas. He grunted and pointed to a similar incision beneath the outside door handle. Then he pointed to the key.

I nodded, smiling a broad smile of gratitude and understanding. Using the tiny key, I would be able to leave and enter the hotel at will, even on Wednesdays!

But just so I did not forget, he shouted at me: "*Mercoledì! Chiuso!*"

On Friday morning, just back from Rome, Barbara came to the Coradetti – to be sure, she said, that I had gotten her message.

"Barbara. I have now been here for four nights. I am the only person staying here, except for the family. And I don't even want to talk about Wednesday. But every time I walk through the front door, the Spirit of Christmas back there asks me what I want. I tell him I want the key to my room. He asks me what room I'm staying in. I tell him room eight. He looks at me as if I've just insulted his mother. Then he stares at me. Finally, he hands me the key. Do you really think he'd give me a message?"

"That's why I came in person," Barbara said. "Because it's very important. Signor Rezza wishes to meet with you in his office at noon."

"Uh-oh. What for? I swear to God, I ate every clam they gave me. Shells and all."

"No, no, it is nothing like that. Signor Rezza would simply like to welcome you officially to Castel di Sangro, and I will be there to translate. I will meet you at *La Società* office on the third floor at ten minutes before noon."

At precisely five minutes before noon, an aide to Rezza materialized and motioned for Barbara and me to follow him. We walked up two flights of dark and narrow stairs and paused outside a heavy mahogany door that offered no clue as to who, or what sort of enterprise, might occupy the interior. The door was very slightly ajar.

The aide, who was wearing dark sunglasses, knocked hard. He then called out, *"Permesso?"*

There was no answer. Nonetheless, he opened the door and walked across a large and heavily carpeted room that – although it contained desks, chairs, computers, and all sorts of other equipment one might expect to find in a modern office – was deserted. At the far end there was another door, this one also only slightly ajar but enough so that the smell of cigar smoke wafted out.

The aide knocked again. *"Permesso?"*

From behind the door there was a grumble.

The aide opened the door fully, motioned for Barbara and me to step inside, then closed it behind us and was gone.

Signor Rezza was seated behind a large desk, the surface of which was absolutely bare. His hard eyes were looking a little rheumy, I thought, through the cloud of cigar smoke in which they were enveloped.

He grumbled again.

"Buongiorno, signor Rezza," Barbara said.

"Buongiorno," I said.

He took a long pull on his cigar, though never moving his eyes, which stared hard at us. All was silent. His bodyguards were not in evidence, but I would have bet a year of my life that there was a button somewhere within his reach that could have promptly summoned them.

He grumbled again. This one was longer than the two that had preceded it.

When he stopped, Barbara said to me, "Signor Rezza would like to know why you are staying in a hotel so unpleasant as the Coradetti."

"Tell him I did it on short notice. It's only temporary. Next week I'll start looking for an apartment."

She repeated this to him, and he grumbled again. "Signor Rezza says you do not have to look. He has one for you."

"Ah! Well, that's, ah . . . convenient. But I think maybe I'll look around a little anyway. You know, to compare prices, locations, and –"

But Barbara had begun to speak before I'd finished. Whatever she said elicited a grumble quite similar to the others.

"What did you say?"

"I told him you were immensely grateful for his hospitality and that you would be ready to move in as soon as you returned from America."

"But wait a minute, Barbara." I was, however, interrupted by another grumble.

"Signor Rezza says that for your convenience, the apartment will be located next door to the one occupied by Mister Jaconi."

"Really? Wow, that would be convenient. Tell him, really, thanks a lot. But is it vacant? And how much do you think the rent will be?"

"Those are merely details. Not to bother Signor Rezza with personally. He has assistants for the details. And it does not matter if the apartment is vacant. Whenever you wish to move in, it will be."

Then Rezza spoke again. This time actual words were distinguishable, though I could not, of course, understand them.

"Signor Rezza is asking if on Monday morning you would like a tour of his mountaintop estate to be followed by a lunch prepared by his cooking staff, and your answer of course will be yes, so I will simply ask him at what time he would wish you to arrive."

"*We*, Barbara. *We!*" I'd already heard about Signor Rezza's security measures, and did not wish to pass unaccompanied through his ten-foot-high steel gates.

"Yes, now Signor Rezza has invited me also, in order that he might be more convivial. He tells us that we should arrive at the gate at nine A.M. Monday and announce ourselves at the speaker. So – oh, wait just one moment, please."

An additional grumble rolled through the smoke toward us.

"Oh, yes. Signor Rezza instructs that under no circumstances, of course, are you to bring either a camera or any sort of recording device. I will assure him that you would never have considered doing so."

"By all means," I said, shuddering at a sudden image of the skinny bodyguard patting me down and discovering my trusty little Canon, and then the big one, Bruno, taking the camera from me and swallowing it whole.

There came from Signor Rezza what I took to be a grumble of dismissal.

"Yes, Signor Rezza says we may leave now, unless you have any questions, and I shall assure him you do not."

"But, wait a minute, Barbara. I do have one."

"Joe! This had better be nothing about the new stadium."

"Barbara, please. I may be crazy but I am not suicidal. I only want to ask if he is going to the match in Foggia on Sunday."

In response to Barbara's query, Rezza actually took his cigar out of his mouth. He grumbled in what seemed a darker tone, then waved us away dismissively.

"No, he will not attend. Signor Rezza says he does not travel to a match when he anticipates an unpleasant result."

Anticipated result notwithstanding, on Sunday morning I rode with Giuseppe to the hotel near Foggia where the team had spent the night before. The players were just finishing lunch when we arrived. My first task involved the dreaded language barrier, but I knew I would have to attempt it or be thought an even greater fool than I was.

All week, I'd felt like an idiot whenever I'd seen Lotti. He would smile at me and even make a point of walking over to me and shaking hands. It was obvious from his manner – not merely with me but in the way he dealt with everyone – that he was a gentleman as well as an exceptional goalkeeper. The pace of the training sessions, however, had not permitted more than a greeting. Now I had to explain to him my mistake.

I found him on the lawn outside the hotel, walking slowly back and forth under a shade tree and, naturally, having a conversation on his cell phone. When the team traveled, the players all wore matching gray suits, blue shirts, and red-and-blue ties – the upscale end of the Soviet Jeans line. On this warm afternoon at sea level in southern Italy, Lotti had his jacket slung over one shoulder as he strolled.

As soon as he'd completed his conversation, I approached him. As usual, he smiled and reached forward to give me a firm handshake. Like most of the others, he was a good-looking man, but what I had begun to notice especially about him was his eyes. They were the eyes of a deer, constantly flicking this way or that, noticing everything that entered the field of vision, constantly on the alert for possible danger. In no other mannerism did Lotti display any sign of nervousness whatsoever. But the eyes told you he had to be one of two things: a professional goalkeeper or a cop.

"*Scusi, Massimo.*" I had practiced this, alone in my cold room at the Coradetti.

"*Sì, Joe. Ciao. Come va? Bene?*" Hi, how are you, okay?

"*Sì, Massimo, grazie. Però un attimo, per piacere.*" However, a moment, please.

"*Certo, Joe. Certo.*"

"*L'ultima settimana . . . ,*" I began. Last week . . .

"*Sì?*" He looked at me in encouraging fashion, as if rooting for me to manage the Italian successfully.

"*Ho detto . . .* to you!" I said . . . but I couldn't handle the pronoun in Italian, so I simply pointed at his chest. I said, "*Ho detto, 'un bel pasticcio.'*"

He laughed and put an arm around my shoulder. "*Sì, Joe, sì. Ricordo.*" He remembered.

"*Quello era un errore.*" That was a mistake.

"*Sì, Joe,*" he said, still laughing. "*Lo so.*" He knew it had been a mistake.

"*Volevo dire . . .*" I was hoping this meant what I thought it did: I wanted to say, "*una bella partita.*"

He'd stopped laughing but was smiling and nodding. "*Lo so, Joe. Lo so.*" He pointed to his forehead with a forefinger. He'd figured that out at the time. Well, of course. He was no idiot. Only I had sounded like the idiot.

• • •

Although Jaconi was still being coy with the press, he had told both Lotti and De Juliis on Friday – and on Friday night he'd also told me – that Lotti would play against Foggia. De Juliis was still number one, Jaconi stressed, but Lotti had played so well in the first match that there could be no justification for making a change so soon.

Knowing this, I handed Lotti a note I'd spent two hours composing that morning, also uttering the new phrase I had learned. The phrase was, *In bocca al lupo!* The literal translation was "in the mouth of the wolf," but for some reason this was the *real* Italian way of wishing someone good luck before a competition of any sort.

"Crepi il lupo!" Lotti replied, as the saying required ("Death to the wolf!"), then gave me a strong squeeze on the shoulder and a big grin. *"Grande Joe,"* he said. *"Tante grazie."* He pointed back and forth between himself and me. *"Noi siamo amici, no?"* We are friends, aren't we? Then he looked down at the note. *"Io la leggo."* I'll read it.

What it said, in the best Italian I could muster, was no more than "I know what it feels like to be an outsider. And I know that even after your great match against Cosenza, you are still an outsider to this team and to Mister Jaconi. This must put extra pressure on you, so please know I will be rooting especially hard for you today, and no matter what happens, I know from what I saw last week that you are a goalkeeper who carries with him the potential for greatness."

I walked back toward the hotel feeling quite pleased with myself. But standing on the first step, just staring at me, was De Juliis.

"Ciao, Robert," I said. For reasons having to do with Abruzzan dialect, people did not pronounce the *o* at the end of his first name.

He nodded but said nothing.

"In bocca al lupo," I said.

"A lui," he said, gesturing toward Lotti. *"Io sono in panchina."* Good luck to Lotti, sure. As for me, I'm on the bench.

Jaconi invited me to ride to the stadium on the team bus. We arrived shortly before 3 P.M., an hour before the match, and walked quickly through a short, dank tunnel into a locker room located beneath the grandstand. As soon as the players dropped off the bags containing their uniforms, they headed down a dark corridor, turned right, then walked up a flight of stairs, and stepped out into the brilliant sunlight that flooded the field.

I quickly joined them. This was, after all – and especially for those who had been with the club the previous season — their Field of Dreams. It was here, only three months earlier, that *il miracolo* had occurred.

I had a hard time imagining it as I gazed around at the 25,000 empty seats and dreary, run-down surroundings. Foggia was not a thriving city, and the stadium, which looked as if it had survived every Italian war since the time of Garibaldi, was definitely not in the high-rent district.

True, down through the centuries, many miracles had occurred amid shabbiness, but it was beyond any mental leap I could make to picture a Foggia team having beaten the Juventus of Baggio here only two years earlier. Yet it had happened. And only a year before that, as Castel di Sangro had struggled in *C2*, Foggia had finished in the top half of *Serie A*. Then, as frequently happens, a shortsighted management had rushed to cash in, selling off all the talent at once, and now here was Foggia, about to face us, having slumped to twelfth in *Serie B* the year before.

I noticed De Juliis pacing the scrubby, dusty field in solitude, pausing occasionally to squat and to rub his hand through the thin patches of grass. I approached him, a bit afraid that he might have been displeased by having observed my sudden cordiality with Lotti.

"Che fai?" What are you doing?

He looked up. Then he smiled at me with what I thought was a trace of embarrassment. *"Sto cercando i quadrifogli."*

I shook my head helplessly. I didn't understand. He stood and brushed off the knees of his trousers. *"Quadrifogli,"* he repeated.

"Scusa, non capisco." I don't understand.

He held up a finger. *"Aspetta, Joe."* Wait just a moment. He bent down again and tore a clover loose from the grass. He held it toward me, counting. *"Uno, due, tre,"* he said. *"Niente."* Then he held up four fingers and smiled.

Ah, of course: *un quadrifoglio* – a four-leaf clover!

"I quadrifogli portano bene, no?" he said. They bring good luck.

"Sì, sì," I said smiling.

"Anche in America?" Also in my country?

"Sì, certo. In tutto il mondo." All over the world. My late nights with the phrase book were already paying off.

But now that we'd begun to quasi-converse, there was something I wanted to ask him.

"Questo campo," I said. *"Per te è speciale, no? Il miracolo?"* This field is special to you, isn't it? Because of last June?

"Ah," he said, suddenly understanding that I wanted him to reminisce. *"Sì, sì, molto speciale."* He placed a hand on my shoulder and guided my eyes toward the substitute's bench at the side of the field. *"Piangevo, piangevo. Quando ho visto Spinosa, ho detto, 'No, no, no!'"* I was crying. When I saw Spinosa, I said, No, no, no! *"Ma. Eccoci qua. Speriamo in meglio."* Yet, here we are. Let's hope for the best.

Just as in June, buses arrived bringing hundreds (though not thousands) of Castel di Sangro supporters. This time, of course, Gravina had not paid. Also, this time the Castel di Sangro supporters were confined to one end of the field, behind a goal, and "protected" by phalanxes of armed police. This was standard procedure at matches in Italy, presumably intended to keep the fans of the home team from assaulting and dismembering the badly outnumbered fans of the visitors. And even though attendance at Foggia had dropped sharply since relegation from *Serie A,* I estimated that our people were outnumbered by at least ten to one.

From the start, it appeared that our players were outnumbered, too. Jaconi had succumbed to what seemed the greatest temptation for all *allenatori* in Italy: to approach a match *fuori casa,* or away from home, with undue caution, if not outright fear. In this instance he had chosen to keep Di Vincenzo on the bench in favor of an extra midfielder, whose presence he hoped would relieve pressure on the defense.

The tactic proved ineffective from the start. In the first three minutes Foggia attacked three times, forcing Lotti to block a menacing shot on each occasion. And after only eight minutes Foggia scored. An attacker dribbled nimbly past the stumbling and backpedaling Cei, then simply pushed the ball past an already prone Lotti, whose frantic dive had come too soon.

From that point forward, matters worsened rapidly. After only ten minutes I wrote in my notebook that Castel di Sangro was "outclassed and outpaced." Nothing that happened later changed my mind. It was only another phenomenal effort by Lotti that held the final score to 2–0.

. . .

THE CASTLE FALLS TO PIECES was the headline in the next morning's *Il Centro*. DEFENSE UNRECOGNIZABLE, TOO MANY ERRORS AND BAD GAME PLAN said the Abruzzo edition of *Il Messaggero*.

Jaconi, while he could not mask the reality with words, had told reporters, "It's only one stop along the way. We'll proceed calmly and think ahead to Cremonese," which would be the opponent the following Sunday.

I admired his attempt to keep an even keel, especially given how deep-seated was the Italian tendency – win or lose – toward hysterical overreaction each week.

At the same time, in my own private moments of hysteria, I feared that the season could be more more *lunga e dura* than anyone yet suspected. Our offense had managed only one goal in two matches (and even that had been a penalty kick), and our defense seemed, in essence, to be composed only of Lotti, fortified by any four-leaf clovers De Juliis might be able to find.

10

Barbara arrived on time, as always, and we were at the locked steel gates, about fifteen kilometers outside and at a considerably higher altitude than Castel di Sangro, at 8:55 A.M. Monday morning.

She left the car to press a button and to talk into a speaker attached to the gate. I noticed two small videocameras mounted on either side of the gate, trained toward us, from the ten-foot level. By requiring that the driver of a vehicle step outside to request admittance, the security system allowed those inside to see, as well as to hear, whoever wished to enter.

All the way up, the private road had been narrow and steep, with many curves. Thick woods bordered it on either side. Where the steel gate ended, a high fence topped with barbed wire continued through the woods. Not a tempting spot for trick-or-treating on Halloween.

Barbara and I were expected, however, and the two massive steel plates soon slid apart. Once inside, a visitor had to travel another two miles up a steeper, twistier, even narrower road. One thing seemed certain: if anyone ever did penetrate the outer layer of Rezza's security, he'd be approaching at minimum velocity.

The morning was clear, the air dry, and the sun, from the vantage point of Rezza's house, was already well up in the sky. This area not only offered a 270-degree view of all that lay for many miles beyond and below but was itself devoid of anything that grew above the knee, so the view of the foreground also was unobstructed.

That meant, of course, that anyone approaching Rezza's house from any direction would be clearly visible from at least half a mile away. There would be no unpleasant surprises here, it seemed, for the man Jaconi called – without apparent reference to Mozart – *il Commendatore.*

Moments after parking in front of the main house, we were approached by a pleasant young man wearing a green jacket with various insignia that would have made him look like a National Park Service ranger if we had been in America. This was Vito, a nephew of Signor Rezza's, and he would be our guide for the morning.

Within a moment, a Land Cruiser appeared. Vito quickly climbed into the driver's seat, taking the place of the man who'd delivered the vehicle, motioned for Barbara and me to get in, and we were off.

The next three hours were strictly Steven Spielberg. I don't know how many thousands or tens of thousands of acres the estate might have covered, but its vastness wasn't the point. For behind his steel gate and the barbed-wire fencing that ran the entire circumference, Rezza had created for himself a self-sufficient world.

His water came from mountain streams. Three separate generators could supply electricity if the main power lines were down for any reason. The main house was heated not only by wood but by natural gas and solar power. He had his own petroleum depot for refueling his fleet of vehicles. He'd erected greenhouses for growing tropical fruit even in winter conditions that approached the subarctic. He had women who did nothing but tend acres of vegetable gardens. He had men who did the same with fruit trees. He had ponds full of trout. And, most of all, he had animals.

As in *Jurassic Park,* the varied species were fenced off from one another; and, as in *Jurassic Park,* some were so exotic that Rezza's estate was the only place in Italy one had any likelihood of seeing them. There were chamois, gazelles, mule deer, horses, sheep, and huge herds of something that looked to me like a cross between an elk and a caribou but that no one ever could precisely identify.

Why? was the first question that came to mind. Rezza didn't seem the sort of man who'd get up in the morning and ask Vito to drive him to the llama patch so he could feed a few out of his hand.

The answer, after much apparent embarrassment on Vito's part but much persistent questioning by Barbara, finally came down to "tax break." By providing a self-sustaining habitat for various species considered endangered by the Italian government, Rezza qualified for tax rebates so huge that it was as if the people of Italy had built and were maintaining his estate for him – which, in a sense, they were. Lure a hundred unicorns from the nearby national park, throw a fence up around them, and the government sends you a check for billions of lire. It was not the worst of businesses.

But even more amazing than the animals was what Rezza had done to the mountains themselves. When he'd first acquired this property some years earlier, he'd selected the site for the house he wished to build, and then examined the sight lines in all directions. To the south the land gave way steeply to the valley in which Castel di Sangro lay. But in other directions mountains rose in the distance above what would be the house. Some of these were in configurations that pleased Rezza. Some were not.

And so, over several years, he had set about changing the terrain. Using dynamite and bulldozers, and maybe even arranging for a small, localized earthquake or two, he put peaks where none had stood before and eliminated those that offended his aesthetic sense. The scale of the operation, as Vito detailed it, seemed beyond not only description but comprehension. Most important, however, was that at the end it should all look natural – at least from the house.

Yes, if one were to drive up close as we were doing now in the Land Cruiser (and no lesser vehicle would have sufficed), one could see the sutures and gaps. Tens of thousands of tons of boulders had been moved maybe three hundred yards and rearranged in a contour that Rezza had found more palatable. This process had been repeated dozens of times, across all quarters of the estate. And tens of thousands of tons of soil had been excavated, carted, dumped, and piled high in dozens of other areas.

Rezza had literally made mountains. And he had, in the space of only a few years, literally destroyed mountains that had been formed over millennia by geologic forces clearly less powerful than him.

The key, Vito said, was importing just the right collection of grasses. Types that would grow swiftly to cover the scars, prove hardy enough to withstand the climate, and be indistinguishable from the natural grasses covering the lower slopes that had remained untouched.

Everything, Rezza decreed, was to look as if it had always been there. Everything had been changed to make it seem as if nothing had changed. With one exception: the sight of rocks – not rock formations that were necessary for building mountains – but just plain rocks, if visible from the front lawn of his house, offended him. He didn't like just plain rocks sitting there.

So the last part of the construction of RezzaWorld involved digging up and moving to a location of his property not visible from the front of his house what turned out to be thousands of rocks, ranging in size from soccer balls to the moons of Jupiter.

Yet even now there was danger, Vito said. Rezza would come to the front yard to take the sun and to look down over Castel di Sangro – his private Lilliput – but then, sometimes after five minutes, sometimes after ten, sometimes not for an hour, but almost every day Rezza would think he saw a rock.

Where? Up there. There? No, over there. Up by those fir trees? No, goddamnit, over there, where I'm pointing, can't you see it? That's a rock. Get it out and get it out now! *Subito!*

And so a crew of six to eight men clambered into Land Cruisers and trucks (they kept their earth-moving equipment in sheds high up the mountainside for just such occasions) and, all the while maintaining radio contact with Rezza's bodyguards below – as the old man sat on a lawn chair, watching through binoculars – would search for what might possibly have been an overlooked rock but what was far more likely to be a figment of Rezza's imagination or a false image conjured by his seventy-seven-year-old eyes.

In any event, they'd stay up there for an hour or two, driving their vehicles across the terrain, getting out, calling in a bulldozer, and eventually radioing back to base camp that they'd spotted it for sure this time, yep, that sucker had been there all right but it wouldn't be there much longer because Uberto or Tito or whoever was coming in now with the 'dozer. By the time they'd come down again, Rezza would have gone in for his nap. And that would be it, until the next time.

In my naïveté, I asked Vito what would motivate a man who didn't like rocks to build an estate in the mountains.

The courteous Vito did his best to answer, this time employing an analogy. "Signor Rezza," Barbara informed me, after listening to a long explanation, "has an estate similar to this one but overlooking

Lake Lugano in Switzerland. Sometimes the color of the lake displeases him, but because it is not his lake, there is nothing he can do to change the color. Also he has an estate of this dimension above the ocean, in Pescara, and he becomes irritated on occasion by the times at which the low tides and the high tides arrive. But again, there has been no way that he has found to alter this. But here, everything belongs to him, and so this is the one place on earth that he can make perfect, according to his vision of perfection."

We returned at lunchtime. Signor Rezza was waiting at the door. He had apparently just concluded a business meeting of some sort, for there were three or four clearly subservient men in business suits and dark ties standing in a semicircle just behind him, jiggling their briefcases nervously, as if eager to be set free.

As I entered, Rezza asked the expected question about whether I had enjoyed the tour. Maybe it was the altitude, or maybe it was my empty stomach, or maybe it had just been the whole scene. In any event, as Barbara began her ritualistic, appreciative response, I reached out a hand and stopped her.

Instead, I spoke myself, at the same time taking a checkbook from an inside pocket of my blazer.

"Just what I'm looking for," I said. "I'll take it. How much?" And I thrust the checkbook and a pen toward Signor Rezza.

At this, the minions sprang like jumping beans. Some to Rezza's side to make sure he would not hear Barbara's translation and to assure him that my producing a checkbook was simply a tasteless joke; others to Barbara, to make sure she would not translate; and still others in front of me, to berate me for my irreverence, making it clear in the most forceful verbal terms possible that Signor Rezza's estate was not and never would be for sale, and what I might have thought was a joke was in fact a profound insult. It was amazing how many people who heretofore could not seem to comprehend a word of English had understood exactly what I'd said.

Through the babble, Rezza gripped his cigar in one hand and with the other reached out and gently took Barbara by the arm.

"Forget these idiots" was what she later told me he had said. "Tell me the words of the American."

And so she did, explaining that of course I'd only been joking, that of course I recognized that the estate which represented the culmination of Signor Rezza's life's work was not and never would be for sale. I stood still, the hand holding the checkbook now lowered to my side, its palm starting to sweat.

But as Barbara translated, Rezza merely put his cigar back in his mouth. And then, looking directly at me, he said, through clenched teeth, words that Barbara translated as "You never know. As with anything, it depends on the size of the check."

The table was set for four: Barbara; Signor Rezza's other niece, named Elena, who had no interest in the soccer team; Signor Rezza, wearing a blue blazer much like my own; and me. Suddenly I was nervous. I could feel myself begin to sweat.

Eight courses were served. Antipasti, first cold, then hot; two pastas; two fish courses; a *secondo,* or main dish, which in this case was inedibly tough lamb killed that very morning – not shot, I was assured, for that would impair the flavor, but strangled by hand – and then, after a sorbet, an impossibly rich dessert of chocolate, custard, and a multiplicity of pastries.

I gobbled. I tried to swallow. I choked. I stuffed my cheeks like a chipmunk. I looked desperately for a housepet to which I could give some of my food, but the German shepherd and Doberman guard dogs were kept outside, on lean rations. I even considered getting up at one point and walking to the fireplace to admire the blaze and, at the same time, tossing a napkinful of half-chewed food into it. Finally, I settled on merely excusing myself for the men's room and flushing as much as possible down the toilet.

Not that there was anything wrong with the food. On the contrary, it was even better than that served at the Sea River Club. But it was also served in far greater quantity, something I would not have thought possible. Besides, it is difficult to chew and swallow when one's digestive juices have dried up at the same rate at which one's testicles have ascended into one's groin.

For me, both processes had commenced just before lunch, as I'd glanced into Signor Rezza's den and seen, amid all the newspapers stacked for his reading, a single hardcover book. I knew that Rezza himself could not read, but I'd been told that his niece read to him each evening.

I stepped into the den and leaned sideways in order that I might decipher the title, as printed on the spine of the book.

And I did. It was in Italian, but I translated it all too easily. It was *The Life and Times of Sam and Chuck Giancana: American Heroes*!

The meal concluded with a chilled bottle of Dom Perignon. This coincided – certainly not by accident – with the unannounced arrival of Gravina, who pulled a fifth chair to the table, swigged half his champagne in one gulp, lit a cigarette, and began to stare at me.

After sending away the empty bottle, Rezza summoned the eighty-proof grappa. Glasses were poured only for him and for me. It was apparently time to talk business, though I could not imagine what kind. Barbara leaned forward, listening attentively.

Rezza began by asking my opinion not of the food or the wines or the estate, but of the team.

"Well," I said, trying to be prudent, "they have achieved much in a short time. To expect more immediately might not be realistic."

Mah! He waved his cigar dismissively. Then he began to speak as quickly as Barbara could translate. One always expects more, he said. Otherwise, what is the point of life? I was a *scrittore americano* and therefore presumably possessed of at least some intelligence. If the team were mine instead of *his* – and with this he jabbed his nine-inch cigar perilously close to Gravina's silk shirt – what would I do to make it better?

I glanced across the table at Gravina, whose province this clearly seemed to be but who was just then not merely studying but apparently *counting* the bubbles in his perfectly stemmed glass of champagne. Clearly, no help coming from that quarter.

So I took a deep breath and said, "Money." I said it was obvious to me from the first two matches, against mid-level teams in the division, that with its current roster, Castel di Sangro could not hope to survive in *Serie B*.

"Money for the midfield," I said. "For defense. For the attack. The team must spend the money necessary to attract better players. Only Lotti seems truly worthy of *Serie B*."

Rezza listened intently to Barbara's translation, then spoke a word of true Italian: *"Esattamente!"* Exactly! But from what source would *La Società* obtain these essential funds?

"As I understand it," I said, wanting to tread cautiously here, "you already have them. I am told that *La Società* received a promotion bonus of at least eight billion lire from the Federation."

Rezza and Gravina both stared hard at me as Barbara translated. Though not precisely a secret, the promotion bonus was not something Gravina encouraged the newspapers to focus on, and neither man seemed pleased that I had already learned of it.

Fueled by Dom Perignon and grappa, I continued. "But you're not spending this on the team," I said. "You have bought only one expensive player, Pistella. And although I have seen only two matches, I would already say that whoever advised you to spend so much money on Pistella either knows nothing about *il calcio* or does not have your best interests at heart."

I paused. Signor Rezza actually placed his cigar in an ashtray, turned in his chair, and glared at Gravina in a manner that could not have made *il presidente* comfortable. Then he mumbled something to Barbara as Gravina motioned to a waitress for more champagne.

"Signor Rezza says Gabriele insisted on the purchase of Pistella. Signor Rezza himself had opposed it from the start and is most interested in the view you have expressed."

Emboldened, I added, "You're not even spending to build the new stadium fast enough. It is shameful that the team must play its home matches in Chieti. And by the way – if you will permit me to put to you one further question – when will the stadium be completed?"

Barbara glared at me, but she was a professional. She translated. In response, Rezza merely waved his cigar and mumbled. Gravina spoke. "The stadium will be ready for the match against Ravenna on October thirteenth, as scheduled."

"But not ready for Cremonese next week?"

He shook his head and repeated, "Ravenna." He was glaring at me in the same manner that Signor Rezza had glared at him a moment earlier.

Then Rezza mumbled to Barbara. "Signor Rezza," she said, her own voice now seeming just slightly strained, "says that while Gabriele's optimism is admirable, it is not always grounded in fact. For Ravenna, he says, maybe and maybe not. But certainly for the match against Padova two weeks later."

"But could you tell Signor Rezza," I persisted, "that I walk past the construction site every day and never do I see any signs of progress?"

She sighed, but complied.

His eyes not the least bit rheumy at this moment but with pupils like two pieces of buckshot, Rezza said, "Tell the American that if there is so little to see, he should not waste so much of his time looking."

In response, I only nodded.

Then Rezza continued to speak, both looking at me and gesturing toward me with his cigar. "Signor Rezza says you should forget about the bonus from the Federation," Barbara translated. "You should pretend that this does not exist. It has been put to different purposes, which are of no interest to you, but it is not available for the purchase of the new players you would like, so where should Signor Rezza obtain the money to buy them?"

"Possibly," I said, "by selling one or two of the players who are on the team now."

A fierce waving of the cigar was accompanied by a short burst of *abruzzese* dialect apparently so coarse that it reddened Barbara's ears. But she said only, "Signor Rezza has used an earthy colloquialism to express his view that our players are not of sufficient quality to attract a buyer willing to spend the money he wants."

Then Rezza mumbled again, and pointed to Barbara with his cigar, meaning he wanted his postscript translated also.

"Ballerinas," she said. "Signor Rezza feels that Gabriele has assembled a squad of ballerinas. And Signor Rezza is not a fan of the ballet."

More smoke and grumbles from Rezza, who now appeared to be openly glowering at me.

"You write a book about my team?"

"Yes."

"And you receive money to write this book?"

"Yes, but it's sort of complicated."

He shook his head in annoyance. When he asked about money, he did not want to hear about complicated.

"*Sì o no!*" For that clarification he did without Barbara entirely.

"*Sì.*"

Another long puff on the cigar. And back to Barbara with a series of questions: How much money? All in a lump sum or spread over time? A fixed amount, or did it depend on the number of copies sold? Was the book to be published in Italy? If so, by whom? How much would they pay? And what about England? And other European countries? And might there not be a large market in South America? And surely there would someday be a movie.

For an uneducated Abruzzan who spoke only dialect, he was certainly asking all the right questions. I felt as if I were in a meeting at Simon & Schuster.

"It is my team," Rezza said. "The American writes book. The American makes money. I make no money. This is –" and Barbara paused a long time before translating the next word as "unsuitable."

Leaning closer to me, but at the same time seeming to sit farther away, she said, "Signor Rezza continues, 'It is my team, so I receive money from the book. Very simple. And very just. Surely, the American, as a guest at my table, would not be so discourteous as to challenge my logic.' "

The sound of her voice betrayed the new dryness in Barbara's mouth as she translated these remarks. By the time she'd finished, there were tiny traces of white spittle at each corner, and she reached quickly for her glass of water.

"Signor Rezza," I said, leaning forward. "Perhaps your assistants have not made you aware that I have forfeited the sum of one million dollars U.S., which I was to receive as payment for writing a book about Mr. O. J. Simpson, in order to have the privilege of writing about the *calcio* team you have created for the village that lies below us in the valley.

"Having done so, unfortunately, I have put myself in a position whereby any payments, except of course for my rent and basic living expenses, are out of the question. While I agree completely with the spirit of your remarks and would receive great pleasure from sharing with such a generous man as yourself any revenues I might receive as a result of writing this book, it is simply not possible.

"In fact, were you truly to deem such payments necessary, I would have to return to America without ever having the opportunity to write about your magnanimity and graciousness – nor about the 'Miracle of Castel di Sangro' for which you deserve so much credit. And I, for one, feel that that would be a terrible pity."

Barbara's translation must have been a work of art. By the time she finished, Gravina was staring at me open-mouthed, while Rezza simply looked me in the eye. Then he nodded in his usual almost imperceptible manner and extended his grappa glass forward until it touched mine.

"Salute!" he said. To your health.

"Prosperità!" I replied. Bless you.

Five minutes later Barbara drove me back to town. We spoke barely a word to each other, but I noticed that she was sweating even more than I was and that her hands were trembling as she gripped the steering wheel.

11

As soon as he arrived at the training field on Tuesday, Jaconi summoned me to his office. At first, I feared that he, too, might want a cut of my proceeds, but his concerns turned out to be more immediate.

"*La squadra è senza umiltà,*" he said bluntly, pointing to my notebook, indicating that he wanted me to write this down. The team was without humility.

But I must have misunderstood. Perhaps there was a word that sounded like *umiltà* but meant something more along the lines of, say, talent? Possibly a word on the order of *capacità,* or ability. This was what he must have meant.

"*Sì,*" I agreed. "*Peccato! Nessuno è molto capace. Forse solo Lotti.*" It's a pity. No one has much ability. Maybe only Lotti.

Jaconi pounded a fist on his desk. "*Umiltà!*" he shouted. "*Non capacità. Ho detto umiltà!*"

Okay, I'd been right the first time: he had said *umiltà*.

"*Sicuro nessuno ha le capacità! Quello non è il problema! E' che mancano d'umiltà!*" Of course, no one had ability! They weren't *supposed* to have ability. If they had ability, they wouldn't be here. It was humility they'd have to learn, he repeated, before they could hope to succeed.

Oddly enough, and based only on my brief observations, if I'd had to choose a word that *would* have aptly described most of the players, "humble" is probably the one I would have selected.

Yes, some, such as Galli (who did not seem likely to play for at least another two weeks), might have had a surface bravado, but almost to a man the Castel di Sangro *giocatori* conveyed most strongly the sense that despite their elevated status in Italian society (and if anyone thought that even minor-league soccer players in Italy were not viewed as semimythic creatures, he would have had only to see their wives and girlfriends in order to correct that misapprehension), they did not consider themselves superior in any significant sense to the nonplayers who populated their daily lives.

Whether it was toward one of Marcella's sons working as a waiter at the pizzeria, strangers stopping them on the street to offer unsolicited advice, or an older man billed as a *scrittore americano,* the Castel di Sangro players exuded spontaneous warmth while both maintaining their own dignity and respecting the presumed dignity of others. To me, this seemed the essence of humility, and I did not grasp – then or ever – Jaconi's point.

Other than seeing them at training and sharing meals with the bachelors at Marcella's, my most frequent contacts with the *ragazzi* (or boys, as they were known collectively, no matter their individual ages) in these early days came simply from chance meetings in town. And when, as was the case in Castel di Sangro, a town consists of only three main streets and one square, such encounters occur with frequency.

Heading out for the papers in the morning, I might encounter Andrea Pistella walking with his young wife, who would be pushing their baby in a stroller. He would greet me warmly. I would hug him as if I hadn't seen him in weeks, though in fact I would have seen him at training the afternoon before and would see him there again in a matter of hours. I would shake hands with his wife, mumbling what I hoped might pass for Italian, then bend over to ogle their baby. On the field Pistella was having a difficult period of adjustment following his jolting transfer from Lucchese, but this did not detract in the slightest from his graciousness to another new arrival.

Two minutes later I might pass Fusco, walking alone, his head down, looking for all the world as if he wanted to be left alone. Thus, I would do so. But my failure to greet him would prompt an immediate and indignant shout, followed by his insistence that even before I bought my papers, I permit him to buy me a coffee.

In the steamy, noisy, crowded coffee bar, Cei might be standing at a small, circular table, looking at the papers and conversing, perhaps with Gigi Prete, the left outside defender, or possibly just with a fan. I would order an *espresso doppio*. The flavor of genuine espresso was unmatchable, but as I'd learned with Lalas in Padova two years earlier, the half ounce contained in the typical Italian cup was scarcely enough to coat the tongue; hence the double.

Even that went down in one gulp. Alongside me, Fusco would nod. This had been no test – merely the offer of a morning coffee – yet somehow I would feel I had risen marginally in his cool estimation.

Cei and Prete would leave, exchanging farewells with those who stayed behind as though the two of them were embarking on a trip to North Africa instead of simply heading back home.

Motioning for me to follow, Fusco would move to their table, where all papers lay already opened to the *Serie B* pages. He would read silently for a minute or two, then sigh, shake his head as if at some inexpressible sorrow, and then say it was time to move on.

Just as we would be leaving, however, Spinosa might arrive and I would decide to stay on for a chat with him. But to properly stand with Spinosa – a wiry and clear-eyed man whose innate decency revealed itself long before what turned out to be his equally characteristic sense of humor – I would have to have another coffee and, at his insistence, a small pastry, too.

Spinosa would have brought his own newspapers, and so we would look at those. (There were chairs at these small high tables, but no one ever sat in them, because if one was sitting when a new arrival approached, one would immediately have to stand and extend the offer of the seat. That the offer was sure to be declined did not matter. It would not do to keep sitting while someone else stood, so one would have to abandon the chair anyway, and given this social imperative, the logical alternative was simply not to sit in the first place.)

With no player was taking coffee a lengthy ritual. For no more than ten minutes Spinosa and I might stand, gazing at headlines and perhaps intermittently mumbling about the unfairness inherent in the fact that all of A.C. Milan's new problems seemed to be being blamed on Baggio. (And almost from the first day I could mumble quite coherently if the subject was unfairness to Baggio.)

Then we would step up to pay – already arguing about which of us would cough up the few lire involved – only to find that Fusco, without knowing what we would order, had paid for both of us in advance.

This – and not only at the coffee shop but everywhere – became a season-long game of tag: trying to pay for whatever had been consumed by the person who had joined you, or whom you had joined. In the end, I'm sure, it came out as even as if everyone had insisted on separate checks, yet it was infinitely more entertaining and left all involved with a sense of well-being, rather than the spiritual cramps that come from counting too closely the change you put back in your pocket.

Despite the drubbing at Foggia, the players seemed unperturbed as they drifted in for afternoon training, the weather continuing sunny and mild. Their awareness that thirty-six matches remained no doubt helped keep both the lows and highs of the early season in perspective. Or maybe they did lack humility.

For several, the day's highlight seemed the opportunity to shoot baskets (with a soccer ball) on a small court that lay between their changing room and the training field. Tonino Martino, the curly blond midfielder who already had struck me as one of the more capable members of the squad, was unquestionably the most enthusiastic of the *basket* players. Permitted for once to dribble with his hands instead of his feet, he would drive toward the hoop, make the simplest of layups, and shout, in the fullness of his love of life and self, "KarrrEEM AbDUL JabbARRRRRRRRRRR!" and then look to me for approval.

For Tonino, the fact that I was a citizen of the same country as Kareem Abdul-Jabbar was the only credential I needed, and from the start his warmth was unrestrained. Invariably the *basket* would start him on a riff that could run anywhere from five minutes to half an hour as, finally tiring of warbling, "Ja-bbarrrrrr!" he would shout to me the names of players who'd been on the American World Cup team in 1994. With "Tony Meola!" he had no trouble, but after that he grew quickly confused. He knew there was a "La-lash" but did not even attempt the first name. And from there he was on to "Cobeeeeee Ra-mosh!" and "Tab-ba Caligurrrrrri" and, my personal favorite, "Werrick Rinalllddaa!"

Soon, he would be joined by the "serious" players of *basket*. Chief among these were Fusco and the new but old midfielder Guido Di Fabio. For them, this was nothing to smile about. They shouted out no names of NBA stars. This was an athletic activity – however peripheral to their professional lives – and they approached it with undiluted intensity.

Until he'd reached adulthood, Fusco had not known that a round ball inflated with air could be intended for use by the hands as well as the feet. He was a true *'sciuscià* – a tough street kid from Napoli who literally grew up kicking, if not screaming. Still, he would focus as intently on the rim before letting fly a ten-foot, two-handed set shot as I imagined he would if taking a match-deciding penalty kick.

Likewise, when Di Fabio missed a shot with a soccer ball from the foul line, his self-directed anger seemed no less than it would be an hour later when he would miss a nearly open goal from the same distance, but in the latter case kicking the ball and fighting for his livelihood.

Di Fabio, thirty-one, had been born in a small fishing village on the Adriatic, about sixty kilometers north of Pescara. His career had been unusual in that, for his first six seasons as a professional (four of which had been in *Serie B*), he could have almost walked to work, the two clubs he played for having each been located within twenty kilometers of the house in which he'd been raised.

After that, however, it had been off first to Sicily and then up north to Piacenza and Siena before returning to his Adriatic roots with *C2* Fermana, with which he had played the previous season. Although he had more than 200 *Serie B* matches behind him, the last had been more than five years earlier, and he recognized this as his last chance.

Di Fabio would turn out to be among the better educated and more widely read members of the squad, as well as the most religiously devout (attending not only Sunday mass regularly but even Novena services with his wife and two children during the week); but there was about him, at first glance, an almost menacing cast.

He had long black hair that was totally unkempt, he seldom shaved, his features did not fall naturally into an expression of geniality, and his voice was both the deepest and loudest of any player's. Not the first man one would head for if seeking directions on an empty street late at night, but his appearance could not have been more deceiving, masking, as it did, a heart rich in empathy and a manner so genteel as to seem positively courtly at times.

On the field? Well, he was in Castel di Sangro, after all. Di Fabio possessed perhaps the most powerful shot on the team, but in only one of his eight prior *Serie B* seasons had he scored more than a single goal, which suggested a certain lack of accuracy. What he offered, in place of flair, speed, or imagination, were steadiness, grit, and a degree of experience that often seemed to put him in the right place at just the right time.

After maybe fifteen minutes of *basket,* someone would spot the bulky Jaconi approaching and the players would dash for the training field. Jaconi's demeanor never varied: whistle around neck, clipboard in hand, scowl on face no matter what the most recent result, he strode toward the field as if it were the place where that very afternoon he'd be engaging in a struggle in which his own life would be at stake. Even when chatting amiably, Jaconi did so in a voice rough and hoarse, and during training sessions Jaconi did not chat amiably.

Each session would open with a harangue as the squad gathered about him in a semicircle, heads bowed, waiting him out. Eventually the shouting would stop and the kicking would start.

Then for the next couple of hours, I would slowly walk the perimeter of the field, or settle myself into the *panchina* in order to scribble some notes. As I basked beneath a warm autumn sun that lit up the snowcapped mountains in the distance, I found myself drifting surprisingly close to a state that could only be called happiness.

It had taken me more than fifty years to get there – and the destination could not have been predicted – but finally I was where I felt I belonged.

Unfortunately, the action on the field suggested that a number of the players were not. All week the squad seemed to grow more inept. Each day Jaconi's rants grew louder, his raves longer. Training seemed only to expose new weaknesses rather than to bring needed improvement. Meanwhile, Sunday's opponent, Cremonese, had played in *Serie A* only the season before and its roster was chockablock with the sort of talent that Castel di Sangro could only dream about.

I did not feel I could sit idly by. After all, I was soon to be Jaconi's neighbor. I'd seen flashes of good form from the new defender Luca D'Angelo as well as from a skinny, twenty-year-old midfielder named Cristiano. It seemed to me that both should start on Sunday. And above all, Lotti *must* remain the goalkeeper.

I tried to approach Jaconi with my insights and suggestions at the Thursday night meal, using Marcella's son, Christian, as an intermediary.

"Could you please tell Mister," I said, "that after the players leave tonight, I would like to speak to him privately."

"Yes, Joe. No problem. But what is this? What is your need?"

I waved my hands back and forth in a gesture that I hoped would discourage further questioning. "It is very private, Christian," I said. "But it is about the team. And about how I can help. And I think it is only proper if I discuss it with Mister first."

"No problem, Joe. No problem. I ask no more." Christian then leaned over and spoke quietly in Jaconi's ear, presumably presenting my request.

But Jaconi's reaction was not what I'd expected. He looked at me quickly, his face grew red, then he burst forth with a huge bellow of laughter and leaned forward and slapped me on the back.

"Americano," he said. *"Famoso scrittore americano."* Again he convulsed in laughter. *"Pazzo, pazzo americano!"* Crazy American. He curled one hand into a fist and pounded it on the table as he laughed.

"Christian!" I said. "What exactly did you tell him?"

"Just what you say, Joe. You needs to speak with him in privates about maybe you can play for the team."

"*Play* for the team?! Christian, I never said anything about playing for the team."

"Joe, you say you help. I think you must mean you play. Is no other way you can help."

"Goddamnit, Christian, I had no intention of asking Mister to let me play for the team! What do you think I am, crazy? Please tell him right away that this is *not* what I said."

"Okay, but Joe – *calma*, please. Everybody has good laugh. You help the team by be funny!"

I buried my head in my hands. Now that he'd mentioned it, I could hear the players' laughter sweeping up and down the table.

Then Jaconi rose and actually rubbed the bald spot on top of my head. This caused him to burst forth with another aria of laughter. Then he put on his coat and departed Marcella's by the rear kitchen door that was reserved for his use.

"Okay, Joe," Christian said. "I tell him you not play. You need talk about other things of team. Okay, okay, he say, tomorrow. Now he must meet with Signor Gravina and discuss the lineup and the tactic for Cremonese."

"But *that* was just what . . ."

"Excuse, Joe? Say again?"

"Oh, hell, Christian. Never mind."

And I got up and put on my own coat. The players banged their spoons on the table and chanted my name: thinking that I had proposed that I might join them. Or that I had pretended to be proposing to join them in order to make Jaconi laugh.

Either way, they apparently felt it was not so bad to have the American around. It might even be fun from time to time. Well, that was fine. Whatever it took to keep up the morale of my *ragazzi*, I would do.

12

At lunch the next day, I approached Jaconi directly. I wanted to tell him I thought a 5-3-2 formation would work well, with Bonomi and Martino on the wings, flanking Cristiano, who would try to push forward whenever possible. He should play both Di Vincenzo and Pistella at forward. In this manner, we could seize the initiative from the start, trusting Lotti and the five-man defense to thwart the inevitable counterattacks. I also thought he might want to consider using the new D'Angelo as a sweeper, given his speed and apparent skill on the ball.

"*Osvaldo,*" I said, as the smell of Marcella's Friday fried fish special wafted through the nearby kitchen doors, "*dobbiamo parlare. Ora. E' molto molto importante.*" We must speak. Right away. It's very, very important.

Again, Jaconi's reaction startled me. He tossed back his head, made a quick gargling sound, then slammed an open palm on the table. Immediately, he jumped up from his chair.

"*Sì, stavo dimenticando!*" he said loudly, motioning for me to follow him. "*Subito! Subito! Vieni, Joe. Sbrigati! Sbrigati!*" I almost forgot! Now! Now! Come, Joe. Hurry! Hurry! And with that, he burst through the swinging doors and trotted across the kitchen toward the exit, shouting to Marcella that he and I would not be having any fish.

He did not seem like a man about to calmly sit down and ask for my insights into the squad's problems and my thoughts as to possible solutions. Rather, he seemed like somebody who just remembered that he'd forgotten to turn off the gas burner on his stove.

This impression strengthened when we ran directly to his apartment building, a three-story white stucco structure located just down the street from the Coradetti. He sprinted toward the main entrance, then took the stairs three at a time. Only slightly out of breath, he paused outside his second-floor apartment.

For a moment I thought he was going to invite me in for a strategy session after all. Instead, he took a different key from his pocket and opened the door of the apartment next to his.

"Per te," he said, *"è casa tua. Dal signor Rezza."* Pushing open the door, he led me inside, to a sparsely furnished corner apartment with living room, kitchen, bedroom, and bath.

He paused, breathing short and hard now. Then spoke in English. "You . . . like?"

"Osvaldo, sì. E' bella. Ma –"

He held up a hand. "No, no! No 'but,' " he said loudly in English. *"Quando torni dall' America, signor Rezza dice che tu abiterai qui. Vicino a me."* When you return from America, Signor Rezza says you are to live here. As my neighbor. He handed me the key.

So this was to be my new home in Castel di Sangro. An apartment right next to Jaconi's, as Signor Rezza had promised. I could see those strategy sessions looming after all, which, in retrospect, seems a strong indication that even then my obsession was beginning to drift toward lunacy.

For his part, Jaconi seemed delighted. He walked around grinning – knocking on walls, flushing the toilet, opening and closing cabinet drawers, sitting on the couch to prove it was sturdy – as if he were a real-estate agent.

Below me, I learned, lived Vito, who had been my tour guide at Rezza's estate and who served as the building's superintendent. Upstairs lived the defender Altamura, with wife and young child. I was so giddy at this sudden upturn in my fortunes – within two weeks I'd moved from the position of total stranger (and *straniero,* or foreigner, at that) to living quarters adjacent to the virtual control room of Castel di Sangro Calcio – that on the way back to Marcella's, I decided to joke with Jaconi.

"You like *'il hip-hop'*? " I asked.

He looked at me, puzzled.

"Gangsta rap?" I said.

"Non ho capito," he said.

I held up a finger. *"Aspetta,"* I said. Wait.

Back in the restaurant I sought out Christian and asked him to translate my questions about musical preference.

Once he understood, Jaconi glared at me and shook his head.

"Mister say he no like the music, but especial not these kind," Christian said.

"Uh-oh," I said. "Christian, please tell him that I am afraid this will be a problem. Because all night I play the hip-hop and the gangsta rap very loud. *Very* loud."

Now it was Christian's turn to look alarmed. "But, Joe, you cannot do this. Mister he no like. And he do like sleep. Very much."

"Christian, don't worry. It's only *uno scherzo*. A joke."

"Ah!" Christian's eyes brightened and he grinned. But when he turned back to Jaconi to explain, he gave no sign that he was in on the joke.

One of Jaconi's most compelling characteristics was the expressiveness of his face. His voice might have had only two settings: the Bill Clinton end-of-campaign hoarseness for normal conversation and the foghorn bellow for everything else, but with facial expressions alone, he could play the full symphony of human emotion.

As in this case. First there was shock. Then a flicker of dismay. Then a shift to stubborn refusal to believe. Then wariness. And finally the realization that this was, after all, no more than my little attempt at a *scherzo*. From start to finish, this progression consumed no more than three seconds. And then he burst forth with a bellow of rich, appreciative laughter. "Heep-hope!" he exclaimed. "Too loud! *Tutta la notte!*" All night!

He threw a beefy arm around my shoulders as he continued to laugh, his eyes crinkling into slits. With his other hand he pointed to me, as he uttered several sentences to Christian and to Marcella and to those few players who had not yet left the restaurant.

"Christian, what does Mister say?" I asked.

"He say you have got the . . . the . . . senses of 'umors, and this is very good because in this season are many time will be *la necessità* for the laughing. And so Mister is happy to be having you in the door next to him."

"I'm glad, Christian. Tell him, 'Me, too.' "

I never did get to talk to him about whom we should play, and how we should play, against Cremonese. But that was all right. I could see – or thought I could – that once I returned from America, Jaconi and I would function quite nicely as a team. Only two matches into the season, and already my grip on reality was loosening.

In Chieti, at sea level, clouds gathered throughout the afternoon and by 4 P.M. Sunday, September 22, it was warm and muggy. The pace of construction in Castel di Sangro had not picked up. Still, Gravina assured me that the new stadium would be ready for the match against Ravenna on October 13.

As the teams took the field, I withdrew into what I was coming to recognize as my unavoidable prematch cocoon of misery. I was suffering from an almost unbearable tension. I did not have hope. I felt only fear, and a sense of claustrophobia – as if awaiting the sentence of a judge, or a jury verdict that I knew would go against me.

Our moment of triumph over Cosenza seemed years in the past. I could think only of how hobbled we'd looked at Foggia and of the far greater potential strength of these opponents. Granted, Cremonese (from the Lombard city of Cremona, population: 75,000) was not of true *Serie A* caliber, but their having been there only last season lent them an aura of invincibility.

My fear, however, arose not so much from their recent history as from their current roster. To name but one, their midfielder Maspero had already scored twenty career goals in *Serie A*. After losing their first match *fuori casa,* Cremonese had beaten mighty Genoa, 2-1, the previous Sunday, with Maspero scoring. Their entire lineup, in fact, was stocked with players of talent, reputation, and experience.

To counter this, Jaconi had made only one change from the week before, returning Di Vincenzo to his starting position in attack in place of the fifth midfielder. Thus, we'd be playing a traditional 4-4-2 – without either D'Angelo or the rookie Cristiano, but to my enormous relief, with Lotti remaining as *portiere*.

The only other question involved playing style. At home – or as close to it as we were likely to get for a while – I still believed we should seize the initiative. And, praise the Lord, that was how the match began, with Castel di Sangro trying to press forward and to exert control over the midfield.

Unfortunately, our players were simply not good enough. After only ten minutes, they reverted to their pattern of unease, compounded by error. Lotti once again was playing as if his real name were Horatio, but not even he could withstand seventy-five more minutes of that sort of pressure at the bridge. Yet time after time we'd lose the ball before even getting it across the midfield line. Then we began fouling: always a sign of a team either fatigued or knowing itself to be in trouble.

And, as always, the fouling only made things worse, giving Cremonese free kicks from dangerous positions. Alberti fouled. Cei lost the ball out of bounds. Prete, clearly beaten, fouled in desperation. Maspero drove a vicious free kick toward the upper left corner of the goal and only in the last nanosecond did Lotti, at full stretch, reach out one glove to tick it wide.

After this, we played as if we knew we were doomed, giving up the ball all over the field, without even being pressured by Cremonese. Even Di Vincenzo seemed a lost boy, contributing nothing. At thirty minutes Cei again kicked a long ball to no one, and in a severe breach of protocol (given my position as honored guest of management), I screamed as loudly as I could, "D'Angelo! D'Angelo! Bring on D'Angelo!" Gravina, again seated to my immediate right, muttered something and made a point of looking away.

Our first shot on goal did not come until the thirty-seventh minute. Taken by the pimply faced and orthodontured *centrocampista* Claudio Bonomi, it was too high, but at least it had been a shot. And now the end of the first half began to draw seductively close. As badly outclassed as we'd been, we'd not yet fallen behind. Like a boxer nearing the end of a round in which he's taken a terrible beating but has somehow managed to stay on his feet, we simply wanted to last the eight minutes to the whistle. And we did.

Even better, the players came out for the second half distinctly uptempo. Jaconi must have spoken effectively during the *intervallo*. We even managed our first truly good offensive play of the season, with Bonomi breaking upfield and passing to the overlapping Prete, who raced into an open corner and then delivered a lovely cross to an open Pistella in front of the net.

Pistella, however, promptly kicked the ball into the grandstand.

But we came back again within minutes, and this time Tonino

Martino found a reserve of energy that carried him goalward once, twice, and then, after a corner kick, a third time.

On that occasion, in the fifty-ninth minute, he passed to Bonomi and then Bonomi, shooting on the run, scored a goal! After 237 minutes of play, we'd finally scored a *real* goal, not one that resulted from a penalty kick. More important, we led Cremonese, 1–0.

The northerners pressed forward with an intensity not seen before. Again it was primarily Lotti who saved us. In those last twenty minutes, there were moments when it seemed one against eleven, with Lotti left pitilessly exposed by his defense.

Finally, however, the ninetieth minute arrived. Now all that remained would be the minute or two that the referee added on to compensate for time lost to stoppages of play such as had occurred when we'd scored, or when a slightly injured player had received treatment without leaving the field.

An assistant held up an electronic sign on the sidelines. *Eight* minutes of extra time. An outrage! Clearly, Cremonese had expected an easy win and just as clearly the *arbitro* had decided to give the bigger, better-known team from the north several unjustified extra minutes during which they might at least salvage a tie.

I threw my notebook to the ground and buried my face in my hands, vowing that I would look only at the second hand of my watch until it had made eight complete revolutions of the dial. If that bastard *arbitro* – whose name was Lana and who came, of course, from the northern city of Torino – had not called a halt at that point, I didn't know what I might do.

Once it was over, all I could say was, Thank God we'd had Lotti in goal. The more frenzied everyone around him became, including Jaconi, his own players, the Cremonese players, the *tifosi,* and the scum *arbitro,* the calmer Lotti seemed to be. Where before his saves had been spectacular, in this unwanted, undeserved overtime they appeared effortless.

And as if to prove that a measure of justice still existed on some plane, as Cremonese pushed forward recklessly in their final assault, Bonomi stole the ball and ran downfield unmolested – accompanied, in fact, only by a certain Verolino, the most lowly regarded among our offensive substitutes, a young man who'd gotten onto the field only as a result of Pistella's having bungled one time too many.

The town. The church at the lower right was the only building to have survived World War II. The new stadium is to the left of the bridge in the upper middle of the picture. The snowcapped mountains are visible twelve months a year. *(Nancy Doherty)*

La squadra at the start of the season. First row (left to right): Alberti, Di Fabio, Martino, Di Vincenzo, Terrara, Cristiano, Michelini; second row: Fusco, Verolino, assistant manager Longhi, Jaconi, trainer Petrarca, Bonomi, D'Angelo; standing: Altamura, Biondi, Cei, Lotti, Spinosa, De Juliis, Galli, Pistella, Prete.

The original "miracle." Spinosa saves the Ascoli penalty kick. Castel di Sangro advances to *Serie B*.

Jaconi *in panchina* during a match.
(Michele D'Annibale)

The president and later "patron," Gravina.
(Fabrizio Gentile)

La presenza occulta, il Signore Rezza.
(Photograph by the author)

Cei, the captain and student of American literature. *(Nancy Doherty)*

Lotti, *il portiere straordinario.* (Michele D'Annibale)

Danilo Di Vincenzo, not long before his death. *(Michele D'Annibale)*

Filippo Biondi, also soon to die, in one-on-one training with Jaconi. *(Nancy Doherty)*

Altamura on the day before the first match against Padova. *(Nancy Doherty)*

Marcella and son Gianmarco in her kitchen. *(Nancy Doherty)*

Just another weeknight during the long, hard season. Left to right: Rimedio, D'Angelo, Cristiano. *(Nancy Doherty)*

The training sessions were never casual. Cei and Cristiano compete for a ball, with Rimedio close behind and Albieri ready if needed. *(Nancy Doherty)*

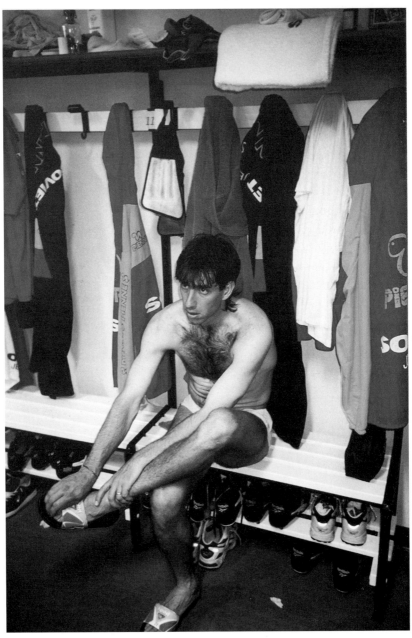

Pistella after another hard day of getting nowhere. *(Photograph by the author)*

As the Cremonese goalkeeper came forward to attempt the virtually impossible – stopping a two-on-zero break – Bonomi, rather than scoring the second goal himself, as he so easily could have done, slid the ball across to Verolino so that the beleaguered benchwarmer (who would soon be thrown back to *C1*) could have a moment of glory.

My estimation of Bonomi as a player had risen throughout the match. Now, my estimation of him as a man rose just as high. Our second goal had come in the ninety-eighth minute of a ninety-minute match. That it had lasted that long was a scandal. But it was a scandal with a happy ending.

As soon as Verolino's shot crossed the goal line, Lana blew his whistle to signal the end of the match and then sprinted for the tunnel that would get him to his private locker room and out the back door and out of Chieti before anyone could catch up to him to ask, perhaps impolitely, why he'd given Cremonese a clearly unjustified eight minutes to tie the score.

It took two or three minutes for my own anger to subside to the point where I was able to realize what had happened: We had *beaten* Cremonese! *Mamma mia!* And *Dio mio!*

Lotti once again had proved impervious to an afternoon of sustained attack. Beyond any doubt, he was our mighty fortress, and inspired by him, we had now beaten a team that had played last year in *Serie A!*

Was it possible that another, even greater miracle might occur?

13

In a word, no. I had to return to the United States for family business that consumed more than two weeks. Nothing out of the ordinary, but I had a son in his last year of secondary school who was starting to visit college campuses, a daughter due to deliver a first child in December, and many domestic details to iron out with Nancy in order that I might from that point forward stay in Italy for the rest of the season except for a break at Christmas.

During that time the squad played three matches and lost them all without scoring a goal.

> Palermo 3, Castel di Sangro 0
> Chievo Verona 2, Castel di Sangro 0
> Castel di Sangro 0, Ravenna 2 (played in Chieti)

By the time I got back, on October 15, we had fallen from being tied for fourth place to being tied for fourteenth.

I'd planned my arrival in Rome for a Tuesday morning, knowing that the players would have had Monday off and that they'd be returning to Castel di Sangro for training. Jaconi had assured me by telephone that he'd have one of the *romanisti* meet my plane, and not surprisingly, the duty had fallen to little Cristiano, nicknamed "Mimmo," the youngest and least experienced among them and therefore lowest in the pecking order.

Cristiano, who stood smiling and waving at the customs gate, was only five foot eight inches tall and weighed but 135 pounds. If the two of us had spent the rest of the day standing at the airport entrance and I'd asked a thousand native Italians to guess the occupation of this twenty-year-old at my side, I doubt that even one would have said *calciatore.*

Yet Mimmo was a veteran of the Lazio youth team and had actually, at the age of seventeen, made two late-season appearances for Lazio itself, first coming on as a substitute and then, in Lazio's final match of the 1995–96 season, starting alongside such players as Beppe Signori, the leading goal scorer in *Serie A* for three years in a row; Pierluigi Casiraghi, who, like Signori, played for the national team; the Dutch international Aaron Winter; and the Croatian star Alan Boksic.

This was, quite frankly, amazing. These men were among my idols. They composed the core of the powerful Lazio squad that Nancy and I had seen in that unforgettable first-ever *Serie A* match at the San Siro. And little Mimmo here had played with them against Sampdoria four months before that!

It had never been intended that he would go directly from the youth team to *Serie A,* but the fact that he'd been given the honor of two appearances showed how highly regarded he had been. Last year he'd played an insignificant substitute's role for Venezia in *Serie B.* Then Lazio, which still controlled his contract, had made him available to Castel di Sangro in the expectation that he would play regularly and gain some of the experience he still needed.

He didn't know, of course, that I'd sought to urge Jaconi to play him against Cremonese, but he had come on in place of Di Fabio for the last thirty minutes in Palermo the following week, although, as he was quick to admit, he had not played well. He was a fast, aggressive, and hugely ballsy kid with a tendency toward recklessness on the field, which too often took the form of foolish, impulsive fouls, which led in turn to a rapid accumulation of yellow cards, which led in turn to brief but all too frequent suspensions.

Off the field, he was probably the friendliest, most cheerful and charming twenty-year-old I'd known since I myself had been twenty, even if I could understand only about 20 percent of what he said. In Rome he still lived at home with his parents. His father, in fact, on this rainy Tuesday was driving him back to Castel di Sangro, along with a puppy he'd acquired for companionship.

Also in the car was a new young defender, Fabio Rimedio, also only twenty years old, who had played with the Roma youth team for the past two years but had refused to go to the *C2* squad to which Roma had assigned him. Instead, he'd spent the early fall auditioning for many teams, including Castel di Sangro.

I'd seen him play in a midweek "friendly" against a nearby *Dilettante* team a few days after the Foggia match and had been impressed by his intelligence, ruggedness, and poise. So much so that when the Castel di Sangro director of personnel asked me, more out of politeness than genuine interest, what I'd thought of the new youngsters given tryouts that day, I'd said, "The *attaccante* wasn't much, but I really liked the kid on defense. He's strong, quick, he obviously has a good head for the game, and he's got so much *carattere*, I could smell it from the *panchina*."

The director of personnel had nodded. "Yes, well, if you like him that much, you can pay for him and then I will offer him a contract."

I laughed. "You talk to Signor Rezza about what I can pay for and what I can't, but if I were you, I'd sign this boy tomorrow."

That had been my first scouting report and, as it happened, my last. But three days later *La Società* had signed Rimedio, and although I never made known to him my early enthusiasm, I took rather a proprietary interest in him from the start.

For his part, he immediately proved to be – while not the best player – perhaps the best educated and most intellectually gifted member of the team. In addition, he had the sort of post-preppy American good looks that would have made him seem as at home on the Princeton campus as in a Soviet Jeans uniform.

He had moved in with Cristiano and the nineteen-year-old Biondi, forming a Three Musketeers unit within the larger framework of the squad. All three were quick witted, deferential to the older players, hardworking, and filled with that unmistakable joie de vivre that comes from being an unencumbered young man doing exactly what it is he wants to be doing and believing himself (and not entirely without reason) to be on the threshold of a successful career.

Once we'd gotten my luggage stowed and I'd been introduced to the puppy and Cristiano's father had maneuvered us clear of the Fiumicino Airport confusion, I wasted no time in asking what had gone wrong.

"Tutto," Cristiano said. Everything.

Rimedio, who spoke rudimentary English, was more circumspect. "I am too new," he said, his clear blue eyes projecting sincerity. "I think for now only to play well enough in training to remain. I have not been even *in panchina* for these three matches."

"And the stadium?"

The two players looked quickly at each other, then shook their heads.

"Surely," I said, "it will be ready for the Padova match in two weeks."

Again, wordlessly, they shook their heads. Finally Rimedio said, "We look every day. Not possible."

"There is still no work being done?"

"Oh, yes. Work. But not big work, not fast. Each day, Signor Rezza comes to look and Signor Gravina comes to look, and they smoke and do not speak and go away."

A cold rain was falling as we reached Castel di Sangro. With help from Cristiano and Rimedio, I was moved in to my new apartment within minutes.

To give the living room a homier feel, I'd brought with me a significant part of my team scarf collection from around the world. It seemed disloyal to hang any from other clubs in *Serie B,* but even without those I had more than enough to fill every available inch of wall space. Borussia Dortmund, Real Zaragoza, Notts County, Bayern Munchen, Olympique de Marseille, Real Madrid, Napoli, Fiorentina, Arsenal, Barcelona, Saint Etienne, Sao Paolo, et cetera, et cetera.

I began the process of hanging them shortly after returning from dinner at Marcella's and I know it could not have taken more than two or three hours, so I was mystified the next day when I heard that Jaconi was complaining that his new neighbor had kept him up all night with incessant pounding and hammering on the walls.

But it was true, as I discovered when I turned up for lunch.

"Boom! . . . Boom! . . . Boom!" he shouted at me as soon as I stepped into Marcella's.

"Osvaldo, scusami, ma –"

"Boom! . . . Boom! . . . Boom! No heep-hope. No rappa. Boom! Boom! Boom!"

I took my regular seat at the table. *"Scusa, mi dispiace Osvaldo, però –"* I'm sorry, but –

"Basta!" Enough! He waved an arm in my direction. *"Mai più! Capito?"* Never again! Do you understand?

"Sì, però –" Yes, but –

"Basta!" He pointed to the plate of spaghetti that had been set in front of me.

"Mangia." Eat.

I looked down at the plate. Then I looked around the table at the players, every one of whom was grinning and trying to stifle laughter.

Finally, Luca D'Angelo spoke up. *"Grande Joe,"* he said. *"Finalmente, il mister grida contro qualcun altro. Non solo a noi."* Which meant, roughly: All right, Joe! Finally, Mister shouts at somebody besides us.

With that, the whole table broke out laughing. And then Jaconi joined in, smiling, leaning toward me and squeezing my shoulder. *"Non c'è problema, Joe. Non sono irritato. Ma che diavolo facevi?"* No problem, I'm not angry, but what the hell were you doing?

"Ho molte sciarpe di squadre diverse. E io . . . io . . . Christian!" Once again, I'd hit my linguistic limit: "I have many scarves from different teams" probably had been understandable, but I could not possibly explain in Italian that I had been hanging them all over my walls. As usual, Christian bailed me out, to the extent that Jaconi insisted I show him this collection right after lunch.

He stepped into my living room and looked at the riot of color and language that hung vertically almost from ceiling height. Slowly, he walked the four corners of the room, as if in a museum. Then he looked at me, whistled softly, and shook his head slowly from side to side. He walked out without saying a word.

I couldn't tell if he'd been impressed or if he was starting to fear I might be dangerously unbalanced. He'd never known an American before, and I was certainly not fitting the stereotype.

The rain continued and even the daytime temperature fell into the forties. The training field was a quagmire. All *basket* was put on hold until the weather improved. But at least I had heat, blessed heat! (Although, as I would notice increasingly as it got colder, the heat came on at 8 A.M. for fifteen minutes and then again at 8 P.M. for the same length of time. Before, between, and after it was no different from the

Coradetti. When I remarked on this to Jaconi, he said, Yes, it was wonderful: such an improvement over what it had been the year before!)

As I continued to settle in to my apartment, I kept discovering more items I needed to buy. Most of these could be acquired at the nearby Acqua & Sapone outlet (this being one in a chain of domestic-supply stores that sold any items relating to soap and water). It carried a full line of cosmetics, toothpaste, shampoo, and shaving cream, but nothing that was intended to be swallowed. Thus, when I realized that I'd forgotten to bring back from America my normal supply of Maalox, I went to a nearby *farmacia* instead.

An hour later I walked into Marcella's for lunch. As soon as she saw me, she pointed an accusing finger. *"Maalox!"* she said. *"Maalox!"* Now all of Castel di Sangro would think that her food was giving me heartburn.

I tried to assure her that she was in no way to blame. Even in America I drank Maalox like orange juice, and had done so for years. It was just part of being a *scrittore*. But then I asked, how did she know about the Maalox?

Well, how did I think? The pharmacy had called her as soon as I'd left. "The American has been in here buying Maalox, Marcella. You must pay more attention to what he eats!"

Then she told me, forgivingly, that there were two pharmacies in town. The one I had gone to always told everyone exactly what each customer had purchased. The other did not. So if it was anything *privato* that I needed, Marcella said – though her voice warned that she would be troubled indeed if I should turn out to need pharmaceutical privacy for any reason – it was to *l'altra farmacia,* the other pharmacy, that I must go.

After dinner that night Jaconi invited me to his apartment. I'd been gone for three matches, things had turned sour, and it was important, he said, that I understand a few facts.

He kept his vocabulary simple, and I was able to grasp his main points. Chief among them seemed to be that only players with an extra degree of determination and commitment could succeed in Castel di Sangro, where there were many deprivations and no diversions. In Castel di Sangro, *il calcio* had to be your life, not only your work. Other cities offered better food, more women, stores, cinemas, better access to other parts of the country. Castel di Sangro offered long, cold winters, Marcella's, and low pay.

But maybe it was even worse if you were married, because good housing was hard to find, your wife was isolated for long periods of time with few friends for consolation, and your children spent much time indoors because of the rain, snow, and cold.

But if you did choose to come, you had better learn to like it fast. Jaconi had no time for unhappy players. All it took was one to spread his disease like the influenza, and soon the entire team would have first one thing to complain about and then another.

This could not be permitted, no matter how talented a player might be. Indeed, to Jaconi, talent was the least important factor among many. First, there must be *il carattere* and then *la mentalità*. Character and the right mentality.

A star player, a gifted scorer of goals, was more likely to harm a team than help it, Jaconi said. Suddenly, this one player was more important than the others. Everything had to be rearranged to suit him. The tactics, the training procedures, maybe even the time of the meals.

Jaconi would not permit this. There could be only one person of importance, one leader, one voice whose commands would be followed without hesitation or discussion: and that person must be the *allenatore*.

Talented players tended to think that because they had physical skills, they also were smart. And it was dangerous for a player to think he was smart. Soon he would be thinking he was smarter than the manager. "Why are we doing it this way, not that way?" One question like that to Jaconi was a one-way ticket out of town. Apparently, *la mentalità* meant being smart enough to know you were stupid.

To play for Jaconi, you had to have *il cuore, il coraggio, la grinta* – heart, courage, grit. You would not win because you were better, you would win because you fought harder. And because Jaconi was your manager. The team came before any individual, but in Castel di Sangro it was not merely a team, it was family. That was why you ate together every day and every night. So the family would be always close and always ready to listen to the father. The married ones had to understand this, too. They could have their wives, they could have their children, but their real family was Castel di Sangro Calcio.

He'd heard me speak admiringly of Baggio. And so he thought he'd better set me straight: if it were artistry, brilliance, or flair I was seeking, then I should go elsewhere immediately. In Castel di Sangro the season would be nine months of trench warfare. It was the only way Jaconi knew and the only way he wanted to know. For those attracted by elegance, for those in need of spectacle, Castel di Sangro was simply the wrong address.

And so our neighborly concern became reciprocal as I began to wonder – as he did about me – whether he was an eccentric genius or simply a madman on the loose.

Having just had a telephone installed – the normal waiting time was six to eight weeks, but because it was an apartment owned by Signor Rezza, the phone arrived the day after I did – I received a call from Barbara on Friday morning.

"I keep hearing from my friends one thing that I think I should tell you," she said, "because if it is true – and I do not know this – it explains maybe the business of the new stadium."

"What is it?"

"My friends say that Signor Rezza does not wish to be in the *Serie B*. It is too expensive, and too much attention is paid to the doings of *La Società*. As I do know, he does not like attention paid to his business. He was more comfortable with the privacy of *Serie C,* where no outsiders knew or cared about anything."

"And so?"

"He thinks this team is not good enough for *Serie B*. And if he is not to spend money to buy good players, why spend it on a stadium for *Serie B?* And certainly he will not do both."

"You mean he doesn't plan to *ever* finish the stadium?"

"Now, Joe. What I say is only rumor. I do not tell you this is true. But my friends say that maybe this was his plan until you arrived with all your questions and your plans for this book, which will be published perhaps in many countries, where people will read about Castel di Sangro.

"For Signor Rezza this presents a problem because, while he does not wish to spend the money and maybe does not wish to stay in *Serie B,* he also wants to cut a *bella figura* in your book, so people will not say, 'Oh, that old Rezza was so greedy, he would not even build a stadium for his team.' "

"So now he is going to finish it?"

"Nobody knows, but now it is probable. But you have stirred up other problems. For example, what might you put into your book? Signor Rezza is said to be very unhappy with Gabriele for allowing you to come to Castel di Sangro without having first consulted him."

"Allowing? But he couldn't have stopped me."

"Joe, in this small town, if Signor Rezza says you are not welcome, your life will be very difficult and unpleasant and soon you will decide to go home."

"But that isn't happening."

"That isn't happening *yet*," she corrected me. "But remember: *la stagione è lunga e dura*. The complication now is that Signor Rezza seems to find you amusing. He thinks you have the, what is the word, the *spine* to say what you think, even to him, which no one else does."

"Yeah, thanks to his grappa."

"Gabriele, on the other hand, is said to regret everything and to be sorry you are here. This is the rumor. Gabriele has not said this to me. What happens next? *Chissà!* Who knows? In Castel di Sangro, if Signor Rezza is known to like you, there is much freedom for you to do many things. It is – how would you say? – you are under his protection."

"But if he changes his mind . . ."

"Ah! Then Signor Jaconi will have yet another new neighbor very soon. But right now the ball is rolling in a favored direction for you. Is that correct? A metaphor of sports?"

"Well, it's not great, but I think I know what you mean."

"For now, it is enough that Signor Rezza smiles upon you. Let us hope that continues."

"Hope? Barbara, in this case I would say, 'Let us pray.' "

14

Whatever might have been the rumblings behind closed *Società* doors, they did not noticeably affect Jaconi's attitude toward me, or that of the players. Indeed, during my absence there seemed to have arisen the belief that I might truly be some sort of *portafortuna*, or lucky charm. It was probably as much for this reason as out of courtesy that Jaconi invited me to ride the team bus north for the Empoli match.

That impression strengthened when I saw Giuseppe's story in Saturday morning's *Il Centro*. Under a headline that took note of my return, he had built his article around the fact that after winning twice while I had been here, the team had lost the three matches played while I'd been gone. "At Empoli, therefore, Jaconi will have an extra man," he wrote.

Often I had read of a home crowd described as a "twelfth man" because of the impact its enthusiasm could have upon a team (as well as the ways in which it could intimidate both *arbitro* and opposition), but I'd not before seen any individual credited with such power. Once people started believing in miracles, however, there was no telling where they might stop.

The bus was to leave at 9 A.M. At 8:45 I set out on the eight-minute walk from my apartment to the departure point, which was a parking lot outside the still unfinished new stadium. I'd scarcely begun when an old and battered car slowed to a halt and its driver, Fusco, motioned for me to jump in.

The morning was crisp, blue and sharply etched, after a week of cold and rain. I climbed into Fusco's front seat, noting that already he'd opened *Il Centro* to Giuseppe's story.

"Adesso tu non sei solo lo scrittore americano ma anche il dodicesimo uomo, eh?" Fusco said. Now you're not only the American writer but the twelfth man? In keeping with his morning personality, he did not smile.

"Ovviamente," I said. *"Ma dove giocherò?"* Apparently – and I smiled when I said this – but where will I play?

Feigning – at least I hoped he was feigning – deepest solemnity, Fusco said, *"Se vuoi puoi prendere il mio posto."* If you'd like, you can take my position. Then, as we entered the parking lot, he sighed deeply and shook his head, his mouth settling into what I already recognized as his typical Neapolitan expression of mistrust and skepticism.

"E' sempre peggio," he said. It gets worse and worse. Not knowing whether he was referring to Giuseppe's "reporting" in *Il Centro* or to larger-scale issues concerning the team or maybe even to life itself, I simply thanked him for the ride and said I would see him on the bus.

He gave my shoulder a squeeze as I got out of the car, a gesture I chose to interpret as one of solidarity. Not having been present during the three consecutive scoreless defeats, I still wasn't quite sure how low morale had sunk.

The parking lot was filled with wives, girlfriends, other friends, and assorted well-wishers. The players, mostly unshaven, wearing sunglasses, street clothes, or training sweatsuits, and carrying newspapers, magazines, and bottles of water or juice, boarded quickly, steadily jabbering to one another, and making – from what I could infer from tone of voice and responses – a series of lighthearted, smart-ass remarks, as equipment managers hurriedly stowed the heavier traveling bags underneath, alongside the rack of gray business suits, blue dress shirts, and striped neckties that all would change into once we reached our destination.

Not all the players had been aware in advance that I'd be joining them. Yet those who were surprised seemed pleasantly so, with the exception of midfielder Roberto Alberti, the one player who from the start had made it clear he wished I'd never heard of Castel di Sangro.

At thirty-five, Alberti was the oldest member of the team. He was also the shortest, though Fusco and Michelini came close. And except for Cristiano, he was the lightest, at 140 pounds. His face seemed to wear a permanently quizzical expression; he never raised his voice, on or off the field; and just as not one in a thousand could have identified Cristiano as a *calciatore,* I would have bet that not one in ten thousand would have guessed that Alberti was entering his eighteenth season in the game.

Most of his career had been spent in *C1,* and there were many, including me, who wondered if, at thirty-five, he would be able to meet the physical demands of *Serie B.* Chief among his supporters, however, was Jaconi, which rendered other opinions moot. At least ten times since I'd first arrived, Jaconi had emphasized to me that the entire concept of *la mentalità* was personified by tiny Alberti.

Like so many others on the team, he had been born near the Adriatic Coast, in the region of Marche. In 261 matches in *C1* he had scored only seven goals, so it must have been primarily on the strength of his mentality that he'd survived. So unspectacular that he could play an entire ninety minutes without an observer even realizing he was on the field, he would often turn out – during a later viewing of the videotape – to have been the only player on either side not to have committed a single error.

He wasn't big, he wasn't strong, he wasn't fast, but he was never caught out of position, and when in possession of the ball – no matter how much pressure he was under – he never panicked. He had a remarkable ability to instantly analyze his available options and, like a chess master, invariably to choose the best. Also, more often than one would have thought possible, it would be Alberti who would stick his leg in and pluck the ball from an onrushing opponent without committing a foul.

Already an appreciator of his cerebral approach to the game, I was quite prepared to become an ardent personal *tifoso* as well, but any attempt I made at conversation was rebuffed. He didn't need me, he would have preferred me to be elsewhere, and he went about his daily business with scarcely a nod of recognition in my direction.

Now, on the bus, finding me seated directly across the aisle from him, he let his pale blue eyes gaze right through me and then turned his attention to *Il Corriere della Sera,* the national newspaper published in Milan, which was generally considered, along with *La Repubblica* of Rome, to be the best in Italy.

Unlike his teammates, when Alberti had a real newspaper in his hands, he did not flip immediately to the sports section. Instead, he read methodically from start to finish, devoting as much time and attention to accounts of the previous day's doings in the parliament and on La Borsa, the stock exchange, as he did to reports of new crises at A.C. Milan.

We were underway quickly, for Jaconi was not a man who meant 9:05 when he said 9 A.M. Departing Castel di Sangro and its magnificent surroundings on an autumn morning with brilliant sunshine pouring unchecked from as clear a blue sky as I'd ever seen, I was reminded first of the glories of Alaska, where I'd once spent a year, and then of the Canadian Rockies.

Throughout the season this scenery never failed to move me, never ceased to thrill me, and continually left me dumb with disbelief that no guidebook anywhere mentioned the mountains of the Abruzzo as an attraction at least the equal of the more fashionable Dolomites, far to the northeast.

The players, of course, had seen it all before, with the possible exception of young Rimedio, who stared out his window, seemingly as awestruck as I was. To them, a bus ride was a bus ride – a necessary if not especially enjoyable part of the job.

They fell quickly to the pursuits most likely to distract them, chief among which were card games and the reading of high-concept comic books featuring the adventures of the Italian equivalents of Superman and Batman: Dylan Dog (who was not a dog but a man) and Diabolik (who despite his sinister name worked exclusively for the forces of good).

I should say that I, too, soon began to enjoy these stories, mostly because I found the vocabulary understandable – at least when accompanied by the drawings. I might not have known, for example, that *"Fuori con le mane alzate!"* meant "Get out with your hands up!" but when I saw the phrase complemented by an illustration of six men pointing submachine guns at a stopped car that had been surrounded by four others, I got the point.

We'd been on the road for about half an hour when Giacomo

Galli, seated in front of me, head twitching, stood and walked to the front. Galli's ankle had healed, and he had reentered the lineup two weeks before, in place of the underachieving Pistella, but had not yet provided any spark.

On the bus, however, he was the man in charge of the most important aspect of the ride – the videos. Like De Juliis sniffing the cheese at Marcella's, it was Galli who sorted through the current cache of videos on the bus and programmed the day's entertainment.

All window shades were ordered lowered, and almost immediately a sound louder than seemed possible came blaring from speakers that seemed to be located directly over *every* seat.

Galli's first choice was *Congo,* dubbed in Italian, of course. In the back of the bus, the card games continued, the players having somehow rendered themselves impervious to the blast of sound emitted by the speakers and not especially interested in the antics of genetically altered gorillas.

From mid-bus forward, however, all attention except Jaconi's was riveted on the small screens at the front, which gave forth a picture of such poor quality that it was often difficult to distinguish between the gorilla and the girl. Jaconi, a veteran of all-day and all-night bus rides from a time long before the videocassette had been invented, kept his eyes insistently closed throughout, his arms folded across his chest and his mouth gaping slightly open, as if he were well and truly asleep.

Our destination was the outskirts of Florence, a five-hour journey in a car driven at less than suicidal (i.e., non-Italian) speed. On the bus, however, it would take nine hours because all buses in Italy – in what had apparently been the first and only governmental step ever taken in the direction of highway safety – had been equipped with devices that held their top speed to 100 kilometers per hour (60 mph).

Thus, Galli was able to squeeze in two complete videos before we'd even stopped for lunch. *Congo* was succeeded by an original Italian film that seemed deeply indebted to American studios for a "plot" that consisted only of random, massive explosions occurring about every five minutes, followed by scenes of the two survivors – always the same man and same woman – embracing passionately and vowing to survive, if not prevent, the next one. Who was detonating the explosions, and where, and for what reason, never became clear. The explosions were the point of the movie; all else was irrelevant.

After lunch Galli – whom I delighted by coining for him the new appellation of Giacomo Impresario – selected first *The Executioner's Song,* but that was quickly booed from the screen for being too wordy and lacking in action. Its replacement was another Italian original in which a bevy of incredibly large-busted young women were employed in a massive laundering establishment whose owner turned out to be a sadistic male who achieved special gratification from watching on hidden video cameras as one of his large machines (which he could apparently shift to "seize, rip, and crush" mode merely by flicking a switch) would swoop an unsuspecting laundress off her feet and devour her.

In each instance, one of her panic-stricken colleagues would throw the main power switch to OFF at the last possible moment before death, thus permitting the sadistic owner to race from his office feigning dismay as the sweet young maiden was slowly disentangled from the machine in a state of blood-smeared disarray, which her employer apparently found sexually arousing.

With only minor variations (i.e., one maiden substituted for another), this same scene was repeated perhaps a dozen times before – for no reason I could discern – the police arrived and arrested the owner, causing the spared maidens to celebrate by stripping off their laundering uniforms and gathering in a communal shower room to wash themselves (and one another) clean of all traces of their trauma.

By the time this was over – with, as far as I could tell, the status of their future employment still unresolved – it was late afternoon and turning dusky and we were nearing the outskirts of Florence on a crowded *autostrada.* A delighted Galli removed the cassette from the machine and brought it back to his seat. This one was too good to leave behind. This one he was taking home for private viewing.

To my astonishment, I learned that we were to spend the night not in a hotel but at Coverciano, the glorious campus on Viale Gabriele D'Annunzio, on the eastern edge of Florence, which served, among many other things, as the official training ground of the Italian national team.

For a lover of *il calcio,* this was the holy of holies, but its cultural history reached far beyond sport. In the Castle Poggio Gherardo, which loomed high above the perfectly manicured playing fields, Boccaccio had set his *Decameron*. About a hundred years later, Leonardo da Vinci stood on the walls of Monte Ceceri, just above Coverciano, and launched his flying machine, which proved about four hundred years premature. In the early years of this century, Gabriele D'Annunzio, perhaps Italy's prototypical poet and political activist, had lived and worked in a villa on the grounds.

This was not a location open to the public. It was not possible to reserve a room here for an overnight stay, or to eat in the facility's restaurant. Like Buckingham Palace, this was very much by invitation only, and the invitations were not freely dispensed.

Jaconi, however, had attended the school for *allenatori* that was held at the Centro Tecnico here each year. Italian *allenatori* cannot get a license to manage at the *Serie A* or *Serie B* level without attending a sixteen-week course at Coverciano. (The result, unfortunately, is that all native managers are exposed to the same courses in tactics, psychology, and training and that all graduate having majored in *la paura,* or fear, and as sworn adherents to the philosophy of *il catenaccio,* the defense-first approach to *calcio* – the word *catenaccio* literally means "bolt," as on a lock – which has been virtually the state religion for more than half a century.)

Given his outgoing personality and innate conservatism, it was not surprising that Jaconi had proven popular at the school. Now that he was guiding a *Serie B* squad that would play a match nearby the next day, the facility had been placed at his disposal.

There are Americans, we have learned, who yearn to spend a night in the Lincoln Bedroom. And no doubt many a cardinal at the Vatican would be delighted if the Pope, in his private quarters, were to say, "That couch there folds out into a bed. Why don't you spend the night, and maybe tomorrow you come out with me onto the balcony."

But I can say truthfully that in October of 1996 there was no place on earth where I would rather have spent a night than Coverciano. I'd never dared to dream of such a privilege, yet here I was! For me, at least, *il miracolo e la favola* lived on, more compelling than ever.

My room was number 308. There was no telling who might have stayed there before me. Baresi, Dino Zoff, Gigi Riva, Tardelli, Gentile, Bettega, Facchetti, Cesare Maldini, Paolo Maldini, or possibly (it was not a mathematical impossibility) even Baggio. I opened the cedar-scented closet: a full row of Armani hangers. And in the bathroom: three different types of hair dryer. No doubt about it, this was the real thing.

I went down to a lounge where the players were sitting while awaiting the call to dinner. Every one of them was as excited as I was. None had ever been here before, and certainly none of these players would ever return as a member of the national team, so for them, too, this would be a night to remember.

After the meal most of the squad settled in the lounge to watch the Saturday night *Serie B* match on television. It featured two teams I'd not yet seen: Salernitana, which had seven points, and Cesena, which, like us, had six. The match was still 0–0 with twenty minutes left when the newly acquired Philemon Masinga, of the South African national team and formerly of Leeds United in the English Premiership, came on for Salernitana.

Speaking with the full authority of someone who had seen him play one match on television two seasons earlier, I informed the players that now they were in for a treat because here was someone who could *really* play the game.

Fusco, in particular, seemed skeptical, and even more so twenty minutes later, after Masinga had lost the ball virtually every time it had come near him. Salernitana won anyway, but the goal came from one of their veteran Italians.

"Non per Serie B," Fusco said of Masinga, shaking his head.

"Troppo presto per dirlo," I replied. Too soon to say.

"No, Joe," Fusco said, lighting a cigarette and preparing to go up to his room. *"Masinga non è per la Serie B. Il suo stile non è per un giocatore da Serie B. Lui è troppo egoistico."*

Well, there it was again. The notion that anyone who played the game with style, with a bit of dash or flash – especially a foreigner, and perhaps even more especially a black foreigner – somehow could not fit into the intensely prosaic world, the inflexible mold of *Serie B*.

Too egotistical? On that opinion I gave Fusco the benefit of linguistic doubt. I suspected that he'd really wished to say something along the lines of "too fancy" but instead chose a word I'd be more likely to understand.

But just that brief exchange had been enough to stir Jaconi's passions, for we'd blundered into what seemed by a wide margin – at least in his conversations with me – his favorite subject.

"*La Serie B è un campionato molto strano, Joe,*" Jaconi explained. "*Troppo difficile per gli stranieri. Il talento non è sufficiente –*"

"*Sì, sì, il carattere, la mentalità. Lo so.*" To interrupt Jaconi, especially when the nature of *Serie B* was the topic, was risky, if not downright rude. But by now I had his speech memorized. *Serie B* was very strange, very difficult for foreigners. Talent was not enough. Character and mentality were what were needed.

But that could be said of any sport, at any professional level. Yet Jaconi had almost a fetish, it seemed to me, about *Serie B* being some special ring in Dante's Inferno in which all normal laws of physics, kinetics, and common sense were rendered inoperable.

Well, I had only myself to blame for having opened the door. But it quickly became clear that neither I nor any of the players still in the lounge was going to bed until Jaconi had once again delivered his lecture about *stranieri*.

Yes, he admitted, many foreigners could and did do well in *Serie A*, but this was because *those* foreigners possessed such extraordinary talent that they could flourish even without the requisite character and mentality.

But you didn't see that kind of foreigner in *Serie B*. The *Serie B* foreigners were, by definition, not gifted with such brilliance; otherwise, they would have been offered a contract in *Serie A*. And in the absence of that transcendent level of talent, they were left to try to cope with the multitude of native Italians who were, quite frankly, *furbi*, or cunning, wily and shrewd in a way no foreigner could ever be, and who possessed far more *grinta* and *cuore* and *carattere* and *mentalità* besides.

What about Goossens of Genoa? I asked. Or Ingesson of Bari? Or Florijancic of Torino? Or Manfred Binz, the new Brescia defender who had played for many years in Germany? And speaking of Germans, had not Oliver Bierhoff played for three years with Ascoli in *Serie B* before moving up to Udinese and *immediately* becoming one of the strongest *attaccanti* in all of *Serie A*?

Jaconi listened, bemused. Then he said, "*Il guaio con te, Joe, è che sai rispondere a tutte le domande anche sei non sai proprio niente.*" With that, he rose, left the room, and went to bed, leaving me clueless as to the nature of his final riposte. Fortunately, Rimedio was in the room.

"Fabio," I said. "I don't think I understood Mister. What was the last thing he said?"

Rimedio answered slowly, wanting to be precise. "He say, 'Joe: the trouble with you is that you knows every thing. But in same times you knows nothing that you talks about.' "

"In other words —"

"In other word, Joe, no argue with Mister because he always right and you wrong."

Ah, but Sunday morning. Once again Match Day throughout Italy. I was still adjusting to the fact I'd be scaling these peaks of ecstasy and agony every week. But never again would a day begin, as did this one, in the *calcio* equivalent of the Garden of Eden. Appropriately, the weather was as close to perfect as weather could be.

Even better, Jaconi was in an expansive mood, bearing no grudge from the night before, and giving me a splendid walking tour of the entire facility, then graciously introducing me to a number of high-ranking *calcio* Federation officials. As late-morning sunlight filtered through the glorious tall trees that lined the driveways that wound through the campus, I began to try to conjure ways in which I might obtain a permanent appointment here, as "American-in-residence" or something of the sort. At that point, in fact, I would have accepted a job raking leaves.

Inevitably, however, we had to leave for the match.

Empoli was another team far more accustomed to *C1* than to *Serie B*. They had, in fact, been promoted from *C1*'s northern division by winning a playoff in June, just as Castel di Sangro had done in the south. Prior to that, their last previous appearance in *Serie B* had been in 1988–89, when they'd lasted only the one season before being relegated again. They had a capable attacker named Esposito, but otherwise, like us, seemed bereft of star-quality players.

The town of Empoli (population: 40,000), lying half an hour west of Florence, was as undistinguished and thoroughly modernized as Florence was not, but the stadium was small, pleasant, open, and entirely free from the police-escort, barbed-wire, fear-of-*ultras* (i.e., gangs of "fans" so extreme that they often instigate violence) atmosphere that plagued so many Italian grounds.

It might have been simply that Empoli was unnaturally tranquil, yet the *tifosi* of Fiorentina, the *Serie A* team of Florence, were known in both north and south to be particularly nasty and prone to acts of violence, not all of which were directed against the opposition. Fiorentina players, in fact, had had their cars set afire and their team bus stoned by their own fans after a particularly galling loss just two years earlier.

The laid-back atmosphere in Empoli, I suspected, had far more to do with the fact that nobody took Castel di Sangro seriously. We were the fairy-tale team. The Lilliputians. We'd be here for a year and then be gone forever. We were not a squad worth getting worked up about.

In *calcio,* you made enemies primarily by going somewhere you didn't belong (such as to another team's stadium, even if you were scheduled to play there) and doing something you shouldn't (like winning). As far as the *tifosi* of the other clubs in *Serie B* were concerned, Castel di Sangro had never been anywhere or done anything. We were children and they were adults, so it would have been not only beneath their dignity but almost perverse for them to taunt us or to instigate violence against our few hundred loyal fans who'd made the trip.

So the ambience seemed as mellow as the weather on what had turned out to be a particularly luscious autumn afternoon in Tuscany. Possibly 5,000 spectators had turned out, leaving the stadium two-thirds empty, which was about average for early season in *Serie B,* especially with so many *Serie A* matches on television.

When the squad took the field, I was pleased to see that Cristiano had been added to the midfield, but less so that Jaconi had opted for a 4-5-1 formation, with Galli as the lone attacker. To me, this seemed tantamount to announcing over the public address system that his highest hope was for a 0-0 draw.

So what happened? *Il calcio* once again displayed its infinite ability to surprise. Eight minutes into the match, with neither side yet having contemplated the possibility of going forward in menacing fashion, Galli, who was taking a solitary wander through the Empoli defense, as if on some sort of one-man goodwill mission, found, to his surprise, the ball rolling freely within easy range of his right foot.

An Empoli defender, lulled by autumnal splendor into a state of near torpor, had been gently kicking it back toward his goalkeeper when Galli emerged directly in the ball's path.

Giacomo Boom Boom didn't even have to alter his stride, such a perfect pass to him it turned out to be. The ball was in the Empoli net behind their nonplussed keeper before the poor *portiere* even had a chance to start cursing his defender.

For a moment I, too, was stunned into silence. That could not have happened. Castel di Sangro could not have scored such a ludicrously easy goal. It had been, however, classic *Serie B* – the result of a gross defensive error rather than offensive brilliance. And so it must really have occurred.

That's when I started to scream. Along with every Castel di Sangro player on the field and *in panchina,* as well as the few hundred of our fans who'd made the long drive to sit in the cheap seats.

It had been our first goal in four matches, our first-ever *Serie B* goal *fuori casa,* Galli's first goal of the season and his first-ever goal in *Serie B*. It also put us in that most unlikely and unforeseen of positions: ahead in a match on the road. The Tuscan hills that formed the backdrop to the stadium could never have looked more radiant in any autumn of any year.

And for the next twenty minutes it appeared as if they might grow more gorgeous still. Cristiano was a dervish, tackling, passing, sprinting, diving from one side of the midfield to the other, and in the process creating such confusion that Empoli suffered another stunning defensive lapse, feeding the ball inadvertently to Martino, only ten yards from goal. Unfortunately, Tonino's surprise reflex was not as finely honed as Galli's, and he booted the ball over the top of the net.

Then one sensed a turn in the tide. Fusco had been shakier than usual on defense, and Empoli was finding a path for the ball down the left side of the field, into his territory. Foul begat foul begat foul, all of which begat Empoli free kicks, the site of each creeping closer to the edge of our penalty area.

And after the free kicks, at the thirty-fourth minute, came a corner. It appeared a dangerous situation, but the ball arced in lazily, not struck with much force, and no Empoli players were in position to play it. Actually, had the Empoli kicker been aiming for the top of Fusco's head, it would have been a bull's-eye, for that's what the ball hit.

But Fusco – inexplicably – instead of heading the ball out of danger, bounced it directly toward the opportunistic and onrushing Esposito, who – just as Galli had done – popped it into the goal without breaking stride.

It was now Lotti's turn to gasp in disbelief. At least until Fusco started shouting at him that he should have come out from the goal and picked up the ball before the Empoli player reached it.

I didn't need an interpreter to understand Lotti's forceful response, which was, essentially, that no defender capable of tying his own shoes could possibly have made a mistake as dumb as Fusco's.

In any event, that Empoli had scored was all that mattered. Especially an hour later, when 1–1 became the final score. One could say that what should have been a win had been only a draw. Or one could say that finally we'd won a point on the road. But if one were hoping to say anything, one would have had to say it very quickly, for within fifteen minutes of our departure on the bus, a *Die Hard* video was blasting at top volume.

We did not arrive back in Castel di Sangro until 1 A.M., but Marcella had waited up. She insisted on taking Jaconi and me for a drink at a late-hours trattoria, where the three of us could sit and rehash the match, something which, at that point, only she had any desire to do. But Marcella was family, and Jaconi knew that one never was discourteous to a family member who was trying to be gracious, no matter how hobbled one might be by fatigue, disappointment, or both.

And so it was well after 2 A.M. before he and I walked across the damp, chilled central square toward our apartments. As we arrived, he said, *"C'è una buona notizia per te."*

Good news for me? What might that be?

"Martedì," he said, *"un nuovo giocatore arriverà."* A new player was coming on Tuesday.

"Chi? Da dove viene? In quale ruolo giocherà?" Who? Coming from where? What position would he play? I wanted to know everything all at once.

Instead of answering, Jaconi sighed deeply, and his warm breath steamed in the cold night air. Then he shook his head.

"Non sembri contento," I said. You don't seem happy.

He made his classic Jaconian gesture of shrugging, tilting his head back so his eyes would point skyward, and raising his opened hands, palms up, to shoulder level.

"Uno straniero," he said. Uh-oh. The dirtiest world in all of Osvaldo's personal lexicon: foreigner. Or maybe the second dirtiest. For after that he said, *"Africano."*

"Africano! Davvero?! Che nazionalità?" Really? What nationality?

"Del Ghana," he said, in a tone that suggested he was confessing to me a long-buried secret from his past. *"Della squadra nazionale."* From the national team of Ghana.

"E quest'anno?" This year? Where was he playing?

"Frankfurt, alla Bundesligia." He was coming from Eintracht Frankfurt, in the German first division. This seemed almost too good to be true. Coming to Castel di Sangro? *Madonna!* I had badly underestimated Gravina. And this Ghanaian must either really hate Germany or have a very bad agent.

"Come si chiama?" What's his name?

"Jo-seph," Jaconi said. *"Come te."*

Like me.

"Jo-seph Ad-do."

"E il suo ruolo?" And his position?

"Non lo so," Jaconi said, not looking like a manager whose team had just won its first point on the road. *"Il difensore, centrocampista, non lo so, non lo so, non so niente."* Defender, midfielder, I don't know, I don't know, I don't know anything.

And, as he said good night, he didn't sound as if he wanted to find out.

15

In the mornings, when the weather was right, if I lay flat on my back in bed and looked out the window facing west, I could see only a russet-colored mountain beneath a bright, untainted blue sky. The uppermost ridgeline of the mountain, perhaps 2,000 feet above me, was rugged and jagged, as one sees in the American West. The golden color of the *abruzzese* fall had begun advancing down the mountain's flank like an army, each day driving back a few meters farther the doomed green forces that had ruled all summer long.

When I sat up, however, the foregound was a parking lot that lay empty, except on Thursdays, when it became the site of the outdoor market, second only to the Sunday match as the most exciting event in a Castel di Sangro week. Beyond the parking lot was a jerry-built, pastel-colored eight-story apartment house bloc (assembled, it appeared, in less time than it was taking to expand the stadium) that provided vacation homes for the middle class of Naples.

Thus, before even rising from bed each day, I could see both the best and the worst of Castel di Sangro. Freed from my cell at the Coradetti, I could much better appreciate the town's charms. Agreed, architectural glory was not among them, but there is more to life than old buildings.

My apartment, for example, overlooked the Sangro River, such as it was – flowing through the town, it was more of a meandering stream – and each morning I was awakened by the honking of geese. Never once by the honking of an automobile horn. Which caused me to reflect that since my arrival in September, I had yet to hear the wail of a police or ambulance or fire engine siren.

There was a sense of peace and ease about the town and its people. No one had high expectations: neither for the team nor for themselves. Hopes, yes; but not expectations. This led to a beguiling absence of frustration. Courtesy, empathy, and even charity came much more easily to people who were not constantly stewing about how they'd just been cheated out of some grand prize that they felt life owed them.

This was, of course, still only October. And the ever growing piles of firewood in the parking lot across the river from my apartment, as well as the fact that almost every store window – whether it was an apparel shop, a butcher, or a pharmacy – now featured electric or kerosene heaters for sale, stood as a stern reminder that if my days of miracle and wonder were to continue, they would be cold.

A more imminent concern was that with almost 20 percent of the season gone, the squad had by no means shown that they truly belonged in *Serie B.* We were, for the moment, in fourteenth place, which would have been a cause for celebration were this the end of the season, but we had a long road yet to travel and all too few players who seemed capable of taking us where we needed to go.

Lotti was clearly the team's most valuable player. Although De Juliis remained immensely popular, while Lotti was considered standoffish, there was no way now that Jaconi could change keepers. Massimo had simply done too much to save us already.

In front of him, the situation was more problematic. The young communist, Luca D'Angelo, whom Jaconi had finally, if reluctantly, inserted into the starting lineup in place of Cei, seemed by far the most graceful and talented of the defenders, and my new neighbor, Altamura, although lacking in speed and finesse, could give out a good thump when needed and played with an almost ferocious intensity.

More worrisome were the outside men, Fusco and the much traveled Gigi Prete. For all their effort expended, neither seemed capable of doing the job he'd been assigned. Without going into adjectival detail, I would note that this opinion was supported by the *pagelle,* which after seven matches showed each of them well below the generally accepted minimum passing grade of 6.

The midfield, as a whole, not only seemed more capable but offered Jaconi more opportunities for flexibility. While both wingers, Bonomi and Martino, were erratic, each had at least a modicum of talent. Bonomi, in particular, seemed still to be improving rapidly.

In the central midfield there were the proven veterans Alberti and Di Fabio (Mind and Matter, as I'd come to think of them), as well as the dashing if untested Cristiano. In addition, the nine-year Castel di Sangro veteran Michelini had begun to see some playing time, not only starting at Empoli but having been perhaps our most effective player in that match.

The true embarrassment lay with our forwards. After three matches, and despite his fortuitous goal, Galli did not look like a reliable *Serie B attaccante*. Too many times he would make the same foolish errors, such as receiving a ball from the midfield and heading it onward – though he *knew* that only opponents lay in wait. He also lacked speed, dribbling ability, a strong or accurate shot, and any knack whatsoever for creating space for himself by working free of defenders.

Di Vincenzo, as much as I liked him personally, had also failed to prove that he could play at this level. There were whole blocks of time – twenty, even thirty minutes – when he would simply seem to disappear from the fray. Worse, after his promising start he'd seemed to weaken steadily, to the point where, at Empoli, Jaconi had kept him on the bench throughout the match.

This left only the Six-Million-Dollar Man, aka Andrea Pistella, exhibit number one in Gravina's case against ever spending real money for (supposedly) proven players. Poor Pistella. I knew he cared, I knew he tried, I knew that his wretched start was tearing him up. Nonetheless, whereas Lotti (the last-minute bargain-basement buy) had proved by far to be our most effective performer, the overpriced Pistella had been clearly our least.

Indeed, he was like a black hole at the front end of the pitch: any ball that fell within his field of gravity simply disappeared until one saw it again on the foot of a counterattacking opponent. Already he'd missed more clear chances for goals than some players see in a year, and like a baseball player in a batting slump, anything he tried to do differently seemed only to make matters worse.

The roster was filled out by the twenty-year-old Rimedio and the nineteen-year-old Filippo Biondi, for both of whom the season looked to be primarily a learning experience. Rimedio had yet to play at all, and Biondi had come on only for an unimpressive eighteen minutes against Ravenna.

It was not a group portrait that inspired confidence – *la potenza della speranza* notwithstanding. Indeed, from my vantage point at Via Peschiera 10 (my new address), the impending arrival of Mr. Joseph Addo of Ghana and Frankfurt seemed like manna from heaven, no matter what position he played.

Marcella's was not officially open for lunch on Mondays, but that morning Tonino Martino had called her to say he was too depressed to make the drive to his home, maybe ninety minutes away, and had asked if she could serve him something.

Well! Had she the time, she would have slaughtered a pig, a calf, a lamb, an ox, or even all four for her Tonino. Since she didn't, he would have to make do with spaghetti and red wine and Sprite: his normal meal at midday.

Marcella saw me walking down the street just before lunchtime and insisted that I come to the pizzeria, too. Tonino, she said, did not need food so much as *una spalla per piangere,* a shoulder to cry on, and two were better than one, especially if both were not hers.

Tonino was sad because he'd played so poorly the day before. Had he only converted his golden opportunity from ten yards out, as Galli had, we would have gone up 2–0 and undoubtedly would have won the match.

He was far and away the most skillful dribbler on the team, but if one wanted to be unkind, one could have said that it seemed also that his brains were in his feet. *La mentalità* was not his strong suit. In fact, he often seemed to hold no cards at all. He played with bursts of energy that frequently amazed, but often as not his dribbling would lead him into a corner where, surrounded by three or four defenders, he'd wind up losing the ball.

He did not have a strong or accurate shot, but that didn't discourage him from using it, often at inappropriate times. And although 90 percent of the time it was he who would throw the ball back into play from the sideline, he never seemed to learn to do it right. More often than not he would throw it either directly to an opponent or to a teammate so well covered by opponents that the loss of ball would be immediate.

I had asked Jaconi why he kept having Martino perform this chore, since he was so obviously unsuited to it.

"He likes to" was Jaconi's response. "If I didn't let him, his feelings would be hurt. And when his feelings are hurt, he cannot play." This was Tonino: jewelry, bleached blond hair, Kareem Abdul Jabbarrrrrrrr, the kindest heart in the Abruzzo, and the emotional maturity of a five-year-old.

Now he was staring dolefully into his wine-Sprite mixture, shaking his head from side to side and saying over and over, *"Aah, Joe . . . Ooh, Joe . . . Ahia, Joe . . . Aaaaah, non lo so."*

Marcella herself was close to tears now, although she had only heard the match on the radio and although Tonino was not the only player to have underperformed at Empoli. (Bonomi and Fusco, for example, had been equally bad, but Tonino was the one who was here, and so it was his pain Marcella felt.)

"Non è colpa sua, Joe," Marcella said. *"Lui non gioca mai bene fuori casa,"* she said. It's not his fault. He never plays well away from home.

These didn't strike me as the most cheering words she might have chosen, but I asked Tonino if he thought this was true.

"Purtroppo, sì, Joe. Sempre." Unfortunately, yes. Always.

"Perché?" Why? I asked him.

But it was Marcella who answered. *"Perché lui è sente la nostalgia."* Because he feels homesick.

Nostalgia? This was impossible.

"Are you telling me, Marcella, that this twenty-seven-year-old *calciatore,* who has been playing professionally for – what, five or six years? – that he can't play well on the road because he gets *homesick?"*

"Sì, Joe. E' vero," Marcella said. It's true.

"But we come home right after the match!"

By now, for some reason, Marcella's son, Christian, had joined us as well, and in his basic but quite useful English, he tried to explain. All the while, Tonino sat with his head down, resting his eyes against closed fists.

"Joe. You must understand. Tonino lives near Teramo. His mother house. Teramo only one hour, one hour *mezzo* from here. So, okay. Here, Tonino close to home. Close to mother. But Empoli? Many hours, many kilometer. He think this, it make him sad. So, like you say, the homesick. *Nostalgico."*

"Tonino," I said. "Is this true?"

He sighed deeply. *"Non lo so, Joe. Non lo so. Ma è un peccato, no?"* I don't know, he'd said. But it's a pity, isn't it?

Then, leaving his spaghetti uneaten and his Sprite-wine undrunk, he excused himself. He was going back to his apartment, he said, to play Nintendo.

The whole scene had been so bizarre that I had completely forgotten to tell Marcella that I would be having dinner at Gigi Prete's house that night, and so I had to stop by the pizzeria again in the evening.

If Marcella knew you were in town and you did not show up for a meal, she would worry. Not that you had taken your custom elsewhere but that you might be lying in bed, your throat so sore and your fever so high that you were not even able to make a phone call. The depth and genuineness of her concern for everyone connected with the team – but especially for those of us who were her "regulars" – was remarkable, and I did not want her needlessly racing to my apartment with chicken soup.

As I walked in, I saw no sign of Tonino, but I did see Paolo Michelini and his wife. They insisted that I join them, if only briefly. After having spent the first four matches *in panchina,* the thirty-two-year-old Michelini – another on what seemed our endless list of players only five foot six or five foot seven inches tall – had started each of the last three and had been the most consistent man on the field for us at Empoli.

Michelini had the unique perspective that came from having played eight consecutive seasons in Castel di Sangro, the first when the club was still at the *Dilettanti* level. Knowing his own limitations – he was small, not terribly fast, not an accurate passer, not blessed with an especially strong shot – he had never expected to reach *Serie B,* and he knew he never would have made it on his own.

Now, he told me, even if he never played another minute all season, he would at least have the privilege of wearing his uniform inside such fabled stadia as the Delle Alpi in Torino, built for the 1990 World Cup and with a seating capacity of more than 70,000; the Luigi Ferraris in Genoa, which seated more than 40,000 and was widely considered the most beautiful in all of Italy; and the futuristic San Nicola in Bari (capacity: 60,000), which also had been built especially for the World Cup and which many visiting teams considered the most intimidating arena in the country.

"So," he said in English, grinning happily, "I . . . be . . . *looky!*"

"*Sì, Paolo,*" I said. "And if you're really lucky, you might someday even see the new stadium of Castel di Sangro!"

Prete's dinner invitation had come as a surprise because until he'd extended it, my contact with him had been minimal. He arrived for training, he worked hard, he showered, he went home.

There was about him, however, a somewhat cosmopolitan air that many of the less traveled, small-town *ragazzi* did not possess, and so maybe it was not so unusual that he would be first among the players to invite the American to his home.

Just as likely, the invitation had come at the behest of his wife, a lavishly sexy Chilean named Vanessa Diaz with whom I'd had some brief conversation at Marcella's and who had already said she was glad I had come to Castel di Sangro because having only *calciatori* to talk to all year long bored her to tears.

Gigi and Vanessa lived in an apartment five minutes from the center of town, which could have been said about three-quarters of the members of the team. The only surprise was that, although childless, they had a Chilean housekeeper, who also prepared their meals. Vanessa explained that she did not like to cook and that the tedium of such chores as laundry and housecleaning sapped her strength, which she preferred to reserve in order that she might "be a good wife" to her husband.

Stroking Gigi's broad shoulders with one hand and his thick brown hair with the other as she said this, Vanessa, who was wearing a very, very short skirt and a very, very tight sweater, left not a great deal to the imagination.

Prete was twenty-nine, had been born near Rome, and had followed a career path similar to that of many of Castel di Sangro's more experienced players: two steps forward, one step back. Two years with the same team in *C2,* then four in *C1,* spread among three different clubs. Annual salary, possibly $25,000 per year. One year in *Serie B* with a team that wound up the season relegated; then a year each in *C1* and *C2* with different clubs. He had been playing with Lotti's *C2* team, Albanova, on the northern fringes of Naples, when Castel di Sangro bought him the previous year.

His was the typical journeyman's résumé: nine teams in eleven seasons and only one, before Castel di Sangro, in *Serie B.* In America no baseball player could afford to devote so many years to what obviously would never be more than a minor-league career, but in Italy both the pay and social status awarded to any professional *calciatore* were sufficient to keep most men in the game as long as their legs held out. Besides, in Italy the work was full-time, with training for the next season beginning no more than a month after the previous one ended.

Prete had acquired virtually no English along the way, but he had a quick mind and what I sensed was an untypically cynical attitude toward his profession. We sipped red wine as the elderly housekeeper began putting meats of various sizes and shapes onto skewers. An open fire was burning in a fireplace, and Prete indicated that the meats would be cooked on the fire, as was the common practice in Chile.

I asked how he coped, year after year, with new teammates, a new *allenatore,* a new style of play, new *tifosi,* a new *Società,* new cuisine, new regional accents, a new climate, and widely differing living conditions.

"Mi sono adattato," he said, smiling. I am adaptable.

But his wife was not inclined to let the question go by so lightly. *"Non è facile,"* Vanessa said, her dark eyes reflecting the glow of the fire. *"Per esempio, questa Società è cattiva."* It's not easy. For example, this *Società* behaves badly.

"Come?" I asked. How?

"Vanna," Prete said to his wife, shaking both his index finger and his head in warning. *"Basta così."* Enough.

"No, Gigi!" And suddenly she was off on a verbal whirlwind within which the Spanish eventually overpowered the Italian, telling him all the reasons why she would not be quiet, why she *would* say the things that she would say, and how he had no right to tell her what to say and what not to say, just as he had no right to tell her she could not stay overnight in Rome when she went there for the classes that were supposed to teach her to give up smoking.

When she had finished, Gigi looked at me wanly and shrugged. She had married him six years earlier, when she was nineteen and he was playing in Calabria, and she was apparently well past the stage where she was content to be an ornament.

"Lui è troppo geloso," she said angrily, pointing at Gigi. He is too jealous. *"Vado fuori casa per un giorno, e lui pensa che è perché voglio fot-*

tere!" I leave the house for one day, and he thinks it's because I want to fuck.

"*Vanna, per piacere –*" Please!

"*Vero o no, Gigi! Sì o no!*" True or not? Yes or no?

"*No, no, ma –*"

"*Sta' zitto!*" Shut up!

Blessedly, at precisely that moment – as if she'd known it would be coming and had waited – the housekeeper-cook carried the skewers of meat to Vanessa for her approval before roasting them over the fire.

Vanessa nodded wordlessly, then lit a cigarette. I took advantage of the momentary silence to ask Gigi what she'd meant about *La Società* being bad, figuring he'd rather talk even about this than about his suspicions of his wife's infidelity.

"*Disonesto,*" he said. "*Per esempio, non pagano ai giocatori il premio per la promozione.*" They were dishonest. For example, they hadn't paid the players the *premio,* or bonus, to which each one was contractually entitled after a season that resulted in promotion. Such bonus arrangements, a standard feature of all player contracts, could be lucrative, sometimes amounting to almost a full year's pay. For Gravina to be withholding them even after *La Società* had received its own *premio* of more than 5 million dollars could not be sitting well with the squad.

Prete confirmed this without hesitation. "*Sì,*" he said. "*Noi non riceviamo niente. Solo parole da Gravina. Molte, molte parole ma non soldi.*" We receive nothing. Only many words from Gravina, but no money.

"*Molte, molte stronzate!*" Vanessa said. Very much bullshit! "*Da quel maiale di Gravina!*" From that pig, Gravina!

"*Vanna,*" Gigi said, almost pleading. This could not have been the sort of evening he'd envisioned. But for the moment she'd made her point. The meats were served, and a salad, and good bread. We washed down the food with an abundance of red wine, and we made polite if primitive talk about my family and my career and my interest in *calcio,* and we laughed our way through some stumbles across the language barrier. By meal's end I felt relaxed and at home with both of them.

And Gigi himself seemed considerably more relaxed as he lit an after-dinner cigarette. "*Vanessa dice che io sono troppo geloso?*" Vanessa says I'm too jealous? "*Ho le mie ragioni. Il pezzo di merda di Gravina è la numero una!"* I have my reasons, and that piece of shit Gravina is number one!

But now it was Vanessa who wanted the subject closed. *"Non c'è nessun altro uomo,"* she said to me. There's no one else: no other man. *"Solo Gigi."* And with that she moved to his lap and began kissing him long enough and hard enough so that his cigarette burned itself out, forgotten. It seemed to me that the time had come to say good night.

It was raining hard, however, and Gigi insisted on driving me back to my apartment. On the way, I thanked him for the dinner. I didn't know how to ask, politely, whether or not the team president was actually screwing his wife, but I thought I should make some reference to Vanessa, so I asked him how he had come to meet and to marry her.

Gigi's grin seemed to freeze on his face. His gaze sharpened considerably, and taking me rather aback, he asked, "Why do you want to know?"

"No special reason. The other married players all are married to Italians. I just wondered how you found a woman from South America and she found you."

Gigi looked at me for a long time as I sat, halfway in and halfway out of his car. His expression was serious, almost grim. Then he said, *"Non è importante. Così è la vita."* It's not important. It's just one of those things. *"Mettiamo che io abbia avuto un colpo di fortuna."* Let's say I had a stroke of good luck.

That was fine with me. But I must say he didn't look any happier about it than Jaconi had the night before when he'd told me that Joseph Addo was coming to town.

16

Joseph Addo, who was not only a member of the national team of Ghana but its captain, arrived on Thursday. He posed for pictures and did a number of newspaper and television interviews as soon as he stepped onto the training field. I enjoyed listening to these because I understood his flawless English, but I felt sorry for Giuseppe, whose attempts at translation were something less than adroit.

> *Question:* *Da dove sei venuto?* Where have you come from?
> *Giuseppe:* From which places you be arrive?
> *Addo:* Well, I could give a lot of answers, depending on just what you mean. Ghana is where I was born, but I went to college in the United States. But if you mean the places I've played professionally, I guess Stuttgart and Frankfurt would be the two most significant, unless, of course, you want to take into account the Olympics in Atlanta last summer, where I played with the Ghanaian national team.
> *Giuseppe (after a long pause): Da Roma stamattina con signor Gravina.* From Rome, this morning, with Signor Gravina.

Then training began. Two hours later, as I left the training field along with hundreds of other Castel di Sangro *tifosi* who'd come to see the new arrival, my heart was singing. Addo had a natural touch on the ball that not one among our players could have duplicated if he were to try for the rest of his life. He also showed, in a brief intra-squad scrimmage, that he knew instinctively where to best position himself as he watched the play unfold and flow around and toward him.

Playing as a defender, he effortlessly dispossessed of the ball any forward or midfielder who came near him. And in the very same motion, it seemed, having already spotted a teammate thirty or forty yards upfield, he would deliver a pass with unerring accuracy.

He was also faster than any other player on the team and quickly showed that his heading ability, both offensively and defensively, was far superior to any that had previously been seen in Castel di Sangro.

Also, he was no prima donna. At least a dozen times during the session, Addo found himself in a position where, were he to make the move that came naturally, he would have embarrassed his opponent. And so he refrained – having enough self-confidence so as not to need to make himself look flashy at a future teammate's expense.

Madonna, it was hard to believe that this man had come to Castel di Sangro and for some reason he wanted to play for us. In the interviews his answers to the question of Why? had been, I thought, deliberately less than informative. I couldn't wait to hear his real story at Marcella's and, being the only person to whom he could tell it in English, I knew I would.

But even before I managed to leave the training ground, Luca D'Angelo ran up to me and literally shook me by the shoulders in his excitement. "Joe, Joe," Luca said, about to make a rare foray into English. "He is so good! He is more the best than any of us!"

Marcella's that evening was even more clamorous than usual, with everyone at the team table wanting to speak to Addo at once, in any language. Everybody wanted to show him something, tell him something, ask him something, to make sure that he knew how happy they were to have him among them.

And, for his part, he turned out to be charming, witty, and intelligent, a man who in only his first training session had won the hearts of his teammates for his personality as much as for his skill on the pitch.

He had attended George Mason University in Virginia for four years on a soccer scholarship. His English was as good as my own, and his sense of humor keen. In Ghana he'd been captain of the national Under-17 and Under-21 teams, as well as of the national team, and one of the three players over twenty-three chosen to play with the Olympic squad in Atlanta in June. Addo had been the cornerstone of a defense that had led Ghana to the semifinals. Beyond that, he'd played two years for Stuttgart in Germany before joining Eintracht Frankfurt over the summer.

"But I don't like Germany," he said. "I am miserable in Germany. It isn't just the racism, although that's awful. The German people are cold even to each other. So I have a friend, he says Italy is not this way, come to Italy, the weather is warm and the people are warmer, and also the football is good. I think I can play one year at this level in order to grow accustomed to Italy and then next year move to *Serie A*."

But why Castel di Sangro?

"Well, first it was to be Padova. But when I got there, I talked to some people – black people – who knew some things. And they said the *razzismo,* the racism against blacks, was very bad in Padova. Every week, they said, I would see bananas thrown on the field and people dressing up in gorilla suits. Hey, for that I can stay in Germany and freeze my ass off for one more year.

"But then my friend in Padova says he knows of one very small team in one very small town that is brand new to *Serie B,* but where I definitely would not find any problems of racism. And Mr. Gravina got in touch with me and invited me here, and this morning he took me to this beautiful mansion way, way up in the mountains to introduce me to an old man, but obviously the one with the money and power, a Signor Rezza."

I laughed. "Oh, yes. He's got the money and power."

"Hey, a little *Godfather* I can live with. But mostly this town is okay?"

"Mostly, it's great," I told him. "And I can guarantee you that you'll never hear a racist remark from anyone. It's just not that way. The people here are really special. And the guys on the team, without exception, they are first-class, number one people all the way, although maybe not the strongest players in Italy."

"Yeah," Addo said, "this afternoon I didn't see many who would cut it in Frankfurt, but that's all right. I'll do my part. I don't claim to be a striker. I'm not going to walk in here and take ten shots a game.

But if part of the problem is, like they were telling me, they need more organization in the back and in the midfield, I seriously believe I can help."

The next day's papers, of course, were full of news of Addo's arrival, and how his presence would transform Castel di Sangro from a team sure to finish at the bottom of *Serie B* to one that now would have a fighting chance for *la salvezza*.

"*Un africano per il Castello*" said the full page headline over Giuseppe's story in *Il Centro*. Beneath it was a picture of Addo, who was smiling, standing next to Jaconi, who was not.

Unfortunately, Addo's paperwork would not be cleared in time to allow him to play against Padova, but Gravina had hired Barbara as Addo's interpreter during final contract negotiations. She told me on Saturday morning that there had been an ongoing but low-key difference of opinion about what constituted a fair salary, but in the end *La Società* compromised and Addo signed.

Thus, I gleefully approached Jaconi after the Saturday lunch at Marcella's. In an hour the team – Addo included (though he could not yet play) – would depart for its usual home-away-from-home hotel in Pescara.

Jaconi stood at a railing, tearing lumps of stale bread from a loaf taken from Marcella's and feeding them to the ducks in the river below.

"*Osvald'*," I proclaimed. "*E' magnifico!*" It's great!

He scowled at me. "*Forse,*" he said. "*Forse, forse, forse e forse no.*" Maybe, maybe, maybe and maybe not.

I assumed that in this instance I knew something he'd not yet learned, so I told him *forse* no longer applied. Addo had already signed his contract.

"*Sì,*" Jaconi said, throwing the remainder of the stale loaf in the river all at once. "*Lui ha firmato, ma La Società non ancora.*" Yes, Addo had signed the contract, but *La Società* had not. And with that, seeming as agitated as the ducks below as they fought over the last lumps of bread, he left me and walked quickly away.

It was strange to see Castel di Sangro take the field against Padova. Two years ago, with Alexi Lalas named one of the five best new *stranieri* in *Serie A,* Padova had defeated Genoa in a postseason "play-out" match to preserve their top-level status.

In 1995–96, however, with Lalas leaving at midseason in order to help launch Major League Soccer in America, Padova had finished dead last and was relegated to *Serie B,* along with Bari, Torino, and Cremonese.

Cremonese we'd already seen and, surprisingly, had conquered. But Padova seemed made of sterner stuff, and destined for a quick return to *Serie A.* Already, they'd accumulated fourteen points to our seven, a total that put them third in the league. And they'd just signed one of *calcio*'s most enduring legendary figures, the goalkeeper Walter Zenga.

For eleven years, from 1983 to 1994, Zenga had served as *portiere* for Inter Milan, and in that time had made fifty-eight appearances for the national team. Leaving Inter in 1994, at the age of thirty-four, Zenga – who was a master showman and an unapologetic bon vivant – had played two seasons for Sampdoria of Genova, though the more recent one had been curtailed by injury.

Clearly in his twilight years, but still casting a long shadow, this figure – who to residents of the Abruzzo had for years seemed larger than life – would be tending goal against Castel di Sangro. His presence alone made this our most important match yet.

It would also have made the most fitting inauguration imaginable for the new stadium, but Gravina had announced once again that "due to materials shortages and delivery problems and unforeseeable delays of a technical nature," the opening would have to be postponed for another two weeks, until our match against Brescia.

Seeing the same ten or twelve men leaning lethargically against the same pieces of machinery day after day, with absolutely no construction taking place, I wondered if the "delays of a technical nature" were not simply code words for Signor Rezza's continuing refusal to spend the money required to bring in the labor force necessary to get the job done.

In any event, we were in Chieti once again. Ten minutes before the match, Joseph Addo materialized in the empty seat to my right. (Consistent with what Barbara had told me about Gravina's already having come to rue my presence in Castel di Sangro, I'd been moved several rows back and a full section to the right of *il presidente.* No more would he have to suffer my exultant punches on the arm each time we scored – assuming we ever did score again.)

I'd just begun to tell Addo how much better I'd feel if he were on the field today instead of sitting next to me when he held up a hand and, with a great gloom spreading across his handsome face, he said, "It will never be."

"What do you mean?"

"Jaconi told me last night. At the hotel. He does not want me."

"What do you mean?"

Addo shook his head wearily. "Jaconi tells me," he said, "and you know his broken English is not so bad that he cannot tell you when he's screwed you – that the club never signed the contract at all. They wanted my signature only so no other team in Italy could sign me, in order that I might never play against them. Jaconi says I cannot play *for* him because it would take me too long to learn his tactics."

"His *tactics!*" I screamed, actually rising briefly from my seat. "That's the biggest laugh of the year. Jaconi's 'tactics' consist of kicking the ball as far away from his goal as often as possible and hoping for a scoreless tie in every match."

"Yes, but Joe," Addo said calmly, reaching for my arm. "You should sit down. That old man from the mountain is staring at you. And besides, nobody is going to change Jaconi's mind."

On that jarring note, the match began. In midfield, Cristiano again proved himself capable of surprise, while Di Vincenzo, starting again in attack, seemed newly energized and ran with a pace and purpose not seen since the season's first match. Meanwhile, on defense, Luca D'Angelo was playing for four, personally thwarting every Padova approach toward goal and giving Lotti, in the early going at least, the easiest afternoon he'd enjoyed all fall.

Indeed, after the first half hour, Padova's expectations seemed to diminish dramatically. It was if they decided, collectively: If this isn't going to be easy, to hell with it. Continually frustrated by D'Angelo's quickness and intuitive reading of their game, Padova ceased to press forward. It seemed that despite their abundance of talent, their manager was as much an adherent of the "draw on the road is as good as a win" school as Jaconi.

As the first half came to a close, it was we – Castel di Sangro –

who were getting off the occasional strong shot; in particular, a blazer from Di Vincenzo, which forced a fine save from Zenga. But as for "tactics" that Joseph Addo might not be able to understand? That was preposterous!

"Kids in a school yard," Addo said to me at halftime. "Kick the ball and run and hope maybe someone kicks it back. These are not tactics, these are ten players each playing by himself. If two of them happen to combine for something useful, it is only coincidence, not a plan. Last night, when Jaconi told me I couldn't fit in, I was shocked and very disappointed. But now, after seeing this, I'm insulted."

When he got up to buy an ice cream, hundreds of unknowing Castel di Sangro fans in the area applauded him warmly and shouted encouragment and words to the effect that once he was out there, everything would be different.

"But for now," Addo told me, returning to his seat. "What I've said to you is private. Jaconi says the *Società* will wish to give it a different 'spin.' Well, you know, he didn't say that in those words, but he made his meaning very clear. And that if I were to complain publicly about my treatment, they could make it very hard for me ever to play in Italy again and maybe even hard to find a job in another country."

"Those miserable bastards!" I could not help standing again and glaring in the direction of Rezza and Gravina.

"Yes, but you know how the world works. Joe, please sit down. I really don't want to make a fuss. I just want to get out of here. So please, for today, for tomorrow, for next week, the truth is only for you. I'm sorry we won't get to know each other. I'm sorry we won't become friends. But after bringing me here, they have sent me away because of Jaconi and now I must get on with my career. I'll try to send you a postcard from Holland. I have an offer from Sparta Rotterdam."

Padova came out for the second half acting as if they'd just been informed that their bus had left without them. They seemed suddenly hapless, helpless, and hopeless. With Luca D'Angelo continuing to assert himself on defense as no one before him had all year, we assumed complete control of the match.

At sixty minutes, Martino, playing at "home" again and hence not *nostalgico,* took a strong header that required an exceptional save from Zenga. For the next ten minutes – no longer in awe of our big-name opponents and sensing a chance for yet a third win in Chieti, and this one the most improbable of all – we continued to surge forward.

Given the flow of play, it seemed more inevitable than shocking when, at seventy-four minutes, Di Vincenzo scored. Seconds before, Martino had crossed a lovely ball in from the corner and Di Vincenzo had headed it goalward. Only Zenga's finest save of the day had prevented a goal.

On the ensuing corner kick, however, the Padova defense simply stood still, allowing Di Vincenzo to dart to the ball as it arced toward the grass and to smash it past Zenga with a volley that no keeper could have stopped.

Total chaos and mania ensued, and despite my anger about the treatment of Addo, I joined in. If it held up for the next fifteen minutes, *this* would be the biggest win in Castel di Sangro history. And there seemed, for once, no question that the lead would hold. The body language of the Padova players on the field reeked of defeat, and the match ended without even a flurry of additional excitement.

Joe Addo and I shook hands for the last time, and he left the stadium for a car that Gravina had hired to take him to Rome for the one-way flight back to Frankfurt. I was shocked. I was outraged. I was appalled.

But on the other hand, *we had beaten Padova!*

17

November. In the blink of an eye, someone changed the stage set. Suddenly the mountains were wreathed in low clouds. The temperature no longer rose from morning lows. The days stayed bleak and raw, and by the time of afternoon training even the nearby hills were obscured by lowering fog.

The shift in mood was no less dramatic. The post-Padova high had lasted exactly two days: until the players returned on Tuesday to learn that Joseph Addo would not be joining them after all.

At first, they were mystified, then angry. *"La Società,"* Gigi Prete whispered to me. Hadn't he told me? Gravina was not only *disonesto*, he was also *un taccagno*, a cheapskate. Addo had left because *La Società* refused to pay him what he was worth.

I knew this not to be true, but it was the story Gravina himself was putting out, although with rather a different emphasis. Agreement had been reached, Giuseppe reported in *Il Centro*, when at the last minute Addo had suddenly insisted that his salary be doubled.

"E' stato un vero ricatto!" an assistant to Gravina announced to the squad. It was pure blackmail! And *La Società* had too much honor, too much morality, to submit to such extortion. I never could determine whether the use of the word for "blackmail" had been an inadvertent or deliberate double entendre, but I knew that the entire explanation was a lie.

I think I would have known instinctively simply from having met

Addo, and even more surely from my brief encounter with Jaconi as he was casting his bread upon the waters (or, less grandiloquently, feeding the ducks behind Marcella's).

In this case, however, I had Addo's personal account to rely upon. I also had confirmation from Barbara.

"He signed it," she told me. "I was sitting right next to him as he did. He even used a pen I handed to him. He was not happy with the money, but he so much liked the other players, how genuine their welcome seemed, and all the good things you had told him about the town.

"I remember that he said of Signor Rezza, 'That old man's a skin-flint bastard,' but then he smiled; he was not angry. And he said, 'Well, I suppose I can make up the difference next year in *Serie A.*' "

"And did anyone sign on behalf of *La Società?*"

"I did not see this, Joe. I do not know. But I know that when Addo left the offices on Saturday morning, he felt himself to be a member of the team. The only talk at the end was about how to bring the rest of his belongings here from Frankfurt."

My anger at the shabby treatment meted out to Addo far exceeded any negative emotion I had felt up to that point. At the start it had been *we* all supporting one another as we set out on the long road toward *la salvezza*. Then it had become *we* and *they* as I gradually learned and came to adopt the players' point of view toward *La So-cietà*. Now, as what I thought of as the A.D. (after Addo) portion of the season began, it was *we* and *they* and *him*. And the fact that *him* – or *he,* for grammatical purposes – was my next-door neighbor made it no better, and maybe worse. Jaconi had much to answer for: not to me, but to his team.

As I walked to training on a raw, gray Wednesday afternoon, I came upon Signor Rezza, his cigar, and his bodyguards, standing at the edge of the construction site, which was finally showing signs of activity, though not enough, in my opinion, to ready it for the match against Brescia.

As I approached Signor Rezza, I noticed that his niece Maria Teresa was with him also.

"Buona sera," I said, the Abruzzo being a part of Italy where this greeting replaced *buongiorno* at some mysterious point in early after-

noon, unlike the north, where *buongiorno* remained in effect until the onset of the evening *passeggiata*.

"*Salve,*" Signor Rezza grunted, a response on the order of "hello," implying neither cordiality nor the absence thereof.

I stood at the edge of the group for a moment, but no one else said anything or even looked in my direction. The cigar smoke hung heavily in the chill November air.

Finally, Signor Rezza removed it from his mouth and gestured toward me. "*Porti bene,*" he said. "*Continua così.*"

So! The old man could speak Italian. And he was also a believer in my magic. You're bringing good luck, he had said. Keep it up. Three wins and a draw from the five matches I had attended; three goalless defeats in those I had not. Soon, I'd be believing it myself.

"*D'accordo, ci provo,*" I replied. Okay, I'll try. "*Ma è un peccato per Addo.*" But it's a pity about Addo. To my right, I heard a sharp intake of breath from Maria Teresa. Quite possibly, this subject was already considered taboo.

"*Senti,*" Rezza responded immediately, making sharp thrusting motions with the hand that held the cigar. "*Lo dici a me? Perchè non lo dici al tuo vicino?*" Listen: you're telling me? Why don't you speak to your neighbor?

And then he waved the cigar in a wide arc that seemed clearly a gesture of dismissal.

I did of course speak to Jaconi about Addo. Several times. And never had the image of throwing pebbles at a bulldozer seemed more appropriate.

At first he said, "Go read the papers. The story is there." When I told him that I knew that the stories in the papers were false – and reminded him that he himself had acknowledged on Saturday afternoon that Addo had already signed the contract – he simply closed down, refusing to speak about it, walking away.

Later he told me that it would have taken Addo too long to have learned to do things the way he wanted.

"Why?" I asked, none too politely. "Because's he's a *straniero,* or because he's *nero?*" I knew that Jaconi had never had a black player on any of his teams, and I sensed strongly that he didn't want one.

"Attento, Joe!" Be careful!

"L'hai mandato via senza motivo," I said angrily. You sent him away for no reason!

"Avevo tutte le ragioni del mondo, ma non devo rendere conto a te." I had every reason in the world, but I am not answerable to you.

"C'è solo una ragione: il razzismo." There is only one reason: racism. I realized that I had now gone from throwing pebbles at a bulldozer to tickling the tail of a dragon.

"Bada!" Jaconi shouted. Watch it! *"Non fare un' altra parola!"* Don't say another word!

And so, for the moment, I did not.

Throughout the raw week, Jaconi appeared unusually unsettled, and not only when speaking to me. Cosenza had just fired its manager, following in the steps of Cesena and Venezia, although the season was only eight matches old. And no matter how many verbal assurances he might have received of a lifetime contract with Castel di Sangro, to have so badly embarrassed *La Società* by sending Addo away after he'd been personally received by Signor Rezza could not have solidified his position.

Nor did the suddenly constant presence of Gravina at the training field have a calming effect. The club president, of course, was no stranger to the training sessions, but during most weeks he would turn up two or three times, always seeming more engaged by his cell phone than by whatever was happening on the field, and leave within twenty to thirty minutes.

Now, however, *il presidente,* seeming jittery and preoccupied, became a fixture on the training field *panchina.* For long periods he would sit alone, hands in pockets, head lowered, speaking to no one. He was pale, thinner, and his panache had been replaced by fretfulness, as if, mentally, he were constantly looking back over his shoulder, expecting the worst, whatever it was. I could not help but sense that something even beyond a pitched battle with Jaconi over the disposition of Joseph Addo weighed heavily in the somber gray air.

One afternoon I asked him my ritual question about whether the new stadium would indeed be ready for the next match, as he was publicly promising. Instead of reiterating, "Of course," or "Without a doubt" as he always had before, however, he looked at me bleakly and responded, *"Ne so quanto te."* Your guess is as good as mine.

This seemed particularly odd because the pace of construction work had quickened noticeably, and Signor Rezza himself now made daily inspection visits to the site. Often Maria Teresa would stand at the side of her uncle, but she was not slow to move forward on her own to question or instruct one of the foremen.

And twice that week she made the short walk over to the training field. When she arrived, however, she took a seat by herself, at the opposite end of the *panchina* from her husband, and the two of them did not speak.

Once, to my surprise, she actually initiated a conversation with me. "You must understand," she said, "that both Gabriele and Signor Rezza wanted very, very much to have Addo play for our team. Gabriele worked very hard to find him and to persuade him to come here. It was Jaconi – all by himself – who refused."

Short, plump, and now with a positively sullen expression on her face, Maria Teresa shrugged. *"Non sapevamo cosa fare."* We didn't know what to do. Then she looked at Gabriele, seated ten feet away, his cell phone active. There seemed neither respect nor affection in her glance.

"Ciao," she said abruptly, forcing a smile as she walked quickly away.

I called Barbara one night that week to ask if she could offer any insight. She'd been giving me regular and extraordinarily helpful instruction in Italian, and also seemed to have gotten caught up in the ongoing drama surrounding the team's attempt to survive in *Serie B*. I'd always found her willing to speak with apparent candor, and this case proved no exception.

Other women had long been a source of contention between Gravina and Maria Teresa, she told me, but recently, on Gabriele's part, there had seemed a new and almost blindly arrogant lack of discretion. You could cheat on your wife even if she was the boss's daughter, Barbara suggested, but what you could *not* do was to flaunt your behavior in such a way as to humiliate either the daughter or the boss. Since the start of the season, however, there seemed to have been an increasing number of instances in which Gravina, swept away perhaps by the heady atmosphere of his *calcio* success – or by who knew what else? – had done just that.

"The women have been a problem," Barbara said, "because Maria Teresa grows unhappy, and Signor Rezza sees this and he tells Gabriele, 'No more women to hurt Maria Teresa. Period.'"

"If Signor Rezza told me that, I might listen."

"Yes, but Gabriele does not. I think he feels that if he always drives fast and talks on his phone and gets good publicity, even Signor Rezza would not act against him. And who can tell? The life of a family is complicated, and many truths are never known by outsiders."

Others I spoke to told me readily that Gabriele's frequent "out-of-town business" would leave him, at the dinner hour, in some small, secluded hamlet such as Pacentro, above Sulmona, which happened to have a particularly excellent restaurant and a particularly discreet maître d'. That he would not dine alone, but rather in the company of an ever changing array of gorgeous women – the wives of certain players whispered to be among them – was accepted as fact by people whom I'd found to be reliable.

As if to highlight the atmosphere of discord – and certainly to increase the pressure on all concerned – Signor Rezza himself, with bodyguards and a fresh cigar, arrived for the regular Thursday afternoon intrasquad scrimmage.

A large space was cleared for him on the *panchina*. The players had already taken the field, but upon his arrival the older ones, the ones who'd been here, the ones who knew more of the true score than did the more recent arrivals, stopped their warmups and trotted toward the sideline and then, led by Prete, one by one stepped forward, executed half bows, and reached out to shake Rezza's hand or just to receive a benevolent half wave. If he'd been wearing a ring, they would have kissed it.

But then the scrimmage began and it was a disaster in every way, as if the entire squad had conspired beforehand to be sure that each player would put on his worst practice performance of the season.

Before he'd smoked even half his cigar, Signor Rezza stood in disgust, motioned to his bodyguards, and walked away, saying good-bye to no one and not even glancing at Jaconi. He was, however, heard to mutter, "They are so bad, they cannot even score against themselves."

And then there was the matter of De Juliis. All season he'd been bothered by a knee injury. It wasn't crippling, but it had affected him and it was worsening. With Lotti now firmly ensconced as number one, De Juliis finally opted for the necessary arthroscopic surgery.

The practical impact was nil, for Spinosa was more than capable of stepping into the goalmouth during training, but even the brief absence of De Juliis from Marcella's seemed to unsettle Jaconi even further, underlining the fact that not all goalkeepers (Lotti being a prime example) worshiped their manager, or even acted as if they did.

In addition, we would be traveling north on the weekend to face Cesena, one of the six teams that lay below us in the standings. This created even more than the usual anxiety for Jaconi. Any match *fuori casa* provoked trepidation, but to travel away from home to play a team *that was supposed to be worse than you were* seemed almost paralytically frightening.

When you lost *fuori casa* against a good team, it was expected; there was no fuss. But against Cesena, which was three points beneath us, we would be expected to come away with no worse than a draw. This additional burden seemed to drive Jaconi nearly frantic.

Especially, I felt, because he knew – even if he would admit it to no one – that Joseph Addo could have been with us, and that with Addo we would have been a stronger team.

Not only Jaconi knew this, of course. The players, having been tantalized by the waving of such a glorious possibility as Addo in front of their eyes, felt his absence even more keenly. And on their behalf I felt it pretty damned keenly myself. What sort of man *was* Jaconi? Not to mention, what sort of manager? Not only would he refuse to seek talent, he would spurn it when it was presented on a silver platter. It was starting to seem – and not only to me but to a number of the players as well – that if he could not win *la salvezza* on his terms, Jaconi would rather not have it at all.

Cesena was a squad that made occasional appearances in *Serie A* but was essentially the stuff of *Serie B,* having finished in tenth place there the preceding season. The city, with a population of 90,000, had peaked in terms of splendor in the fourteenth century but was pleasantly situated in the region of Emilia-Romagna, enabling us to spend Saturday night in the coastal resort city of Rimini, much favored by film director Federico Fellini and the site of, among others of his films, *Amarcord*.

We reached Rimini just as dusk fell, and drove along wide boulevards and past the Grand Hotel used in the filming of Fellini's movie. We were staying a few blocks away, in one of the many four-star hotels that stood largely empty (or shut down entirely) in fall and winter but that from May through September were filled to capacity by beachgoers. A fog settled in just as we did, and the sound of foghorns was louder than any noise of automobiles – quite the opposite of summer months.

Through the evening, I let the sense of unreality wash over me. Drifting toward sleep in the town where Fellini had grown up, I found myself feeling that Jaconi's big problem was that his thinking was too linear, and thus constricted. Like Fellini, he should open himself to outlandish possibility, break free from the conventional, explore the world of fantasy (or at least try to sign a *fantasista*). Less structure, more freedom, that was the ticket. Perhaps Jaconi and I should watch a few Fellini films together. It was going to be, after all, a long winter.

But the next day the sky fell. Not just one or two pieces, but the whole bloody thing. Cesena won the match, 1–0, but the true catastrophe was an injury to Lotti's elbow that was expected to sideline him for three months.

Overly defensive and fearful from the start (*la paura* having drifted in with the fog), Jaconi had again opted for a 4-5-1 formation, with Galli as the lone attacker. No matter how many times this approach proved unsuccessful, Osvaldo seemed bound to it, insisting that because it had worked last year in *C1*, it should work this year in *Serie B*.

After pressuring us constantly throughout the first half, Cesena scored only three minutes into the second. Again, Claudio Bonomi (seemingly intent on proving me wrong for having believed him capable of quick improvement) was having a wretched afternoon out on the wing, while the homesick Martino failed to threaten on the other side. With half an hour left, Jaconi sent on Di Vincenzo in place of Di Fabio, which finally gave us two *attaccanti,* although in this case we might as well not have had any, so little did either see of the ball.

The final flicker of hope was extinguished late in the match when, for reasons unknown, Jaconi took off the ever more dangerous Cristiano and sent on Roberto Alberti. Down by a goal with only ten minutes left, with both your attackers seemingly reachable only by cell phone, and with your star winger's lungs collapsing under the weight of too much nicotine, was *not,* in my opinion, a propitious time to remove your most energetic, effective, and unpredictable player.

I had little time to brood, however, because only three minutes later Lotti, diving to make a save at his left post, hit the metal upright full force with his left elbow. He lay untended and writhing in agony for minutes, while it slowly sunk in to Jaconi that now, when he finally had the chance to send in De Juliis, there was no De Juliis to send in – Robert being home, recuperating from his knee surgery.

Eventually Lotti, face contorted in pain, was carried off on a stretcher and taken to a hospital nearby. In the meantime, Spinosa, who had retired in glory the previous June, was forced to take up position in goal.

But by then it didn't matter. While Cesena showed no urge to rub salt in the wound, Castel di Sangro, for the remaining ten minutes, continued to self-destruct. We were in total disarray, without a semblance of leadership on the field or from the bench, without focus, poise, or any awareness that we were still down by only one goal and might – by invoking even a *minor* miracle – eke out a tie.

That night Lotti couldn't even ride back on the bus. His elbow was so badly damaged, he had to remain in the hospital in Cesena.

I wound up wishing I'd stayed there, too. For on the ride back, the communist defender D'Angelo began grilling me about America's role in Vietnam.

For better or worse, I'd made it clear from the start that politically, in America, I was *di sinistra,* a left-winger, but that I felt it would be inappropriate for me to express opinions (such as that Berlusconi was a greedy, corrupt, fascist pig) about the political affairs of Italy.

On the ride back from Cesena, therefore, D'Angelo decided the time had come for a more extensive discussion of America's role in Vietnam. I had *gone* to Vietnam, had I not? And not once, but twice?

Yes, Luca, I explained for at least the fifth time since mid-September, but this was only as a journalist, not as a soldier, and, in fact, the dispatches I'd filed were considered controversial, inflammatory, and even unpatriotic at the time because they had made clear my belief that America's involvement not only was doomed to fail politically and militarily but, first and foremost, was absolutely immoral.

"Comunque, Joe, hai protestato contro la guerra?" Had I protested against the war?

"I miei articoli erano la mia forma di protesta." My articles were my form of protest.

"Non era sufficiente," he said. Not enough.

"E' facile parlare! Ma ti facevo più intelligente." It's easy to speak. But I thought you had more sense. *"Facevo il mio meglio."* I was doing my best.

He looked across the darkened aisle at me and shook a finger from side to side. *"No, Joe. Tu dovevi intervenire per fermarla. Non dovevi solo scrivere."* No, you should have acted to stop it, not only write about it.

"Forse, Luca, ma oggi tu dovevi intervenire per fermare gli attaccanti, non dovevi solo parlare." Maybe, Luca, but today you should have acted to stop the attackers, not only talk.

At this, Galli, who'd been twitching his head in front of me for an hour, suddenly leapt to his feet.

"Bravo, Joe," he said. But then he pointed an accusatory finger. *"Ma la bomba atomica contro Hiroshima? Hai lottato contro quella?"* The atomic bomb against Japan? Did you fight against that?

"Giacomo, per favore! Avevo solo due anni!" Please! I was only two years old!

"Davvero?" Really? Galli said. It seemed his first inkling that World War II and Vietnam had not been fought in the same year.

"Ho-Ho-Ho Chi Minh! . . . Ho-Ho-Ho Chi Minh!" D'Angelo began chanting. " 'Ey, 'ey, Elle Bee Zhay, 'ow many kids you kill today?"

"Basta!" Galli said, and since he was already standing, he walked to the front of the bus to put in a new video.

Thus, I was spared further political discussion, but at the cost of *Kickboxer 4: The Aggressor.*

The bus returned to a cold and desolate *cittadina* well after midnight. I fell into bed and felt so depressed all day Monday that I could barely shower and dress. And though I called to assure her I was fine, I didn't even go to Marcella's on Monday night. Addo was gone, Lotti would be out for weeks, no one could score, and we still had no stadium.

Some fairy tale. Not even Fellini would have been tempted to try to turn our sorry story into art.

18

Gravina announced, through Giuseppe in *Il Centro,* that due to "unforeseen delays in delivery of materials and bad weather," the stadium would not be ready for Sunday's match against Brescia. As one resident said to me of Signor Rezza, "He didn't get rich by paying overtime."

It was clear, however, that rapid progress *was* being made with the stadium and that completion would not be far off. I found it hard to credit Barbara's view that my arrival – and Rezza's concern about how he might be portrayed in a book (better than Sam but worse than Chuck?) – had been a factor.

More significant, I felt, was Gravina's oft-stated desire to use Castel di Sangro's success and ensuing moments of fame as a springboard for his own larger ambitions. A supporter of the right-winger and ex–prime minister Berlusconi (owner of A.C. Milan and most of Italy's private television stations and many newspapers as well), Gravina nurtured the hope, according to those who claimed to know him best, that he might be given a cabinet position in a resurgent Berlusconi government.

Thus, in the eyes of the people he wanted most to impress, his failure to have built an acceptable home for his team (because his "uncle" wouldn't give him the money) made him look inadequate, and possibly even ridiculous.

In the end, the equation was simple: no stadium equaled no political future for Gabriele. The new playing surface and the six thousand additional seats were the dues he had to pay for admittance to the ranks of the plausibly ambitious.

Signor Rezza, of course, might have preferred to have Gabriele at least partially dismembered, but family comes first in Italy and so, however grudgingly, he had finally given primacy to the interests of Maria Teresa and her children and had parted with enough of the multimillion-dollar bonus from the Federation to have the construction completed. (Still, however, the players had not received the bonuses due them.)

Meanwhile, for the fifth time, it would be off to Chieti for a "home" match. And this time without Lotti or even De Juliis. This time, with the suddenly unretired Spinosa in goal, playing a full ninety minutes for the first time since 1994 in *C2* and for the first time ever in *Serie B*.

But Spinosa was a man with considerable if unspoken pride in his abilities, and he inspired confidence in others. He seemed energized by the situation and eager to face the challenge, even if it would be coming from powerful Brescia.

At the same time, all Castel di Sangro was rejuvenated by a sudden change in the weather. September-like temperatures brought every baby age nine months or younger outdoors in a stroller. The sky had never been bluer; the mountains, both close and distant, never more cleanly drawn; the sun – though low in the sky and setting early – never sweeter.

And so, inspired by this most unseasonable gift as well as by the example of Spinosa, I once again succumbed to the power of hope.

Wednesday night at Marcella's I was approached by the Three Musketeers – Cristiano, Rimedio, and Biondi – who told me they would like to visit America after the season.

I told them immediately how welcome they would be, how I would pick them up at the Boston airport and drive them to my home, how they could stay as long as they liked, and how beautiful the surroundings were in summer.

They smiled politely. Then Biondi got to the point. "But where will be the women?"

Oh, I said, not so many in my small town, but we are only three hours from Boston and three hours from New York, and there you will find more women than you have ever seen in all of Italy.

"But beautiful?" Biondi asked, his thin lips forming a wry smile.

"Pippo," I said. "Not only beautiful, but I know for a fact that there are thousands of them – thousands – whose only true desire in life is to meet a genuine Italian *calciatore*."

"And they are not too shy?" Rimedio asked. "Even if we speak not so good English?"

"*Shy?* Listen, every day the papers in New York and Boston are filled with the stories of beautiful young women who say their strongest desire is to unlace the boots of a true Italian *calciatore* and kiss his feet."

"*Sì!*" Rimedio said, immediately captivated by the image.

But Biondi was a cooler customer. He said, "That is their *strongest* desire? If that is their *strongest* desire, maybe we do better in Sardinia."

"No, no," I assured him. "I know young people in both cities. And in other cities as well. I have children your age. And I have taught in college. I can tell you that you would not regret a minute of your trip. And that when you were exhausted by the women, Nancy and I would welcome you back at our home for sleep and good sunshine and good food."

By the end of the evening it was agreed: Pippo and Mimmo and Fabio would come to America at the end of June and would stay for two or three weeks. I would plan their itinerary, making sure that plenty of "woman" time was factored in. Just how I would come up with the legions of lovelies so eager to unlace their boots, I had no idea, but June was still a long way off.

In an attempt to paper over the damage done by the dismissal of Addo, Gravina reclaimed from *C1* a player named Luca Albieri, whom he knew Jaconi would not disapprove of, although, except for having been born in Italy, he fit none of the criteria Jaconi stressed as essential.

Albieri was not experienced, being only twenty-one and having played about only sixty matches in his career, evenly divided between *C1* and *C2*. In twenty matches with Castel di Sangro the year before, he'd scored only one goal and in September had been considered not fit for the move up to *Serie B*. So far this year he'd played only three games in *C1*.

So what suddenly made him desirable? He was available cheap, he was a known quantity (however minute that quantity was), and his arrival would presumably encourage the townspeople, reminding them of happier times even as they were dreading the imminent arrival of Brescia.

The Brescia team represented one of the least appealing cities in Italy. It was *bruttissima,* the Italian word for very ugly, and not only architecturally. It was said to house a higher percentage of unhappy and even mean-spirited people than any other city in the north. It was an industrial morass with a population of 200,000, the vast majority of whom gave every indication of wishing that they lived someplace else.

The club was a *Serie B* perennial that had enjoyed occasional, disastrous flirtations with *Serie A*. This season Brescia had been notable underachievers, compiling only fourteen points to our ten.

Yet looming so large over everything that it was simply easier not to talk about it was the question of the admirable Spinosa: Could he serve, even for a day, as a *Serie B portiere?* Almost twenty years of his printed performance records made the point that until this mid-November Sunday in 1996, he had never even been asked to try.

The Sunday drive to Chieti, made on yet another unseasonably *bella giornata* (beautiful day) was slowed by an *autostrada* blockage caused by a fatal accident. As the car I was riding in finally edged past the scene, I saw that one body had been pulled from the wreckage and lay, sheet-covered, at the side of the road. A fellow passenger looked carefully and then said, *"Solo uno,"* nodding in apparent satisfaction. Only one. Not so bad. Like so much else in Italy, it was simply a matter of perspective.

It had finally sunk in, even to Jaconi, that Galli alone on attack was about as useful as a totem pole, though perhaps not so artfully crafted. And so, once again, Di Vincenzo was slotted alongside him.

In the defense, captain Cei was omitted for the fifth consecutive match, the burgeoning talent of Luca D'Angelo being something from which Jaconi could no longer avert his eyes, no matter how much personal distaste he harbored for the young, long-haired communist. Fusco, Altamura, and Prete filled out the back four.

In midfield, Jaconi chose Cristiano and the feisty Michelini to start alongside each other for the fourth consecutive week. Di Fabio was dropped to make room for Di Vincenzo at the front, and the slumping but speedy Bonomi and the erratic (but at least close to home) Martino remained on the wings.

Nonetheless, we looked outclassed from the start. Within the first five minutes Prete, Di Vincenzo, Martino, Martino again, D'Angelo, Di Vincenzo again, Michelini, Prete again, and Cristiano all lost the ball without our advancing even to midfield. Plus, Fusco picked up a yellow card. (The yellow card is shown to indicate the referee's disapproval of a particularly violent foul. Two yellows in the same match equal a red card, which brings immediate expulsion.)

In the next five minutes the ball losers were Galli, Galli, Martino, Galli, Galli, Cristiano, Prete, Galli, and Michelini. That was eighteen losses of ball in the first ten minutes. Who says soccer is a game without statistics?

Di Vincenzo was fouled in the penalty area in the seventeenth minute, but the referee, a man named Rossi from the town of Ciampino, close to Rome's Fiumicino Airport, who had been blowing his whistle for phantom fouls at least once per minute, did not deem this one worthy of attention. No penalty kick was awarded.

Brescia was playing like Padova the week before – as if they'd been forced to inhale chloroform in their locker room. This at least kept the pressure off Spinosa even if it was not exactly stimulating for the fans. (For me, by this point, there was no such thing as a dull match because at any moment disaster could strike Castel di Sangro. Each contest thus was composed of ninety minutes of simultaneous feelings of pain and dread, interlarded with veins of fury, disgust, and ultimately either despair or the most unexpected sort of ecstasy.)

Almost half an hour passed without Brescia having shown the slightest awareness that the object of the game was to score. This meant we were only fifteen minutes shy of still being 0–0 at the half, which meant – in my newly warped view – that it had been a glorious thirty minutes of football.

The only off note continued to be the *arbitro,* Rossi. He was like a three-year-old who'd just been given a whistle for his birthday. The foul calls were constant, with neither body contact nor even proximity to an opponent seeming a prerequisite.

As the result of his call of one such nonexistent foul, Brescia was finally forced into taking a shot: a free kick from twenty yards out that sailed menacingly past our wall of defenders and bounced off the left goalpost as Spinosa, looking suddenly very, very small in that big space, dove toward it far too late.

Having squandered that opportunity, Brescia slumped back into their sluggish defensive posture, which consisted mainly of standing virtually still while the Castel di Sangro players – who were ostensibly trying to pass the ball to one another – continually bounced it into Brescia laps instead.

Shortly thereafter, Spinosa was actually required to make a save, which he did without difficulty, and then, *miracolo dei miracoli,* exactly at the forty-five-minute mark, Martino recovered a loose ball and passed it directly to Galli, who stood unmarked and apparently unseen less than ten yards in front of the Brescia goal.

The Brescia keeper, paralyzed by the shock of such an unlikely event, stood stock-still as Galli turned and shot. Defying all known laws of vector physics, however, Giacomo Boom Boom sent the ball at least ten yards wide to the left. And that was the first half. I could exhale.

To start the second, Jaconi sent on the new arrival, Albieri, to replace Di Vincenzo, who had, inarguably, been ineffective once again. Almost immediately Albieri stole the ball at midfield, danced his way through a bevy of Brescia defenders, ran on into the penalty area in full stride and in full control of the ball only to be tackled viciously from behind by a Brescia defender.

Even as Albieri rolled on the ground in agony, all of us Castel di Sangro *tifosi* were on our feet cheering. Albieri, no doubt, would recover. We were rejoicing because the penalty kick, if made, would give us a 1–0 lead.

But play had not stopped! With Albieri curled in a fetal position at the edge of the Brescia goal, the ball was coming back toward the Castel di Sangro end, with Mr. Rossi trotting blithely alongside as though one of the ugliest, most cynical fouls I'd ever seen had not just been committed in the Brescia penalty area.

Surely, he was about to reach into his pocket and take out an additional yellow card to punish Brescia for playing on after he'd called for a penalty kick. But no . . . but no . . . was it possible?

This was unthinkable. This was unspeakable. This was theater of the absurd as directed by the Marquis de Sade. But, God in heaven, it was true! No foul. No penalty. No goal. No 1–0 lead. Only a limping Albieri.

Well, now, this was a different matter altogether. A wretched, squalid 0–0 draw, that was one thing. That would have made for a highly satisfactory afternoon. But now this Rossi, now *he,* rather than any of the players on either side, became the focus of attention. By a factor of ten, he was the worst referee I'd ever seen work a match in what were now the four countries in which I'd seen matches.

At the sixty-minute mark, Albieri was again the victim of a flagrant foul – this time at the very edge of the penalty area – and again no call was made. Instead, Rossi spun on his heel and whistled down some harmless shuffling that the eye in the back of his head had seen at midfield.

Still, at sixty-five minutes, we threatened again. Three gorgeous passes (a first!) left Galli open once more in front of the net. Again, with all afternoon to choose the pace and placement of his shot, Galli missed. Only Brescia's almost insulting level of indifference to these events gave me hope that we would pull off a 0–0 draw after all.

But then, for no apparent reason except that possibly he'd misplaced them earlier and was rushing to make up for lost time, Rossi began to wave yellow cards as if trying to flag down a train. One to Brescia, two to Brescia, then one to Cristiano (his fourth in four games, meaning that suspension would follow), one to Bonomi . . . but none of them had even committed fouls!

I began to wonder – and not frivolously – who, if anyone, had the power to suspend a match because the referee had suffered a nervous breakdown in the middle of it and could not be permitted to continue. For this had ceased to be a match of any sort. Rossi had turned it into a shooting gallery, with his cards the ammunition and, increasingly, Castel di Sangro players his primary targets.

BANG! At seventy minutes, card to Altamura, and not a yellow but a *red.* Free kick for Brescia at the edge of the penalty area. This one was quickly converted into a goal, which meant the end for us, because among our many incapacities, we reserved a special place of honor for the inability to come from behind.

It was also the end for Altamura, who would now be suspended for the next two matches. He had brushed against a Brescia player while both were going for the ball, but this was the very essence of defensive play. If a foul had been committed, the Brescia player could just as easily have been found at fault. But under no circumstances had it been the sort of play that merited a card for either man, and absolutely not a red card.

I was so stunned by this that I scarcely paid attention as we moved the ball back to the Brescia end. I did perk up when I saw Galli break free and Martino lob a pass toward him. And I was focused intently on the scene as Galli fought off the predations of an onrushing Brescia defender and shot, for once powerfully and accurately, and . . . scored!

Yes, yes, yes, he did! Galli actually scored a goal! For once, he had not missed! Oh, my God. Oh, my God. Who would believe it? I looked down briefly and could see my chest wall giving ground under the savage and relentless pounding of my heart.

But wait. Rossi was racing down from midfield, where he'd been badly out of position, and was waving his arms in a manner indicating that Galli's goal would be disallowed.

Amid explosive bursts of fury from every Castel di Sangro player on the field – not to mention an ominous surge toward the fences by thousands of Castel di Sangro supporters in the stands – Rossi decreed that Galli had committed an *offensive* foul in making sure that he, the intended target of the pass, did not allow it to go astray and wind up in the control of the Brescia defender.

I saw police rushing to take up posts at the edge of the field in case any of our *tifosi* managed to scale the wire fence or in case several hundred managed to push through it, as they were trying to do.

Well, somebody had to do something to this man and do it fast. I mean, *hurt* him. *Hurt him physically.* How I wished I had some heavy metal object in my pocket. I'd have run down from the *tribuna d'onore* to the edge of the field and would have let fly. I would have aimed for the head and prayed for a direct hit. And nothing that happened to me after that would have been of the slightest consequence whatsoever because at least I would have made that bastard pay.

Then Rossi gave a yellow card to Galli for "dissent." Knowing Giacomo's tongue, and that both he and Rossi probably spoke Roman dialect as well as Italian, I was sure the *arbitro* had just had a few new holes bored in his verbal memory bank. But words alone, however hurtful, could not suffice.

For the match was essentially over. After the nullification of Galli's goal, we simply fell back on defense, dazed, demoralized, disgusted, and waited for the final whistle. Brescia, now realizing they could do whatever they wanted with impunity, suddenly sprang forward with vigor.

A Brescia forward dribbled into the Castel di Sangro penalty area. Cristiano slid at his feet and knocked the ball cleanly away. A whistle. A penalty. Rossi had apparently decided that Brescia should be rewarded for their first burst of offensive effort by being given a penalty kick, which they made, sending the score to 2–0.

Losing all control, Fusco charged at Rossi as soon as the ball went into the net, spewing foam and Neapolitan curses in equal amounts. Teammates grabbed him before he could make physical contact, but out came the red card and Fusco, too, was sent off.

At ninety minutes, seemingly only for the perverse fun of it, Rossi awarded Brescia yet another penalty kick. Not one person in the stands, not a single player on the Brescia team, not the Brescia manager, and, one suspects, not Rossi himself, had the slightest idea why. It seemed an act of sheer, demented whimsy.

The kick was good, the score was 3–0, and as soon as the ball was back out of the net and in Rossi's arms, he whistled the game to an end and ran as fast as he could for the tunnel that would take him out of the stadium before any of what had now grown into a furious mob of several hundred Castel di Sangro supporters could have at him.

Since I had been in the good seats, I was not one of the first to arrive at the barbed-wire fence that would have to be scaled, but when I approached it, I saw that some Castel di Sangro *tifoso,* more crazed with rage than even I was, had already made it to the top and was balanced there, one hand gripping the mesh on either side of the barbs, as police on both sides climbed up after him, smashing at him with their clubs to dislodge him. And then I saw who it was: *Christian!*

· · ·

It was hours later, back at Marcella's, before either Christian or I was calm enough to speak coherently in any language. (In order to avert a riot, the police, heavily outnumbered by Castel di Sangro fans, had spared Christian a clubbing once they'd shaken him loose.)

Our conversation, once it began, centered not surprisingly on referees, and on the worst examples of the breed.

"This was very bad," said a man whose name I did not know but who had played for Castel di Sangro in the 1960s. "Very bad. Maybe the worst since Celano."

I had seen road signs for Celano, an Abruzzan town west of Sulmona, just off the *autostrada* that led to Rome.

"Celano? When was that?" I asked. "When did Castel di Sangro play Celano?"

"Oh, no, this is many years ago. Maybe 1978, 1979. And Castel di Sangro did not play. But the *tifosi* of Celano, they think the *arbitro* that day, he was worse even than this Rossi of today."

"Not possible," I said.

"Yes," he nodded. "Possible. So . . . they have a . . . don't know in English . . . a *linciaggio*."

I called to Christian for help. "Christian, for a bad referee . . . what is this *linciaggio?*"

"Oh, you mean at Celano? Maybe twenty years past?"

"Yes, what happened?"

"To the *arbitro?* Yes, a *linciaggio*. You know, with the tree and the rope around the neck. The hanging. Like in America you did to the Negroes in the South."

"You mean, they *lynched* him?"

"I think so, *sì*. I don't know this 'lynch,' but I know *linciaggio*. Yes, yes, they put the rope on the tree and put his neck in the rope and, yes, he dies. And maybe this is wrong, but I hear the stories and is not so bad because only by the *linciaggio* they be sure he never do again to another team what he do to them. So it was in, how do you say, the good interest?"

"The public interest?"

"Well, for Celano public, yes. But is something else."

"In the best interests of the sport?"

"Yes, that is it. *Esattamente*. In best interest of this sport. For if they kill him, he can never be bad *arbitro* again."

"Well . . . well . . . what happened to the fans? Was anybody arrested? Was anybody prosecuted? Did anybody go to jail?"

"I don't know," Christian said.

But my original informant remembered clearly. "Oh, no," he said calmly. "That could not happen. You see, the police, the *magistrati* from Roma, they all knew that the *arbitro* had been at fault."

19

Each morning, Italy's daily newspapers produce large posters that a news dealer can paste outside his shop, highlighting in huge dark type the biggest story of the day.

On Monday, *Il Centro*'s poster proclaimed: ARBITRO SCAN-DOLOSO.

And no one, at least not in Castel di Sangro, disagreed. The Brescia match had been a defeat for us, but it also had been a defeat for fair play and decency. The *pagelle* were irrelevant after such a match: only the rating assigned to the *arbitro* was significant. And *La Gazzetta dello Sport,* the only paper that really mattered in a case like this, gave Rossi a 3. A *three!* Never before had I seen a player, manager, or *arbitro* receive less than 4, which in itself indicated disgrace.

Well, it seemed time to learn whether my upstairs neighbor Altamura did or did not have a sense of humor. For Christmas the year before, my son James, then twelve, had given me an authentic referee's kit consisting of a red card, a yellow card, and a pad on which the official can write the name of the offending player, the nature of the infraction, and so on.

I'd been carrying the red card and yellow card, contained within a folding plastic wallet, everywhere I went, even using it in place of a regular wallet, stuffing it with credit cards, crumpled lire, phone numbers, and the like.

I arose early on Monday morning and walked out to Altamura's automobile, parked at the curb.

I tucked the red card beneath his windshield wiper, along with a scribbled note that said in Italian: *Meant to give you this yesterday, along with the first one. Best wishes, Signor Rossi of Ciampino.*

Having bought the newspapers, I was back in my apartment when I heard Altamura call good-bye to his wife, Sabrina, and head down the stairs with Niccolò, their four-year-old son, whom he was taking to day care.

I heard him come down from the third flight to the second (where I lived), and then to the first, all the while talking to Niccolò in calm and fatherly tones as the little boy babbled the sort of pre–day care talk that little boys babble on Monday mornings.

I heard them exit through the small lobby and head for the car. A moment later I heard the lobby door slam open and then Antonello's mad thundering up the stairs. (He must have left Niccolò secured in his car seat.)

He was still a flight away when he began screaming, *"Sabrina!"* I heard her worried voice call back as she opened the door to their apartment. The door slammed shut again but did not damp the voice of Antonello, who was bellowing like a dying bull. Then I heard fists pounding on the wall. As his cursing rose in volume, and as I thought of Niccolò strapped into his car seat alone, I figured I had better confess.

So I walked upstairs, knocked on the door, and said in Italian, "I am Rossi of Ciampino. I hear that you're looking for me."

The door swung open. As soon as Antonello and Sabrina saw me, they realized I'd been behind the joke. Which of them screamed more loudly with laughter was hard to tell, but as they both pulled me forward to embrace me, it was definitely Antonello who was stronger. *Accidenti,* what a crazy American they had as a neighbor. One who not only knew *calcio* but knew also how to make them laugh, even on a very bad Monday morning.

While Castel di Sangro was my main focus at all times, it was not possible to live in Italy in the fall of 1996 and not be aware of the travails being suffered by Baggio.

The sale to Milan had not worked out well. Their new Uruguayan manager seemed to find a fresh reason each week to keep *il Divino Codino in panchina.* Meanwhile, the arrogant, vain, sadistic, megalomaniacal, and utterly incompetent national team manager Sacchi had coldly and arbitrarily excluded Baggio from the *azzurri,* the national team.

In early qualifying matches for the 1998 World Cup, Italy had managed to squeak by such pathetic foes as Moldova and Georgia but, *mamma mia,* had looked execrable in doing so.

Now, on November 6 they were playing an *amichevole,* or exhibition match, against Bosnia in Sarajevo. One would not have thought that Bosnia had eleven able-bodied men to field as a team, nor that the *campo* in Sarajevo would be safe to play on, but the match went forward nonetheless.

Given the time difference, it was shown in early afternoon in Italy, and I watched before going to the Tuesday training session. To the horror and astonishment of all – except me, for I felt that this would prove the last straw for Sacchi, and in doing so might give new life to Baggio's international career – Bosnia beat the Italians, 2–1.

I skipped my way to the practice field, singing to myself, "Ding-dong! The witch is dead!" Yes, I remained furious about Rossi of Ciampino and disconsolate about Lotti's injury, but I knew that Lotti would recover, while I suspected that Sacchi would not.

Luca D'Angelo was one of the first players I saw on the field.

"Luca, Luca! Two to one!" I shouted.

He trotted over, looking puzzled. Where had I gotten my figures, he wanted to know. He said the results of early exit polls showed Clinton beating Dole easily, but not by a two-to-one margin.

Election Day in America. I'd totally forgotten. Here was I, the American, exulting over an Italian defeat in Bosnia because it would work to the long-term advantage of the Italian soccer player I most admired, while an Italian soccer player standing right in front of me was relieved and delighted that the American right wing had suffered such a substantial setback in the polls. He'd been watching election returns on CNN while I'd been watching the *calcio* from Bosnia.

Work on the stadium was progressing feverishly now, around the clock. Signor Rezza himself was at the site constantly. Indeed, I would have been only mildly surprised to have seen him don a hard hat. It was definite this time: the new stadium would be officially inaugurated on December 1, the day we played Genoa.

Il Centro, however, published on Wednesday Gravina's surprise announcement that the gates would be opened even sooner. The next day, in fact, as the field was used for an exhibition match that would introduce to Castel di Sangro the *attaccante* whom Gravina had just purchased for a huge sum of money from Leicester City of the English Premiership: Robert Raku Ponnick, of Nigeria.

Come un fulmine a ciel sereno – like a bolt from the blue – the news hit the town like nothing ever before. A Nigerian forward from the Premiership, England's equivalent of *Serie A?* This was by far the boldest move *La Società* had ever made, and one shuddered to think of the cost. But even Gravina must have come to recognize that *la potenza della speranza* was not enough for *Serie B;* a team needed a goal scorer as well.

Additional facts and statistics about Ponnick – such as age, goals scored, previous clubs, et cetera – were hard to come by on short notice, Giuseppe wrote in *Il Centro,* but Ponnick himself would be presented at a news conference to be televised live from Pescara on Wednesday night, and he would play in the next day's *amichevole.*

The story was featured on national newscasts by noon. Tiny Castel di Sangro, the team of *il miracolo* and *la favola,* had rocked the world of *calcio* once again. News of Ponnick's signing was sent out worldwide by ANSA, the official Italian news agency. The *Società* office was swamped by phone calls from national newspapers and magazines, all demanding privileged seating from which their representatives could witness Ponnick's debut.

Granted, Leicester City was not one of the Premiership's stronger clubs, having just been promoted this season, but a quick check of the records showed that Ponnick would be the first Premiership player to come to Italy since Lazio had bought Paul Gascoigne in 1992, and that he would be the first ever to play in *Serie B.*

At Marcella's it was standing room only to watch the press conference at 7 P.M. Sure enough, there he was, Robert Raku Ponnick, seated between Gravina and the semibilingual local journalist, Leopoldo Gasbarro.

Already wearing a Soviet Jeans jersey, Ponnick was tall, thin, and had a totally shaved head, a style that was becoming increasingly popular among players. Like Addo, Ponnick spoke flawless English, which gave me a rare advantage.

And a good thing, too, for if someone had been translating for me,

I would have been sure I'd misunderstood. Ponnick didn't wait for questions, or even for an introduction from Gravina. He just started talking, while Leopoldo translated into Italian as fast as he could. And I could hardly believe what I heard.

"I know I come late to the season," he began, "but still I will score the most goals in the league. But that is nothing. I have seen this *Serie B* and I am so far superior, it will be a joke. I will score the most goals that anyone has ever scored in *Serie B*. I don't know how many that is, but it does not matter. I will do better."

Leopoldo then asked Ponnick if he thought his presence would assure Castel di Sangro of *la salvezza*.

"You mean *stayin'* in this rinky-dink B division? Shee-it. Forget that, my man. That be negative thinkin'. We going to *Serie A!* You got my word on that. This year. No question. Now that I'm here, Castel di Sangro is a *Serie A* team. There's no one who can stop me. And if my team won't pass me the ball, I'll just go get it for myself. I can dribble, I can shoot with both feet, and I give great head."

Ponnick leered as he delivered the double entendre, which was lost on his Italian audience, but not on me. *O Dio mio!* What would happen when this man's blood was tested for drugs? Then he began what was almost a rap monologue, leaving Leopoldo in the dust, and leaving all in Marcella's demanding that I translate immediately.

"I got to warn the people of this Castel whatever-dever. If you value your women, keep 'em inside. 'Cause if they be sweet-lookin', I'm gonna fuck 'em. And I don't care who they are. I don't care whose daughter, I don't care whose wife. To score my goals, I need my pussy. And I tell you right now: I got the biggest dick in Italy. So get ready, ladies, get ready. Your magic moment and magic man have arrived. Robert Raku Ponnick will rake you over the coals and entertain you like you never been entertained before. And I mean on *and* off the pitch."

No. *Non è possibile,* I said to myself. This could not be happening. Gravina, not understanding a word of English, remained oblivious. But Leopoldo was looking as if his shirt collar had just become six sizes too small, and obviously *someone* in the studio knew enough of what Ponnick was saying to send a technician rushing forward in order to prevent him from saying more.

"Hey, what the fuck, man!" Ponnick shouted, as the technician tried to pull a lapel microphone from his jersey. Gravina looked on, dumbfounded. Then all sound was cut off. Then the screen went blank. Marcella's was in chaos, with me taking the cowardly way out, clapping my hands over my ears, claiming, *"Non capisco!"* and fleeing as fast as I could.

Chaos was rampant by the next afternoon. An hour before the exhibition match was due to start, 5,000 people were surging at the new stadium's shiny gates. Large TV trucks with satellites on top clogged the new parking lot.

As usual, I went in through the players' entrance, but when I walked down the hall to the locker room, I found my way barred by Jaconi. "Only for today, Joe," he said apologetically. "No one is permitted. We don't want Ponnick to be nervous." As he spoke, sweat poured from him in a way I'd never seen before, and for the first time since I'd met him, I could tell he was acutely uncomfortable. I didn't argue.

Back up in the *tribuna* there was a mob scene. No admission was being charged for Ponnick's debut, and at some point someone had simply thrown open the gates, letting the 5,000 people surge into an area that contained only 3,000 seats. Only the fact that these were almost all townspeople – friends and neighbors – prevented a riot from breaking out.

Scanning the mob for familiar faces, I spotted the unlikely figure of Giacomo Galli, dressed in a suit so elegant, it put Soviet Jeans' finest to shame, and wearing a monogrammed shirt with cuff links and an extremely expensive silk necktie.

This was strange enough, since he was supposed to be taking the field within fifteen minutes, but stranger yet, tears were streaming unchecked down his broad, handsome face.

When he saw me, he reached out and embraced me, sobbing into my shoulder.

"Ciao, Joe," he said. And then in English, "Good-bye." As I hugged him, I spotted Christian standing nearby and asked what was wrong.

"La Società," Christian said glumly. "To pay for Ponnick, they must sell a player and they choose Giacomo. Because Ponnick will now score the goals, Giacomo goes to *C1* tomorrow. He is no longer a member of the team."

Jaconi, apparently, had approached Galli only an hour before and told him to clean out his locker and not to dress for the match. He'd been sold to a *C1* team whose identity could not be disclosed until this evening. But it was official: Giacomo had eaten his last meal at Marcella's. Robert Raku Ponnick would be taking his place.

Galli was grief-stricken. For all his faults as a player, lack of heart had never been one. All he'd had – insufficient though it might have been – he'd given to Castel di Sangro, and he was now telling Christian he could not imagine life anyplace else.

Sticking with Giacomo in his hour of torment, Christian and I squeezed into seats alongside him for the start of the match. Who were the *dilettanti*, I wanted to know, but no one seemed to have an answer. That was odd, because *amichevoli* – matches whose results do not count in any standings – are scheduled well in advance, and the identity of the visiting amateur team is always known. But these people seemed to be strangers.

Not that it mattered. Robert Raku Ponnick was all that mattered. As the players filed onto the field, Ponnick pushed his way forward in the line and ran on ahead by himself, waving and grinning to the crowd, which responded with a standing ovation.

As the match began, the crowd had eyes for him and him alone. He had long, loping strides that led him all over the pitch, regardless of the position of the ball. Jaconi was not going to like that. Ponnick seemed oblivious to *any* sense of tactics. He also tripped two or three times and fell down in a tangle of limbs, getting up and pointing to the pitch as if it were not fit to play on. At one point, ignoring the play going on all around him, he bent down and picked up a handful of turf, holding it at arm's length and shaking his head before throwing it back down with disgust.

But then he decided to join the action. Immediately it became clear that all he wanted was the ball and that, as he'd said the night before, he really wasn't willing to wait for a pass. He ran to Michelini and kicked the ball out from under his legs, giving Michelini a hard shove in the process. The whistle blew. The referee ran over, waving a yellow card at Robert Ponnick. For having fouled *Michelini!*

"Christian," I said. "Can you get a yellow card for fouling your own man?"

"I don't know," Christan said, sounding worried.

Next to him, Galli had buried his head in his hands. This was more than he could bear to watch.

When play resumed, Martino threw the ball in to Ponnick, who immediately set off for the opponents' goal, closely shadowed, but not impeded, by two defenders. From about thirty yards out he let fly with a shot – which missed the goal by more than thirty yards.

Around us, fans began looking at one another and shaking their heads. The *dilettante* team seemed even worse than the usual run of amateurs, turning the ball over immediately to Castel di Sangro. Martino passed to Ponnick, who was standing, back to the goal, in the middle of the penalty area. The ball bounced off his knee and Ponnick fell down without having been touched by an opponent.

Another whistle, and the referee ran forward to indicate a penalty kick. It was as bad a call as any made in the Brescia match, but apparently this *arbitro* had been instructed to give Ponnick every chance to strut his stuff.

Di Vincenzo stepped up to take the penalty kick, as he usually did for Castel di Sangro, but Ponnick would not give him the ball. Instead, the Nigerian angrily waved him away, and when Danilo did not retreat, Ponnick threw the ball down and lunged at him, beginning to grapple. Half a dozen Castel di Sangro players rushed up and pulled them apart. Cei, the captain, was looking desperately to the bench for instructions. Jaconi's shouts and waves indicated that he did, in fact, want Ponnick to take the penalty.

Cursing volubly and kicking the grass, Di Vincenzo stepped back to join his teammates. The referee placed the ball on the spot. Ponnick stood over it. But then, instead of taking a step or two backward and coming forward and kicking it, the tall Nigerian bent down and moved it six inches to the left.

This was not permissible. There was one spot and one spot only from which a penalty kick could be taken. The referee ran up, shook a warning finger at Ponnick, and moved the ball back to the spot. Then, walking backward slowly, he kept his eye on the ball to see that Ponnick did not move it again. He whistled for the kick to be taken.

But Ponnick suddenly clutched his right side, doubled over as if in severe pain, wobbled backward three steps, and sank to the ground. Immediately, the trainer and team doctor sprinted onto the field, as other Castel di Sangro players, and some from the amateur team, gathered around to see what had happened. Even the opposing goalkeeper came forward, concerned that Ponnick might have suffered some sort of serious attack, or might possibly have been hit by an object thrown from the stands.

As soon as he saw the open net, Ponnick sprang to his feet, took two quick strides toward the ball and kicked it into the goal, after which he immediately began a jog around the field, grinning and waving his arms in jubilation and inviting the fans to join him, though none did, nor did his befuddled teammates.

No goal, no goal, of course it was no goal! And now the referee ruled that Ponnick had forfeited his opportunity to take the kick. Enraged, the Nigerian sprinted across the field toward the official. Only Altamura and D'Angelo together were able to restrain him.

Then he appeared to spit in Altamura's face. Altamura took a step backward, glaring. D'Angelo shoved Ponnick away. Altamura now took a step forward, pointing to his face with one hand and waving a fist at Ponnick with the other. The whole squad was now milling about as reserve players began to run onto the field, closely followed by Jaconi.

Into this mass of cursing, heaving bodies, the referee plunged, trying to restore some semblance of order. But Ponnick reached toward him and pulled from his pocket the little black book containing both the yellow and red cards. He threw the book to the ground but waved the red card in Altamura's face.

With that, Altamura exploded, and threw a right-handed punch, which landed squarely on Ponnick's jaw, knocking him to the ground. Jaconi presssed forward and tried to help the Nigerian to his feet, for which *he* was rewarded by an ugly shove. And then Ponnick pushed through the ring of players all around him and started to walk toward the sideline.

The referee, meanwhile, having retrieved his red card, caught up to Ponnick and showed it to him, making clear that an expulsion had occurred.

But Ponnick seemed beyond caring. He walked toward the Castel di Sangro sideline, and as he approached, the thousands who had gathered to cheer him began to boo. This man was an utter disgrace! He was a lunatic! Ponnick raised his middle finger high, pointing it at all sectors of the stands. The jeering fans began to throw soda and water bottles, but by then Ponnick had disappeared into the dressing room.

Pale and shaking, Galli pushed past Christian and me and ran for the nearest exit. But at the same moment the entire *dilettante* squad proceeded to the middle of the field, holding hands. They spread into a single line and began to applaud, facing our crowd. And then, loping toward them, was the unmistakable figure of Robert Ponnick. He shook hands with each of them, then turned to wave to the crowd. The public address announcer asked for a warm greeting for the Guastafeste Professional Acting Troupe and their star performer, Robert Raku Ponnick!

The whole game had been a charade. And the climax, as it were, occurred when the fake referee also ran onto the field, pulled down his shorts, and mooned the shocked and baffled residents of Castel di Sangro.

It took a few hours to sort things out, but by that night at Marcella's I finally understood what had happened. All the players except Galli had been told upon entering the locker room that Ponnick was only an actor and that Gravina had arranged the whole farce in order that he might be featured in a three- or four-minute segment on one of the weekly *calcio* programs that were broadcast all over Italy. ("A man of imagination who is not afraid to dream!" was the title he himself had suggested for the segment.)

The players were indignant and in some cases enraged, but Jaconi made it clear that they had no choice but to go along. Gabriele considered this another step forward in his bid for national attention, and as employees of *La Società,* they had no choice but to assist.

Every aspect of the Ponnick story had been fraudulent. There was not, nor had there ever been, a player named Ponnick at Leicester City, much less one purchased by Castel di Sangro. Indeed, Ponnick wasn't even Nigerian, but an actor born and raised in London. Yes, it was too bad that Galli had had to be played for a fool, but it had been only temporary and, in any event, all for the cause. Or so Gabriele maintained.

But by the next morning the whole thing blew up in his face. The press, which will so often make a fool of itself, does not react well when made a fool of by others. In particular, the Italian national news agency ANSA was not amused at having been duped.

From all quarters reaction poured in, and it was unanimous: Gravina had not only made himself seem an idiot but had disgraced

La Società and the entire sport of *calcio,* which in Italy was not something ever to be treated as a joke.

Gravina, said *La Gazzetta dello Sport* (in an article not written by Giuseppe), had shown himself incompetent to direct *Società* affairs by treating it as his personal "plaything." Other papers added that he had insulted his own players and fans, who now justifiably were responding with "venomous" words; that he had squandered much-needed money on an *"errore grossolano"* – a boorish, vulgar mistake – had committed a "huge blunder," had thrown *un autentico boomerang,* and had proven himself guilty of *"pessimo gusto"* – execrable taste.

Seeing the public reaction, Gravina tried at first to deny any involvement or even awareness. *"Non sapevo nulla,"* he said. I didn't know anything. Then he ordered Giuseppe to put out a press release saying that he, Giuseppe, the lowly PR man, had been solely responsible for the entire disgrace; that he, Giuseppe, deeply regretted any inconvenience or offense his words or actions might have caused; and that he, Giuseppe, wanted to apologize especially to the Castel di Sangro president, Signor Gravina, and to all the fans and players of Castel di Sangro.

Of course, no one believed that story for a minute, and by the end of the week Gravina was forced to admit that the fiasco had been his doing from the start.

He continued to insist, however – and quite angrily – that his had been a wonderfully clever idea that press and townspeople, and even his own players, had just not been sophisticated enough to appreciate.

I suppose I shouldn't have taken it so personally, but *calcio* does tend to drive one to extremes. The more I stewed over it all day Friday and Friday night, as cold November winds began to howl down from the mountains, the more disgusted I grew at the whole Ponnick sham.

Beyond the flagrant racism (a "blackface" joke to make people forget the reality of Joseph Addo), Gravina had, in essence, defecated all over the *miracolo* at the same time that he tried to use it to promote himself as a man worthy of serious national attention.

I arose early on Saturday and clipped from the previous day's *Il Centro* a large photograph of Robert Raku Ponnick, clad in Soviet

Jeans jersey, striding insolently off the grass of the new stadium and giving the middle finger held high to three-quarters of the adult population of Castel di Sangro.

Using the copy function of my fax machine and the printer connected to my computer, I managed to create a series of not terribly artistic but nonetheless unambiguous 8 × 11 posters that reproduced the Ponnick "finger" photo on the top and proclaimed beneath it, in large black letters, BENVENUTO A CASTEL DI SANGRO. Welcome to Castel di Sangro.

I stuffed half a dozen in envelopes and addressed them variously to the town mayor (a man long on ceremony but seemingly terrified of doing anything that might irk either Gravina or, worse, Signor Rezza), to both the provincial and regional tourist offices, and to a few national newspapers and magazines.

To each I appended a form letter that said, in Italian:

> I am the American who is writing the story of *la favola del calcio* of Castel di Sangro. However – although I retain the greatest respect, admiration, and affection for the players – the ownership and management of this team has come to disgust me. This photograph is one example of why. It seems that the president, Signor Gabriele Gravina, will do anything to obtain publicity for himself, no matter how insulting it is to his players or to the loyal supporters from this wonderful town, which already I have come to love. Possibly, this is none of my business, but such things as this make me so angry that I must tell people now, and not only later in my book. Thank you for considering the views of one visitor who loves both *il calcio* and *l'Italia* very much.

At first light I left my apartment and, in near-freezing rain that had blown in overnight, walked to the post office to place my missives in a receptacle that promised quick dispersal.

Then I walked to the center of town and taped one of the posters to the door to the offices of *La Società*. Returning to my apartment, I taped one to my own door and one to Jaconi's. Still later, at the brief morning training session, I handed out a dozen or so to various players.

Reaction was not long in coming. As I walked into Marcella's at noon, she told me in a voice heavy with worry to call *La Società* immediately. When I did, I was informed by an assistant to Gravina that I would not be permitted to fly south with the team that evening for the next day's match in Reggio Calabria. Indeed, I would never be permitted to travel with them again.

"Bello!" I said, having learned that this could also be taken ironically as the equivalent of "fine!" But I made it clear that I would proceed to Reggio Calabria on my own.

"Io faccio l'autostop!" I shouted into the phone. I would *hitchhike* to Reggio Calabria and back. And, if necessary, to every other away match of the season.

This was, of course, ridiculous, especially in regard to Reggio Calabria, a city located on the very tip of the toe of the boot that was Italy, so distant that a portion of Sicily actually lay to its north. So distant, in fact, that *La Società* was even springing for plane fare from Rome rather than making the players ride the bus. But I didn't care. The honor of my *ragazzi* seemed at stake. And no mean thing is the fury of a *tifoso* who feels that his team has been wronged (see "Celano, 1978, *il linciaggio*").

In any event, only minutes after I'd returned to my apartment, Marcella called. She said that both Gravina and Maria Teresa had arrived, eager to speak to me. I walked back to the pizzeria. Gravina got right to the point: his assistant had overreacted and had misspoken. I would be as welcome to travel with the team that afternoon as I'd always been, and this would remain the case for the rest of the season.

I thanked him, of course, and in a manner that I hoped appeared gracious. But even as I did so, I viewed his act as no more than pragmatic. The fact was, as we moved toward the year's darkest days, it was only my presence in Castel di Sangro that continued to bring Gravina and the team the favorable publicity he craved.

I state this simply as fact. Far from having been proud of it, I was embarrassed. I was not striving for publicity, merely trying to be cooperative. Two or three times a week, as my Italian began to improve, a representative of *La Società* would inform me that a new interview had been arranged.

Then, in person or by telephone, with newspapers, television stations, and magazines, I praised the town and its warm and caring people; the team members, who were not only committed athletes but gentlemen of the highest order; Jaconi, who was the best neighbor a man could hope for and – as his past record demonstrated undoubtedly – a fine manager, too; and even Gravina, whose vision and whose faith in the improbable had created the whole rich, rewarding stew.

I was scrupulous about saying only the most benign things. One could, I suppose, view this as hypocrisy on my part, but I felt that my more complex, not to say negative, reactions were works in progress and that they were strictly my business until the time came for me to write my book. It was enough for the moment to tell the people what they wanted to hear: that I'd come to the Abruzzo to write a beautiful story about wonderful, humble people who had dared to dream and who'd then seen their dream become reality.

This was made to order for mass media consumption, and I was photographed and interviewed in almost every locale Castel di Sangro had to offer: sitting on a park bench; walking through the Thursday morning marketplace, engaging in badinage with the merchants; chitchatting and cavorting with the players on the training field; and embracing Marcella, whose fairy-godmother spirit increasingly struck me as the most genuine element in the whole, crazy business.

Thus, Gravina continued to use me, even as he grew to despise me. And I played along willingly, even cheerfully, sharing the full contents of my mixed bag of true feelings only with the players, toward one and all of whom I felt myself drawing closer as the cold and blustery November winds roared down from the mountains and stretched the very fabric of our days.

20

In regard to Reggio Calabria, I was not sure Gravina had done me a favor.

Foreigners and even northern Italians considered the Abruzzo unappealing, but the Italian government itself, in a recently completed "quality of life" survey that involved more than 125 cities, had ranked Reggio Calabria dead last. It was impoverished, still heavily under Mafia domination, and as ugly as vice and corruption could make it.

Worse, on the flight down from Rome, *Società* underlings were made to walk the aisle of the filled-to-capacity plane, handing out copies of a new comic book that Gravina had had produced. The title was *Squadra Speciale: Operazione Simpatia – un'avventura di Serie B.*

The cover featured an illustration of Gravina in James Bond–Special Agent 007 mode. Superimposed on him (but not blocking any portion of his face) was a seductively posed, large-bosomed, and scantily clad blonde, who looked to me very much like Vanessa Diaz, the wife of Gigi Prete. If the object of the operation was to gain *simpatia,* or affection, for the Castel di Sangro squad, the comic book seemed a very strange – even bizarre – way to go about it. And coming on the heels of the Raku Ponnick fiasco, it appeared almost ludicrously tasteless.

Yet Gravina was apparently quite taken with the image of himself as a swashbuckling adventurer, who even if he failed to obtain a cabinet position might someday aspire to the stature of Dylan Dog or Diabolik.

By chance, I was seated next to a pleasant young man from Ravenna, whose name was Ottavio Piretti and who was flying to Calabria, he told me, because the next day he would be refereeing a professional soccer match between the teams of Reggio Calabria and Castel di Sangro.

"E quale ti piace di più?" I asked. And which do you prefer?

There I was, on the very brink of pulling off a massive *Squadra Speciale* intelligence coup all my own, when just at that moment there arrived at our row the *Società* employee who was passing out the comic books on our side of the plane.

Calling me by name, he said, "Well, I don't suppose you need another one," even as he pressed a copy into the hands of Signor Piretti.

Needless to say, that brought an abrupt halt to my conversation with the *arbitro,* who was scrupulous about following Federation instructions that referees are not to converse with interested parties from either side once the announcement of their assignment to a given match has been made. I noted, however, that after only the briefest of glances, Signor Piretti discarded the comic book and did not take it with him when he left.

The next day, at the ancient, decrepit, and crumbling stadium, thousands more of the comic books were handed out to Reggina supporters and instantly discarded, some after being torn in half, others after being spat upon. It did not seem to me that whoever was advising Gravina during this particular portion of his personal public relations campaign was playing at the top of his form.

As usual on Sunday, however, I had more immediate concerns. As dark clouds gathered, I took my seat in the *tribuna*. Rain began to fall before the match, and as it did, the temperature dropped. Loud and badly outdated rock music blared from cheap speakers, and the sound echoed off row upon row of empty concrete benches in the grandstand. (Even a half-full 12,000-seat stadium can make for a lot of bare concrete.)

And then came the match: that ninety-minute pearl at the heart of the oyster. As the teams took the field, I was dismayed beyond words to see that against an opponent that was winless in ten matches, and with his own squad lacking not only two starting defenders but the increasingly able Cristiano in midfield, and with De Juliis, however esteemed, making his first-ever *Serie B* start in goal – circumstances that bellowed for at least the pretense of an offensive formation (if not to score, then at least to keep the ball in the Reggina end for a respectable portion of the match) – Jaconi *still* had plunged headlong into his 4-5-1 bunker, which on this occasion required using what was indubitably the slowest central midfield trio in all of *Serie B* – Alberti, Michelini, and Di Fabio – the grandfathers of the Three Musketeers.

Granted, this ensured that the recently traumatized Galli would have a full ninety minutes to regain his composure in solitude, spared the anxiety of any ball coming his way, but it also meant that we would not score and that any goal against us might as well have been ten.

La favola. Il miracolo. La potenza della speranza. Mamma mia, what a load of crap. Add the eleven players he fielded to Jaconi himself, and you had probably the dozen dullest drudges in all of professional *calcio*. And it was to this bunch that I'd tied my fate. Now, of course, it was too late to do anything else. I was as committed to the goal of *la salvezza* as any of them. But there was nothing I could do to help. Instead, I could only suffer.

For the first fifteen minutes there was little to indicate that the match was actually under way. The two arteriosclerotic and overcrowded midfields took turns giving the ball away and kicking it out of bounds. At twenty minutes, I wrote in my notebook, *Reggina a terrible team!* Worst of year! *But chance of a CdS goal today likely as announcement of life on Mars.*

And you know, when that's really what you feel, deep down inside, way down there where only the notebook knows – that the chance of your team scoring in a match in which seventy minutes remain is no more likely than the discovery of life on Mars – it is, and I mean this sincerely, very, very painful and discouraging.

At the thirty-five-minute mark I noted, *CdS actually worse since start of season.* And they were: Where once we had tried for shots on goal, now we seemed to consider it a job well done if we kicked the ball across the midfield line. Only Bonomi was even running. But in his case this did not work to our advantage.

"The trouble with Claudio," someone once told me, "he's the sweetest guy in the world, but with Claudio you don't find too much above the braces." With each passing week, despite his natural talent, he was coming to seem more and more like a rat in a maze. How long will the same rat run up the same blind alley before he realizes it will not get him to the cheese? Answer: How many matches are there in a season?

And so, in summary, I wrote: *WORST HALF I'VE EVER SEEN!* . . . *Must be the most wretched football on earth! WORSE THAN AMERICA!*

Then came the second half. Jaconi, of course, made no changes. The only change, in fact, had been in the weather, which was improving. The rain stopped, a pale November sun began to shine, and a light breeze picked up from the south.

This apparently felt so soothing on the skin of Davide Cei that from almost the moment play resumed, he turned his face to it, closed his eyes, and just let himself feel one with nature . . . *while a goddamned Reggina attacker drove straight past him before he could even manage to shift his weight from one leg to the other!* A shot. A save by De Juliis? Not a prayer. Reggina 1, Castel di Sangro 0. Which meant, of course, game, set, and match to Reggina. Because for us 1–0 was no different from 10–0. The 0 would always be 0. Jaconi's "tactics" would see to that.

At the airport, poor Tonino, who'd received a yellow card in the second half, suddenly realized that this meant he would not be able to play in our first match in the new stadium against Genoa the following week. He started to cry, because his mother would be coming and she had so much wanted to see him play.

He continued to cry, too, until Signor Piretti, the *arbitro* (who was about to experience the joy of flying back to Rome with us and receiving yet a second comic book), came over and talked to him and said that if he'd realized it would mean suspension for the historic inaugural match, he probably would not have given the yellow card. He then offered to buy Tonino a drink, proving that all *arbitri* were not filthy scum like Rossi of Ciampino.

On the flight I sat next to Luca Albieri. The new young reserve had replaced Martino for the last twenty minutes and, as he had against Brescia, had played with a flair and originality that made me wish he'd been in the match from the start.

I noticed that he had not fastened his seat belt. As we began to taxi toward takeoff, I pointed this out. But Albieri only shook his head in warning fashion, got a very serious expression on his face, and explained to me in great detail how he never fastened his seat belt on an airplane because to do so would be bad luck.

Later he told me that what really irritated him on airplanes was hearing the announcement that cell phones should not be used during takeoff and landing because they interfered with the plane's navigational system. How could a little thing like a telephone – which wasn't even connected to anything – cause a problem for a big thing like an airplane? It was all bullshit, he said. Just more of the stuff the government told the people to keep them like slaves. And here, on this flight, he would prove it.

I had thought he was kidding, but I should have known better. About sixty seconds above the airfield at Fiumicino, Albieri pulled his cell phone from his pocket and dialed a number. The plane swung sharply to the left just before hitting the ground, then bounced hard, then bounced again, before finally settling on the ground.

Albieri covered his mouth with one hand, as if to say "oops!" But he was too late getting his cell phone back into his pocket. A steward who'd taken a seat across the aisle from us for landing jumped up as soon as the plane was safely on the ground and began shouting, *"Sei in arresto!"* – you're under arrest! – and tried to lunge across me to get to Albieri.

I unstrapped my seat belt, pushed my way past the steward, and hurried to the front of the plane to get Jaconi. "Trouble," I told him. "Luca Albieri. You go. *Subito!*"

Jaconi succeeded in keeping the police out of it and in getting Albieri off the plane unshackled, but another little bit of my sanity snapped as we were waiting for our luggage and I said to Jaconi, "Tell me again? *Il talento non è importante? Solo il carattere e la mentalità? Sì, sì, come Albieri. Bravo!*"

He just looked at me. He was too tired and discouraged to even tell me to go to hell. Finally he shook his head, raised his eyes skyward, and, as the luggage carousel began to move, said, *"Aiuto! Per fa-*

vore, mi aiuto! Subito!" And he clasped his hands together as if in prayer, as indeed he had been as he'd cried out, Help! Please help me! Now!

But I suppose things could have been worse. As Kierkegaard once said (this was, apparently, not long after he'd given up the winning goal to lowly Brondby during his brief tenure as goalkeeper for FC Kobenhavn), "The nature of despair is precisely not to know one is despairing."

Jaconi and I, at least, knew.

With still only ten points, we had dropped *into* the dreaded relegation zone. And our unchanging total of five goals – now after *eleven* matches had been played – was by far the worst in *Serie B*. In the future, instead of sending out Pistella and Galli as our attackers, Jaconi might just as well walk onto the field with a shovel and simply dig two holes in the ground.

And so on the long bus ride back into the now frigid mountains, I could not avoid contemplating the irony of my position. In my attempt to immerse myself even more deeply in the sublime, the artistic, the noble and grand that I'd discovered in the world of *calcio,* I'd committed myself not to a year at the San Siro, watching Baggio dance and dart and dazzle, but instead to a season in *Serie B,* a realm where, as described by the soccer historian Peter Alegi, "the most cynical, gruelling, stressful, tasteless, destructive, gloomy, dull, calculating, close-minded, foul and tragicomic interpretations of football reign supreme."

And he had written that without ever having seen Galli or Pistella.

With the new week, however, optimism took hold once again.

On Tuesday, in an unprecedented and thoroughly unexpected act of diplomacy, Pope John Paul personally received Fidel Castro at the Vatican. Luca D'Angelo could scarcely restrain his jubilation.

"Fidel . . . Fidel . . . ," he kept saying. *"Joe, viviamo in un mondo in cui tutto è possibile."* We live in a world in which everything is possible. *"Forza Castro! Forza il Comunismo! Io dedicherò la mia stagione alla gente coraggiosa di Cuba!"* I will dedicate my season to the brave people of Cuba!

. . .

Also on Tuesday, Gravina finally announced that the new stadium would be officially inaugurated the following Sunday, December 1.

True, December was not September, and the months of delay had taken a toll on everyone, but finally – just like the real teams – we would have our own stadium in which to play our home matches.

Moreover, the inauguration promised to be the greatest event ever to occur in Castel di Sangro. Hundreds of dignitaries from all over the country, trailed by journalists, would flock to the Abruzzo for the occasion. Above all, it promised to erase the sour taste that had permeated so many of these early days and to be a moment of supreme personal triumph for Gravina.

What a shock, then, to wake up two days later and learn that Gravina had resigned.

21

When I went out to get the papers Thursday morning, I found the area surrounding the news kiosk swarming with chattering townspeople in a way I'd never seen before.

Across the street the number of old men taking the morning sun as they leaned against the facade of the Bank of Napoli building in which the offices of *La Società* were housed seemed to have tripled within twenty-four hours, and their normal desultory conversations had been replaced by impassioned utterances and energetic gesticulations.

Edging my way through the crowd, I caught the eye of Pierluigi, the news vendor, a man normally so laconic that I often wondered whether he sedated himself before entering his cramped and dusty quarters for the day.

Not this morning, however. As he gathered together the five papers it was my custom to purchase each morning, he said to me in a voice fraught with excitement, *"Una vera bomba, no?"* A real shocker!

"Sì, sì," I agreed for the sake of convenience, though I had no idea what he was talking about.

It did not take long to find out. A brief glance at the front page of *Il Centro* explained the extraordinary animation all around me: Gravina had resigned as president of *La Società!*

Impossibile! Incredibile! Inconcepibile! I could not have been more stunned if the Pope had announced his conversion to Buddhism. I immediately suspected another hoax. Its purpose was not clear to me, other than to gain Gravina more publicity in the days leading up to the stadium's long-belated opening, but obviously he had not simply decided to "resign."

The official version, as presented by Giuseppe in *Il Centro,* placed an even greater strain on credulity than did the announcement itself. This had been a long-planned and carefully timed transition, Giuseppe wrote, and the announcement of it only three days before the Grand Inauguration was simply one more example of *il-*about-to-be-ex-*presidente*'s unerring ability to choose *il momento giusto* (the right moment) for a bold and dramatic act.

The resignation was "the logical culmination of the progress I've achieved over the past several years," Gravina was quoted as saying. Because he would soon be seeking a post high within the power structure of the National Federation, he said, he felt he should resign at the earliest opportune moment in order to avoid even the appearance of a conflict of interest. It was, he said, the only "morally correct" thing to do.

He stressed that with the stadium completed, his decade's work with Castel di Sangro Calcio was essentially done. While he would remain involved in team business with the new title of *il patron,* his successor as president would be one Luciano Russi, rector, or president, of the University of Teramo, where Gravina occasionally taught a course titled Fiscally Sound Management of a Professional *Calcio* Enterprise.

For the first time, Gravina proclaimed in print, the worlds of academe and football would be united, something that had been a goal of his for many years. The "high culture" of the academy, through its merger with the "popular culture" of the football world, would produce an entirely new, muscular, yet refined aesthetic: that of *alto calcio,* or "noble" or "lofty" football, which in turn could serve to unite Italy as nothing had done since the armies of Garibaldi.

As an example, he said, a string quartet already had been engaged to perform Vivaldi's *Four Seasons* upon the conclusion of the match against Genoa.

Open snickering mixed with lurid speculation as to the nature of *la vera storia,* the true story, all day Thursday and Thursday night. Then, in Friday morning's *Il Tempo,* Luigi Liberatore, the best and most independent journalist to cover the workings of *La Società,* stated baldly that Gravina had been removed against his will by Signor Rezza. The word *dimissioni,* and its close cousin, *dimesso,* both of which Liberatore used in his story, were unambiguous in meaning.

The reasons, Liberatore wrote, were abundant. There was, to start with, the failure of the team on the field and the failure of Jaconi on the bench. *"Gira, gira, Osvaldo Jaconi"* – he spins and spins, turns and turns – "but in the end to trust once again only the *'vecchi giocatori,'* " the old players, whose limitations had been so pitilessly exposed once more against Reggina.

Gravina's misplaced faith in Jaconi was one factor. Another had been his inability to place a proper valuation on players purchased from other teams (i.e., Pistella) and, in the aftermath of that disastrous acquisition, his sudden attack of cold feet: or, as Liberatore put it, his *"poca voglia di spendere dall'altra"* – his small wish (i.e., refusal) to spend any more on other new players. This was, Liberatore wrote, *"un cocktail micidiale"* – a deadly mixture – as *la classifica* made all too clear week after week. "While common sense requires a return to the marketplace," he wrote, "even to talk about this subject at *La Società* remains *tabù.*"

Liberatore saw Rector Russi as someone brought in solely for cosmetic purposes. And not even truly brought in, for Russi quickly made clear that he had a university to run and would continue to live in Teramo, almost two hours to the north. Thus, he would not even be a convincing figurehead.

But even all of that constituted only the outer layer of the onion. And in Italy (and not only in the world of *calcio*) the truth, or even *a* truth – just as with the true flavor of an onion – was not typically encountered until at least a few layers had been removed.

In Italy, and especially in the world of *calcio,* a state of crisis is considered the norm. So much so that the word *crisi,* as applied to some player or team, can be found almost every day in *La Gazzetta* or in one of the other sporting papers. In a country in which fifty-six governments have fallen since the end of World War II, the people become accustomed to *crisi,* and like *voce* (rumor), only one in a hundred ever amounts to anything in the end. Even 90 percent of impending or supposed events reported as *quasi fatti,* "almost facts" (a splendid phrase, by the equivalent of which the English language would be greatly enriched), fail to materialize. And so it is only when something is deemed *un fatto* – a fact – that one *begins* to think it *might* be true, and even then it is best to form a judgment slowly, bearing in mind that the adjectival form of the word – *fattibile* – is translated merely as "feasible" or "possible."

Some players and even townspeople cited as the real reason for Gravina's ouster his continuing and – despite Signor Rezza's repeated warnings – increasingly indiscreet infidelity to his wife.

For the first time, I was told about a particularly sordid episode that had occurred in October and that, because it involved one of Gravina's better-known mistresses, no doubt would have been brought promptly to Signor Rezza's attention.

It seemed that several team members – not all of them unmarried – had traveled to a not terribly distant village for the purpose of engaging in sex with a young, married German woman.

The woman's availability for such a form of recreation arose from the fact that her husband was serving an extended prison sentence for cocaine smuggling.

Gravina had been seeing her frequently, and when he learned of her "infidelity," and that it had involved five members of his own team, he apparently had flown into a rage and plunged into a funk simultaneously, not a posture from which he could govern the business of *La Società* effectively. One result had been Robert Raku Ponnick; another had been the comic book, for the cost of printing which he might have acquired an *attaccante* capable of scoring twenty goals.

Besides – at least in the somewhat conventional mind of Signor Rezza – certain lines were not to be crossed. By having had sex with the same woman as at least five of his players – and a woman with known drug connections at that – Gravina had crossed them: not only by adding a new layer of humiliation to the many already borne by Maria Teresa and their two sons but by endangering the good name of *La Società* as well.

Then there was the entirely separate problem of the playing surface. No matter how fine it might look from the *tribuna* where the *pezzi grossi,* or grand pooh-bahs, would sit, the new field was essentially a bottomless pit, not fit to play on and a danger to any player who might try.

It seemed that Gravina – concerned, as always, with creating *una bella figura,* or good impression – had made a disastrous mistake. He wanted for his new field the greenest grass not only in *Serie B* but in all of *calcio*. Despite the harsh climate of Castel di Sangro, he had told his groundskeepers that he wanted grass as green as the grass of a cemetery. Such grass would make a fine impression on all the dignitaries who would attend the inaugural ceremonies and would surely impress the powerful men who ruled *La Federazione*.

From one consultant he learned of a chemical fertilizer that – if spread just under the top layer of soil – would enable the grass above it to stay bright green in any weather. Immediately, he ordered that this fertilizer be applied. Then, as usual, he quickly turned his attention to other matters. Unfortunately, in his haste, he'd failed to ask a vital question: Just how did this fertilizer work?

Had he asked, he would have been told that its distinguishing characteristic was that when it came into contact with any sort of moisture – such as rainwater that would leach through the topsoil above – it developed a consistency that was almost plasticlike in its impermeability. In other words, no water could penetrate beneath the barrier that this chemical would create only several inches below the surface of the field. The grass above it indeed would be green, bathed as it was in a constant pool of moisture, but the soil beneath that grass would, with the first rain, turn to the consistency of pudding because any water that fell on it simply would have no place to go.

It was only after all work on the pitch had been completed, and after several days of rain had ensued, that Gravina finally recognized the awful truth: The field was not and might not ever be fit to play on. This was no *campo* but instead a bright green swamp, or *pantano,* and the whole thing would have to be torn up in order for a new surface and subsurface to be laid.

Invitations, however, had already been mailed for the December 1 opening. Gravina's image could not survive further delay. But Signor Rezza was displeased, to say the least. The first estimate he received was that it would take up to three months and would cost at least $500,000 to undo the damage Gravina had done. Thus, one more reason for the sudden resignation. Such an incompetent, Signor Rezza was said to feel, could not be permitted to hold the title of *il presidente* on the day of the Grand Inauguration.

. . .

La Società, of course, did not want the public to be aware of this problem, and so the public was not. The players, however, knew all about it, and – unlike the October orgy – wanted to be sure that I did, too.

As soon as I arrived for Thursday afternoon training, Michelini grabbed me by the arm and asked me to walk the pitch with him. It did look beautiful. In fact, I had to admit, despite my growing skepticism about the ability of *La Società* to accomplish the tasks required of it by promotion to *Serie B,* the field, up close, looked as lovely as any I'd seen anywhere, and far better than any I'd seen so far this season.

The grass was a fresh, bright green, neatly trimmed, and because it had not yet had to withstand the scraping and tearing and digging of a real match (only of the Ponnick farce), resembled a fairway, if not a putting green, of a world-class golf course.

As Michelini and I set forth across it, however, he pointed out area after area where the footing beneath that picture-perfect grass was substandard at best and, in many spots, positively treacherous. Even without there having been a prolonged spell of bad weather recently, the base was cuppy and muddy, soil clinging to our shoes like wet clay, and water oozing from just below surface level at every step.

"Una spugna per l'acqua," Michelini said. A sponge for water. *"Non è buono. Non è buono. Questo campo è molto pericoloso per i calciatori."* This field is not good, and it is very dangerous for the players.

It was apparent – especially after I'd taken a step that plunged my right foot more than six inches into the muck, resulting in the temporary loss of a shoe – that a serious problem existed.

Michelini stood still and shook his head. *"Disastro,"* he said. *"Disastro."* He then pointed at the sky to the west and said, *"Sta per arrivare il maltempo."* Bad weather was coming, to make it worse.

I nodded. *"Sì."*

But this apparently had not been reaction enough. For again, he grabbed me by the arm. *"Joe,"* he said. *"Un diluvio!"* I shook my head. This was not a word I knew. *"Per sabato e domenica,"* he said, *"ci sarà un grosso acquazzone! E un vento forte! Una tempesta! Una burrasca! E molto freddo. Ci sarà una nevicata! E molto ghiaccio!"*

I'd never seen Michelini so agitated. And it had been some time since I'd been at such a loss as to what someone was trying to tell me. Obviously, it had to do with the weather. And obviously it wasn't good. That something about *grosso acqua* sounded like, maybe, a lot of rain was coming. But his intensity – and vocabulary – seemed to indicate even more.

Blessedly, at that moment, young Pippo Biondi limped past. A knee injury would keep the teenager from playing on Sunday, even in the unlikely event that Jaconi would have wanted to use him, but he was nonetheless interested in testing the condition of the field for himself.

His usual wry smile was not in evidence, and I could see why. If you were a player, each competitive step on such a field literally threatened to be your last. It was one thing to walk slowly and sink in, but to be running as fast as possible and suddenly hit a spot where one foot plunged six inches into the muck while the rest of your body kept going – well, that would be the end of the ligaments in *that* knee. See you next year. Maybe. Or, if the knee injury was bad enough, maybe not.

I called Pippo over and then asked Michelini to repeat his warnings. The short blond midfielder did so, using even more gestures than he had with me. Biondi nodded. "Big storm coming," he said to me. "Big wind. *Burrasca* – like 'urricane, no? And very cold. The rain, he exchange into snow. The water get freeze – make *il ghiaccio* – the ice. Very bad. Paolo say, *'Sarebbe la fine per il campo.'* It puts the field to an end. *Non sarebbe possibile giocare qui.* Is per'aps not possible to play 'ere."

Pippo, Michelini, and I looked up at the sky together. And an ominous sky it was, darkening fast as the wind blew harder and grew colder.

"We wait to see, no?" Pippo said. "Still three day."

On Friday, however, the wind began to blow harder and, as if responding to Michelini's cue, the coldest rain of the season began to fall. I retreated to my apartment immediately after a very subdued dinner at Marcella's, feeling uncharacteristically lonely.

I was also colder than I'd ever been at the Coradetti. The morning and evening breaths of heat were arriving as usual, but on this night the north wind made it seem as if the radiators had not even grown warm. For not the first time, I glanced forlornly at the mini-fireplace in my living room. It was functional, Vito had assured me, but it would not accept pieces of wood more than twelve inches long, nor would its poor draft permit the creation of a blaze from much more than kindling, neither of which – through lack of foresight – I'd acquired.

Suddenly my doorbell rang. And there stood Antonello Altamura, bearing three large sacks of firewood, the logs cut into the special small size that would fit into my fireplace. I'd never mentioned either to him or to Sabrina that my corner apartment, with floor-to-ceiling windows, tended to be intolerable when cold winds blew.

But he must have known, and on his own he'd done something to reduce my level of discomfort. I said, No, Antonello, you can't do this, but he said, Yes, yes, I must, and besides, I have more sacks upstairs, plus an extra gas heater, and I said, But, Antonello, still, it is not right, here, at least let me pay you –

Thump-thump-thump!!! The three sacks of wood dropped to my floor. Altamura looked genuinely angry. I'd said the wrong word: pay. "Joe!" he commanded. "Sit down! Pleeess!"

So I sat on the couch and started to laugh, still holding in my hand the first lira note I'd grabbed from my table, which happened to be 10,000 lire, the equivalent of about a five-dollar bill.

He took the note from me, took a matchbook from his pocket, struck the match, and set fire to the L 10,000. *"Finito,"* he said. *"Tu hai pagato. Capito, Joe?"*

"Sì, Anton'. Capito. E grazie." Yes, I understand. I have paid. And thank you.

"Niente," he said. It's nothing. Then he pointed upstairs. He wanted me to come up to his apartment. It was warm, he said. We could have a drink.

"No, Antonello, I cannot intrude on Sabrina with no notice."

It would not be an intrusion, he said, for neither Sabrina nor Niccolò was there. She had left for her family home in Fano, three hours to the north, in the Marche region, bringing Niccolò with her. As he said this, the broad grin quickly vanished from his face.

She had gone home, he said, because she was *abbattuta,* meaning despondent or depressed. Facing the onset of her fifth consecutive winter in Castel di Sangro, and with the team slumping badly and Jaconi growing ever more abusive to all around him, I could see why.

But no, it was even worse than that. As soon as we entered his apartment, he said he had just called Sabrina's parents and had been told that she'd been placed in a hospital after bursting into an uncontrollable crying fit upon her arrival. Now she would undergo tests and treatment for *"troppo stress, troppo ansia. Un disturbo da stress, colpa dell'ansia. Capito, Joe?"* Understood, Joe?

Yes, I did understand: stress, anxiety, and what sounded like possible depression. Sabrina had always been high-strung and edgy, and now apparently – at least temporarily – she'd tumbled over the edge. He said he did not know when she would be back. Certainly not before Christmas. But for the next two weekends, since he was suspended anyway – as a result of his *cartellino rosso* – he'd be going home to see her.

And then this roughest and least polished of all the Castel di Sangro defenders – a man quick and proud to show off the bulldog tattooed on his bicep – said with considerable embarrassment that the real reason he'd invited me up (though not the reason he'd brought me the firewood, he stressed) was to ask if I would watch with him the videotape that had been made on the day he and Sabrina had been married.

He wanted to watch it, he said, to remind himself of how beautiful she was. If I would do him the honor of watching with him.

And so we watched the videotape. It ran for an hour and a half. It would have been only an hour, actually, if he had run it straight through. But no. Every time a new second cousin came on the scene, Antonello paused it in order to explain to me the precise relationship between the newcomer and all those who'd already passed before the camera.

"Capito, Joe?"

"Sì, sì, capito, capito: è suo cugino, sì, e anche il suocero della sorellastra della figlioccia del suo fratello maggiore." Yes, yes, I understand, he's the cousin, yes, and also the father-in-law of the stepsister of the godchild of his older brother."

"Capito, Joe?"

"Assolutamente, Antonello. Assolutamente."

Of course, when Sabrina herself appeared – and, even five months pregnant, she was extraordinarily beautiful – we went to slow motion, instant replay, freeze-frame, every trick in Antonello's VCR book, of which there were many. And as he watched her, he cried.

"Solo quattro anni fa," he said. *"E adesso . . ."* This was only four years ago. And now . . .

I tried to console him. I said I was sure she'd be fine, although I still had only a vague idea of the severity of her illness. Still, I tried to promote the idea of antidepressant medication, which apparently was not widely prescribed in Italy. He promised he would call her doctor in the morning. But for now, for now, let us just look at her, Joe, look at how beautiful she is.

"Certo, Antonello. Certo." Certainly, she is beautiful.

"E adesso," he said, *"che macello!"* And now, what a mess!

Weeping, he hugged me as the videotape ended. I tried to mutter reassurances. Then I went back downstairs to my bitingly cold apartment, more conscious than ever that the ninety minutes of *calcio* played each Sunday were having less and less to do with my experience of Castel di Sangro.

I must have slept, because I was conscious of waking up. I recognized also that my ears, nose, and toes seemed on the verge of frostbite. The warmth of the tiny living room fireplace did not carry to the bedroom. The bitter wind did. And it was now making a noise, gusting through the louvers of my shutters, that I imagined a dozen cats might make if strangled simultaneously.

I pulled open the shutter and for just a very few seconds, in that hallucinatory state that sometimes separates sleep from full wakefulness, I believed myself to be back on the ship on which I'd once traveled from the southernmost tip of Argentina to the Antarctic coast. All the world around me was in whiteout. I could not see a foot outside the window, so fierce and dense was the sleet that shot past my window.

But I could hear. I heard the sounds of a fierce winter storm. I could also feel the freezing wind blowing through uninsulated walls. Shivering so hard that my eyeglasses fell off, I dressed as quickly as possible, falling back on my Arctic and Antarctic experiences, which had taught me the layering technique: as many as possible without restricting movement; first cotton, then wool, then a windproof material, then more cotton, more wool, a solid outergarment of down, with a waterproof layer over that.

Thirty pounds heavier, I wobbled out my door and down the stairs. As I opened the front door, the gale and sleet hit me full force, blowing me back against the rear wall of the apartment house lobby. I crouched and scuttled sideways, pulling my parka hood forward in order to protect my eyes from the sharp darts of sleet, and managed to make it out the door.

No wonder, I thought . . . no wonder the Brazilians are the best in the world at this game. They play with the rhythm of the sunshine and the samba and the undulating tan bare bellies of the most gorgeous women in the world. They probably never even see newsreels of weather like this.

I slowly made my way up the street toward the newsstand. From sheer force of habit, I expected it to be open. Instead, it was barely still standing. The wind had blown down tree limbs and electrical wires and had swept away trash cans, outdoor Christmas lights, and any and all Castel di Sangro flags that had been affixed to the outsides of buildings.

For the first time, I looked at my watch. I have no idea why I had not done this before. I was amazed to see that it was already 10 A.M. The inaugural festivities had been due to start at the stadium at eleven. But obviously, there would be none. Just as there would be no festive luncheon, no match, no Vivaldi.

Knowing that if I managed to build a small fire in the living room and dragged a mattress from the bedroom and lay down near the fireplace while keeping almost all layers of clothing intact, I'd be able to pass a few hours with a minimum of discomfort, I did a quick pirouette in defiance of the gale and began to slowly sidestep back the way I'd come.

The team had been scheduled to eat a prematch spaghetti brunch at Marcella's at 10:30. Undoubtedly, this, too, would have been canceled, but partly from habit and partly from the desire to get relief from the wind and sleet, I slid down the icy driveway that led to the pizzeria. Possibly Marcella would have battled her way there, if only to be sure no permanent damage was being done by the storm.

The door was unlocked. I pushed it open and fell inside. To my astonishment, there was the team, eating spaghetti. I immediately approached Jaconi and asked why, since obviously the match would not be played.

"*Perché no?*" he said. "*Noi abbiamo una possibilità migliore. Queste cattive condizioni ci dano una possibilità in più per ottenere tre punti, o un punto, no?"* Why not? These bad conditions give us a better chance for three points, or even one, don't they?

Genoa had arrived at their Roccaraso motel the night before. It would not be possible for them to return home until the storm had abated, so they'd said they'd be willing to play. And the Castel di Sangro squad seemed of one mind: Let's do it! Despite knowing how physically painful and dangerous would be the chore of playing ninety minutes of football in conditions that might have forced a postponement of Alaska's Iditarod dogsled race, no one expressed a single reservation.

The reasoning was simple. On a decent field, in good weather, we would have scant chance to beat, or even tie, Genoa. But today? In these conditions? The team with the warmest socks wins. While the sleet storm would make the match a mockery, it also would provide us with an unexpected opportunity to collect a precious point, or, with luck, even three.

At the stadium, to my further amazement, a curtailed version of the inaugural ceremonies was under way. The cardinal had been replaced by a bishop, and the general by a colonel, and so on, but neither that nor the absence of an audience prevented a full slate of speeches from being made.

The expected joyous throng of townspeople had stayed home, close to their fires. They were not willing to risk either frostbite or influenza to hear politicians congratulate themselves and one another upon an occasion to which they'd contributed nothing and of whose very existence they'd been unaware until receiving a last-minute instruction to proceed to this most desolate of locations.

I'd long been of the view that only people in positions of power from which they cannot be easily unseated – they, and the mentally deranged – will talk for half an hour or more when it is obvious to everyone except themselves that no one is listening. I didn't want to pin any labels on the roster Gravina had assembled, but the fact was that despite there being no audience, and despite the fact that any words uttered were instantaneously scattered to oblivion by the gale, the speechifying went on for so long that we were forty-five minutes late for the Grand Inaugural luncheon across the street in the seldom used indoor sports arena.

· · ·

The scene there was a sodden mess, with half the honored guests having slipped and fallen as they'd tried to make their way across the parking lot. Meanwhile, Gravina was trying to pretend nothing was wrong. He must have changed clothes in the men's room, because while everyone else sat huddled together for warmth and trying to find some heat source near which they could thaw, if not dry, at least some of their outergarments, the ex-president of Castel di Sangro Calcio resembled nothing so much as the maître d'hotel of a four-star restaurant on the French Riviera.

Toward meal's end, three trim and grim-faced men entered the dining hall and made straight for Gravina. There was much gesticulating, and more than one voice was raised. These were, I learned, the *arbitro* and his two assistants. They were explaining to Gravina that they'd just completed a close examination of the field and that they were of the opinion that the combination of unendurable wind and sleet, coupled with the wretched condition of the pitch itself, had persuaded them that no match could be played here on this day.

I never did find out exactly what happened next. And I certainly saw no money change hands. Nonetheless, after being closeted for twenty minutes with not only Gravina but Signor Rezza, the *arbitro* made a stunningly quick *voltafaccia,* or about-face. Immediately, Gravina announced that it was time to clear the dining hall, for the match was about to begin.

And at precisely 2 P.M. the two teams took the field. The white-clad Genoese trotted confidently from the tunnel that led from the dressing room to the sideline, but as soon as they traveled beyond its protective cover, they began slipping, sliding, sinking, and falling as if they were part of a circus act.

By contrast, our starting eleven tiptoed carefully to the positions they would adopt. A moment later they were joined by the referee who, Signor Rezza's persuasiveness notwithstanding, continued to look extremely skeptical.

And why not? Neither the wind nor the sleet had lessened one whit in ferocity. I'd heard at lunch that Genoa almost hadn't made it down from Roccaraso because, just ten kilometers up the road, the sleet had fallen as heavy, wet snow, and their team bus had been stuck in it up to the hubcaps. As I looked out upon their shivering, miserable players, who could not believe that even *Serie B* could impose hardships like this, it seemed obvious that they were wishing that the bus had never broken free.

Our players, who knew better than to jump up and down to stay warm because they knew that on the down cycle they'd plunge into freezing mud up to midcalf, just quivered in place, already sensing that if they could merely endure, they would not be beaten on this field on this day.

Jaconi had taken what for him was a gamble, reverting to a 4-4-2. Fusco, D'Angelo, Cei, and Prete gave him an experienced defense – perhaps the most important factor of all under the prevailing conditions – while he sent forth also the most experienced midfield available to him: Bonomi, Michelini, Di Fabio, and Alberti. The "gamble" was using two forwards: Galli and Pistella.

His hope was that under these conditions one long ball from the defense might find its way to a forward's foot, that the Genoa defenders would either sink or swim as they tried to retain strong position, that one of the forwards might *somehow* manage an accurate shot on goal, and that the Genoa keeper would fall either forward or backward the first time he tried to move across his ice-slicked goalmouth.

None of this, however, came to pass. Nothing even resembling football was played on that field that day. Except for the prohibition against the use of hands, one might have thought it was a bizarre form of water polo. Finally, after twenty-five minutes, with players from both teams turning blue even as they watched their limbs stiffen, the referee took the ball to apply the classic test.

Holding it at arm's length in front of him, he let it drop from shoulder height. The general rule was that if it bounced, the pitch was still fit to play on. If it lay still where it fell, the match would be canceled.

In this case, strictly speaking, it did neither. Instead, it sank halfway out of sight, plunging beneath the several inches of freezing water that by now had pooled above the grass, and lodging firmly in the muck beneath.

Players from both teams made for the dressing rooms as if their lives were at stake. The match would be replayed in its entirety sometime after January 1. Gravina's first stubborn attempt to be a *patron* instead of a *presidente* had degenerated into just one more ridiculous failure.

An expert was flown down from the north on Monday, and by

Tuesday morning he and his crew were at work, assessing the damage to the field and considering options for repair. This expert was said to be the top man in all Italy in matters pertaining to soccer-field construction, maintenance, and repair. He had been personally hired by Signor Rezza, without consultation with Gravina. Money, for once, was said to be no object: only the quickest possible restoration of the field. Because there would be no answer, the question, Where was he in July? was never asked.

The players returned for training on Tuesday afternoon, under a mockingly warm sun that seemed only to intensify their distress. They gathered in small, silent groups to stare at the mud-soaked, waterlogged expanse that they had expected to be their new field of hope, at the least.

"*Il miracolo è svanito,*" Di Vincenzo said to me as I took a seat next to him on a locker room bench. His expressive face showed undiluted sorrow. "*Il sogno è sparito.*" The miracle has vanished. The dream is gone.

Slowly and sadly, feeling absurdly out of place in the carpeted comfort of their new locker room, the players dressed for training. Now each day, in order to reach their raw and bumpy training pitch, they would have to come out of this new room and stare at the field on which – having been betrayed by the negligence of those who presumed to pass judgment on them – they might never play a single match.

"*Non era una favola, Joe,*" Fusco said as he walked past me. "*Una frottola!*" It wasn't a fairy tale. Just a lie.

22

The predawn arrival of the Thursday morning marketplace vendors – most of whom drove up from Naples and all of whom parked their trucks in the lot directly beneath my window and then noisily but joyfully unpacked and assembled the stands from which they sold everything from whole pigs to sausages, chickens on a spit, hundreds of different cheeses, as well as fresh fruit, vegetables, and fish – ensured that on this day I would wake up in the cold of my solitary bed long before the day's newspapers were available.

But I welcomed the din. The sounds were those of vitality and enterprise. To me, the cries of the vendors, one to the other and later to the early arrivals for whose business they vied, became a more deeply ingrained part of the Italian experience than did visits to churches or museums. This was not art, but something of even greater value – life itself.

Because I did so little cooking, I bought almost nothing at the market, yet I enjoyed walking among the crowds in the morning, nodding or chatting briefly with acquaintances, stopping for a free sample of this or that, occasionally even buying something that I would later wind up giving away, absorbing the texture, the woof and warp, of this small fragment of the Abruzzo, a part of Italy I'd come to love like no other.

On the frigid first Thursday of December there were predawn sights as well as sounds: fires lit by the vendors, who used their packing crates for fuel, and then clustered close to the flames, waiting for the first rays of the warming morning sun. At 8 A.M., as I prepared to leave for my regular newspaper pickup, I looked down and saw something else new: for the first time, Christmas trees were for sale.

September now seemed almost lost in the mists of history. Yet Castel di Sangro still had not played a genuine home match, nor would we until at least December 15, no matter how rapidly and successfully the expert from the north might work, for on Sunday we would travel to Venezia.

And what might I say of Venice? For hundreds of years painters, composers, poets, and writers of prose have been lured into that enchanted realm of canals and lagoons, each to try his or her best to capture its essence. In the past century photographers and film-makers have joined the parade. But no one, in any form, has been more than fractionally successful in conveying the nature of the Venetian experience.

I'd been there before: in 1994 by myself (the city being only a short train ride from Padova), and in January of 1996 with Nancy. On Saturday I'd be returning with my *ragazzi,* this time strictly for business. Canals, lagoons, cathedrals, great works of art? *No, grazie.* We would be coming in search of points.

Before the trip, however, I was given a new job, and it taught me convincingly how invisible and how easily crossed is the line between the famed and defamed, the honored and the scorned in *calcio.*

Jaconi had scheduled only a light workout for Friday afternoon. The eleven who would start in Venice were spared even this. So the training boiled down primarily to a five-on-five match, for which suddenly I found myself the *arbitro,* as Jaconi tossed me his stopwatch and whistle. He said he just wanted to sit and watch, to concentrate on individual strengths and weaknesses among these bottom ten, and so he needed me to referee.

He may well have been doing this more for me than for himself, in order that I might see the game from a different and more difficult perspective – having to decide on the spot what was a foul, when to award a penalty kick, when to accuse a player of a dive.

The game would be divided into two fifteen-minute halves, with extra time added on at my discretion. Offsides would not be called, but I would have to rule on every out-of-bounds play, when to award a corner kick or free kick, and when to say the attacking team had been at fault and make them turn the ball over to the defenders.

The players and I were all friends; it was only a five-on-five match at the end of a light Friday afternoon; the next day we'd all be traveling together by bus and by plane to Venice – this would be fun, I thought.

Instead, from the moment I blew my whistle to start the mini-match, it was apparent that the players had forgotten they'd ever met me before. I was simply the *arbitro* and, as such, was their enemy, for I had within my power the ability to deprive them of their just rewards and to grant their enemies undeserved opportunities.

Cristiano caused my first problem. He fouled Albieri as the seldom-used *quasi-fantasista* dribbled toward the goal that Cristiano's five were defending. I blew the whistle and signaled for a free kick from the spot of the foul.

But Cristiano screamed at me that it had not been a foul, that Albieri had faked it and had fooled me. I walked away from him shaking my head, but he followed, still protesting, and with language I knew well enough to realize was inappropriate.

I wheeled to face him, *"Basta, Mimmo! O ti espello per dissenso!"*

"Cazzo!" he replied, which was a curse that would have given me reason to expel him, but he walked away as he said it, so I let the matter drop. But I became aware of the anger I felt toward him for arguing so heatedly. I found myself thinking, *Just wait, Cristiano. Wait until the next close call. And see which way that one goes.*

Oops. Referees are not supposed to do this. They are supposed to remain unemotional and detached throughout a match. To mete out punishment for an offense as committed, but never ever to carry a grudge against a player forward into the remainder of a match.

Even worse than Mimmo was my beloved neighbor, Altamura. He was being given the chance to play on attack in this little intramural kickabout and, oh, did he ever undergo a change of perspective. Any and all contact, or even the threat of contact against him as he went up for a ball or dribbled toward the goal, was a foul.

"Fallo! Fallo!" he would shout, turning toward me, arms raised, palms up, in an imploring gesture. I would simply shake my head and would not even look him in the eye as I kept moving with the flow of the play.

I decided that two minutes of extra time would be appropriate for the first half. I was about to blow my whistle to end it when I saw Altamura run toward the goal defended by Lotti, who was trying to work himself back into shape ahead of schedule. Time was up and I should have blown the whistle, but I did not. Poor Antonello, he was suffering so much from the illness and the absence of Sabrina. Maybe I should just wait to see what would happen.

Fully ten seconds after the half should have ended, he leaped forward, received a splendid pass from Rimedio, and headed it past Lotti for a goal. I immediately whistled the half to a close. The score was 1–0, the result of a goal that should not have counted. I'd allowed it through what I had wanted to think of as compassion but what, in truth, was probably more akin to cowardice.

Lotti walked past me silently, changing sides, carrying the ball that had just been driven into his net. His only gesture was to tap his wrist in the area where his wristwatch would have been, while raising his eyes quizzically in my direction.

I simply looked at him and shrugged. And he simply shook his head and looked back at me in disappointment. He knew the truth, as did I.

There was a five-minute pause at halftime, during which Cristiano approached me to complain further. I'd called two other fouls against him. I said, "Mimmo, it's not my fault if you don't know how to play the game without committing too many fouls. This happens with you every Sunday, too!"

Well, that was something I shouldn't have said. To criticize his performances in real matches on the basis of his arguing with me here was indefensible. And Mimmo knew it. He got right in my face, or as close to it as he could, given the nine-inch difference in our heights, and followed me, his hand grabbing my arm, as I again turned and walked away.

Finally his pals, Rimedio and Biondi, came over and calmed him, but Biondi shook a warning finger at me and then said to Mimmo, "Calma, calma. L'arbitro è fuori strada." The arbitro is off the beam, out of line, or, literally, "off the road."

In the second half Albieri, whose team trailed, 1–0, tried to seize an advantage by dribbling and diving as soon as he came into contact with anyone. I resolutely refused to call a foul, telling him to get up and get on with it.

But then he took a beautiful pass, dribbled two steps into the penalty area, and just as he was preparing to shoot, received a hard but I thought fair tackle from Rimedio. Now Albieri was screaming for a *rigore* louder than Cristiano had ever screamed. I shook my head and said, "Play on," so tense that I found myself lapsing into English. I thought I'd been right, but I wasn't sure.

Nobody wanted to play on, however. They all wanted to run at me, arms waving, demanding a penalty kick for the foul against Albieri or else demanding that Albieri be sent off for having faked it. Again, I simply trotted away, indicating with an arm signal that the ball was in play.

Altamura took advantage of this moment of chaos to move the ball downfield and, with only Biondi defending against him, prepared for a hard shot against Lotti at point-blank range. Biondi lunged into him, elbows first, his knees clipping Altamura in the thighs. Now *that* was a penalty, and I so indicated by blowing the whistle and pointing to the spot from which the penalty kick would be taken.

Now it was Biondi's turn to charge at me, eyes bulging and arms waving. Nope, nope, nope, I would hear none of it. This was to be a penalty kick. And then I pointed to my watch, to indicate that the minimatch was almost over and that I wasn't going to add on extra time to make up for what had been lost through squabbling.

Altamura took the kick. Lotti saved it. The score remained 1-0. But now Altamura was screaming again, accusing Lotti of having moved illegally before Altamura's foot had made contact with the ball. I dismissed that complaint summarily, and again whistled for play to resume.

By now virtually every player on both teams was furious with me. As the second half drew to a close, I said, *"Due,"* and held up two fingers, indicating that there would be two minutes of extra time played.

The cries of anguish in response to that must have been heard by Signor Rezza on top of his mountain. *Only two minutes!* shouted all the players from the team that was trailing 1-0. *"Impossibile!"*

"Basta!" This was quickly becoming my favorite Italian word.

Jaconi had been watching silently from the stands. But for these last two minutes he came to the edge of the field. My watch was ticking off the final fifteen seconds when Di Vincenzo sprinted furiously forward from the edge of the penalty area and, as he tried to reach a pass that had arrived slightly too far in front of him, shoved Altamura out of the way.

Jaconi, standing right behind me, yelled, *"Fallo!"* as Altamura regained his balance and stood still, hands on hips, waiting for the play to stop after Jaconi's call of foul. Di Vincenzo, however, continued on and blasted the ball past De Juliis for the tying goal.

I blew my whistle. That was the end of the match. One to one. But, oh, the weeping and wailing and gnashing of teeth! Not to mention the cursing and shoving and spitting. No goal! No goal! It could not have been a goal! Jaconi had yelled, *"Fallo!"* and play had stopped.

"Scusami," I said. *"Oggi, per questa partitella, Mister non è l'arbitro. Sono io. E solo l'arbitro ferma il gioco."* Today, for this little match, Mister is not the referee. I am. And only the referee stops play.

Altamura was so enraged that I thought for a moment he might hit me. My own neighbor! And De Juliis, while not about to attack me physically, was standing six inches from my face and spluttering curses so vile and thick with *abruzzese* dialect that I couldn't understand any of them.

I took a step backward and held up both arms. *"Zitti!"* I shouted. Shut up! *"Anton',"* I said to Altamura. *"Fermati solo quando senti il fischio."* You stop playing only when you hear the whistle.

In response, Antonello tore off his perspiration-soaked outer shirt and threw it at me. It missed and I let it lay where it fell.

"E' corretto questo, Mister? Sì o no? Fermarsi solo quando si sente il fischio?" Is this correct, Mister? Yes or no? You stop only when you hear the whistle?

"Certo," Jaconi said. *"Però era un fallo."* Absolutely – however, it was a foul.

"Non credo," I said. I don't think so.

"Perché sei uno scrittore, non un arbitro." Because you are a writer, not a referee.

"Comunque, neanche tu sei un arbitro." However, you're not a referee, either.

"Meno male," Jaconi said, suddenly laughing. Thank goodness.

And, for the most part, that broke the tension. Di Vincenzo stepped up to me quietly and said, "You were right. Mister was wrong. It was no foul." And Lotti, treating this as if it had been a game played in front of 20,000 on a Sunday afternoon, did what he always did with a referee after a match, no matter how good or bad he'd thought the calls had been. He said, *"Grazie, arbitro,"* and shook my hand formally, as if we'd never been introduced. That was Lotti. Class all the way.

Of all the great cities of Italy, the one least associated with *il calcio* is, by a wide margin, Venice. I was aware that many Americans – indeed, undoubtedly a majority – came to Italy, visited, left; or came to Italy, lived there for months or even years, and still left without associating *any* of its great cities with *calcio*.

They could not spend much time in the country without being aware of its existence, but to many it seemed just another of Italy's inexplicable, sometimes quaint but often annoying peculiarities, such as the closing hours of shops, the rudeness of public servants, the pervasiveness of cigarette smoke, the high incidence of petty theft, or the unchecked pollution of the air.

And at least *calcio* was possible to ignore. One could give wide berth to the stadia where it was played, skip over the sports sections of the newspapers (and not buy at all, of course, any devoted entirely to the sport), make it a point never to watch television on Sunday afternoons, remain studiedly ignorant of the objectives of both *Totocalcio* and *Totogol*, the national lotteries, and throughout one's stay associate only with other Americans or with that self-strangulating upper crust of the Italian social hierarchy that considered *calcio* exclusively the province of ruffians.

Still, in Roma, Napoli, Milano, Firenze – the cities, other than Venezia, most visited by tourists of all nations – *calcio* was a palpable presence. The teams of those cities traditionally were among the strongest in the world, and if one were to spend significant time in any of them, conscious effort would be required to pretend that these teams did not exist.

I was aware that many Americans – particularly women and academics – made just such an effort, believing that they'd be risking their lives by attending a match and convinced that even if they did survive, they'd be somehow soiled by the passion of the lower classes and forever after somehow less worthy to gaze rapturously upon the ceiling of the Sistine Chapel or the like.

For them, Venice was a safe haven indeed. In a way not possible in Rome, Naples, Florence, or Milan, one could spend weeks in

Venice and leave the city entirely unaware that it was home to a professional soccer team.

In part, this was historical: the Venice team had never been a national power. In its ninety years of existence, it had played only 15 percent of its matches in *Serie A,* and none during the past thirty years. All sorts of odd cities, most entirely unknown to American tourists – Ternana, Varese, Ascoli, Catanzaro, Pescara, Avellino, Catania – had had their brief fling at *Serie A* glory since Venice had last been relegated.

In equal part, however, it was geographical. One could spend a full year in Venice without stumbling across a clue either that there was a stadium where a soccer team played or, if there was, where among those myriad lagoons and canals it might be. And should one ask – and I've known this to happen – it was far more likely that one would be, in all good conscience, directed to Mestre on the mainland and be told that *that's* where the professional soccer stadium could be found. (And, indeed, it would be, for Mestre has had a team in *C2* for the past twenty-five years.)

And, finally – this third part being, in my view, somewhat more equal than the others – it was cultural. Not the simple snobbery that might be found in Rome or Florence, but the more delicate and subtle sense that Venice had not only a history but a contemporary identity separate and unique from the rest of Italy and that, to the extent this was true, *calcio,* that quintessentially Italian athletic activity, did not belong. Thus, while tolerated as long as it did not make a nuisance of itself, *il calcio* was relegated to the outermost fringes of Venetian life: not only a secret from the tourist but all but unknown to the majority of Venetian citizens themselves.

We stayed in the Lido, the beach area whose hotels in December offered rates far below those in the city proper and from which the stadium would be much easier to reach the next day.

Sunday morning was dark and raw, with a most unwelcoming wind blowing hard from the east, typical of Venice in December. The stadium in which we would play was unique in all of Italy in that it was accessible only by boat.

We loaded our gear in our launch soon after lunch. From the stadium the same craft would take us directly to the airport, from where we would fly back to Rome, then board the trusty old bus for the slow, late-night slog back to Castel di Sangro. Some of us, at least. Many a player had sought to have his car driven from Castel di Sangro to Fiumicino so that he would have independent transportation either into Rome or to another destination of choice late Sunday night.

In any event, cars were the last thing on our minds as we crowded aboard our chartered water taxi for the ride across the choppy channel. A few of the players seemed notably uncomfortable as we pitched and yawed during the twenty-minute voyage. Di Vincenzo, in particular, seemed green around the gills as he muttered, *"Immagina: infortunato per il male di mare!"* Imagine: unable to play because of seasickness!

Jaconi, old salt that he was, told everyone the story of how he'd once played at this stadium and had won, 2-0, and how then his team had been forced to take evasive action in the lagoon to avoid the many small craft filled with irate Venezia supporters apparently intent on ramming it.

I asked Jaconi if his tactics for the day included a nautical escape route. He laughingly said that if necessary, he'd take the helm himself and that if worse really came to worst, we could jettison unnecessary cargo and throw overboard someone who might seem a valuable prisoner of war. Luca Albieri was his first suggestion, but Albieri, in a genuine panic, said he could not swim. All the better, said Jaconi, the pursuit craft would have to stop to search for his body: It was the law of the sea.

This was the hidden heart of *Serie B:* the camaraderie, the jesting, the repartee. As Luca D'Angelo once said to me: *"Serie B* — never a dull moment except during the ninety minutes of the match!"

The giddiness of December 8 might strike some as being out of place given that Castel di Sangro and Venezia were tied for next-to-last place. But there's something about approaching a soccer match by motor launch that lends an aura of unreality to the proceedings. And there were, of course, the inevitable jokes about how closely the lagoon we were crossing resembled the pitch on which next week's match against Lucchese would have to be played – unless, as seemed likely, we were forced back to Chieti instead.

In addition, there was a very real feeling in the hearts and minds of many of us – though I'd heard nothing from Jaconi to indicate his own awareness of this – that finally, on this day, in this place, Castel di Sangro would win a road match. However many hours after midnight it might be, we finally would return home with three deserved (and absolutely vital) points and would at last begin the climb from the depths of despair into which the most recent few weeks had thrust us all.

For Venezia was as sorry a squad as one was likely to encounter. They'd won but three of six home matches, during which they'd scored only seven goals, and all season they'd seemed an unusually spiritless bunch, at least if one could judge from television highlights and newspaper accounts. They were already on their second *allenatore,* but he'd produced no better results than the first.

And the day itself smelled of a Venezia defeat: dark clouds scudding low across choppy water, and an attitude emanating from all whom we encountered upon arrival – from locker-room attendants to the Venezia players themselves – that their primary objective was simply to get this match over with so they could get back to the cheerier sections of the city and either warm themselves by their fires or pursue some of the many loose ends that still lay before them in the run-up to the Christmas break.

Without the suspended Altamura and Martino, we were at less than full strength, but since I'd now become a sworn member of the "Martino Can't Play *Fuori Casa*" society, his absence did not trouble me. And a back four of Fusco, D'Angelo, Cei, and Prete seemed adequate, even with De Juliis in goal.

Unfortunately, however, Jaconi froze solid at the last minute, and while keeping Cristiano, Albieri, and Di Vincenzo *in panchina* – any one of whom might have broken the match open all by himself – he once again resorted to the Grandfathers of the Three Musketeers, putting the leaden-footed Michelini, Alberti, and Di Fabio together in midfield, along with his pet, Bonomi. At least he'd paired Pistella with Galli up front rather than leaving poor Giacamo to wander off alone into a canal, but this was *still* a lineup indicating that Jaconi's fondest wish was a 0-0 draw and that he was sacrificing in advance the chance for the crucial three points.

So, as all too often in the recent past, I took to my seat already damp and disillusioned, notwithstanding the picturesque sailboats visible beyond the far stands, their masts jiggling in the raw wintry wind. There were nineteen opponents in *Serie B,* but none that offered the attractive inducement to go for the win *fuori casa* like Venezia, which played in a dreary stadium surrounded by oil tanks and in which 12,000 of the 15,000 seats remained unoccupied.

For ninety minutes the match remained not only scoreless but shotless. So pathetic, in fact, was the play on both sides that afterward both De Juliis and the Venezia goalkeeper got *s.v.* (meaning *senza voto*, or "no rating") on their *pagelle* because neither of them had been required to do anything.

At the end, the referee's assistant held up a sign saying that four extra minutes would be played. No one could figure out why, and no one – players included – seemed eager to endure even one more minute of what I could now say was far and away the worst soccer match I'd ever seen.

With two minutes remaining, and feeling as if I'd just spent an afternoon in Perth Amboy, New Jersey, I stood and walked toward the dressing room, largely in an attempt to restore some circulation to my feet.

Back and forth and side to side the ball went, as players from both teams looked expectantly toward the referee, awaiting the whistle. By now darkness had fallen to such an extent that it was almost impossible to see the field, and the Venezia *Società* was not about to squander money on a match as sorry as this one by turning on any lights.

I had reached ground level and was looking at my own watch, wondering how long four minutes could possibly take, when Galli tried one futile shot, which bounced off the leg of a Venezia defender, who then booted the ball high in the air and toward the other end of the field.

Surely, now, the *arbitro* would blow his whistle. Yet he did not. And the ball, in full flight, bounced off the head of another Venezia defender, who had set off toward our goal even before the match was over, either to keep his feet warm or simply because it was in the direction of the locker room.

Startled by the ball, he raced toward it, and as our defense stood and stared, he stuck out his leg in an effort to bring it under some control. It took a tricky bounce on the uneven playing surface, however, bounced against the front of his shin, just below the knee, and caromed directly into our net. In the same instant, the *arbitro* blew his whistle, ending the match. Venezia 1, Castel di Sangro 0, although De Juliis did not yet seem aware of the presence of the ball in the back of the goal he'd been guarding.

Instead of entering our locker room, I walked directly to the pier and stood there in solitude as raw, damp dusk descended in full. There had been losses. There had been bad losses. There had been losses attributable to the *arbitro*. There had been more losses attributable to Jaconi's poor tactics and personnel choices and to the equally poor performances of those players he did choose, but never had there been a loss so needless, so breathtakingly stupid and so unnecessary as this one.

Our boat was at the end of the pier, waiting to take us to the airport, any fears that evasive action might be required now obsolete. Just as the whole season seemed suddenly obsolete. Just as life itself seemed scarcely worth living, if these were to be the conditions.

Di Vincenzo, who had not played and who therefore had no need for a shower, was first out of the locker room. He saw me standing at the end of the pier, walked toward me, tossed his equipment bag on the boat, and then gripped my arms with both hands.

"*Aiuto, Joe!*" he said. Help! "*Non possiamo andare più avanti così.*" We can't go on like this anymore. He looked utterly beaten and desolate, and I could understand why: rare was the player whose spirit would not have been broken by his having had to sit helplessly on the bench throughout an entire match as poorly played as this one had been, only to witness the tragicomic ending.

I didn't know what to say. So I fell back upon my usual vague, scarcely credible encouragement.

"*C'è ancora la speranza che le cose possono cambiare.*" Still, there is the hope that things can change.

Di Vincenzo smiled a bitter smile. Then he hugged me quickly and said, "*Ah, Joe, sì, quando gli asini voleranno.*" Yes, and pigs might fly.

As others began to drift out of the locker room, he retreated to a corner of the pier in order to deliver his personal report, by cell phone, to his lovely fiancée, who lived in Florence.

De Juliis arrived on the pier, smoking and talking on his cell phone as if he were advising his broker to short Castel di Sangro in the morning. I'd seen enough of him now to know that he was not and never would be nearly the goalkeeper that Lotti was, but it was impossible not to feel sorry for an essentially good-hearted, competitive player, immensely popular among his teammates, who had given up only two goals in 211 minutes of play – and for neither of them could he be faulted – yet had to show for his efforts only two losses and one cancellation, as the ten men playing in front of him had failed to score even once.

The team, in fact, had not scored since Di Vincenzo had beaten the mythical Walter Zenga in the Padova match on October 27. Including the Genoa annullment, we had gone almost 400 minutes – *more than six and a half hours!* – without scoring.

And Danilo Di Vincenzo, the man who'd scored our first goal of the season and also our most recent – though it had been *six weeks* ago – seemed now a permanent fixture *in panchina* for reasons known only to Jaconi, who had taken to fielding lineups better suited to shuffleboard than to *calcio*.

For me, this was a new low. And obviously I was not the only one. More than half the squad bailed out at Fiumicino, whether they had fixed destinations or not. They just couldn't tolerate that last long leg back to frigid little Castel di Sangro, for which they'd done nothing on that day, and whose *Società,* all season long, had done less than nothing for them.

As we collected our luggage in Rome, I again encountered Di Vincenzo. He was one of those who would not be taking the bus. Instead, he'd be riding to Florence with Biondi, whose family lived there, in order to see his fiancée.

Again I said something to the effect that from this low point, matters could only improve.

"Non si sa mai," he said, managing a smile. One never knows. Then he said good night, and that he would see me on Tuesday.

23

Rain fell all Tuesday morning, so when Davide Cei walked into Marcella's shortly before noon to find half a dozen players and me gathered early for lunch, I thought at first that it was rainwater running down his cheeks.

Then I realized it was tears.

He stopped in the middle of the room. With one arm he motioned to the television set, which as always was on and as always was turned up too loud. Fusco picked up the remote control and turned it off. The room fell silent, except for what we could now hear were Cei's sobs.

He said a few words very quickly. I did not understand them, but everyone else did. And except for the absence of blood, it was as if each player in the room had been shot. Instantly, they sprawled into varying positions of shock, pain, and grief and remained immobilized as Cei, their captain, stood, still sobbing, still alone.

With the greatest trepidation I told him I had not understood what he'd said.

He nodded, and with the utmost courtesy, he repeated it slowly for me.

Di Vincenzo and Biondi were dead.

They'd been killed in an automobile accident only one hour earlier, on the *autostrada* south of Florence, as they'd raced back toward Castel di Sangro in Biondi's Volkswagen Golf in order not to be late for training.

Di Vincenzo had been driving the car. Biondi had stopped at Di Vincenzo's fiancée's house to pick him up, and Danilo, laughing, had said, "Here, it's late, we have to hurry, so let me drive because I've had more practice driving too fast."

And they had been driving too fast. And through rain. Di Vincenzo had lost control of the car on a curve, and it had slid on the wet pavement and had bounced off a center guardrail and then had spun across three traffic lanes into a shallow roadside rest area, where a tractor-trailer had been parked. Both players had been killed instantly as the small car crumpled against the unyielding steel of the trailer.

Cei, of course, did not say all that. The details emerged later. And if God were in those details, his face was well hidden.

For some reason, I cannot even remember which players were in the restaurant. I vividly remember Fusco, perhaps because his face, in such torment, took on the cast of a footsoldier in Caesar's army, wounded in an ancient war. And I remember Marcella, of course, the heaving of her shoulders as she wept and wept and wept. And Cei: who had carried out this most onerous of a captain's tasks with unforgettable dignity.

I am almost sure Cristiano was there, and Rimedio. And I seem to remember Luca D'Angelo. And Tonino Martino was almost always an early arrival for lunch. But the faces fade, and I recall only the contorted postures of the bodies and the long and awful silence that preceded the first of the curses, questions, and moans.

One by one the players drifted out, to be alone, although if Cristiano was there, he and Rimedio might have left together. Marcella, of course, did not leave but only cried harder than the rain fell. I wanted desperately to be gone, but I could not leave her alone. At some point, Christian or Giovanni, or maybe both, arrived. I remember one of them saying that he'd come to bring her home.

Then I did leave. I lay all afternoon on the bed in my apartment, hearing the steadiness of the rain, and once in a great while the honking of a goose from the very small river below.

Just as darkness began to fall, I suddenly remembered Friday and my brief service as *arbitro*. And it was through that vein of memory that the full force of grief rushed into my heart in all its ferocity. I'd refereed the last match in which Pippo and Danilo had ever played. It was with that recollection that my own tears began.

The funeral service, in keeping with Italian custom, was held the next day. The players, all wearing suits, neckties, and sunglasses, carried the caskets the full three kilometers from the stadium to the church in the center of the square. It was – how could it not have been? – a dark and windy and bitterly cold afternoon.

Everyone in the town lined the sidewalk or stood on a balcony or crowded into the square outside the church. No one spoke. As the caskets passed a particular location, the townspeople standing there would slowly and solemnly applaud.

As the players, and their burdens, moved on toward the next corner, silence again would fall, to be replaced by the same staccato clapping of hands a block farther on. And so the procession slowly advanced, to the steps of the church and then up the aisle.

At the end of the funeral mass, the process was repeated in reverse. Other than muffled sobs, and one terrible keening wail from Di Vincenzo's fiancée as she collapsed to her knees, no human voice was heard outside the church – only the saddest and most dignified applause that any performer, of any kind, dead or alive, could ever receive.

The bodies were buried the next morning: Pippo's in Florence and Danilo's in Rome. Training resumed that afternoon. Jaconi had printed a message – in English, for some reason – on the locker room blackboard.

SHOW MUST
GO ONE

I did not correct him. We played a 0-0 tie against Lucchese and we lost, 1-0, at Torino. Then it was time for Christmas, and I went home.

Part II

24

I was disoriented from the moment I set foot in America. Castel di Sangro had dropped to last place; we had gone six consecutive matches without scoring; we had made only five goals all season long (Lecce, by contrast, had twenty-six), and two of those had come from a player who was now dead. Yet when I went for a haircut, all I heard was "How about those Patriots!"

It was as if I'd been in Narnia. In the "real" world, the adventures I'd had there, the life I'd been living, the crises I would face on my return – these simply could not be explained. Yet it was on the far side of the door that I felt my real life to be.

It was not as if I had ceased to love my family. While in Italy, I missed my wife and children with an intensity that sometimes proved crippling, and now I had a first grandchild as well. But I had less and less in common with once-close friends, and virtually no interest in the public life of America.

My heart and mind were with my team. The Uruguayan novelist Edoardo Galeano writes of the "melancholy I who had been we" as the end of a match forces disengagement and the fan "returns to his solitude." But for me, in Castel di Sangro, there was no such separation. I and the team were now one all week long and – however ridiculous or even pathetic it may sound – it was that union which gave passion and meaning to my life.

Call me irresponsible. Call me juvenile, irrational, selfish, foolhardy, and neurotic. *Forse così.* Maybe so. I make no defense. I have none to offer. I could no more control my obsession than I could reverse the direction of the tides.

In a further description of the *calcio* fanatic, Galeano refers to "the remains of the shipwreck that once passed for his mind." In most instances the words went unspoken, but it was evident that this was all they saw when those who had known me best looked in my direction now. How little sense they had of the richness of the life I led as a stranger in a strange land.

My presence was required in America until mid-January, by which time a second "miracle of Castel di Sangro" seemed to have occurred.

On January 5 we beat first-place Lecce, 2–1. Goals by Galli and Bonomi.

On January 12 we beat Salernitana. Goal on a penalty kick by Bonomi.

On January 15, in the makeup of the canceled match, we beat Genoa, 1–0. Goal by Altamura.

Altamura! When I heard that, I rushed back as fast as I could.

Playing three matches in eleven days, the squad had earned nine points, after having collected only eleven in the 111 days before that. Granted, all three wins had come at home (the matches played on the new field, which was perfectly serviceable as long as the temperature stayed below freezing), but nonetheless this *scatto,* or spurt, had lifted us from last place to a tie for twelfth, with Foggia. And if Altamura could score, our possibilities seemed limitless.

I arrived back in Rome on Saturday, January 18. Christian met my plane. My first question was, How? How had this group of grief-stricken, despondent, Lotti-less mediocrities transformed itself into a team capable of beating Lecce, Salernitana, and Genoa within two weeks?

"Is Pippo and Danilo, Joe. They are the reason."

"What do you mean?"

"They spirit. It lift up us all. The players say, 'We 'ave now the memory of Pippo and Danilo, and to this we must give all of our *cuore,*' no? 'We cannot make the *disonore* of they names.' "

"You mean they've been inspired?"

"Ispirati, sì. You remember when Giuseppe write, 'We 'ave the

twelve man now because Joe is return?' Well, don't be insult, but with Pippo and Danilo is the truth, not just the bullshits of Giuseppe. And we 'ave now not the twelve but thirteen man – Pippo and Danilo. Every match is dedicate to them, so every match we win because they *ispirano* we from *paradiso*."

I waited for Christian's wink, and his wry, knowing smile, for this young man was no credulous naïf. But nothing of the sort was forthcoming. "We are *i lazzarati,* Joe," he said earnestly. "The death of Pippo and Danilo have raise us from the dead. You think I jokes? You wait, Joe. Tomorrow you will see, in Pescara."

Having come to think of Pescara primarily as the home of Signor Rezza's luncheon club, and as the place one would reach if one kept going past our old "home" field in Chieti, I'd paid scant attention to its squad. It was a strong one, however, currently in fifth place in *Serie B* and boasting a teenage goalkeeper named Morgan De Sanctis, who was number one for Italy's national Under-21 team.

Moreover, Pescara was located in the Abruzzo. This meant that our match against them would constitute a "derby," the name given to any match between two teams of the same city or, failing that, the same province or, failing that, the same region.

For a host of historical, political, and socioeconomic reasons, certain derbies were of naturally furious intensity. That between Lazio and A.S. Roma, for example, pitted the team of the suburbs and upper middle class against those who considered themselves the true workingmen, and thus the heart and soul of Italy's capital. In Milan when Internazionale played A.C. Milan, it was a battle – to oversimplify, but not egregiously – between the political left and right wings of the country.

In Turin there was burning rage when Torino, representing the downtrodden masses enslaved by the assembly lines of Fiat's trillionaire Agnelli family, played rich, powerful, and pampered Juventus, for whom old man Agnelli could acquire any player he desired merely by lifting an eyebrow.

And in Genoa it was those who still imagined in their veins the salt water of their seagoing forebears, and the dockworkers who tasted daily the salt of their own honest sweat, who supported the Genoa team – the oldest in all of *calcio,* having been founded in 1893 by the British sailors who imported the game to Italy – against upstart Sampdoria, a haven for the nouveaux riche, which wasn't even a real name but only one formed by the 1940s merger of two other clubs (Sampierdarenese and Andrea Doria).

The passions of the latter two derbies lay temporarily dormant because of the unlikely demotion of both Torino and Genoa to *Serie B*, but their roots remained as strong as ever and no one doubted that a reflowering was close at hand.

When one got out of the cities and into the realm of the intra-provincial or intraregional derbies, it was only natural that one found less bloodthirstiness (though I was often told that if Napoli should ever find itself in the same division as Salernitana, the team from the nearby city of Salerno, by match's end, inside the stadium the living would be outnumbered by the dead).

Our derby seemed to fit the category only technically. It would be the Abruzzo's first involving teams in *Serie B*, and as such it had taken on more the air of a festival than civil war. The truth was that between Pescara – a beach resort and fishing port with a population of 125,000 – and Castel di Sangro – a tiny village of pig farmers, truffle hunters, and small merchants tucked high in the mountains more than 100 kilometers away – there simply was no shared blood through which a bond of hatred might have formed.

Thus, an air of celebration reigned on the sunny and unseasonably warm Sunday of the match. The sense of good fellowship had received an additional boost from the announcement that *Le Donne Biancazzurre,* the women's fan club of the Pescara team (whose blue and white colors explained the name), had arranged a mass in honor of Pippo and Danilo, to be celebrated only hours before the match. Di Vincenzo's family remained too deeply in mourning to attend, but the mother and sister of Biondi would be there.

My wife, Nancy, had visited Castel di Sangro in October. A professional photographer, she had taken many pictures, including a portrait of Biondi. I'd brought this back with me from America, and on the day of the derby I carried it to Pescara, along with a short note in my best Italian, to give to Pippo's mother.

I rode to the church with Gabriele and Maria Teresa. Gabriele, however, did not plan to attend the mass. He wanted to arrive just as it was ending, so he could jump from his car, dash up the church steps, and quickly embrace Biondi's mother in order to provide an emotionally affecting picture for the next day's papers.

Either we'd left too soon or he'd driven too fast, or the mass took longer than expected. We had to circle the church five or six times – Gabriele growing more irritable and glancing at his wristwatch more frequently on every pass – before the doors finally swung open and those who had attended stepped back out into the midday sun.

He gave his embrace, and when he was done, I handed the picture and note to Pippo's mother. It did not seem right to embrace her, or the sister, who was only about a year younger than Pippo, but neither could I just turn my back on them. So I stood there not knowing what to do, and finally blurted out in Italian, "When Pippo died, I felt I had lost my own son."

With that, they both began to sob and hug me. And then the three of us – I, a total stranger to them before this moment – stood on the church steps in the bright sun and cried for what seemed a long time.

By midafternoon Pescara felt like southern California in June. I slowly wandered the pleasant perimeter of the stadium, soaking up both the sun and the most unusual county-fair atmosphere. To my surprise, I came upon Fusco, in sports shirt and sandals, standing with an attractive young woman.

"*Squalificato*," he explained, meaning he'd been disqualified from play in this match because of an accumulation of yellow cards. Then he proudly introduced the woman as his new *fidanzata*, the engagement having become official in Naples at Christmas.

He had not been standing idly under a shade tree outside the stadium in the hope that I might wander by. Instead, he was waiting for Alberti, the elder statesman, who was also *squalificato* for the day.

At that news, I would have moved on, for I had no desire to have the spirit of the day spoiled by yet another snub from Alberti. Before I could go anywhere he arrived, accompanied by his wife and ten-year-old son.

Alberti ignored me, as expected, but a complication immediately presented itself. *La Società* had apparently told him that Fusco would have three tickets for him, but there were only two. And it was now less than half an hour before the start of the match, and the Pescara crowd was swelling at the gates.

I must say I was not thinking of Alberti. But I soon thought of his ten-year-old son standing next to me. The boy had been looking forward to sitting with his father at a big match for perhaps the only time in his life. My own ticket was for the *tribuna d'onore,* as were Fusco's and the two that Fusco had been given for Alberti. The boy was just beginning to understand that there was a problem when I pressed my ticket into his hand and disappeared into the crowd. *Cosa posso dire?* What can I say? It was my day for good deeds.

But now how would I see the match? By the time I reached a *curva* gate, where the last of the standing-room tickets were being sold, play had begun. And before I could struggle past the hundreds of Pescara fans clogging the stairwells that led to the upper deck, a roar of jubilation exploded all around me. Pescara had already scored!

With a frantic, final effort I reached the standing-room area and hoisted myself two steps up a light tower to get a better view. The first thing I saw was Bonomi blasting a shot from twenty yards out that even Morgan De Sanctis could not block. A goal! By God, it *was* true. We were *i lazzarati.* I let out an unrestrained yelp: *"Claudio, Claudio, bravissimo! Bellissimo! Forza Bonomi! Forza Castel di Sangro!"*

Instantly, I became aware of the silence around me. And then of the openly hostile stares. Actually, they were glares. So much for the county-fair atmosphere. When one drew the very bottom line, this was definitely a derby. And I had just done the most insulting (and reckless) thing possible for a *tifoso* to do at any match: I had cheered my team's goal while surrounded by supporters of the opposition.

Rumblings from clusters of bare-chested young men wearing blue-and-white scarves around their necks brought home the peril of my position. My exultation had been not only inappropriate but provocative.

Mumbling, *"Permesso . . . scusi . . . permesso . . . scusi, per favore . . . ,"* I wriggled my way through the worst of the crowd even as the growling behind and above me grew louder. Stepping on toes but never stopping and not once – not once – looking back, I made it to the bottom of the stairs and back out of the stadium within ten minutes.

My sense of relief was quickly replaced by the realization that while I was now safe, I was also not watching the match. Instead, I was at the edge of a parking lot, bareheaded under a blazing sun, and without any means of reentering the stadium, since all ticket booths had long since closed.

It was halftime. Having heard no further cries of anguish or jubilation, I assumed the score was still 1-1. Soon I heard a steady but controlled rise in crowd noise, indicating that the teams had returned

to the field. At that point I realized I would have to listen to the remainder of the game from the edge of the dusty parking lot. And "listening" not through the magic of radio but solely by evaluating the
volume and pitch of the crowd noise, much as a dog in the woods
cocks his ears at the sound of a cracking branch.

So, measuring each of the next forty-five minutes on my wristwatch, I sat attentively on the grass at the edge of the parking lot and
determined – with what I later found was considerable accuracy –
that Pescara surged repeatedly toward the Castel di Sangro goal but
failed to score.

Granted, I missed some fine points, such as Altamura's being sent
off early in the second half, which forced us to play a man down for
thirty-five minutes, and the fact that it was another stunning defensive
display by Luca D'Angelo rather than any spectacular saves by De
Juliis that preserved the draw, but by the end of the match I knew the
result as surely as if I'd still been standing on the tower.

Alberti and his son found me easily in the small group that had gathered outside the Castel di Sangro locker room afterward. Alberti simply shook my hand and said, *"Grazie."* His ten-year-old son, however,
speaking almost impeccable English, said, "My father is sincere, although he is shy. And I thank you also. I was heartbroken if I did not
see this match with my father."

"No problem," I said. "I think we were just lucky to get a draw
without your father playing, because he is such an important member
of the team."

"Yes and no," the boy said. "It is true he is smart and has much experience. But there are many skills he no longer possesses as he once
did. And according to me, Michelini played so much lovely today
that my father was not being missing. Do this be also obvious for you?"

"Yes, of course. But I think it is always better when your father can
play."

"For our family, certainly. Because in one year later my father can
no more play from he too old. And I don't know in this case is how
will be our life. My mother and father talk very much about this thing
and also I am worrying."

"Oh, I'm sure you'll be fine. Your father is a very intelligent
man. He'll make a good life for you even after his career is over."

"Yes, he is intelligent. But how do you know of this? He says he makes the point of never speak to you because he think you act too much like the idiot."

Blessedly, Marcella arrived at my side just at that moment, offering a ride back to Castel di Sangro. Gravina had already told me he would be staying on for a celebratory dinner in Pescara, and to ride back with Marcella would be much faster than taking the team bus. Besides, now I was desperate to get away before hearing anything else Alberti might have said about me.

The Monday newspapers were filled with good news. A headline in *Il Messaggero,* for example, said MCGINNISS: "ANOTHER UNFORGETTABLE PAGE FOR MY BOOK." I read on. "When I left for America," I saw that I had said, "Castel di Sangro had only heart. Now I see a squad tactically decisive and well prepared, and with more heart than even I could have imagined. I'm so happy, I almost have to wipe the tears from my eyes." Standards were slipping. This time, they hadn't even interviewed me before making it up.

Still, the newspapers were useful. From reading another, I learned that Antonello's wife, Sabrina, had returned. She'd been interviewed by telephone on Saturday night, after Antonello had gone to Pescara with the squad. Even allowing for invented quotations, I feared Sabrina had not yet found the proper combination of medications.

She had told the journalist that ever since his death, Di Vincenzo not only appeared regularly in her dreams but that he had begun "speaking to me like Jesus. He tells me not to be afraid. He says Castel di Sangro will gain *la salvezza.* He says God has told him this directly." Danilo also had asked her, she said, to assure all his friends that he was playing well in *"Serie Infinita."*

In yet a third paper Jaconi took the *lazzarati* motif and raised it a notch. *"In paradiso ci vanno i santi ma anche gli uomini di buona volontà."* Not only saints go to heaven, but also men of goodwill. I gathered that after the team's ten points in four matches, he was including himself among their number.

Well, the Pescara match had been played on his fiftieth birthday, so he was entitled to at least a brief contemplation of eternity. And God knows, even with three wins and a draw so far in January, Castel di Sangro did not exactly qualify as a garden of earthly delights.

25

I quickly learned that not everyone in town subscribed to the *lazzarati* theory. Indeed, a strong body of secular opinion held that all three home wins could be attributed to two factors, neither of which had involved divine intercession. The first was January and the second was Claudio Bonomi.

The January factor was simply this: It had been bitterly cold and relentlessly windy in Castel di Sangro. Lecce and Salernitana, coming from the deep south, could not adapt. And even Genoa had a comparatively mild maritime climate, not to mention recent frightening memories of the Abruzzo.

The effect of the weather should not be underestimated. Castel di Sangro trained every day in such conditions – and at 3,000-foot altitude, which, while not La Paz, was not sea level, either. One would not question the emotional boost supplied by the "win-this-for-Pippo-and-Danilo" mind-set, but if the two tragically dead athletes were to be considered players numbers twelve and thirteen, then the wind, the cold, and the frozen condition of the field could be termed fourteen, fifteen, and sixteen.

As a bonus, we'd had Roberto Alberti at his best. Unquestionably he had *mentalità* in any weather, but in January this linked synergistically with his slight build, short strides, and fine sense of balance. As others slipped and fell on the ice, he kept both his head and his feet. Indeed, in the *pagelle* from the magazine *Guerin Sportivo,* Alberti had been our most highly rated player during the winning streak, receiving a 7 for each match.

In those same ratings, in fact, which covered all matches played from the start of the season through our January 15 win over Genoa, three of *Serie B*'s top ten players were ours. Stranger than fiction, given that we'd been not only winless but scoreless throughout all of November and December, but true nonetheless.

Tonino Martino, who had benefited most of all from our three home matches in succession (his *nostalgia* being temporarily in remission), was ranked tenth. Alberti was fifth, while Bonomi, who had burst into bloom like an out-of-season flower, was now rated as the second-best player in *Serie B*.

Claudio's surge (as recently as the loss in Venice he'd received only a 5.5 *voto*) had been as sudden as it was inexplicable. The speed had always been there, but its efficacy had been minimized by the not-much-above-the-braces factor that often left him in splendid position but with no idea of what to do next.

He had known in Pescara, however. Watching on videotape Monday, I saw his goal clearly. It had come from a curling, swerving, high-velocity shot taken from full stride at a distance of more than twenty yards as he split two Pescara defenders. It was the sort of goal normally seen only in *Serie A*.

In his first three seasons with Castel di Sangro, all in *C2,* Claudio had managed only one goal in seventy-eight matches. Last year, in *C1,* he'd scored four, a total he'd already matched this season, with three of them coming this month.

And it was not only the goals. As a midfielder, Claudio never would rank among any league's leaders in goals scored. It was the sum total of his game: the way he pressured defenses with his speed and dribbling, his seemingly newfound talent for using that speed to dash free of enemy defenders when he did not have the ball, thus creating space for himself as well as opportunities for others, in addition to his powerful shot, which he would take unpredictably.

Obviously – and he was first to say so – the deaths of Pippo and Danilo had inspired Claudio to rededicate himself to his work. This new focus and passion had led to a rate of improvement that could be charted almost by the hour. Having compiled a composite rating of 6.04 in the twelve matches of 1996, Claudio had jumped to 6.87 for January. (An American reader might wish to compare this to a base-

Pietro Fusco, the Neapolitan. *(Nancy Doherty)*

The author prior to a training session at the new stadium, enjoying yet another explication of tactics by Jaconi. *(Nancy Doherty)*

Neighbors at Via Peschiera, 10: the author and Altamura.
(Nancy Doherty)

Soul brothers – and looking like twins – Bonomi and Cristiano. *(Nancy Doherty)*

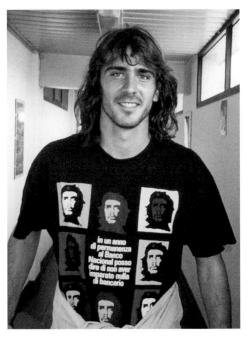

Luca D'Angelo in the hallway outside the locker room, reporting to work in his favored Che Guevera T-shirt. *(Photograph by the author)*

Claudio Bonomi in full dress: suit, necktie, black leather cap. *(Nancy Doherty)*

Gigi Prete.
(Nancy Doherty)

Alberti and Martino, facing one of a player's least favorite moments: an imminent "free kick" from only ten yards away. *(Michele D'Annibale)*

Jaconi in his customary training-session pose. *(Michele D'Annibale)*

Marcella's daughter Rosita with Prete, her personal favorite among the members of the squad. *(Nancy Doherty)*

Franceschini and Albieri, *in panchina* before a match. In uniform, they would remain there during most of the matches as well. *(Nancy Doherty)*

The locker room after the win over Pescara. Left to right: Franceschini, Rimedio, Michelini, Martino. *(Photograph by the author)*

Townspeople swarm onto the field, flares alight, to congratulate the team in the first moments after the victory over Pescara. *(Photograph by the author)*

De Juliis, on a cell phone, at the swimming pool the night before the Bari match. *(Photograph by the author)*

Spinosa, son Andrea, wife Fabrizzia, at the ice cream parlor as they were during the author's final confrontation with Gravina. *(Nancy Doherty)*

ball player whose batting average had been .304 suddenly hitting at a .387 rate.)

Claudio had just turned twenty-four. Given his new intensity, his future suddenly seemed to contain a degree of promise that would have been inconceivable for any Castel di Sangro player of the past, or even for Claudio himself in September.

At the same time he remained Claudio: quick with a hug and a smile but maybe not so fast when it came to problem solving. Until they were gone, one would always be able to tell what Claudio had eaten for dinner the night before by looking at his braces in the morning. And if all *calciatori* could be divided into two groups – those who removed their caps when they sat down at table and those who did not – Claudio looked to be a lifetime member of the second.

And by the very next night it seemed that Claudio's future might already have arrived. My first awareness of straws in the wind came at Osvaldo's fiftieth birthday party, held, of course, at Marcella's.

About the party itself, perhaps the less said the better. The general tenor can be summarized by the description of a single gift: a grotesquely swollen, even malformed ceramic penis in a state of full erection, which in this case meant more than eighteen inches long.

"Galli! . . . *Galli!* . . . *Galli!* . . ."* the squad began chanting as soon as the gift was unwrapped. Reflexively, Giacomo looked down at his lap to make sure that all was as it should have been, and then looked up smiling, but not sure whether to feel proud or insulted.

The present, which had been given to Osvaldo by the young girl-friend of De Juliis, perhaps out of gratitude for his having kept De Juliis as number one even though Lotti's elbow seemed healed, was clearly the work of someone whose imagination (or fantasy life) outpaced his or her skill in ceramics.

It was accompanied by a card, signed by us all, which said, *"La stagione è lunga e dura, ma per te la sola domanda è quanto è dura e quanto è lunga?"* The season is long and hard, but for you the only question is *how* hard and for *how* long?

Either you had to be there, or you should be glad you weren't.

Barbara, however, was among those who did appear briefly to pay respects. Almost as soon as she entered, she called me aside and asked in a low voice, "So what do you think?"

"Well, I've been to worse parties, and this one will probably get worse because they've just finished the grappa, and now Galli is opening a bottle of tequila."

"Not the party. About Claudio?"

"I think he must be playing great, like everyone says. He certainly scored a magnificent goal in Pescara."

"Joe, I mean the news about Claudio."

"What, he bought a new cap?"

"Please. I cannot stay long. I mean about Claudio being purchased by Fiorentina."

"What? Excuse me, Barbara, but that's ridiculous." I looked across the room to where Claudio, wearing a silly birthday hat, was gleefully guzzling about his tenth beer of the night while working his way steadily through a pack of cigarettes.

"Joe, I am told this on the best authority."

"Barbara," I said, an unfortunate note of condescension creeping into my voice, "you might know Castel di Sangro better than I do, and better than I ever will. But, believe me, I know *Serie A*. And I know very well Fiorentina and their needs. In their midfield they have not only Rui Costa and Schwarz, but Cois. And beyond them, Serena and Piacentini and Bigica. Not to mention, of course, Robbiati, who can also play in attack, where they already have, in addition to the great Batistuta, both Oliveira and Baiano, as well as Morfeo, a most promising *fantasista*.

"And so, Barbara, what Fiorentina needs least – and this is even assuming that Claudio could play at that level, which, much as I love him, I assure you he can't, at least not yet – is an attacking outside midfielder. So whoever told you that Fiorentina is interested in making an offer for Claudio is, I'm afraid, someone who knows nothing of *calcio*."

Barbara nodded politely. "Thank you for explaining that to me," she said. "Because when Gabriele and Maria Teresa told me only one hour and a half ago that Fiorentina was offering more than one million dollars for Bonomi, I did not realize that they must have been mistaken. But now I can tell them that it must be simply a misunderstanding, or else that Mr. Cecchi Gori, the president of Fiorentina, who called Gabriele personally, was only, how would you say, pulling his leg?"

"*What?!* Gabriele and Maria Teresa told you this? Cecchi Gori called himself?!"

"Yes, but there is surely no reason to grow excited. You have just explained to me why this would never come to pass. I do think I should inform them, however, because I'm quite sure that in their ignorance they believe the offer to be real."

Just at that moment, Gabriele himself arrived at the party, in a distinctly unfestive mood. He immediately led Osvaldo into the kitchen for a private talk. But their chat had scarcely begun when it was interrupted by the sound of the louvered bathroom door being ripped from its hinges and flung halfway across the room by Galli, upon whom the tequila was having an immediate effect.

Gabriele stepped back out of the kitchen just in time to see the wife of his number two executive, a woman who'd also been rapidly undone by the tequila, plunge face first into Osvaldo's four-foot-by-four-foot birthday cake, which had been meticulously frosted so as to resemble a *calcio* stadium. In doing so, she not only wrecked the cake before it had been presented to Osvaldo but spattered green frosting all over the new suede jacket Gabriele had gotten for Christmas.

At that point, I slipped out and went to bed, thinking it would be better if I were not there when Gabriele discovered that I'd been the one who'd brought the tequila to the party. But Claudio to Fiorentina? Impossible. No way. It had to be just another hoax.

The next morning, however, *Il Corriere dello Sport* reported that Fiorentina would sell the veteran Baiano and replace him with Claudio. And arriving at training half an hour early, I saw Claudio already there, waiting outside Osvaldo's office. Before I could even ask a question, Osvaldo opened the door and told Claudio to enter, making it clear he did not want me to follow.

Tears suddenly sprang to Claudio's eyes. *"Grazie, grande Joe,"* he said, and hugged me as hard as any man ever had before. *"Sentirò la mancanza di tutti,"* he added, sobbing. I will miss everyone.

So it was true. Suddenly Gabriele came striding down the corridor at top speed. Brusquely, he grabbed Claudio by the elbow and steered him into the office, quickly slamming the door behind them.

I waited. After twenty minutes the door opened. Claudio was first out. He walked directly to me and hugged me again. *"Sì, magari! A*

Dio piacendo, lo farò." And how! God willing, I'm going to do it. He then headed for the locker room, and I stepped outdoors into the sunshine. The first person I encountered was Maria Teresa, who was giving orders to the grounds crew working on the field.

"Great news about Claudio," I said, forcing a smile. "At least great for him. Maybe not so good for the squad."

She stared at me, eyes hard as stones. *"Non è vero. Non è vero."* Not true, she said. *"Claudio non ci va."* He wasn't going anywhere. Then she left me and hurried inside through the doorway from which I'd just emerged.

Two minutes later Giuseppe came out. "Is not true," he said. "Claudio does not be sold. Never can 'appen. And very bad for *Società* if you tells people these be true."

"Why?"

He made a gesture that seemed to fall somewhere between the dismissive and the contemptuous, as though I were hopelessly naive for having asked such a question. "Not enough yet the lire be offer at Fiorentina. Until more, we pretend always no, no, no, Claudio is not possible."

"Ah," I said. "So it is true that there has been an offer. But Gabriele is holding out for more money."

"No, Joe! You not be understand. Just forget of this. Not your problem. You not worry. Tomorrow I write these true story at *Il Centro*. Claudio stay here, okay? You always remember this be true. That way, no problem."

Thus instructed, I pretended not to notice anything unusual when Claudio did not participate in the training session but instead ran wind sprints up and down one side of the field while three men I'd never seen before timed him with stopwatches.

And when I stopped by the locker room afterward to have a paper cup of champagne in ongoing celebration of Osvaldo's fiftieth, I pretended not to get the joke when Michelini broke out in song: *"A Lei, Fiorentina . . . ,"* the well-known theme of the Fiorentina *tifosi*.

But as I walked to Marcella's for dinner that night, it was hard not to notice the red Fiat parked at an angle to the curb, facing the wrong way on the one-way main street. Especially when I recognized the car as one in which I'd had many short rides, mostly to and from training. And even more especially when I saw Claudio at the wheel, talking animatedly on his cell phone.

I knocked on the window. He looked up and grinned, but also gave me a finger-across-the-lips gesture, and so I left him to his business. But I noticed that Osvaldo did not come to Marcella's for dinner that night, nor did Claudio's two best friends on the team, Fusco and Martino – and neither of them *ever* missed a meal at Marcella's.

Therefore, I paid little attention to Giuseppe's story the next day. Of course Claudio was for sale. Every player was for sale. As Signor Rezza had said when I'd jokingly handed him my checkbook after my tour of his estate, "You never know. It depends on the size of the check."

In this instance, I learned that Gravina, having received a bid of $1 million – probably ten times more than he'd ever before been offered for a player – was insisting on $1.5 million. Fiorentina eventually raised their offer to $1.2 million, but Gabriele would not budge.

By the end of the week Fiorentina announced the acquisition of the Russian international Andrei Kanschelskis from England for a far higher sum. Having failed in the bargain basement, Cecchi Gori apparently had decided on the penthouse instead.

When I saw Claudio on Saturday morning, I said, "I hope you are not too disappointed."

"No, Joe," he replied. "I know that I will get to *Serie A*. And in my heart I feel my place is here. We have lost Pippo and Danilo. I think maybe is too much to lose me." The utter disingenuousness of that last remark almost brought me to tears. Pure Claudio.

In any event, we hugged a hug of reunion, although the separation had never occurred. And I walked away feeling that whatever it was that *carattere* meant, Claudio had it *in abbondanza:* in spades.

La Società had not been entirely inactive since Pippo and Danilo had died. Although Jaconi had rejected a gifted Liberian attacker named Robert Zizi, who had dazzled during a late-December tryout, he'd grudgingly accepted the arrival of two young Italians whom Gravina had managed to obtain on loan.

Daniele Russo was a tall, thin, twenty-three-year-old midfielder from Rome who had played with Perugia in *Serie B* the year before. When Perugia had won promotion to *Serie A,* they'd felt that Russo was not quite ready and had sent him to a *C1* club for further seasoning. Thus, while still the property of Perugia, it was from *C1* that he'd arrived.

He had not played against Pescara but had seen action briefly in the three earlier January matches, replacing a fatigued Bonomi for the last fifteen minutes against Lecce, coming on for Di Fabio as part of a run-out-the-clock effort in the last two minutes against Salernitana, and being inserted in place of Pistella with twenty minutes remaining against Genoa. The consensus among his teammates was that he had talent but needed regular playing time, which Jaconi seemed unlikely to give him because of Russo's tendency to occasionally enliven his game with *fantasista*-like flourishes, behavior that turned the manager's face dark red with anger.

The other new arrival was Daniele Franceschini, also a native of Rome and a more defensively oriented midfielder who had celebrated his twenty-first birthday two days before the match against Genoa. For reasons unknown, Jaconi seemed to have taken an even quicker and stronger dislike to Franceschini than to Russo, so this Daniele had not yet been used. Like Cristiano (who'd gone into sudden eclipse as Alberti assumed command of the frozen midfield), Franceschini was a product of the Lazio youth system, where he'd been impressive enough to be rewarded with three token appearances in *Serie A* the previous season.

He struck me as an extremely hard worker in training and, like Russo, off the field seemed an affable and easily absorbed addition to the team, particularly to that portion that dined at Marcella's. The early consensus of the full-season players was that Franceschini probably had even more quality than Russo but that his greatest strengths lay where we already seemed to have them, in midfield, thus making it all too easy for Jaconi to write him off as redundant.

In fact, given that we had three midfielders ranked among the top ten players in *Serie B* – and with Di Fabio, Cristiano, and Michelini having proved capable in the position as well – it struck me as odd that Gravina would add two more while ignoring both our defense and attack.

"*Tangenti,*" Gigi Prete told me one night, rubbing his thumb and forefinger together. He meant kickbacks. It was Gigi's belief that Gravina had received private payments for having accepted the two players, whose real clubs were interested primarily in seeing them receive the *Serie B* playing time that would help them hone their skills most effectively.

Thus, if each had been "rented" for – as an example – $5,000 per month, some percentage of that would be returned *sotto il tavolo,* or under the table, not to *La Società* but to Gravina personally.

I had no way of knowing whether this was true, but Gigi laughed off any skepticism I displayed as just another example of American naïveté. Such transactions as those he'd described – and far worse – were everyday practice, not only in Castel di Sangro but at all clubs, at all levels of *calcio.* The only distinction he drew was between north and south, saying that, as with other types of crime, both violent and non, these *pratiche illecite,* corrupt practices, were far more common in the regions south of Rome.

It struck me that Gigi had learned a lot during his travels through the nether regions of the *calcio* world. But maybe all players, after ten years in the game, knew just as much, and the only difference was that Gigi was willing to talk about it.

In any event, we did get a new *attaccante* that week. Gionatha Spinesi, eighteen years old, born in Pisa and owned by Inter Milan, arrived on loan just in time for the match against Bari, which regardless of the result, would close the most successful month in Castel di Sangro history.

From the start, it was apparent that Spinesi was regarded as someone special, not least of all by himself. There were good reasons for this. He'd debuted for Pisa at the highest *Dilettante* level at age seventeen. He scored four goals in ten matches there before Inter Milan bought his contract. Since then, he'd been playing for their youth team, for which, at eighteen, he was still eligible.

Inter, however, considered him a striker of such promise that they wanted to blood him professionally as soon as possible. And after having watched Galli and Pistella in action a few times, Inter scouts reported that were Spinesi to be loaned to Castel di Sangro, he would be virtually certain to play every minute of every match.

The Spinesi buzz began even before the Bonomi buzz had faded, but the young man himself, as befitted a player of star quality, refrained from any such formalities as a tryout and instead waited in Milan until Gravina and Inter officials agreed on a loan price.

He made his debut against Bari and didn't show much, but then neither did anyone else. Having already earned ten points for the month, we could not feel too bad about losing to Bari, a team loaded with talent, just demoted from *Serie A* and clearly intending to get back up there as soon as possible.

We managed to hold them 0-0 through the first half, but six minutes into the second their German midfielder, Thomas Doll, scored a goal. A perfect example, I thought, of a successful *straniero* in *Serie B,* as was Bari's Swedish midfielder, Ingesson, not to mention their Colombian *attaccante,* Guerrero.

That Jaconi would have found reasons for dismissing all three as unsuitable for Castel di Sangro was cold comfort on a cold afternoon. Claudio was fouled in the penalty area and made the kick to tie the match at 1-1 (the fifth consecutive match in which he'd scored), but Bari surged back and, despite Fusco's finest performance of the season, simply overran our defense to add two more goals before the end.

And thus ended *l'andata.* The first half of the season was over. The following week, in February's chill gloom, would commence *il ritorno,* the second half, which would carry us forward – under increasing tension, or else despair – into the hellish heat and humidity and punishing sun of late June.

In any event, *la classifica* at the halfway point looked like this:

Lecce	38
Torino	34
Pescara	31
Brescia	31
Bari	29
Ravenna	27
Empoli	27
Genoa	25
Lucchese	24
Chievo Verona	24
Foggia	24
Padova	23
Venezia	21
Cosenza	21

26

The *ritorno* was simply the *andata* repeated, except that each match that had been *in casa* would now be *fuori,* and vice versa. Thus, for us, it began with an eight-hour bus ride to landlocked Cosenza, in the middle of Calabria, halfway between Bari on the Adriatic Coast and Reggio Calabria to the west.

In September Cosenza had meant my first tentative steps in a new and wondrous world, lunch at the Sea River Club with Signor Rezza, and an ecstasy-inducing winning goal by Di Vincenzo. In February it meant two consecutive showings of an Italian-dubbed *Independence Day* on the bus. (Galli hadn't understood the plot the first time through and so insisted on playing it again.)

Cosenza was not a city that a person – Italian or American – would be likely to visit by choice. One had the distinct sense that those who could get out already had and that the 80,000 left behind were there by necessity, not choice. This was *Serie B* at its grungiest: thirty-seven hours spent riding a bus, eating, and sleeping in the most cheerless surroundings imaginable, solely to play a ninety-minute match.

Altamura remained suspended, while Cei had had to rush his infant daughter to a Perugia hospital after her influenza turned to pneumonia. The baby was in intensive care, and Davide and his wife were at her side. To make matters worse, Jaconi had decided to protect our new prize, Spinesi, from Cosenza's potentially abusive defenders and sent out instead Galli and Pistella, which, for us, was like playing the match with nine players and two birdbaths. De Juliis, of course, remained in goal.

Our die appeared to be cast – not to mention our doom sealed – only fifteen minutes into the match when an inattentive Prete found himself beaten inside the penalty area and clumsily fouled the Cosenza attacker, thus giving the home team a penalty kick that De Juliis merely blew a kiss at as it went by. So it was 1–0 to the *padroni di casa*, as the home team is often called in Italy.

In the *andata* we'd played nine matches away from home, losing seven, managing to draw only twice, and never coming close to a win. (No wonder Galeano could write of the *tifoso's* "mania for denying all evidence." With emigration and suicide offering the only viable options, such a mechanism seemed the very essence of mental health.) For us, however, even more appalling than the 0-7-2 mark was that in the nine matches we'd scored only *two* goals. There had been the gift presented to Galli at Empoli and then only last Sunday Bonomi's blistering drive in Pescara.

And at no point during the ninety minutes in Cosenza did we look capable of scoring even if Cosenza were to send on inflatable dolls as substitutes. Only occasional runs deep into the opposition half by the suddenly indefatigable Bonomi and by lanky Daniele Russo, who was starting for the first time, relieved even briefly the pressure on our defense. And only the fact that Cosenza's forwards were no better than ours kept the score close. Prete, in particular, was a sorry sight from start to finish. And when Osvaldo did send Spinesi on for Pistella in the second half, the youngster simply could not adapt himself to the rhythm of the match (quite possibly because there was none) and would have been better off left undisturbed *in panchina*.

Three minutes of extra time were added on at the end. These, too, were passing without incident, and I'd begun to gather myself for the slow, sad trek to the locker room when we were awarded a corner kick. Bonomi took it, and Luca D'Angelo outfought two Cosenza defenders to get his head on it and knocked it in the direction of Russo, who had somehow positioned himself just to the right of the Cosenza goal. Russo instantly – *just like a professional soccer player* – kicked it past the Cosenza keeper at the very instant the *arbitro* blew his whistle.

Cosenza protested long and loudly (causing me to feel an empathy with the *arbitro* that I would not have had if I had not been in an almost identical position in December; nor, of course, if the goal he allowed to stand had been scored *against* us), but he stood his ground, and we walked off the Cosenza pitch rather stunned by our sudden achievement of a 1–1 draw.

It was still a long ride back, but bearable. And made even more so for me by the fact that I sat directly in front of quiet, shy Russo, who was softly exulting into his cell phone, telling parents, *fidanzata,* ex-teammates, and boyhood friends the same thing over and over again: "I cannot believe it! I scored a goal with only two seconds left to tie the match! My first goal for my new team! *Sono contentissimo!*" I am so happy!

Both Russo and Daniele Franceschini seemed not only talented *giocatori* but likable and sensitive young men. Though neither had known either Di Vincenzo or Biondi, both were acutely aware that they were in Castel di Sangro only because the two others had died. They never pushed for acceptance and sensed instinctively that their new teammates were still recovering from a terrible and recent trauma. Not that they tiptoed on eggshells day and night, but it was clear that they carried within themselves a genuine sense of sorrow in regard to their predecessors.

There was, for example, the matter of Di Vincenzo's chair. While Pippo had sat on one side of the table, next to Cristiano and Rimedio, Danilo had from the start of the season taken the seat at the foot. After his death, the chair first was left empty and then one day simply removed. I'd never heard a word spoken in regard to this. It had seemed to arise naturally from the players' communal sense of decency and respect. Marcella simply rearranged the table settings, and that was that.

When Russo and Franceschini arrived, they took their seats along with everyone else. It never occurred to either of them to drag a chair up to what had been Danilo's end of the table, or if it did, someone must have quietly explained.

But Spinesi was different. The first night he ate with the team, he asked why there was no place set at the foot of the table. It was Luca D'Angelo, I believe, who said that Di Vincenzo had sat there.

"Non più." Not anymore, Spinesi said, and pulled over a chair from an adjacent table and called to Marcella for a place setting.

Well, he was only eighteen and he had come from Milan and he carried with him the weight of high expectations. Any of these could be seen as an excuse for insensitivity.

After seating himself, Spinesi looked around the table, as if defying anyone to challenge him. No one did. Not out of fear, certainly. Nor because of any diminished grief over Danilo. I felt, and I think the others did, too, that we simply had to play on and that incidents like this one were part of the process.

In time, Spinesi would grow up. With luck, he would also score enough goals to earn the place he had appropriated.

Antonello had gone home with Sabrina for the weekend. Since her return in January, she had seemed somewhat brittle. More than once she'd emptied her handbag on a table in front of me and lifted her various pill bottles and explained to me what each one was for, and how the combination had brought under control her agitation, anxiety, chest pains, depression, dizziness, headache, irregular heartbeat, numbness in extremities, sleeplessness, and crying jags.

I felt bad for her, but also bad that my friend Antonello was married to a walking side effect. Despite her arsenal of medications, Sabrina would soon complain of one or more of the symptoms just listed and would grab my hand and tell me – or Marcella or anyone else available – that she despaired of ever truly feeling well again.

On Monday night Antonello called. He told me he'd injured himself while working out over the weekend and thought he could receive better physical therapy in Rimini, which was not far from Fano, and so would not be coming back this week for training.

I asked him if he'd broken this news to Osvaldo. He said yes but that the response had been profane and insulting. Osvaldo had accused him of staying in Fano only because "crazy Sabrina" insisted. Then Osvaldo had said that Sabrina was destroying Antonello's career, or whatever slight career he might have had without her.

Antonello asked me what he should do. I advised him to come back immediately and report for training tomorrow, leaving himself in the hands of Castel di Sangro's trainer and doctors. At least that way Jaconi could not accuse him of malingering.

"But there ees problem, Joe," he said in English. Then he told me in Italian that what he hadn't told Jaconi was that Sabrina had decided that all her pills were useless and that the only cure for her maladies would come from acupuncture. God only knew from what magazine or television show she'd gotten that idea, but she planned to begin treatments immediately and wanted Antonello to stay with her at least through the early days.

"Acupuncture, Anton'? In Fano?"

"Chissà!" he replied. Who knows! It was what Sabrina wanted, so it was what Sabrina would have. And both her mother and father, with whom they lived when they were in Fano, thought it imperative that Antonello remain. (More than once he'd hinted to me that her parents had not yet forgiven him for having gotten her pregnant before they were married.)

"Che cosa devo fare?" he asked. What should I do?

"Come diavolo dovrei saperlo?" I responded. How the hell should I know?

It wasn't the most supportive thing I could have said, but sometimes when conversing in Italian, especially on the telephone, I would just throw out the first generally appropriate phrase that came to mind rather than go through the slow, stressful process of searching for the words that would convey what I really wanted to say.

"Ah, Joe," he said, this twenty-five-year-old minor-league Italian soccer player who was becoming one of my closer friends on earth. *"Le tribolazioni della vita."* The trials and tribulations of life.

"Infatti," I replied, which meant, more or less, You said that right! And the long, hard season wore on.

I realized I hadn't seen Signor Rezza since I'd been back. It occurred to me, given his age and the uncertain climate, that the old man might have fallen ill.

Nothing of the sort, Barbara assured me. He was on his annual winter vacation, which he took each year in Saudi Arabia.

"Saudi Arabia?"

"Yes," she said, "apparently the scuba diving is particularly fine there in a certain portion of the Red Sea."

"Barbara, you're not telling me that Signor Rezza goes scuba diving!" The weight of his sins alone, I was sure, would cause him to plummet to the bottom as surely as if his feet were encased in cement.

"No, Joe," she explained. "Obviously, Signor Rezza himself does not go under the water, or even in it. But his other niece, Elena, she is an avid scuba diver, as is her husband, the oral surgeon."

"But why Saudi Arabia?"

"It is my understanding," Barbara said, "and this is yet one more thing I would not ask about if I were you, that Signor Rezza has business interests in Saudi Arabia."

"What's he doing, building a mosque for King Fahd?"

"Joe, I hope you stop to think before you speak to others as you do to me. Certain of your comments could be perceived by some as inappropriate. Also, it may well be that it is at Signor Rezza's pleasure that you continue to enjoy the cooperation of *La Società.*"

"It's not a problem, Barbara. For one thing, I still don't know how to be sarcastic in Italian."

"Meno male," she said. Thank goodness. "But still I feel that matters were simpler when you could understand no one and no one could understand you."

Cei's baby, thank God, was making a full recovery, but as his wife stayed with the infant in hospital, *il capitano* became a temporary patron of Marcella's.

One night, slow to leave, I noticed him sitting alone, reading intently. As I walked past his booth, I paused to see the title of the book. It was, to my surprise, *The Great Gatsby.*

"Ti piace?" I had the presence of mind to ask him. Do you like it?

He put it down, and a smile broke over his sturdy face. I don't think he'd realized I was still in Marcella's, but at this moment I was exactly the person he wanted to see.

"Sì," he responded, tapping the cover. *"E' bellissimo e offre un intuito acuto della natura umana."* It is very beautiful and offers a penetrating insight into human nature. Which, in my opinion, seemed about as good as one-sentence descriptions of *Gatsby* got.

But Cei had a specific question. He motioned for me to take a seat. Quickly, he began drawing on a paper napkin with a pen.

"Isola Lunga," he asked, *"è a est o a ovest di New York City?"*

"Est," I said confidently. As long as we stayed on geography, I was safe. Long Island was most assuredly east of New York City.

He slid the napkin toward me. I nodded. Cei had drawn an accurate, if basic, representation of the geographic relationship between Long Island and New York City.

"E' corretto," I said. This is correct.

But Davide shook his head.

"Nel libro, sono due uova, no?" he asked.

"Scusa? Non capito, Davide."

"Due uova," he repeated. *"L'Uovo Est e l'Uovo Ovest."*

Oh, of course! East Egg and West Egg. *"Sì, sì,"* I said.

"Comunque," Cei replied, *"mi confondo."* He was confused. I looked more closely at his map. He had drawn ovals where the beach towns of East Egg and West Egg would have been located had they been real. He could understand East Egg, he said, but how could a place called "west" also be east? If it was "west," it could not be east of New York City, and hence not adjacent to East Egg.

Madonna, how could I explain to a man born and raised within 100 kilometers of Florence that in America a town could be called "west" simply because it was west of an adjacent town with the same name, even if both were east of the city?

I tried, but between my poor language and his strict logic, I don't think I succeeded. Finally, I said, *"Davide: credimi! E' giusto."* Take it from me. It's right.

He looked at his map a moment longer but then crumpled it and nodded at me, smiling. Okay. In this instance, my word would suffice. After all, I was a *scrittore americano* and Fitzgerald had been a *scrittore americano,* so presumably I was privy to the same arcane secrets of American geography as the earlier author had been.

America cropped up again the next day when Lotti approached me, saying he was so frustrated by Jaconi's refusal even to speak to him, much less to let him play again, that he was prepared to leave the team, even to leave Italy, if he could be assured of a first-team position someplace else. Then he asked me about the new professional league in the United States.

The only team with which I had any connection whatsoever was the New England Revolution, and even that was highly tenuous, based as it was solely on my acquaintance with Lalas, who now played there. It turned out, however, that Lalas's agent, with whom I'd had dinner several times while in California for the O. J. Simpson trial, was also the agent for the new manager of the Revolution. He told me that the new man, Thomas Rongen, had said his greatest need was for a first-class goalkeeper.

Thus began my own brief foray into the world of agentry. I faxed to Rongen an enthusiastic letter about Lotti. He replied immediately, urging Lotti to send him videotapes of several matches. Within forty-eight hours Rongen had viewed them, and this time he contacted me by phone instead of fax.

"The guy looks wonderful," Rongen said. "Almost too good to be true. But tell me again why it is that he's on the bench even though he's recovered from his injury?"

"Coach Rongen," I said, "you may find this hard to believe, but it's true. The only reason Lotti isn't playing, which is the only reason he's interested in playing for you, is that the manager here has some sort of father-son-type relationship with the other keeper and simply won't give Lotti his job back."

"That's ridiculous," Rongen said. "Pardon me for being blunt, but no professional manager anywhere could be stupid enough to keep a better goalkeeper on the bench just because he happened to like the worse one. I've been in this business now for quite a few years and let me tell you: If I had to field every year a team made up only of players whose personalities appealed to me, I'd still be looking for my first eleven."

"I understand. But our man here, Mister Jaconi, well . . . his decisions are not always easy to explain."

"No, no, no," Rongen said. "With all due respect, Jim —"

"Joe."

"Excuse me?"

"My first name is Joe, not Jim."

"Oh, I'm sorry. But you see, that's part of the problem. Your judgment comes highly recommended, but I don't really know you from a hole in the wall, and something about this situation just doesn't sit right with me. If the man is as good as he looks, and if he is really recovered from his injury, I just can't understand why he's not playing."

"Coach Rongen, neither can I. And neither can anyone else on the team. Or in the town. But you see, the manager here and this other keeper — well, for example, his girlfriend gave the manager an eighteen-inch penis for his birthday."

"*Excuse* me?"

"Oh, never mind."

"Wait a minute," Rongen said. "Now you've got me interested. *Which* goalkeeper has the eighteen-inch penis?"

"No, no, it's the manager."

"God*damn*," Rongen said. "An eighteen-inch penis, and this guy is coaching in *Serie B?* He must *really* be devoted to the game."

"No, no, it's only a joke. For his birthday. He was fifty."

"*Fif*teen? I thought you said eighteen."

"I did, but Coach Rongen, the point –"

"Listen, Jim, I think we're getting off the point. Let me bottom-line this right now: The fact that this Lotti isn't playing worries me. If he gets off the bench, send me more tape. If he's still as good as he seemed to be, then I might fly him over for a look. But not while he's not even playing over there."

Needless to say, when I reported this to Lotti, he was not pleased. His face turned pale with anger, and he began clenching and un-clenching his fists. I was trying desperately to think of something that might make him feel better.

"Did you ever hear of *Catch-22*?" I asked, although I knew his reading tastes ran more toward the Italian horseracing form than to literature.

He shook his head.

"Well, it doesn't matter. But the point is that if you want to play in Boston, you've got to play here again first."

"But if I play here, I don't need Boston."

"Massimo," I said, "that's Catch-22."

27

The geese woke me early on Saturday. Again, the day was sublime. Under a cloudless sky and with only a slight breeze, the temperature had climbed to fifty degrees Fahrenheit by 9 A.M.

I strolled down to training and walked the new pitch with Michelini and Bonomi. We were surprised by its good condition. The weather had helped, obviously, but there was no doubt that the expert from the north had known his stuff. The field would provide almost perfect footing for the next day's match against Foggia.

Sunday itself was just as fine. Even the morning was balmy, with the temperature pushing sixty and an utter absence of wind. I joined the squad at Marcella's for the 11 A.M. match-day brunch of pasta, cookies, and fruit. Then I slowly worked my way through the crowded town square. The atmosphere was so carefree and high-spirited that if I'd had enough hair, I might have been tempted to wear a flower in it.

The shock came as I walked through the stadium gates and looked at the field. It was virtually under water! Overnight, it had again become the sodden mess that the expert from the north had been brought in to remedy, no matter what the cost.

Half the squad was already there, and more players were arriving by the minute. I stood in their midst. In December, after the Genoa debacle, there had been sadness about the condition of the field. But today there was only anger as, one by one, they learned from workmen what had happened.

Fearing that Foggia possessed a better, stronger, faster team, Gravina – who despite his "resignation" seemed more directly in charge than ever before – had sent out a work crew, under cover of darkness, to flood the field. It was his hope, apparently, that wet, mushy, slippery footing might negate Foggia's superiority.

This was a slap in the face of every player on the team. It was his, Gravina's, way of telling them – despite the miracle, despite their astonishing performance in January, despite the fact that the bond among them was now so strong that I did not doubt that almost any one of them would have laid down his life for any other – they would not stand a chance in a fair competition.

Such a mockery this made of the gorgeous day, the warm sun, the spirits that had been so naively rising. And such a mockery it made of the ideals of *alto calcio* which Gravina espoused whenever a microphone or televison camera came within hailing distance.

The field had been so saturated through the night that even at 1:30 P.M., only an hour before match time, water still glistened on the surface. The arriving Foggia players were aghast. Wearing suits and dress shoes, those who ventured onto the playing surface sank to their ankles in mud.

Eventually, their questions and complaints grew so loud that one of Gravina's minions had to come forward and say that there had been a sudden, hard frost the night before and that what had been ice was now quickly melting. This produced only hostile and skeptical glares. But the Foggia players were professionals. They had come to do a job and they would do it, especially now that they'd been given a bit of extra incentive by such an obvious, underhanded attempt at gamesmanship.

Foggia won, 3–1. It was our worst *in casa* display of the season, not surprising given the state of shock into which the players had fallen at the sight of the field. But by the time it was over, there were only two teams beneath us in the standings.

And so on Monday, feeling once again that somehow my own honor was at stake, I composed a *polemica,* just as I'd done in objection to Robert Ponnick. This one, however, was less gracefully worded.

My Polemic Regarding the Flooding of the Field

What bullshit! This was an act of folly!
The stupidity of some people evidently

has no limit.
Osvaldo speaks of character and of the
proper mentality. What a pity that La Società
does not listen.
Instead, they have the mentality of dilettanti.
They resort to every type of trickery. However,
in doing so, they lost not only the match,
but their honor.
"As you sow, so shall you reap!"

I signed my name, of course. I left a copy for Gravina (in a sealed envelope) in the *Società* office. I posted one on the wall of Marcella's. I slid one under Osvaldo's door. And that afternoon, before training, I went to the locker room and taped two or three to the wall there, as I'd done with my protest over Ponnick.

When Jaconi arrived, he did not seem put out in the least. He left my *polemiche* undisturbed. Fifteen minutes later, however, Gravina entered the locker room to give what he hoped would be an inspirational talk. He immediately spotted my little posters and removed them personally, folding each and putting it into a jacket pocket. We exchanged neither glances nor words.

Two days later the false spring ended. The late afternoon was windy and cold, and darkness fell like a curtain. I was walking quickly back to my apartment after training when, to my surprise, I found myself being hailed by the oral surgeon, husband to Signor Rezza's other niece. He had an office on Via Peschiera, only a few doors down from my apartment, but we'd never before encountered each other on the street.

Perhaps he had just been leaving for the day, but it seemed equally possible that he'd been waiting in his doorway, knowing I was likely to walk by at about this time. In any event, he had a copy of my *polemica* in his hand.

The oral surgeon, who probably was about fifty years old and had slicked-back black hair and a dark mustache, could not have been more cordial. When I asked him how the scuba diving had been in the Red Sea, he launched into a five-minute paean to the especial beauties of those waters. He was smoking a cigar (though not nearly the size of Signor Rezza's) and offered me one, which I declined. Finally, he held up the copy of my *polemica.*

"This is interesting," he said, smiling. "Do you really think that that's what happened?"

"I know it was," I said. "And so do the players. My reaction does not matter, but theirs does."

"Ah, my friend, that's where you're wrong," he said, smiling even more broadly. "Your reaction matters greatly, especially when you express it in a tone so . . . so . . . *stridulo.* I am sorry, I do not know the English for that word, but no doubt you get the idea." I did. The word meant "strident" or "shrill."

"Well, I felt strongly about it. I still do."

"Yes, but, Joe, my dear friend and virtual neighbor," he said, looking across the street at my apartment – this man with whom I'd not exchanged a hundred words all season – "the creation of a document such as this might cause some to think that in your book you will treat harshly *La Società.*"

"I might," I said. "Or I might barely mention it. Much depends on what happens in the future."

The oral surgeon spread his arms wide and glanced at the sky, as if my words had been divinely inspired.

"Esatto," he said. "So much depends on the future. You speak with great wisdom. And you realize, I hope, that Signor Rezza feels this way also. No one, not even he, can foretell the future. For this reason, Signor Rezza prepares for every *evinienza* I think you would say, 'eventuality.' "

I noticed, in the near-darkness, that he was no longer smiling. A quick gust of wind caused me to shiver.

"A proposito," the oral surgeon continued, "Signor Rezza has asked me to extend to you his regards. Everything is comfortable in the apartment?"

"Very comfortable," I said. "And please convey my deepest respects to Signor Rezza."

"Without fail, my friend. Signor Rezza will be pleased to know that you remain aware of his continuing interest in your work."

Then he crumpled my *polemica* in one hand and touched the ash end of his cigar to it until it began to smoke. In only a few seconds a flame appeared, and he dropped it quickly to the street. We both stared at it in silence as it burned.

"*Caro,* Joe," he said, "I must be going. But I hope you remember why you first came here. It was to write about the miracle of the football team, as I recall. It would be unfortunate if you lost sight of that point."

"Thank you," I said. "Of course, I shall not lose sight of that point. And I hope very much that no misunderstanding has arisen that has caused Signor Rezza to think otherwise."

He looked down at the smoldering remains of my *polemica. "Non si sa,"* he said. One never knows.

Then he looked back at me as if suddenly remembering a long-forgotten fact. "Joe," he said, smiling again, "I have been intending to tell you that if ever you have trouble with your teeth – any trouble – I would be honored if you would seek treatment from me first. Do not let my title alarm you. For you, surgery would be the last resort, performed only if absolutely necessary."

He unlocked his car door and climbed in. The car was the finest of the models made by Audi, and very new.

"Four-wheel drive," he said, smiling up at me as he started the engine. Then he tossed his cigar into the street. It landed within inches of the ashes of my *polemica.*

"Four-wheel drive," he repeated. "In these mountains one must take every precaution." Then he flicked the switch that closed his window and drove off.

For a moment I thought back to September, when life had seemed simple and *calcio* had been only a matter of scoring goals. Then I crossed the street and climbed the dark stairway to my cold and empty apartment.

Over the next three weeks we lost away to Cremonese, 2–1 (goal by Bonomi on a penalty kick); beat Palermo at home, 1–0 (a first goal, in his fifth match for us, by Spinesi); and played a 0–0 draw *in casa* against Chievo Verona. De Juliis remained our *portiere.* We had six teams beneath us in *la classifica,* but even the bottom one was within four points. Thin ice, indeed; but we had no choice except to skate on.

In the Chievo match Luca D'Angelo had been injured in a jarring collision with an opposing forward. No ill intent involved, but Luca had clearly gotten the worst of it. Nonetheless, he had insisted on playing out the full ninety minutes and had done so with a grimace but with no loss of effectiveness.

On the following Tuesday he arrived for training early, bearing a large manila envelope. Inside were X rays he'd had taken at the Pescara hospital the day before. They clearly indicated a fractured jaw. He'd played the last half hour Sunday with a broken jaw, yet not a word of complaint.

In Pescara some tentative wiring of the broken bone had been done, but he was clearly in need of further medical attention and, just as clearly, would be unable to eat solid food – much less play – for some time to come.

When Jaconi arrived, Luca approached him and showed him the X rays. Jaconi held each plate up to the sun and stared at it with what he seemed to assume was the practiced gaze of a radiologist.

Then, his face turning the dark red that accompanied his most rabid anger, he hurled the plates to the dirt below and began bellowing at top volume.

"Sei una fica! Una fica di strada! Un pompino viglacco!" You're a cunt! A filthy slut! A cowardly cocksucker!

Luca calmly bent over and picked up his X-ray films before any further damage was done to them.

"Vattene!" Jaconi yelled. Get out! Beat it! Keep out of my sight!

It was not until dinner that I dared ask Osvaldo what, other than his ill-disguised contempt for D'Angelo, had triggered his rage.

To my surprise, he explained it quite calmly. Even more to my surprise, he appeared to consider both his reaction and explanation perfectly rational. Luca should not have gone to the hospital in Pescara. Luca should have waited until he returned to Castel di Sangro and had the X rays done here.

Here, the radiologist could have showed them to the team physician, who could have showed them to Osvaldo, who would have viewed the fracture as so insignificant – after all, the bone was not sticking through the skin! – that he would have told D'Angelo that the X rays had been negative and ordered him to train as usual.

Confronted by X rays that showed the fracture so clearly, however, he could not do so, and he knew D'Angelo had known he would not be able to do so, and that was why the *fica comunista* – communist cunt – had gone to the Pescara hospital in the first place.

Well, Osvaldo said, if D'Angelo was afraid to play a man's game, no one would make him. He could spend the rest of the season *in panchina* or *tribuna*. Osvaldo said that back in November he had tried to ship D'Angelo out to *C1* because he, Osvaldo, could see that Luca lacked the *grinta* necessary for a full season at Castel di Sangro.

He'd been overruled by Gravina and Signor Rezza, and in the wake of the Addo brouhaha he'd not fought them as hard as he should have. But this craven behavior on D'Angelo's part – actually going to get his own broken jaw X-rayed the day after he'd played a full match despite sustaining the injury – this should convince any-one who might be still on the fence – me included, Jaconi warned, waving a finger at me – that, like all communists, D'Angelo lacked *carattere*.

Later that night I received a fax from Coach Rongen. It said, *Your man is still on the sidelines, so we're making an offer for Walter Zenga in-stead*. Three days later it was announced that Zenga would leave Padova for Boston, where he would receive a salary of $500,000 for the season. Lotti, who was ranked higher than Zenga in the *Corriere dello Sport* goalkeeper rankings, and who also was seven years younger, would have gone to America for one-tenth of that.

Lotti took the news better than I did, telling me not to worry, thanking me for trying, even giving me a solid gold pen as a sign of his appreciation. *"Sta' calmo, Joe. Sta' calmo. Mi adatto."* Stay calm, he was telling me. He would land on his feet once again. He had *la risolutezza,* he said: strength of purpose. I didn't doubt that, and for the sake of the squad – which by this time was also for my own sake – I was glad he was staying. Now if only Jaconi *rivedrebbe –* would see the light.

Frankly, the player about whom I worried more was Gigi Prete. All season, he'd been the weakest among our starting defenders, but his experience had counted for something, both on the field and in the locker room. But he'd become the newest of the regulars at Mar-cella's because his wife, Vanessa, had not returned from Chile after Christmas.

On the field he'd never recovered from his execrable showing in Cosenza. He'd had to be removed in favor of Franceschini and was not even *in panchina* for the following week's folly against Foggia. He'd played a full match, without distinction, at Cremona but was again excluded against Palermo and came on only for the final twelve minutes of our scoreless draw with Chievo.

One night at Marcella's it occurred to me that Gigi might want to use my fax machine in order to keep in closer contact with Vanessa. She'd been gone now for more than six weeks, telephone rates between Italy and Chile were not cheap, and Gigi was not one of our higher-paid players, earning perhaps $35,000 for the season. So I told him that anytime he wished, I'd give him the key to my apartment and he could go there and send a fax to Vanessa in total privacy and I would simply keep the cost on my bill.

He looked up from the empty coffee cup at which he'd been staring disconsolately and stubbed out his umpteenth cigarette. He smiled, but only wanly.

"*Grazie, Joe, ma non è necessario.*" Thanks, but it's not necessary.

Ah, merda! Shit! I suddenly realized what must be going on: a marital crisis of some sort. Obviously, it was none of my business, and I immediately felt foolish for having even made the offer, which had put him in the embarrassing position of having to decline what had seemed, at face value, a true favor.

"Well," I said, rising quickly from the table, "when you speak to Vanessa next, please give her my warm regards."

"*Certo, Joe,*" and he gave me a half wave as I departed.

I believe it was the next day, though it might have been the day after, that I arrived early at Marcella's for lunch, walking in at the same time as the postal worker who delivered what passed for Express Mail in Castel di Sangro.

"*Prete,*" he called out, holding up an envelope. Marcella signed for it, as was the custom. The players had a good deal of personal mail – which, for one reason or another, they did not want *La Società* poring over – delivered to Marcella's. Even when Nancy sent me something express, I used Marcella's address because it was far more likely that there would be someone to sign for it there than at my seldom-occupied apartment.

"*Aaah! Bene, bene,*" Marcella said, examining the envelope and grinning. "*Un espresso da Vanessa.*" An express letter from Vanessa. Certainly, this would boost the spirits of Gigi, about whose well-being she fretted as if he were one of her own sons.

The postman, however, as he took the receipt, said, "*Guarda il mittente.*" Look at the return address. "*Non è l'America del Sud ma è*

Roma!" And it was true. Vanessa had sent Gigi an express letter from Rome, although, according to him, she was still in South America with her sick sister.

Marcella blanched. She threw a hand to one cheek. *"Mamma mia! Che cosa significa?"* What does this mean?

"It means Vanessa is in Roma, not Santiago," I said.

"O, Joe, questa è una brutta notizia." This is bad news. I tended to agree. There could have been a perfectly plausible explanation that would have turned the letter into good news, but in domestic matters Marcella's instinct seemed infallible.

Her hands were trembling now as she held the envelope. *"Che guaio! Che guaio!"* she repeated. This was big trouble.

Gigi did not turn up for lunch at Marcella's that day, so I never learned precisely when, where, or how the envelope had been delivered to him. And of course I never mentioned that I'd seen it. If he was telling me his wife was in Chile, it would not do for me to say that I knew her to be in Rome.

But during the last few days before our departure for the March 9 match at Ravenna, Gigi seemed to come thoroughly unglued. At training he was distracted, unfocused, withdrawn. The legs were still there but the *cuore* was not, and his mind seemed many miles away.

At the Wednesday training session, two days before our departure for Ravenna, I wrote in my notebook, *Gigi is either pissed purple or scared shitless, but in either case* calcio *does not seem to be the cause. Trouble with Vanessa? More and more, I have to think so.*

Right for the wrong reasons, one might say.

Gigi ate at Marcella's on Thursday night and once again lingered after the meal, as did I. Not feeling that the question of Vanessa was one I should raise, I asked instead if he felt, as I did, that his play had deteriorated in recent weeks.

During the *andata* he had played in eighteen of our nineteen matches, more than any other defender on the team, and although his 5.92 composite rating was the lowest among them, he'd at least been consistent, never receiving below a 5.5. In the five matches of the *ritorno,* however, he'd played enough to receive a rating in only two: a 5 in Cosenza and a 6 at Cremonese.

He shrugged, as if this were a matter of scant importance. Then, abruptly, he launched into a tirade against Jaconi, *"una testa vuota, una testa di zucca"* – a fathead, a pumpkin head – who he felt posed the greatest impediment to the squad's hopes of *la salvezza*.

"But, Gigi," I said, coming to the defense of my neighbor, "isn't it always true that when a team is near the bottom, the players blame the manager and the manager blames the players? Just like everyone wants to take credit at the top?"

"No!" he said with almost startling vehemence. It had not been like this at any other club he'd ever played for, and he'd played for some bad ones through the years. Jaconi was far and away, *senza dubbio,* the worst manager for whom he'd ever played. He was *falso,* a highly derogatory term whose English meanings included false, deceitful, and fake.

But it wasn't only Jaconi, Gigi hastened to say. The entire ambience of Castel di Sangro was the same: counterfeit, bogus, not at all what it appeared on the surface. Underneath, it was *sordido,* especially *La Società,* and most especially that *arruffone* and *arruso,* Gravina. (It did not take me long to learn that the first word meant "swindler," but it was weeks before anyone could or would explain that the second was, in Sicily, about the most offensive term one man could use to describe another: a homosexual who received pleasure from the sensation of having a penis thrust into his rectum.)

Out of breath from his torrid denunciations, Gigi asked me to pass him my notebook. I handed it to him and he drew a sketch.

CASTEL DI SANGRO

VERO

Its meaning seemed plain enough: What was true could fit easily into one very small portion of the surrounding *cazzate,* or, bullshit that to him was Castel di Sangro Calcio.

But he wasn't finished. On the next page he printed:

$$JACONI = FALSO \; n.2$$
$$GRAVINA = FALSO \; n.1$$

Then, under Gravina's name, just so there could be no possible mistake, he drew an arrow and where the arrow ended he printed, PEZZO DI MERDA. Piece of shit.

He tapped the name JACONI with my pen. *"Un bugiardo, Joe. Un falso amico."* A liar. A false friend.

Then he started jabbing at the GRAVINA he had printed. *"A lui,"* he said, his voice suddenly rising, *"dico solo 'mortacci tua.'"* To him, I say only *mortacci tua.* I never did obtain a precise translation of this phrase, which was of Roman rather than Sicilian origin, but it ranked right up (or down) there with *arruso* as a verbalization fraught with consequence. If you think of someone telling you to fuck your dead mother and then the corpses of all the other dead members of your family, you would have the general idea.

"In June," Gigi said, "when the season is over, then we can speak the truth. You remember: In June I will tell you the whole truth, and then you will know many things you do not know now and you will feel differently about many people."

He rose quickly, put on his winter jacket, said a quick *ciao,* and was gone. An angry man. But what eluded me completely was how terrified he also must have been.

28

At ten o'clock the next morning – the Friday we were to leave for Sunday's match in Ravenna – a squadron of law enforcement officials composed of Italian Criminalpol and Interpol agents, directed by members of a special anti-Mafia task force based in Rome, kicked in the door of Gigi's apartment, handcuffed him, and whisked him off to the notorious Regina Coeli prison in Rome.

He was charged with being a member of an international ring, based in Chile, which allegedly had smuggled more than $25 million worth of cocaine into Italy. Vanessa had already been arrested. She in fact had been arrested on *December 30* at the central train station in Rome while disembarking from a Milan express, a fact that Gigi had been aware of since it happened and news that he had shared immediately with Gravina and his closest friend on the team, Giacomo Galli.

Far from lingering at the bedside of a sick sister, Vanessa had left Santiago the day after Christmas, returning to Italy by a circuitous route that had taken her through Brussels and Amsterdam and then to Milan. When arrested in Rome, she was found to have in her possession 1.5 kilograms of pure, uncut cocaine. She'd immediately been incarcerated in a women's prison in Rome, where she remained, denied bail and undergoing persistent interrogation.

In a raid timed to coincide with Gigi's arrest, additional law enforcement agents, equipped with a search warrant, had entered the home of Gravina. Whether he'd been tipped in advance was never determined, and maybe it was only coincidence, but on that particular morning Gravina was not to found at his home. He'd driven to Rome, in fact, and it was later learned that apparently he'd consulted with lawyers who would be able to defend him if any criminal action was brought against him.

The agents, in any event, scoured both his home and the offices of *La Società*, seizing strongboxes and safes that a spokesman said "were believed to contain information relevant to the investigation." One report described the Gravina home as having been "turned upside down" in the search.

When finally located later in the day, Gravina was not arrested but received an *avviso di garanzia* – an official warning that he was under criminal investigation. The anti-Mafia task force director, Dr. Nicola Cavaliere, said at a press conference that Gravina faced "grave accusations" to the effect that he had "aided and abetted" the smuggling ring. In response to a question, Dr. Cavaliere said that both Gigi and Gravina were believed to be "significant members" of the criminal enterprise.

Authorities disclosed also that undercover agents posing as *tifosi* had been working in Castel di Sangro and at the discotheques in nearby Roccaraso for several months and that since January 1 wiretaps had been placed on Gravina's telephones.

An additional investigation had been launched into the possible connection between cocaine for which Gigi might have been the source and the recent deaths by heart attack of Franco Grava, forty-three, and Giovanni Pennacchioni, thirty-seven, two former Castel di Sangro players known to have been his close associates.

We were, then, rather a flustered group as we boarded the bus for Ravenna at 1 P.M. The press had assembled in numbers never before seen in the town – not even for the debut of Robert Ponnick – and all gates surrounding the stadium had been locked, driving the journalists and cameramen into a frenzy.

Three guards stood at the parking lot gate and granted entrance to the cars of the players, as television soundmen tried to push microphones through closed windows, reporters shouted questions, and cameramen swung their heavy equipment like clubs. I'd been walking, but fortunately Spinosa picked me up a few hundred yards short of the gates.

"Che casino," he said, shaking his head. A hell of a mess.

"E' vero?" I asked. Is it true?

"Ogni ver non è ben detto," he replied, taking his eyes off the road long enough to hold mine with his own as he said it. This was a proverb that meant, All truths are not to be told. It was his polite way of telling me not to ask stupid questions, or at least not to expect truthful answers if I did.

Once we'd boarded the bus, Cei went up and down the aisle, making certain that everyone understood that for the moment the answer to any and all questions, no matter who asked them, was to be simply, No comment.

In earlier times the bus would have provided at least a temporary refuge from the chaos, but not in the day of the cell phone. Every player had one, and it seemed that all were ringing simultaneously from the moment we departed from the parking lot. Ravenna was on the coast, fifty kilometers north of Rimini, which meant that this would be only a five-hour ride, but even that allowed wives, girlfriends, and others to call the players each time a news broadcast contained a new *fatto* or *quasi fatto* or *voce:* and no one aboard seemed able to distinguish among the three.

In the first hour came word that Gigi would remain in prison for three to five years before even receiving a trial. Because he was considered high risk in terms of the likelihood that he would flee, as well as because of the seriousness of the charges, at no time would bail be a possibility. This meant that none of us on the bus might ever see him again. For all practical purposes, he was as dead and gone as Pippo and Danilo.

The second hour brought reports that the wiretap on Gravina's phones had enabled police to compile a list of the allegedly extensive promises he'd made to Gigi in return for Vanessa's continued refusal to name names. Beyond any question, a prosecutor said, Gravina was part of a *coinvolgimento,* which was to say, he was "involved."

In the third hour there was further amplification of the extent of Gravina's alleged involvement. In one phone call to Gigi he had said, according to authorities, "Don't worry. We can fix this." That he had not managed to do so by the night before, when Gigi had cursed him so vilely at Marcella's, seemed to me at least a partial explanation for the player's anger.

There was a *Società* official riding in the front of the bus. This man was essentially a *cammello,* a camel who carried water in his hump for whenever Gravina might grow thirsty. Throughout the ride, this assistant was apparently maintaining close contact with Gravina.

During the fourth hour he came back to my seat and said it was desired that I grant a cell-phone interview to the Rome newspaper *La Repubblica.* Desired by whom? I asked. Cei had made it very clear that "no comment" was the order of the day. The *cammello* did not answer. Instead, he put a finger to his lips and, raising his eyes skyward, jerked his head up and down sharply, as if his shirt collar were too tight.

"Non capito," I said. I was not especially fond of this *cammello.*

Then he leaned down so close to me that I thought he was going to bite my earlobe. *"Dall'alto,"* he whispered, so softly that I was not sure I'd heard him.

"Dall'alto?" I said in a normal tone of voice. The *cammello* jumped as if he'd just been goosed and looked around the bus frantically to see who might have overheard my indiscretion.

Rimedio had, for one. He leaned across the aisle and said, "Joe. From high," and pointed upward. Then Spinosa, who was seated behind me, leaned forward to say softly, *"Supponiamo che sia il signor Rezza."* Let's assume it's Signor Rezza.

At the sight of Spinosa's lips mouthing the name of *una persona di cui non verrà fatto il nome* – a person who shall be nameless – as if this were something out of the Talmud, the *cammello* threw his hands up to cover his eyes.

By now the whole farce was becoming irritating. I said I would take my orders from Cei and Cei alone. The *cammello* immediately beckoned the captain and when Cei arrived whispered a few words in his ear. I saw Cei shrug. Then he turned to me with a thumbs-up gesture. "Is okay, Joe. This one. *La Repubblica.*"

I guess he considered me reliable. I had after all persuaded him that, at least in the mind of F. Scott Fitzgerald, both West Egg and East Egg lay to the east of New York City.

More to the point, if this was at Signor Rezza's behest, arrangements undoubtedly had been made to ensure that the reporter would ask no questions that would prompt me to say anything injurious to anyone.

I was handed a cell phone within minutes. The interviewer was already on the line, or whatever one is on via cell phone. He spoke no English, so the entire conversation took place in Italian as the crowd around my seat began to grow.

As it appeared in the next morning's paper, the interview, translated into English, read:

Q – You wished to tell a happy story, but now . . .

A – I tell the reality, so I will also do this time.

Q – Before this, did you think there was a curse associated with Castel di Sangro being in *Serie B?*

A – No, I thought it was a miracle. I still do. However, we suffered a terrible tragedy in December, with the deaths of two players in an auto accident. Now we have another unhappy experience. For sure, it is no longer a fairy tale. Right now, it seems more of a nightmare. But I have faith in the valor of this team, which is simply extraordinary.

Q – Do you know well the player arrested?

A – Gigi is a special friend. A friend who is in trouble now. And I would do anything possible to help him. I had dinner with him only last night. I believe he is innocent and I know he is a fine player. I'm sure he'll soon have a chance to demonstrate both.

Q – Did you know that since December his wife was in jail?

A – I had not seen Vanessa during this time. I thought she was in Chile. I didn't push with questions, because it did not seem my business. I am just very sorry for Gigi and his wife.

Q – And what is the reaction of the squad?

A – They are very determined, very concentrated on the match in Ravenna. If anything, this has even increased their desire for *la salvezza.*

Well, the last answer was obviously bullshit. The Ravenna match was the furthest thing from every mind. But it was true I would have done what I could to help Gigi. While he had been far from candid with me, I'd grown fond of him nonetheless. Besides, innocent until proven guilty and all that.

By the fifth hour of the trip, I was told that radio stations were broadcasting the "news" that I'd claimed to have proof of Gigi's innocence. (And, indeed, there was a headline the next morning: THE AMERICAN KNOWS THE TRUTH: PRETE IS INNOCENT!)

Well, that was simply normal Italian journalistic exaggeration. But what struck me as odd at first – and then didn't – was that the interviewer had not asked a single question about Gravina. If he'd been going to, I soon realized, the *cammello* would not have been urging me to do the interview. Indeed, it would never have been arranged *dall'alto* – from on high.

Toward the end of the ride, I thought back to my dinner with Gigi and Vanessa in the fall, and to Gigi's quick response when I'd asked casually how he had come to meet Vanessa: *Why do you want to know?*

What had he thought? That I was an undercover Interpol agent pretending to love *il calcio* in order that I might track him and Vanessa more closely? That hardly seemed likely. But then again, neither did anything else.

Darkness was falling and we were already drawing close to our hotel when Roberto Alberti beckoned me to sit beside him. Since saying *grazie* to me in Pescara, the veteran with the soft voice and expressionless face had treated me with discernibly more warmth than before, but we'd still not actually had a conversation. Nonetheless, I responded, as much out of curiosity as courtesy.

As soon as I was seated, he started talking, though continuing to look straight ahead all the while and speaking so quietly that no one even a single row behind us, or in front, could have guessed what was taking place.

"You gave your ticket to my son," he said. "Since then I think of you as family, and now I talk and you just listen, as if I am telling a story to my family. It started five years ago when Gigi was in Calabria and had just married Vanessa. Her family had the cocaine in Chile and wanted the *collegamento,* the pipeline, to Italy. Gigi was a *C1* player with no money, no future, and not such a brain. But big balls.

"You have seen Reggio Calabria. No money stays in the city, but the smuggling of drugs there is on a large scale. Big people run things. Giacomo Lauro for many years. Gigi maybe made some friends that he should not have.

"You will notice that after Reggina Gigi never stayed more than one year with any club. People talk. Things happen. Maybe he's not worth the risk. But some men need risk. Did you know that Gabriele flies a helicopter? It is kept in Pescara. No one will ride with him more than once.

"There is risk in the helicopter if it is flown in reckless fashion. There is risk in sex with other men's wives. And of course there is risk in cocaine. But with cocaine the money is *illimitato* – virtually infinite. So Gigi stays a second year in Castel di Sangro. Why? To ride in the helicopter? For our success in *Serie B?* You have seen Gigi play many times. You also have seen Vanessa. Which one do you think Gravina prefers?

"And if a man has *la cocaina* to give him better sex with the women and if he has the money from *la cocaina* – then this man can feel *al settimo cielo,* like he's on top of the world, in seventh heaven. And that is without even taking the drug. I understand you feel also that way – briefly – if you take it.

"For a long time, people are watching, very quietly. But one day they act. Vanessa goes to prison, and one point five kilos of *la cocaina* does not arrive to those expecting it. That is very much money *andato in fumo,* gone up in smoke. This makes problems. Suddenly one looks for the exit. But maybe it's closed.

"Do you know? As soon as Gravina learns Vanessa is arrested – and this is at the same time Gigi learns, which is December – he tries to sell Gigi to Avellino in *C1.* But this only makes Gigi angry. He tells Gabriele, 'You think you solve your problem by getting rid of me? No, not until Vanessa is free. And if ever I have a problem myself, you will, too.'

"So maybe, Joe, you are wonder what will happen. Do not wonder too much. And there is no point in asking questions, for those who answer do not know and those who know do not tell. Besides, it is probable that much has not yet been decided.

"But did you know that fifty years ago, when Signor Rezza first came to Castel di Sangro from the south, he arrived on the back of a mule? It is true. And if Gigi's freedom can be arranged, Gigi, too, might ride through Castel di Sangro on a mule. But not like the young Signor Rezza – more like Jesus. Indeed, we will have to have palm leaves brought up from the south to line his path.

"Also, did you know that Dante wrote all of his great work after he was exiled from Firenze? He made the mistake of being on the wrong side in politics and was forced to leave the city, and for twenty years, until his death, he stayed away. Now in Firenze they claim Dante as their own, but to me Ravenna has the stronger claim. After much wandering, he settled here and here he completed *La Divina Commedia,* and here he is buried. This is true, but in Firenze they do not like to tell this truth to *i turisti.* But, you, Joe, are not *un turista* anymore, and so I tell you these things. Ah, look: now we arrive at the hotel."

All the while, Alberti had been starting straight ahead, as if watching firemen arrive at a blaze. Never once had he varied the volume, pitch, or inflection of his voice. And his timing – as on the field – had been impeccable, for now everyone was standing and moving around and preparing to get off the bus. Alberti was a man of subtle skills.

Given our distractions, one could say we played a decent match. We lost, only 1–0, on a goal that Jaconi blamed on Altamura but that I thought had been more the fault of De Juliis.

We still had five teams beneath us on Sunday night, but we were the only one with a starting defender in prison and an *ex-presidente* openly suspected of involvement in a $25-million-a-year drug-smuggling operation.

29

And matters worsened. *Il Corriere della Sera,* which along with *La Repubblica* was one of the two most widely respected newspapers in the country, reported that Gravina was under investigation not only for "aiding and abetting" the smuggling of *la cocaina* into Italy but allegedly for providing it to certain of his players for use in various *feste a luci rosse,* or red-light parties, more commonly referred to in English as orgies.

These parties, the newspaper said, had featured *his* German girl-friend, whose husband just happened to be in prison for drug smuggling. *Il Corriere* went so far as to identify by name the village where the parties had taken place – Alfedena, only ten kilometers from Castel di Sangro but in a direction not commonly traveled.

Also on Monday, Giacomo Galli went to the Castel di Sangro hospital for treatment of a sprained ankle, which he'd incurred during the final training session before the match in Ravenna.

Because Giacomo was known to be the only player in whom Gigi had confided – although no one besides the two of them knew how much had been said or what names had been mentioned – a tremendous sense of suspense was building in anticipation of his return to the training field on Tuesday.

Unfortunately, he never made it. Galli was given an injection by an unsterile needle and immediately developed blood poisoning so severe that it threatened his life. He had to be rushed to a private clinic in Rome, where he was said to be in critical condition, by no means certain to live.

In announcing this, Gravina used the phrase *incidente inevitabile,* or inescapable accident, as if it were another tragic automobile crash. But this was not Burkina Faso or Bangladesh. And this was the late twentieth century, not the nineteenth. Granted, the hospital in Castel di Sangro might not have been state-of-the-art, but one still might have presumed the use of sterile needles on its premises. And this dirty needle had been used by a Castel di Sangro physician known to be an avid supporter of the team. And used on the one Castel di Sangro player whom authorities might have wished to question regarding the extent of his knowledge of the activities of the drug-smuggling ring with which Gravina had been publicly said to have been "involved."

Given these circumstances, Gravina's use of the term "inescapable accident" in regard to the blood poisoning had a certain jarring, off-key quality to it, as if somehow the poisoning had been the work of *il destino,* or fate, instead of a horrific and inexplicable error committed by an experienced local physician. The third possibility – that Giacomo's misfortune had been the result of neither accident nor error – was one that no one even wished to whisper.

Thus, once again it was a spate of unsettling news that greeted the players upon their Tuesday return to a Lilliput that no longer seemed quite so quaint or charming. The most recent medical bulletin from the unspecified private clinic in Rome to which Giacomo had been taken was that his chances of surviving were *una probabilità su due,* or fifty-fifty. In addition, it was understood that only Gravina was in contact with the clinic's unnamed director and thus would be the sole source of medical news for the foreseeable future.

"Do you see, Joe," Luca D'Angelo said, "why I get my X rays in Pescara?"

I made a brief tally: from the original squad of twenty who had been here when I'd arrived in September, three had been sold to teams in *C1,* two were dead, one was in prison, and one was in critical condition.

It was only March, yet one-third of the *ragazzi* were dead or gone, and the team's president, having resigned, now faced the threat of serious criminal charges. It seemed to me that the oral surgeon, whom I was confident had never used an unsterile needle on a patient, and his inscrutable *padrone* on the mountaintop had more serious concerns than my occasional, ill-tempered *polemiche*.

Nor was life tranquil within the confines of Via Peschiera 10. On Wednesday Jaconi spent forty-five minutes of training berating Antonello for having been at fault on the goal Ravenna had scored the previous Sunday. The attack was angry and highly personal, with Osvaldo concluding by saying that from that point forward, Antonello should go to day care with his four-year-old son instead of coming to training.

Antonello left the field in a rage and went straight home. By the time I got there, Sabrina was already standing in the hallway outside my apartment, terrified that in his fury Antonello would say or do something to Jaconi that would forever end his career.

"Talk to him, Joe! You're the only one he will listen to!"

"But Sabrina," I said. "That's because I'm the only one he can't understand!"

In such a state of disarray, we lost at home, 0–2, to Empoli. Again, a third consecutive match without a goal, and the loss dropped us into a three-way tie for nineteenth place, only one point above rock-bottom Palermo.

Then spring arrived, announcing itself in the Abruzzo a few days later by way of a storm that brought the heaviest snowfall of the year to Castel di Sangro. Osvaldo looked out his window and saw that it would be impossible to train here for the remainder of the week. And so on the morning of Wednesday, March 26, we departed by bus for Padova – in the north but at sea level, where no snow had fallen and where the grass was rumored to be already turning green. (We would play in Padova on Saturday because the next day would be Easter Sunday, the only day of the year in Italy on which religion took precedence over *calcio*.)

On this bus ride I learned that, to a man, the players were anticipating Gigi's imminent release. On what grounds, I kept asking, demonstrating over and over again, and in the most embarrassing way, my naïveté. No one, of course, wanted to come right out and say it, but eventually it seeped through my constricted American view of criminal-justice systems that Signor Rezza could arrange it with a phone call.

For Gigi alone, he might not have lifted a finger. Certainly for Vanessa he had not. But for Gabriele, father of Maria Teresa's two sons? The equation seemed simple: Either Gigi came out or there was a risk that Gabriele might go in.

The weather in Padova was glorious, our suburban hotel an unexpected delight, and the training field, which was within walking distance, one of the finest we'd seen all year.

The players were ambling toward the field in twos and threes, preparing for the day's first training, and I was standing at its edge – taking note, as it happened, of how many daisies were already springing up amid the grass – when, at precisely 10:30 on the morning of Holy Thursday, March 27, I heard the chirp of Osvaldo's cell phone.

I was standing less than twenty yards from him and heard him murmuring without being able to understand the words. The conversation lasted less than a minute. Then he slipped the phone back into his pocket and walked toward me.

"Gigi è libero," he said. Neither the tone of his voice nor his facial expression conveyed any emotion whatsoever. But Gigi had been set free.

"Non è possibile!" I exclaimed.

Osvaldo shrugged. Then he lifted his eyes toward the sky. *"Dio fa i miracoli,"* he said. God works wonders.

"Qualche divinità," I said. Some divinity. *"Dio o il signor Rezza."* Either God or Signor Rezza.

He looked at me sharply. Then he said, "Gigi is the good news. Signor Rezza transmits some bad news also."

"Che c'è ora?" I asked, with visions of a sheet being pulled up over the eyes of Giacomo Galli. What is it now?

"D'ora in poi, Lotti gioca." From now on, Rezza had ordered, Lotti plays.

"Evviva!" I shouted. Hurray! It may have been inappropriate, but that news caused me far more jubilation than did the announcement of Gigi's release.

Osvaldo looked at me, then placed a strong hand on my shoulder and said, *"Buona Pasqua."* Happy Easter.

And then he went off to tell the squad.

· · ·

Lotti was magnificent in his return. *"Il Super-Lotti,"* one paper called him the next day. Another headline proclaimed LOTTI: GRANDE PROTAGONISTA, UN VERO GIGANTE! Great hero and true giant.

His indomitability under constant pressure – in his first appearance in four and a half months – kept us in the match until Luca Albieri (the young man who maneuvered airplanes with his cell phone and who'd not played enough to even earn a *voto* since November 10) came off the bench and scored his first goal of the season to give us a 1–1 draw. "They have the legs of pianos but the hearts of lions," one Padova journalist wrote.

The next day, Easter, prompted the people of Castel di Sangro to refer to 1997 as *L'anno delle due risurrezioni:* the year of the two resurrections. Forget the *lazzarati*. This was the real thing: Gigi was free! The rock had been rolled back from the tomb! Could there be any doubt now? Could there be any doubt ever again? Miracles *were* forever.

Tuesday – it was April Fool's Day in America – was wintry, the sky still spitting snow. A crowd even larger than the one that had gathered on the day of his arrest pressed against the gates of the stadium parking lot, awaiting Gigi's triumphant return.

To some extent, the welcome had been orchestrated by Gravina, who was openly delighted by Gigi's return. (Galli, incidentally, was said to have taken a sharp turn for the better within hours of the news of Gigi's release.) Children of *Società* officials were given signs to carry that said WE LOVE YOU, GIGI! and WE NEVER LOST FAITH.

I'd walked down after lunch at Marcella's and arrived at the stadium well before training time. As it happened, I was standing in the parking lot when I spotted Gigi's nondescript car approaching. No donkey, no palm fronds, just the same old battered Fiat. Quickly, and with minimum fuss, he was admitted by the men at the gate.

He parked about five feet from where I was standing. When he got out of his car, I was the first person he saw and the first person to see him. Instinctively, I rushed toward him and we embraced. I was surprised by how happy I was.

I told him I was glad he was free, and he told me he appreciated what I'd said about wanting to help him, and then the mob was upon us, camera lenses and microphones protruding.

Many newspapers the next day ran the picture of the two of us hugging, with a caption or headline that said, DA MCGINNISS IL PRIMO ABBRACCIO. From me, the first hug. The timing had been accidental, but the feeling was real.

Within moments Gravina arrived. Immediately *he* grabbed Gigi and, spurred by eager photographers, spun him around like a dancing partner, holding him for the longest time in a ridiculously tight embrace. Only God knows what feelings passed between the two, or which of them was the more relieved.

In any case, my prior joy evaporated and I suddenly felt soiled and cynical and angry. Knowing there was no place here for such emotions on this day, I walked out of the parking lot and back to my apartment. Two resurrections? The Prodigal Son? Or the fine but unclean hand of Signor Rezza.

It was not that I begrudged Gigi his freedom. And I could understand the joy of both players and townspeople. Pippo and Danilo had been snatched from us suddenly and violently and could never return. Giacomo, too, had vanished overnight under circumstances that could most charitably be described as mysterious. Thus, Gigi was the true *lazzarato,* his prompt and unlikely return to us standing as proof that all loss need not be permanent.

Yet the mood of unfettered celebration seemed, at best, premature. In writing the order for Gigi's release, the examining magistrate had stressed that "the evidence was sufficient to require the arrest." He had discharged Gigi, he wrote, only because "there is no certainty that this evidence, *in its current state* [emphasis added], would necessarily lead to conviction at trial." That hardly seemed a ringing affirmation of innocence.

And prosecutors made clear that the investigation of both Gigi and Gravina would continue. Indeed, they suggested that no inferences regarding the guilt or innocence of either party should be drawn from the action of the court. And, I, of course, could not suddenly banish from my mind the detailed account whispered to me by Alberti on the bus.

In addition, there were the two "suspicious" (i.e., drug induced?) heart attacks suffered by close friends of Gigi's, which, in this gleeful atmosphere, nobody wanted to talk about. But there was no denial from any quarter that the "red-light parties" had taken place in Alfedena as described, with or without cocaine supplied by Gigi. And no doubts were raised about the presumed guilt of Vanessa, nor in these festive moments was any concern over her continued incarceration voiced by anyone, not even by Gigi.

Moreover, whatever might prove to be the extent of Gravina's criminal involvement, if any, it was indisputable that he had known of Vanessa's arrest since the first of the year and had offered assurances (during wiretapped conversations) of "help."

Yet between first learning from Gigi that Vanessa had been apprehended with more than a kilogram of cocaine in her possession – cocaine she was attempting to smuggle into Italy from South America – he had permitted Gigi to keep playing.

Inarguably, in a court of law, the presumption of innocence exists, but in the world of *calcio* the appearance of impropriety, as well as the notion that one should not act in such a way as to "bring the game into disrepute," as the English somewhat quaintly express it, is an equally relevant concept.

Once Vanessa had been arrested on such a significant charge, it seemed to me, Gravina could have chosen one of three courses: (a) he could have made a full report to the *calcio* Federation and asked for guidance concerning Gigi's continued eligibility; (b) respecting Gigi's wish to keep the matter private as long as possible, he could simply have announced that Gigi was taking leave from the team for personal reasons but that his salary would continue to be paid in full and that he would return at the earliest possible moment; (c) he could have advised Jaconi privately of what had happened and instructed that while Gigi be permitted to continue training with the team, he must not be allowed to play in any matches until it became clear that he was not under investigation.

Instead – and here the question of whether Gravina had been involved in the drug smuggling directly or whether his alleged *coinvolgimento* had begun only at the time Gigi first made him aware of the facts was irrelevant – the *patron* and *ex-presidente* had chosen a more furtive course: forming a secret alliance with Gigi.

Meanwhile, Gigi had played in seven matches since Vanessa's arrest, while his teammates, team supporters, league officials, and the millions all across Italy who wagered on *calcio* through such lotteries as *Totocalcio* and *Totogol* were kept in the dark, unaware that the wife of a still-active player had been arrested for smuggling cocaine.

Indeed, Gravina also had permitted Gigi to lie about Vanessa's whereabouts, doing or saying nothing that would contradict the "sick sister" story that so many believed and because of which so many expressed to Gigi genuine, if misplaced, sympathy.

Gravina's actions did not seem to me those of a man with clean hands. Gigi, meanwhile, had at the least a less than clean conscience, while Galli had almost died from unclean blood. *La primavera,* or spring, hardly seemed a season of renewal and rebirth – at least not in Castel di Sangro.

But the very next day I received an unexpected letter from an unexpected source, and this did more than anything else could have to restore perspective and to remind me of why I had come here in the first place and of what the true spirit of *calcio* was, or could be. Handwritten and in English, it was from the sister of Pippo Biondi:

> I write to thank you for the love you have shown: the gift of that photo has been an important action for us, because it has proved again how much Filippo had been loved.
>
> His death has caused a terrible sorrow, almost impossible to accept. This tragedy, so violent and so abrupt, has destroyed the serenity among us. It's a sorrow that our mind is able to accept with difficulty.
>
> We remember you continually. We remember you in the words of Pippo. We know a bit of you, and what we know is thanks to him. He spoke of you, of your cleverness and simplicity, of your kindness and helpfulness, continually.
>
> I remember when Filippo told me that this summer he should come in America, in Boston. He was so deeply moved, so light-hearted, because he had never been there and goodness knows what he imaged.
>
> You inspired confidence and a great liking into him, you were a great friend. I remember when my mother and I came to visit him, he was so happy: happy because we were all together, because he was no longer alone, and happy because he wanted to show us his new country, his new team. Even if sometimes he felt alone, he felt good in Castel di Sangro. He liked it too much. He admired the nice people; they were so available. He loved the environment, the mountains, the snow, the clean air. He adored his team, his companions.

Sometimes he was homesick for us. He didn't like lone-liness. He was very sensitive and he suffered too much when we were sad. He always behaved as a father with me, he has always protected me in each moment. It was really a mutual love, admiration and pride, and it's sure that all this will never finish.

It's difficult to accept the loss of a brother so dear, but maybe it's also harder to accept the loss of a son, and you, that you are father, surely will understand it. When I look at my mother's eyes I perceive only a deep sorrow, a pain and sadness which will never disappear from her face.

Pippo was and always be one of the only happiness of her life, now a part of herself is gone. However, we feel his living and strong presence here among us, a strength so deep which makes us to go on, to continue to live.

30

April may be many things in Italy, as elsewhere, but in *Serie B* it is the time when, grammatically, the mood shifts from conditional to indicative and the tense from future to present. It is in April that newspapers start to publish a "Road to Salvation" statistical box, displaying the matches yet to be played by each of the teams for which *salvezza* remains in doubt, and it is when *la stagione lunga* can suddenly seem all too short.

Dissatisfied with the rudimentary nature of the statistical analyses published in the newspapers, I began to devise my own. The most pertinent, I felt, involved no more than totaling the points already won by a given team's future opponents. We were one of six teams at the bottom of the table, only two of which would escape relegation. Each of us had eleven matches to play.

As of April 1, *la classifica* showed the following:

Cesena	29
Palermo	28
Lucchese	28
Cremonese	27
CASTEL DI SANGRO	27
Cosenza	26

This was not especially promising, particularly when one bore in mind that of the eleven matches remaining, three of the relevant teams would play six at home while we and two others would be *in casa* for only five. (And given that our team theme song might well have been "Why Can't We Do It on the Road?" this discrepancy weighed heavily against us.)

But that wasn't the worst part. My relative-strength-of-future-opponent table displayed the worst part:

Cesena	358
Palermo	377
Lucchese	380
Cremonese	382
Cosenza	395
CASTEL DI SANGRO	407

The eleven teams whom we had yet to face a second time had accumulated, collectively, 407 points as of April 1. That was *twelve* more than the team with the next most difficult remaining schedule, Cosenza, a difference that to me did not seem inconsequential. And Cesena, our next opponent, would face opposition that had tallied forty-nine points fewer than ours had.

I showed these figures to Fusco and explained them. He shrugged. *"Eccheffai?"* he said. This was a catch-all Neapolitan response along the lines of, "So, what's one to do?"

I showed them to Lotti. He studied them as I'd seen him study horseracing charts. Finally, he shook his head grimly and said, *"Sì, ci troviamo in difficoltà. Joe, se fossimo un cavallo, io non scommetterei su di noi."* Yes, we're in trouble. If we were a horse, I wouldn't bet on us.

I showed them to Spinosa, and he actually copied them down and then thanked me for having taken the trouble to compile them.

Finally, at Marcella's on Tuesday night, I showed them to Jaconi. I explained them very carefully in order to be certain that he understood what the numbers represented. He listened and looked without changing expression.

Then he looked at me almost as if he were angry. *"E' tempo sprecato,"* he said, pointing to my calculations. This is a waste of time.

"Non è un problema," I said. It's no trouble. I was misreading his mood here, thinking he might be concerned about how long it had taken me to compile the numbers.

But then he tore my paper in half. And he leaned across the table and glared. *"Non andare in cerca di guai,"* he said. Don't go looking for trouble! And with that he was up and out the door.

I decided he must be angry with me because Signor Rezza had ordered him to reinstate Lotti as *portiere*. As if I could so influence Signor Rezza – *magari!* But I felt also that Osvaldo had become over-stressed as a result of the Gigi situation and was no longer seeing things clearly. And I *knew* that virtually everyone else in town, except Gravina and Rezza, was afraid of incurring his wrath.

Therefore, though I had not sought it, I felt that a certain weight of responsibility had come to rest on my shoulders. For who else could see – or would say – that Bonomi had been slumping ever since the Fiorentina deal fell through? That Alberti's form had fallen off badly since the ground thawed? That Spinesi had not yet come close to living up to his billing?

In this frame of mind, I worked myself into a total swivet about the upcoming match against Cesena. We would be playing at home against a team we could jump ahead of in *la classifica,* but only with a win, something we had not enjoyed since Spinesi's lone goal against Palermo in February.

Obviously, I would have to try again with Osvaldo. Maybe my statistics had confused him. This time, I would speak only of names, not of numbers. But for the good of the squad, for our hope of *la salvezza,* he and I would have to put differences aside and have a talk, neighbor to neighbor, man to man, heart to heart. After all, it would be for his good as much as for my own.

Fits of pique I could well understand. This was *calcio,* after all, and I had indulged in a few this season myself. But now necessity cried out for us to follow the path of reason.

Despite their lowly standing, Cesena was a worrisome side. They had fired two managers already this year, but with the third they seemed to be getting it right. Since the newest man had taken over, they'd earned eleven points to our six, moving from four behind us to one in front. And given the difficulty of the rest of our schedule and the comparative ease of theirs, we absolutely *had* to beat them, I felt, in order to maintain any real chance of *salvezza.*

They could be expected to field a 5-4-1 formation. Their most in-timidating player was a big, strong, and exceptionally capable forward from Trieste named Dario Hubner, who'd not yet been given a chance in *Serie A* but whose goal totals for Cesena the past four years had gone from ten to twelve to fifteen to twenty-two.

I spent many hours late at night in my apartment that week, puzzling out the best approach to take against them. By Friday I thought I had it, but I knew that convincing Jaconi would be no easy task.

Nonetheless, on Friday night I approached him again at Marcella's. But even before I could start to explain my lineup choices and preferred tactics for Sunday, Jaconi began pounding the table with his fist. He said there were only two things I needed to know. First, De Juliis was good while Lotti was merely lucky. Second, that "my friend" D'Angelo would remain benched indefinitely because of his poor judgment in having his broken jaw X-rayed professionally, because of his cowardice – which was all the X rays really showed, Jaconi continued to insist – and because of his *modo arrogante,* or arrogant manner.

This seemed to me unadulterated madness. Just as Lotti was currently ranked third by *Il Corriere dello Sport* among all the goalkeepers of *Serie B* (well ahead of Zenga, who had departed Padova for his lucrative contract with the Revolution), Luca D'Angelo stood fourth among all *difensori laterali.* I was convinced that Luca was being punished primarily for his communism, in continued retaliation for Fidel Castro's meeting with the Pope. But I tried to stay calm, imagining how Baggio might handle a situation like this: what Zen techniques he'd employ.

After Osvaldo had spent himself temporarily, I calmly proceeded to explain that on Sunday we should go for the throat of Cesena from the start. Attack, attack, attack, this meant – but at the same time, respecting Hubner, we should reinforce our defense.

It seemed evident to me that we could best accomplish this by employing a 5-3-2 formation: Fusco, Cei, Altamura, D'Angelo, and Franceschini in defense; Bonomi, Martino, and Cristiano in midfield; Spinesi and Russo in attack.

Granted, both Russo and Franceschini had been more frequently used as midfielders so far, but Russo seemed to me a natural forward, while Franceschini, who had great speed and fine ball skills, could play anywhere and, specifically, in this formation, could move up quickly on the flank from his (normally Gigi's) outside defender position.

Larger questions aside, Gigi himself would not be a factor, for he had not yet regained his fitness. The key elements in my strategic plan, therefore, involved the reinsertion of D'Angelo on defense (for he was strong and quick enough to mark Hubner individually) and the utilization of the scrappy and quick Cristiano in midfield.

Mimmo had played an outstanding match against Cesena in November but had been almost a forgotten man ever since, until being used effectively against Padova the week before. The presence of Russo in a forward position would prevent Cesena from ganging up on Spinesi and might allow Gionatha the time and space he needed to score. I'd been over this a dozen times in my mind, and it was sound. By Friday night I'd convinced myself it was necessary.

Jaconi sat, looked, and listened until I'd finished. That in itself was no small triumph. But then, even before he spoke, his thick mustache seemed to bristle, almost as if he were a porcupine sensing danger.

"*Parli sul serio?*" he said, pointing at my sheaf of papers. Are you serious?

"*Oh, sì, altro che!*" Oh yes, absolutely.

"*Dunque, sei un perfetto idiota.*" Well, then, you're an absolute idiot.

He picked up one of my pencils. Pressing so hard I thought he'd break the point, he obliterated the name of D'Angelo. Then, applying only slightly less pressure, he crossed out Cristiano, too. He shook his head, still staring at the paper. Then he wrote in the names of Di Fabio, Alberti, and Michelini and with a sharp arrow pushed Russo back to midfield.

"*Sei centrocampisti,*" he said. Six midfielders. Then he tapped Spinesi's name with the pencil point. "*Solo una punta.*" Only Spinesi up front. Then he put the pencil down, folded his arms, and glared at me. His mustache *was* actually moving as the lip beneath it quivered with rage.

"*Che diritto hai di dirmi cosa devo fare?*" he asked. What right have you got to tell me how to do my job? This was a question to which, under the circumstances, the only correct answer could be "none."

"Osvaldo, I –"

"*Questo non lo sopporto!*" he suddenly shouted. I won't put up with it!

"I'm only –"

"*Fatti gli affari tuoi!*" Mind your own business! Then he leaned back in his chair, cast his eyes toward the heavens as he'd done so often before, and cried out, "*Gesù Cristo! Non so che farne di lui!*" Jesus Christ! I don't know what to do with him! Then he stood, grabbed his coat, and even as he was putting it on, picked up the pencil again and scribbled angrily until one could no longer see the name Lotti.

"Punto e basta!" That's that! And yet one more time he walked through Marcella's kitchen and out the back door.

We managed to beat Cesena anyway, 1–0, and in the least likely fashion imaginable. After eighty-five minutes of some of the dreariest and most frustrating football of the year (although in this category, admittedly, the competition was fierce), Roberto Alberti, who had not scored in his last 160 matches, stretching back over five years, acquired the ball in the Cesena third of the field, dribbled forward while looking for someone to pass to, continued to dribble as he saw no one available, and kept right on dribbling until he found himself at the edge of the penalty area with no Cesena defenders anywhere near him.

He kicked the ball toward the goal. It sailed past the Cesena keeper and into the net. Suddenly what had been yet another afternoon of dispiriting mediocrity (except for Lotti's performance in our goal, where he denied Hubner on several occasions) was transmuted into a vital, if not glorious, win.

Good Lord, first Albieri and now Alberti. We were pulling goals down from the dustiest shelves in the barn. But they counted. And with our win over Cesena (which could have been achieved far more easily if we had used my lineup and formation, though I did not intend to debate this with Jaconi) we leapfrogged over four teams. Now, with thirty points, we had five squads beneath us in the cramped quarters of *la zona terrore.*

No one expected us to add to our total the following week, and we did not. We played at Brescia, the most unpleasant city in the north, against a team that had opened a five-point lead over Lecce at the top of the table. Brescia was clearly going to make one of its periodic returns to *Serie A,* and we were the most insignificant of stepping stones along their way.

The dramatic highlight of the weekend, in fact, came not during the match but at lunch the day before, when a *Società* official rushed into the team dining room at our hotel, waving a just-faxed copy of a story from *La Repubblica.*

CALCIO & COCA: 11 ARRESTI IN CILE the headline said. The story, datelined Santiago, reported that in the "second phase" of Operation Vanessa Diaz, as this particular foray into the international drug wars was now known, eleven members of Vanessa's family had been arrested in one swoop.

According to the story, Vanessa herself had been carrying just the tip of the iceberg. The new report quoted Chilean police as saying that the operation had been designed to smuggle more than $100 million worth of cocaine into Italy, using Vanessa as courier and Gigi as one of the central distributors.

Gigi left the table as soon as he read the fax, and I did not see him again until the next day. When I asked if the new arrests had come as a surprise, he gave me a cold look and said, "No comment." I was beginning to doubt that the "truth talk" he'd promised at season's end would take place.

On the field, after a scoreless first half, we surprisingly took a 1–0 lead at the start of the second on Claudio's first goal (not counting penalties) in almost three months. But we were playing without Cei, who was *squalificato,* and D'Angelo was so weakened by influenza that he should never have even made the trip. Midway through the second half Alberti was sent off for having deliberately blocked a shot with his hand. Once they had the extra man, Brescia ran all over us, fully deserving their 3–1 win.

Nonetheless, for myself I counted the match a minor victory: Luca D'Angelo had played again. It was the atmosphere surrounding the match that troubled me. Specifically, an unsettling conversation I'd had with Roberto Alberti about Gigi the night before.

The previous week, when he'd scored his goal, Alberti had made a big point of not accepting any hugs of congratulations from teammates until he'd run to the sidelines and hugged Gigi. Later, he told the press that he'd dedicated his goal to Gigi in memory of all the unfair hardships Gigi had endured. Given the monologue about Gigi's drug-smuggling career that Alberti had delivered to me on the bus to Ravenna, his subsequent actions and words were puzzling.

But when I raised this question, he looked at me with as blank a gaze as I'd ever received from another person. "You must be confused, Joe," he said. "Gigi is free; therefore, Gigi is innocent. And he had suffered unnecessarily. Of course I would dedicate my goal to him, as a tribute to the suffering he endured."

"But Roberto," I said. "You told me yourself. In very plain and simple words. Gigi was guilty. Gigi and Vanessa together had been smuggling cocaine into Italy for maybe five years."

Alberti's eyes were a very pale blue. At certain moments the color seemed to vanish entirely. This was such a moment.

"*Ti sbagli, Joe.*" You are mistaken. "*Non ho detto una sola parola. Di fatto, dall'inizio ho creduto che Gigi era innocente.*" You are mistaken. I did not say one word. In fact, from the start I've believed that Gigi was innocent.

"That's not true."

"You have misunderstood, Joe," he said in his almost unnaturally soft voice. "But do not misunderstand this: Never did I speak one word against Gigi. You must remember *that* as well as you remember your own name. I have always had love and respect for Gigi. And I welcome him back as a brother, as a teammate, as a friend."

"Roberto," I said, "I don't understand."

"And I don't understand how rockets fly to the moon. No one is meant to understand everything. *Non preoccuparti, Joe.*" Don't worry about it. "*E' un affare che non ti riguarda.*" It's not your problem.

31

I did not return from Brescia with the team because I had been in-vited to the *Guerin Sportivo* annual awards dinner the following night. In Italy this was the closest one could get to an Oscar ceremony. A lavish dinner would be served to hundreds in a sixteenth-century cas-tle in the countryside outside Bologna, and awards such as "Player of the Year" and "Manager of the Year" would be presented.

The magazine had invited me, I presumed, because it had re-cently published an article about me and therefore must have con-sidered me a minor celebrity. But I had other reasons for wanting to be there. As mentioned earlier, Danilo Di Vincenzo had been chosen *C2* player of the year the previous season, and it was at this dinner that he was to have accepted his trophy. In his stead, it would be pre-sented to the fiancée from whose home he had left on the morning of the fatal accident. Second, Jaconi was to be honored as "Minor League Manager of the Year" for having guided Castel di Sangro to *Serie B* the year before. Most of all, however, I wanted to be there to see Baggio.

The Unequaled One was having a difficult season, as he'd had, in fact, the year before. In my view, he'd never fully overcome the trauma of having missed the last penalty kick of the World Cup in 1994, thereby allowing Brazil to become champions.

I actually had met Baggio briefly while I was in Padova with Alexi Lalas. Juventus had arrived on Saturday night for a match against Padova the next day, and by displaying a degree of persistence that bordered on the manic, I'd been granted a ten-minute audience with him in the cocktail lounge of the Holiday Inn where the Juventus team was staying.

It is hard to convey the passionate regard Italian *tifosi* have for Baggio, but the only two examples of equivalent hysteria I've ever experienced in America were when the Beatles first arrived from England and, a few years later, when Robert Kennedy ran briefly for president. Baggio is the one Italian popular hero who transcends the bitter north-south divide by which the country is riven, and it seems that both his successes and the string of indignities imposed upon him by a cold, uncaring destiny work equally to intensify the degree of adulation he inspires.

Nor is it easier to describe the reasons why Baggio is so rapturously exalted in foreign lands. There were suicides in Sri Lanka when he missed his penalty kick in the Rose Bowl. Earlier, there had been riots in Bangladesh when the malevolent manager of the Italian national team had replaced him with a substitute midway through a first-round match against Norway.

That he is one of the finest players in the world provides, of course, the necessary point of departure. But Baggio's is as much a triumph of style as of substance. "His game is mysterious," Galeano writes. "His legs have a mind of their own, his foot shoots by itself, his eyes see the goals before they happen."

He is one of the greatest *fantasisti* ever to play the sport: a player gifted with such magical abilities that he appears, at times, to be functioning in four dimensions simultaneously and to possess, on the field, true extrasensory perception, so imaginative and creative is his vision.

Born in Caldogno, a village just north of Vicenza, Baggio played his first professional match at age fifteen, scored his first goal at sixteen, and at eighteen was purchased by *Serie A* Fiorentina. Before he ever played a match for them, however, he suffered the first in a series of damaging knee injuries that have haunted him throughout his career.

Recovered, and having begun his study of Buddhism during his time of pain and solitude, he blazed across the Florentine sky for three glorious years before management provoked large and violent riots by selling him to the wealthiest of the wealthy, the most powerful of the powerful, the Juventus team owned by the Agnelli family.

After sparkling for the Italian side in the 1990 World Cup (played in Italy), he enjoyed four more glorious seasons in Turin, the city of Juventus, and then made the world his stage as never before with his astonishing performance in America.

"He flows forward in an elegant wave," Galeano writes. "Opponents harass him, they bite, they punch him hard. Baggio has Buddhist inscriptions written inside his captain's armband. Buddha doesn't ward off the blows but he does help Baggio suffer them. From his infinite serenity, he also helps Baggio discover the silence that lies beyind the din of cheers and whistles."

It is that last element, I think, that aura of mysticism within which Baggio seems to function, that has caused him to achieve a stature far beyond that of sports hero or cultural icon. It is as if he has, with his self-effacing dignity, blessed all Italy with a quality of timelessness that did not exist in the country before him. Through his *anima,* in Jungian terms, he enables others to draw closer to the infinite.

I, unfortunately, made an utter fool of myself during the short time he had agreed to share with me in 1994. For some reason – a wish-fulfillment fantasy, no doubt, or maybe just the unconscious belief that anyone who played soccer with Baggio's degree of skill would naturally be able to speak every language in the world – I'd developed the notion that he was fluent in English.

"Ciao," I said, taking a seat next to him at a round cocktail table. "I understand you speak English."

He smiled at me warmly and looked at me with lively eyes. "No problem," he said.

Up close, he seemed just a boy. A Buddha-child, five foot six inches tall, weighing less than 150 pounds, and wearing a black leather baseball cap backward, so the bill would obscure his ponytail.

I launched immediately into an enthusiastic monologue about how my wife, Nancy, and I both admired him not only for his abilities as an athlete but for having the strength of character to pursue the path of Buddhism in such an overwhelmingly Catholic country as Italy, for his obvious devotion to his wife and two children, for his loyalty to teammates and friends, for all the ineffable qualities that had so quickly made him such a special figure in our lives.

He listened with what seemed great attentiveness. When finally I paused, he nodded, smiled again, and said, "No problem." At that point a Juventus club official leaned toward me to say, "You under-stand, of course, that Robi does not speak a word of English."

Allora . . . the conversation ran rather steeply downhill from there and out of gas. Yet he willingly wrote a gracious note to Nancy, posed for a picture with me (the film was still in my camera when it was stolen at the Padova stadium the next day), and generally seemed to survive my onslaught of idiocy with his serenity intact.

The next day he scored on a ferocious free kick but limped off soon afterward, having reinjured the thigh muscle he'd first strained at the World Cup. The injury plagued him for the rest of the season, at the end of which Juventus shocked the football world by selling him to A.C. Milan.

Although adoration by the *tifosi* occurred spontaneously and in-stantly, as it has wherever Baggio has played, the Milan *allenatore,* a gruff and autocratic ex-defender, set out to prove that he was a bigger man than Baggio by keeping *il Divino Codino* (the Divine Ponytail) *in panchina,* by forcing him to play out of position when on the field, and by constantly denigrating him to the press.

The result was misery all round. The *allenatore* went off to coach in Spain the next year, my year in Castel di Sangro. His Uruguayan successor lasted less than half a season and was replaced by the former Milan manager – and Baggio's great nemesis as manager of the national team – the vain, megalomaniacal, heartless, petty, pig-headed, and arrogant Arrigo Sacchi, a man whose desire from the start seemed to be to humiliate Baggio in every way possible, with the performance of the team only a secondary consideration. (Milan fell to tenth place under Sacchi and he left in disgrace at the end of the season, while Milan's fans voted Baggio their favorite player on the team.)

As his thirtieth birthday neared in mid-February, Baggio had seemed lost in gloom. The few interviews he gave were heartrending. He was forlorn in Milan. Nancy and I put together, transatlantically by fax, a birthday message for him, which included every public comment I'd made in Italy about what a demigod I thought him to be.

I faxed it to him but never expected he would see it, since he re-ceived more than 5,000 pieces of mail per day. Yet only a week after his February 18 birthday I came back from training to find a fax from Vittorio Petrone, Baggio's well-known agent and confidant.

The message said, *Robi has tried to call you several times to thank you and your wife for your good wishes, so obviously heartfelt. Unfortunately, he has reached only your answering machine. Therefore, he has asked me to send you this fax, telling you that if you are able to attend the* Guerin Sportivo *dinner in April, he would be delighted to see you again.*

I would have attended the dinner if I'd had to crawl there from Brescia on hands and knees.

And the event was splendid in every way. It was heartbreaking to see Danilo's fiancée, Silvia, walk up the aisle to accept his plaque with tears flowing down her face. I had not spoken to her since the day of the funerals, and then the encounter had been brief. Here, I was able to tell her how much everyone in Castel di Sangro missed Danilo, not just for his ability as a player but for who he had been as a man.

Silvia thanked me but then told me that from the delegation of *Società* officials (which did not include Gravina, who was still lying low, close to home) who had made the trip north from Castel di Sangro to see Jaconi receive his award, not one had bothered even to greet her, much less to ask how she was, much less to say a word about Danilo.

"Dilettante da mentalità," I said. *"Non hanno classe."* No class. She nodded, but said, *"Ma perchè neanche il Mister?"* Why had not even Jaconi acknowledged her presence?

I did not know, though I had come to sense that he considered any display of sentiment a sign of womanly weakness and, more harshly, that by the time of Danilo's death Jaconi had already given up on him as a player and so by now it was almost as if he had never existed. I said only, *"Non lo so, Silvia."* I don't know. Then we hugged briefly, but long enough for me to feel at least a passing connection to Danilo again.

Osvaldo received his award in the presence of his wife and two daughters, who during the season did not get to share much of his life. Later, the master of ceremonies introduced me among a number of others in the audience. I stood from my seat long enough for Baggio to spot me. He waved. Then, as soon as the ceremonies were over, he came down from the stage and embraced me as if I were an old friend. He also was kind enough to say it was a pity that Nancy could not be here and to suggest that when she visited later in the spring, perhaps we could all have lunch in Milan.

I slept overnight in the castle, as did Jaconi and his wife and daughters. The next morning – one filled with the soft glow of spring sunshine and the bountiful, sweet aromas of new growth – we headed back to Castel di Sangro, with a stop at Jaconi's home in Civitanova to drop off his daughters and wife.

It was strange to see him in a family setting. His single-minded, monastic existence in Castel di Sangro often caused me to forget that he even had a wife and children. Both girls were sprightly and clearly very smart. His wife was a thin woman with a demeanor as placid as his was volatile, but she seemed, at first impression, just slightly worn down by the years.

Civitanova was no place to write home about. Of course, if it was home, you did not have to. And such was the case with Jaconi. It was here that he had pulled up lame, more or less, at the age of thirty-five, a milk horse who'd made his last run. Except instead of shooting him, the club named him manager, and the milk horse had become a bulldozer in this utilitarian city of 35,000, located in that coastal region east of Umbria and north of the Abruzzo known as Marche.

Though built directly on the Adriatic coast, Civitanova did not feel like a beach town. Nor was it, in essence. Industry, not tourism, work, not play kept the heart of the city beating steadily. It was one of the country's leading centers for the manufacture of shoes. Not the Bruno Magli loafers favored by O. J. Simpson, or those to which other stylish designers attached their names: rather, the shoes of Civitanova were for work – in the factories, in the fields, or even in the office. Like a team coached by Jaconi, they were made to do a job, to last a season, not to transform their wearer into a spectacle.

The family lived in a featureless apartment house, one of thousands of similar, undistinguished design that stretched along the Adriatic coast to compose, collectively, perhaps Italy's most striking monument to the postwar triumph of greed over taste.

As was Jaconi himself, his wife was from the region of Lombardy, in the north, and longed to return there. Jaconi did not seem to care where he or his family called home. His life was his work. *His* home was whatever town he happened to be managing in during a given season or run of seasons.

So they were "temporarily" living in Civitanova, though for the daughters it was the only home they knew or could remember. The years had snuck by, one after another, always with the return to Lombardy better put off for one more, until now the girls were in high school and for the foreseeable future it seemed hopeless. Besides, with Jaconi in Castel di Sangro, at least Civitanova was accessible by car in a way that Lombardy would not be.

In any event, his wife had long ago taken her stand: not for her the vagabond life, packing up children and belongings and following her husband wherever his career led him or forced him to go. Castel di Sangro was the sixth place he'd coached since leaving Civitanova in 1984, and it was the first where he'd stayed for more than three seasons. So for better or worse, for her and her daughters, Civitanova was home.

We paused there only long enough for his wife and daughters to hurriedly pack a suitcase for him. As they did, Jaconi took me to his study, the main feature of which was a set of bound volumes, each one containing every newspaper clipping he'd been able to find and save from every season in which he'd either played or coached. It was like a mini–Library of Congress, with Jaconi the only name to be found in the card catalogue. I said that one day I would have to return and spend time looking through these, to better appreciate the full scope of his career as both player and manager. He beamed. That, certainly, would not be hard to arrange.

The sense of spring remained profuse all the way down the coast and even inland until we had climbed well above Sulmona. But to reach Castel di Sangro from Sulmona, one must pass through a long tunnel. This tunnel carries one up more of a grade than is apparent and at the end opens onto a high plateau that extends on either side of the road for almost five miles.

At this time of year, passing through that tunnel was like taking an unwanted trip back in time. To, let us say, mid-February. All luxuriance, all hints of springtime were left behind as we emerged. The car was suddenly buffeted by strong winds; dark clouds descended upon us even faster than Jaconi drove. Within thirty seconds it was snowing.

Next to me, Jaconi shook his head sadly and pursed his lips. We had shared a special moment the night before, and for him it might have represented the pinnacle of a long and trying career. But that was gone now. We were back.

"Un altro mondo," I said, pointing back with a thumb. Another world.

He made what he probably thought was a laughing sound but to me seemed more of a snarl. *"Sì, sì, certo,"* he agreed. *"Infatti. Un altro mondo, e migliore."* Indeed: another world, and better.

32

It continued to snow through midweek, and each day grew colder than the one before. Low gray clouds had moved in from the mountains, making even the noon hour seem like dusk. Such weather did nothing to lift the spirit. And, unmistakably, *la stagione lunga e dura* was taking its toll.

Montagne russe was the Italian term for roller coaster. Months ago Jaconi had said the season would resemble such a ride, because of the inconsistency of players at this level. But now it was as if several *montagne russe* were operating simultaneously, and one could never be sure on which of them one was riding.

There was, *sicuramente,* the team's inconsistency, as Osvaldo had said. Lotti was always reliable and often spectacular in goal, but not one of the defenders could be counted on to play with the same degree of skill and focus two weeks in a row. The midfield was an even worse mishmash, with Alberti and Di Fabio perhaps showing the least deviation from the norm, but from a norm that was borderline for *Serie B*.

Claudio, meanwhile, would follow flashes of brilliance with a performance of school-yard quality, made even worse by his habit of carrying on a running dialogue with Jaconi during the match.

Claudio would sprint down the sideline with the ball and then inexplicably kick it over the end line with not another Castel di Sangro player in sight.

A vile eruption would occur on the bench.

Claudio would look at Osvaldo helplessly. "So, what do you want me to do?"

"Cazzo, vaffunculo!" Fuck you! Fuck you!

Claudio would continue to gaze open-mouthed at the sideline as yet another possibility for dropping back on defense eluded him. And this was not September; it was April. And Claudio was our million-dollar man. Yet because he was a favored pet, Jaconi would praise, above all, Claudio's *mentalità*.

Spinesi was another whom Osvaldo would single out for praise no matter how poorly he played. And again he would cite *mentalità*. But here was an example of Spinesi's: like any Italian teenage male enjoying a testosterone rush, Gionatha had decided to celebrate his goal against Palermo by ordering an expensive new car. The vehicle had just been delivered to Castel di Sangro. Only then did it become known that Spinesi did not have a driver's license; in fact, he did not know how to drive.

Nonetheless, the car was here, it was his, and he was free to lean on it whenever he wanted and to admire his reflection on its highly polished surface. This got to be a running joke. Every day I'd ask him if he'd started his driving lessons yet.

"Finalmente," he would say. Eventually. *"Non c'è fretta."* There's no hurry.

It was my theory that he was reluctant to drive an expensive new car through town until he'd scored at least another goal or two, which indicated a healthy sensitivity, if not precisely brilliance, on his part.

There was also Jaconi's own roller coaster, which seemed to be operated by an entirely different mechanism. Surly and withdrawn on certain mornings, volcanically angry at lunch, he would suddenly turn boisterous and jolly in midafternoon, then, in a flash, fly again into a rage so strong that more than once I thought he was about to hit a player. Two hours later, at a private dinner in a mountain village (to which he'd made sure I was invited, as he'd made sure from the start that I was invited to everything, no matter how much we might quarrel about tactics), he was the charming raconteur.

If he was aware of the contempt in which so many of his players held him, he did not speak of it to me. Instead, he spoke only – and repeatedly – of his contempt, disdain, distaste, dislike, and lack of respect for each and every one of them, save the half a dozen he considered the "old guard."

His sheer irrationality could be terrifying. One afternoon he grabbed Franceschini by the arm, yanking him away from the circle of players among whom he'd been standing, and proceeded for forty-five minutes to excoriate this young man in every vile and venomous way imaginable. *Perchè? Boh.* Why? No one knew, least of all Franceschini.

Others he'd taken to simply ignoring. Weeks had passed, for example, since he'd last exchanged a word with Russo, though the two were together for lunch, three hours of training, and dinner every night. To Cristiano he'd grown nastily condescending, and to Luca Albieri downright insulting, calling him a number of crude names used to refer to homosexuals.

I had no idea what Albieri's sexual orientation might be, though I presumed that the majority of the players would have known if it was different from theirs. Not once, either to his face or in his absence did I ever hear a player make a snide remark in this regard. Yet Jaconi did everything but spit in the poor boy's face.

Luca D'Angelo was a bit too big and strong to be bullied, but out of his earshot Jaconi would go on verbal rampages against him, almost always closing by looking at me and calling D'Angelo "that long-haired, sissy, communist friend of yours!"

The atmosphere had never been so tense and strange. As the spring days grew longer, the number of weeks left until the end of the season dwindled, thus causing *la primavera,* counterintuitively, to be a time not of rebirth, of joyous release from the burdens of winter, but instead the time of the tightening of the vise. And nowhere did that vise seem to press more forcefully or painfully than against Osvaldo's skull. The *allenatore* might get the plaque if things went well, but he tended to get the sack far more quickly.

Adding to the sense of slightly malignant unreality was the scope of the *festa* Gravina was preparing for Gigi's return to action when we played Reggina on Sunday. While I remained fond of him, I'd grown pretty cynical about the Gigi-as-Jesus myth (all the while wondering how Galli really was, and where he was, though Gravina now assured us he was recovering).

At dinner on Saturday night I suggested to Fusco and Martino that for such a special occasion as Gigi's return as an active player the next day, our north end *ultras* ought to be given a new chant.

They both nodded, noncommittally.

"Dunque," Fusco said, waiting. So? Well? What should it be?

"Il delitto paga," I said. Crime pays.

"Aaaaaaah!" Tonino put his hand to his forehead and leaned sideways in his chair before starting to laugh uproariously. *"Grande Joe! Grande Joe!"*

Fusco, however, the native of Napoli, the son of a sausage maker, the kicker of rolled up socks in back alleys, for whom in his formative years the *Camorra* had been more than a myth, did not even smile. Instead, he placed an index finger vertically over his lips. Looking me straight in the eye, he shook his head slightly from side to side.

As expected, Gigi's appearance on the Castel di Sangro field brought forth the loudest roar of approval and joy I'd heard since my arrival. It was true. Crime *did* pay. As long as you had someone on your side to make the payments.

Gigi played the full ninety minutes and played well. Spinesi scored for us on a superb pass from Martino only seconds before the first half ended, and Lotti barred the goalmouth door all afternoon. And so we won, 1–0. A happy ending to a difficult week.

At the match for some reason there was a reporter who said he was from National Public Radio in America. I wasn't convinced of his bona fides, but while conducting a short interview, at least he let me speak English.

"You know," I said, "we had ten other players out there today who have not even been *accused* of smuggling twenty-five million dollars' worth of cocaine into this country. It would have been nice to have heard an ovation for one of *them*."

The next morning's papers, however, surrendered unconditionally to Gigi-mania. Of the five I checked, two gave him a *voto* of 8 and two more a 7. To me, he merited a 6.5, the same as Cei, among our defenders. But Gigi's ratings were obviously some sort of multiple of his performance and his time spent in jail.

If he'd spent four weeks, I wrote to Nancy, *he would have got an 11.*

. . .

Monday was as nasty a day as I could remember since midwinter. In early evening, I wrote a letter to a friend:

> The gray of a raw dusk settles once again upon this frigid mountain outpost as the day's relentless rain prepares for its nightly transformation into treacherous sleet, and the beleaguered and impoverished inhabitants – their winter's supply of firewood long gone – again face the unyielding choice between burning yet another piece of furniture for warmth or killing still one more of their dwindling herd of sheep, in order to provide themselves with an additional bloodsoaked layer of wool to lie beneath as they pray with frosty breath and ever-diminishing faith that the morrow's dawn might for the first time since one freakish Sunday in February bring with it the warmth of the sun.
>
> But are they complaining? Hell, no! Because yesterday we beat Reggina, 1–0. Thirty matches down, eight to go, and despite our many and varied misfortunes there remain six teams in *Serie B* with records even worse than ours (and we need finish only above four in order to assure *la salvezza*).

But then, as frigid north winds scattered snow squalls across the face of every afternoon, and as low, dark, hard-winter clouds obscured even the nearest of the hillsides, our long-untended training field finally succumbed to the repeated onslaught of the weather.

Since early December all resources had been applied to the stadium field, but it remained as fragile as an orchid, requiring two full weeks of resuscitation after a single ninety-minute match. Training there was out of the question, and now the practice field, too, lay under two to three inches of semifrozen muddy goo that made play on it impossible.

Ten kilometers down the road, however, was a long-abandoned dirt field strewn with rubble that bordered a low-income housing project called Villa Scontrone. It was a booby-trapped rectangle on which not even project residents had tried to play football for years. Yet now the squad was forced to travel here each day for training.

Shards of glass, old tires, and discarded, rusting appliances lay everywhere, as well as embedded rocks that could break an ankle in an instant. Moreover, *scontrone* meant "scene of a bloody clash," or, simply, a site where "moroseness, peevishness, surliness, rudeness, and bad temper" ruled.

One might have thought that the win over Reggina, which kept us clinging by our fingernails to a *classifica* spot just above the relegation zone – and which also had enabled Spinesi to finally begin his course in driver's education – would have brought at least temporary relief from the corrosive tension and confusion that had set in upon the news of Gigi's arrest. His quick release, however, had done nothing to alleviate those feelings – except in the case of Roberto Alberti, whose about-face both mystified and disturbed me – and in fact made them more acute for many. The whole mess seemed to have put *una macchia,* a blemish, on the grit, heart, and unselfish honor that had brought the team to *Serie B* in the first place.

No blood was shed during the morose, peevish, surly, rude, bad-tempered – and utterly futile – training sessions that were held at Villa Scontrone during the week, but the wrack and ruin all around caused the players to feel that *Serie B* had been just a mirage and that each and every one of them was stuck back at the absolute low point of his career and would be forced to remain there forever, with Jaconi bellowing curses from the sidelines. My own mood, too, seemed in free fall after the giddy heights reached at the *Guerin Sportivo* dinner.

This time it was Pietro Spinosa who checked my descent. Toward the end of the week I was riding back to town with him from Villa Scontrone. The miraculous moment of his penalty-kick save was now more than nine months behind him, but the further into the season we went, the more I came to believe that it was he who possessed the *carattere* and *cuore* and *mentalità* that kept this whole haphazard operation from falling apart.

Without him to calm the players, there might have been open revolt against Jaconi. Without him to calm Jaconi, there might have been wholesale destruction of the squad. In addition, I'd come to feel so comfortable with him over the months that by now it was almost as if he were a brother I had brought with me to Castel di Sangro.

Because he was a man of such discretion, however, and of total loyalty to Jaconi, he would not share with me his feelings, or even a small percentage of his knowledge, about all that swirled around us in these chaotic days after what I believed to have been *l'acquisto,* the purchase of freedom for Gigi. Indeed, he steadfastly insisted that any talk of impropriety could be no more than speculation, and reckless speculation at that. Still, I felt that if push ever truly came to shove, not only here but anywhere in the world, Pietro Spinosa was the first person in whom I'd place complete trust.

On this particular afternoon he was going to loan me some newspaper clippings about the match of the previous June and so, at last light, he was expertly guiding his station wagon through the narrow cobbled alleys that led to his home opposite the thirteenth-century church that had not been bombed in the war. He was concentrating totally on his driving, often brushing with no loss of speed through stone-arched passageways that I would have deemed too narrow even to try.

"How do you do that?" I asked when we'd reached his house. "You go through those arches as if you had the width of a field on either side."

"Sono un portiere," he said, smiling. *"Ho gli occhi buoni."* I am a goalkeeper. I have good eyes.

"And good ears," I suggested.

"Sì, Joe, ed anche una bocca che è buona perchè non fa un gran rumore." Yes, and a mouth that is good because it does not make a big noise.

"Come la mia," I said. Like mine.

At this, Spinosa smiled and placed a hand lightly on my leg. *"Lo so che le giornate stanno per finire. Chissà cosa succederà. E so che per te e per me, è meglio non dire niente."* I know the days are closing in. I know there's no knowing what may happen. And I know that for you and for me, it's better not to say anything.

He paused, studying me with those goalkeeper's eyes. "Even if our miracle is not what you expected," he said, finally, "you are still a very lucky man. Because a squad like this – and I speak not of talent but of the *cuore e grinta e carattere* that exist no matter how angry some players might be – this is once in the life, and once only, for anyone involved with *il calcio.*

"And for you, Joe, to pass the season among these kinds of men – *quello è il vero miracolo."* That is the real miracle.

33

One morning in the spring of 1893 a group of British sailors who had been too long in port brought a round leather ball ashore in Genoa and began to kick it about. As usual, the dock area was filled with Italian idlers sipping coffee, making lewd remarks about women, and looking for pockets to pick. After watching the sailors boot the ball back and forth for about fifteen minutes, the Italians said to one another, "*Cazzo!* We can do better than that." And thus was born *il calcio*.

Now, 104 years later, it was both exhilarating and intimidating to be traveling to the place where it all began, to play against a club whose history stretched back more than a hundred years. The fact that we'd beaten Genoa, 1–0, in the makeup match in January (thanks to Antonello's unlikely bicycle kick) did nothing to take the edge off. If anything, it raised the stakes a little higher.

For Genoa, they already were high enough. Two years earlier the team had been relegated to *Serie B* after losing a postseason playoff match to Padova. Since the organization of *Serie A* in 1929, however, Genoa had been a staple of the top division, compiling a cumulative record that was among the ten best in Italy. For this team and its supporters, *Serie B* was a land of exile, an embarrassment, a blot on the escutcheon, and the failure to have returned to *Serie A* immediately was considered scandalous.

Heads had rolled after the club's seventh-place finish in *Serie B* last season, and the crowns were unsteady on several more this year.

A win over us, however, would put Genoa back among the top four in the *classifica* and on track for a return to what was almost unanimously felt to be its rightful level.

We took the bus to Fiumicino. After a *Società* functionary had passed out the plane tickets (and had checked to be sure that lower-level functionaries had brought with them a sufficient quantity of Gabriele Gravina–Vanessa Diaz comic books, the plot not updated to reflect recent events), we began ambling through the domestic terminal toward our gate, when suddenly we were confronted by an apparition.

Clad in all white – and not medical white but a highly stylish white linen suit – was Giacomo Galli! Here, among us, in the flesh!

The shouts and hugs of reunion were extravagant, heightened by the element of surprise. Even I had missed him more than I'd realized. Maybe he hadn't taken any goals with him when he'd been rushed by ambulance to the private clinic in Rome, but the level of laughter in Marcella's seemed to have been cut in half by the absence of his free-association monologues.

Galli didn't look poorly, but on closer inspection neither did he look well. Since we had assumed he was still hooked to tubes and respirators, however, it was both a delight and relief to have him suddenly appear among us as if he were just another traveler, dressed for summer, passing through Rome on his way from one point in his journey to another.

He'd driven to the airport from his home, he said, simply to say hello, to feel again the joy of being among his teammates, and to alleviate at least some of the anxiety that he knew we were feeling over him. But most of all to wish us *in bocca al lupo* for Sunday. To my mind, his brief moments with us were the finest augury that we could have hoped for.

He had brought with him, however, some bad news. He would play no more football this season. There remained significant problems with his blood. These would be cured in time, he said, but not soon enough to allow him to regain his strength and fitness by June. So this was hello and good-bye all at once.

Yes, he would try to drive to our remaining home matches in order to watch, but everyone knew it would not be the same. Whatever the truth behind his bizarre misfortune, Giacomo was yet another casualty of the long, hard season, and I think we all felt a pang of sadness as we boarded the Alitalia jet, looking back and waving as he stood by the counter, waving back and trying to keep the smile on his face.

I sat next to Fusco on the plane. Here was a player who never once had criticized Jaconi, at least within my hearing. Fusco actually seemed to like the *allenatore*, as well as to feel grateful for having been kept on board throughout the whole marvelous ride from *C2* to *Serie B* – though Fusco had more than earned his own passage.

"*Cinque anni, Joe*," he said now. "*Ne ho abbastanza. Per me, e ora di andar via*." Five years. I've had enough. For me, the time has come to leave. He gestured out the airplane window. We were seated on the left side, flying north along the coast, and could see clearly the beautiful coastline and beyond it the island of Elba and farther in the distance, Corsica. His contract would expire at the end of the season, and he did not plan to sign an extension.

Fusco made clear, however, that his desire for new horizons was not the result of bitterness or disillusionment. He loved Castel di Sangro. But after five years he had wearied of playing in the same small mountain town only two hours from his Naples home. The travels involved in *Serie B* competition had awakened in him, at age twenty-four, an urge to see more: if not of the world, at least of Italy.

I understood. But then I foolishly said, "So for you, *la salvezza* is not so important, because you will be leaving anyway."

His eyes snapped instantly to attention. I knew no one else whose expression could shift so quickly from one of tranquillity to one of glittering ferocity and then, when the moment of provocation had passed, back again.

"Do you understand nothing, Joe? Even now? For me *la salvezza* is more important simply because I *am* leaving!" The town and the team, he said, had given him so much. The least he owed in return was to leave with the squad remaining in *Serie B* – *not* as a member of the team that had failed to measure up.

Not for the first time, someone less than half my age had proven himself twice as wise. I apologized as well as I could, but I continued to ponder: If players like Fusco – the younger members of the Castel di Sangro old guard, so to speak – were about to move on, then this season would surely prove unique. Even if the team did achieve *la salvezza*, the players who had brought Castel di Sangro to *Serie B* and then kept it there would be gone. Not only the disgruntled but the loyalists such as Claudio would be leaving, while those such as Cei, Alberti, and Michelini were surely near the end of their careers. And if *salvezza* were achieved, Osvaldo, too, presumably would be offered a better job by a stronger club.

Thus, the trip to Genoa took on an almost elegiac quality. While there would be one additional bus ride into Tuscany, this was the squad's last venture into Italy's true north: the last confrontation with a team not only historic in itself but representative of one of the great cities of the republic. The experience would be repeated the following season if *salvezza* were achieved, but in the equally likely event that it was not, it might be many, many years, if ever, before Castel di Sangro again played football in a city as renowned as Genoa.

Saturday morning was warm and muggy. The ride to our training field from the inconveniently located Novotel Ovest took us through dozens of tunnels and over many bridges that twisted and wound through the hills. A soft drizzle began to fall during training and it was possible to truly smell the grass, so far advanced was the Genovese spring.

That aroma, which seems the same the world over, for some reason triggered a burst of premature nostalgia for my own experience that, in less than two months, would be ending. I didn't want to think about having to say good-bye to these *ragazzi*.

In the afternoon I rode a city bus from our remote location into the heart of Genoa. The streets near the port were aswarm. I walked for two or three hours, just wanting a visceral sense of the place. The sky above me darkened, the air grew thick and still. No alleyway or street was less crowded than the one before it or the one that came next. The noise was tremendous, though this was not the noise of traffic but the noise of thousands of people on foot in narrow spaces.

There seemed an unruly aspect to Genoa that lay just beyond my ability to identify or define. A quick comparison to Venice was inevitable, if only because the two cities had been for centuries the great seafaring and warring republics of the north. I found myself thinking of Venice as being like the sedate and elegant Upper East Side of Manhattan, while Genoa evoked a sense of the funkiness, energy, and unpredictability of the West Side.

Eventually, I came upon a used-book store and spent the rest of the afternoon there, browsing among worn Italian volumes that bespoke a history and a depth of understanding of the culture that I knew I could never achieve.

Glancing outside, I saw the sky had turned almost black, although it was not yet 5 P.M. I left the store quickly to make the long trek back to the hotel, bringing with me a copy of an ancient and gloriously illustrated history of the voyages of Columbus.

I knew that it was Alberti's thirty-sixth birthday and that he was one of the few players who would truly appreciate the quality of such a gift. His about-face regarding Gigi still disturbed me, but I couldn't know what pressures he might be facing in that regard.

Back at the hotel – which I reached just before the storm broke in all its fury – I inscribed the book in an Italian that, to my surprise, turned out to be error free. The English translation was "In the city from which Columbus embarked upon his search for a new world, I wish you fulfillment and success as you prepare to enter your own new worlds, which will lie beyond the fields of *il calcio*."

On Sunday I awoke to the worst match-day weather of my life, not counting Castel di Sangro's first attempt to play Genoa, which, in the end, did not turn out to be a match day.

It seemed that all the rain that had fallen on Genoa since the beginning of time was falling again that morning. And not falling vertically, either. I looked out my Novotel window, which gave a splendid view of the entrance to an *autostrada* and a special sign lit to warn drivers of *freddo vento forte* – a strong, cold wind – which they'd be facing once they entered.

I took the elevator down from my room at 10:15 but encountered only Pietro Spinosa in the lobby. He simply shook his head and said, *"Molto cattivo."* Very bad. Then I spotted Luca D'Angelo, seated alone in a far, dim corner.

But Luca was so *sconsolato* that he simply waved me away with one hand. He didn't want to talk to anybody. Outside, the sky grew darker, a reminder – to me, anyway – that it would be 3 A.M. Monday before we'd be home again, and that the chances of anything pleasant happening in the meantime were, in Claudio's phrase, *sotto zero* – less than zero.

I do not know how low barometric pressure can go, but I can say without hesitation that if it can go lower than it went on that Sunday morning in Genoa, I wouldn't want to be around when it did.

I wrote in a notebook: *The strangest year of my life begins just when I thought it was ending.* I wasn't even sure what that meant. I think now that I might have been searching for Shakespeare's line from *The Tempest* – clearly the play for the day – "What's past is prologue." I don't know.

I stayed in the lobby for half an hour. Each new arrival of the elevator brought one or more players, looking pasty and frightened and eerily two-dimensional in the strange light of the day.

By noontime the rain had abated somewhat, but televisions in the lobby carried the sound of urgent voices warning that this was only the eye of the storm and that far worse conditions would beset the city later in the afternoon. There was a brief snippet of sunshine as we boarded the bus for the stadium, but the ride was taken in total silence. For the first time all year I had the feeling that we were not going to a match but to an execution – our own.

Walking the field with the squad upon our arrival, I saw that the stadium – widely considered the most beautiful in Italy – was every bit as magnificent as advertised. I also saw that a fully professional grounds crew had protected the turf from the worst of the downpour with plastic sheeting and an intricate system of runoff pipes. Possibly, conditions would not be so bad, after all – which was not, from our standpoint, an advantage.

Osvaldo, still at the mercy of his most conservative instincts but unable to satisfy his equally strong desire for experience by using the classic 5-4-1 formation of *la paura,* had opted instead for a 4-5-1.

In front of Lotti were Fusco and Prete on the outside, with D'Angelo and Cei in central defense. Thrown into the midfield, essentially to congest it, were Martino and Bonomi on the wings, with Di Fabio, Cristiano, and Alberti in the center (the use of Mimmo instead of Michelini being Osvaldo's one concession to the hope and promise of youth). This left Spinesi as our one and only *attaccante,* which was asking a lot of a lad who had turned nineteen only one month before.

The sky continued to darken, and at the moment the ball was put into play, blankets of rain, not merely sheets, came hurtling in from the north, straight from the Matterhorn it seemed, dropping the temperature twenty, maybe thirty degrees within ten minutes and causing the players to jump around like fleas on a skillet as first one gust of wind, then another overpowered them.

For the first fifteen minutes they battled the elements more than one another. But at seventeen minutes Tonino Martino kicked the ball out of bounds off the leg of a Genoa defender to give Castel di Sangro a *calcio d'angolo,* or corner kick. Claudio took it and curled the ball nicely into the area just in front of the Genoa goal, where, amid some frantic slipping and sliding and pulling and holding and lunging and stumbling, the unlikely figure of D'Angelo appeared like an avenging angel sent down from the darkened sky. He headed the ball directly into the net.

This was a goal for Castel di Sangro! Against Genoa! In Genoa! It was Luca's first (and would prove his last) of the season. I was seated alone, surrounded by Genoa supporters, and my blood-curdling cries of joy drew a number of unappreciative stares. But I didn't care. I didn't care about anything, except that Luca had scored to put us ahead.

The goal not only shocked everyone in the stadium, but as *Il Corriere dello Sport* wrote, "It seemed to send a wake-up call to the gods, for the bottom fell out of the heavens as the sky turned black and thunder and lightning immediately crashed everywhere in the stadium all at once as the downpour became a deluge."

Lightning flashes crackled over the field with such withering intensity that for the first time I considered that the image of lightning bolts being hurled at earth by angry gods might not be entirely metaphorical. Within the confines of the stadium, the sound of the thunder seemed as strong as that of artillery fire.

I was, quite frankly, terrified. Seen through the storm, the players on the field now looked like tiny figurines, viewed from an insurmountable distance. It seemed impossible that play could continue. Thousands of spectators in seats not protected by the overhanging upper deck scrambled toward the rear of the stadium in a frantic quest for shelter.

All was chaos. Bolt after bolt of lightning burst upon us. The cold rain blew with the force of a monsoon. The plastic seats of the *tribuna* were literally rocked by the explosions of thunder.

Yet "play on" the referee signaled, and so they did. And, as if in defiance of the elemental forces besieging us, Genoa switched on the stadium lights. The sky above remained midnight black, but it was now at least possible to see the players and, more important, for the players to see the ball.

Not that the ball was easy to control, given the conditions underfoot. So much rain had fallen so quickly that water was ankle deep above the grass. But not for long – as the storm's intensity diminished again, the *Serie A* drainage system beneath the *Serie A* soil of the field began doing its job. What a difference from Castel di Sangro!

Indeed, while lightning and thunder continued and the chilling rain settled into a steady, if penetrating, rhythm, conditions on the field improved rapidly. In fact, a bit too rapidly for my taste. Midway through the half, Genoa was able to launch "an interminable and exhausting assault" *(Il Tempo)* at the Castel di Sangro goal, which lasted until the halftime whistle blew. Only a series of phenomenal saves by Lotti ("a Martian in the midst of a community of mortals," said *Il Tempo,* apparently fearful of invoking an image any closer to the Deity) preserved our lead.

Yet only seconds before the whistle, even Lotti was powerless to stop an inadvertent deflection by Fusco, who, in the process of trying to block yet another in the barrage of Genoa shots, instead sent the ball into a far and unprotected corner of the net. This made the score 1–1 at halftime. In terms of its psychological impact, however, the one goal might as well have been three.

Once again, it seemed, no matter how dramatic the circumstances and no matter how "incomparable" *(Il Corriere dello Sport)* the efforts of Lotti, we simply were not destined to win a match away from home. Having tied the score, Genoa surely would come out for the second-half kill, and our stressed-out defense would crumble entirely. Meanwhile, with only Spinesi up front, we did not seem likely to get even another shot at the Genoa goal.

"Tremendous blows" *(La Gazzetta dello Sport)* were struck by Genoa from the first minute of the second half. Time after time, they swept forward, winning the ball in midfield and quickly confronting our outside defenders, the hard-pressed Fusco and a Gigi Prete who was playing with more furious energy than I'd ever seen him display before.

Only five minutes into the half, Luca D'Angelo's back seized up, and he had to be carried off on a stretcher. This suddenly brought

Antonello into the fray, despite Jaconi's newly developed distaste for him. Perhaps he wasn't quite up to the standard set by Luca, but Cei, alongside him, was at his steadiest, and so the defense held firm.

Then Cristiano got sent off for his second yellow card of the match, leaving us a man short. After that, we did crumble. For Genoa the match became little more than target practice. Shot after shot boomed goalward, from close range and far, from left, right, and center, shots high and shots low, shots directed with precision toward the farthest corners of the goal and shots blasted straight down the middle. Yet Lotti did not flinch, nor did he let a single one go by.

As *La Gazzetta dello Sport* wrote, "Lotti displayed, in one match, all the great saves he must have been dreaming of for months." *Il Messaggero* called him simply, "Super-Lotti." And *Il Tempo* summarized by calling him "a champion clearly with the stature for *Serie A*." It was the most astonishing performance by a goalkeeper I'd ever seen.

So mesmerizing, in fact, was Lotti's command of his craft that midway through the second half the Genoa fans simply accepted that they were witnessing something far out of the ordinary. And they responded as true sportsmen. Each new Lotti save brought first oohs and then aahs and, eventually, chants of *"Ole!"* – the highest verbal tribute a *tifoso* can give.

At a certain point, with perhaps twenty minutes of the match remaining, I suddenly *knew* that Lotti would not let Genoa score. For the first and only time all season, I ceased to either hope or fear: At some instinctual level, I simply knew.

This was the day toward which all the frustrations and disappointments of Lotti's season had been building. This was the day that would wipe the slate clean. And it would, in fact, do far more: It would call his name to the attention of every team in *Serie B* and *Serie A* in a way that would ensure that he would never again be ignored or taken lightly.

We were going to obtain a draw at Genoa. We were going to win a vital point in the city that was the birthplace of *calcio*. There was tremendous satisfaction in knowing this.

The rain again began to fall in buckets. The wind rose sharply once more. The sky again darkened in a fashion most menacing. Yet when I looked across to the far side of the field, I saw Jaconi – almost unrecognizable under so many layers of rain gear – having come off the sheltered *panchina* to stand at the edge of the field, and as the storm renewed itself with near-biblical magnitude, by God, he looked like *Noah!*

Fifteen minutes remained in the match when there occurred, within six minutes of each other, the two least likely events I could have imagined. First, Claudio scored a goal to put us back in the lead, 2–1.

And then *Pistella,* who had come on as a substitute for Spinesi, scored only his second goal of the season. *We were leading Genoa, 3–1.* And Lotti would not permit Genoa to score. *We were going to win the match.* We hadn't won one match all season away from home, but we were going to beat Genoa in Genoa!

And so we did. Castel di Sangro, from a tiny and obscure mountain hamlet in the Abruzzo, had won a match in the home stadium of the most storied team in all of Italy.

On this day of April 27, in this place, under these conditions, against all odds, the miracle had truly renewed itself.

"O brave new world," I said aloud, as the tempest put me in mind of *The Tempest.* "O brave new world, that has such people in't."

And then I raced across the field as fast as I could to join in a changing-room celebration that I knew no one would ever forget.

We were an hour and a half in leaving the stadium. It was as if no one wanted to go; everyone wanted to linger just a little longer, to stay in this storied ground where, whatever the future might bring, Castel di Sangro had entered the annals of *calcio* history.

"I feel like I *belong!*" Osvaldo cried out, then unexpectedly breaking down and crying in my arms. "For the first time, I feel I am a true *allenatore.*"

And then there occurred perhaps the most amazing part of the day, and for me the most memorable moment of the season. As our bus pulled out, behind police escort, onto the one-way street that led away from the stadium, we saw that on both sides Genoa fans were standing six deep for as far ahead as we could see.

Someone yelled, "Down! They're going to stone us!"

Nothing could have been further from the truth. As our bus

slowly accelerated and moved past them, the Genoa *tifosi* on both sides of the street burst into applause.

They recognized history when it was made, even at their own expense. And they had waited for ninety long minutes, swallowing their own disappointment, simply in order to pay tribute to the men from the mountains of the Abruzzo, who would never be considered little again.

34

In Italy no higher compliment can be paid to an event or live performance of any kind than to say that it was like a movie. And *come in un film* was what a number of the national papers proclaimed the Genoa match to have been.

"We would want probably a western in the style of the 1950s," one journalist wrote, "to properly re-create the images, the feelings, the mighty tide of emotion." But what cowboy hero could have portrayed Lotti? John Wayne in his prime? No, even then he would not have had the reflexes.

That night, as we stood waiting for our luggage – all of us, players and watchers alike, exhausted and emotionally drained to the bone – Lotti asked me to ride back in the car with him and his *fidanzata,* Manuela, instead of taking the team bus. (Actually, I think what he asked was whether I might *prefer* to ride with them – a gesture of simple courtesy – but I persuaded myself that he truly wanted my company, perhaps so we could rehash his afternoon of a lifetime, notwithstanding my limited rehashing ability in Italian, so I accepted immediately.)

Among the personal qualities of Lotti's I had come to admire was his steadiness, his evenness of demeanor. He did not lack passion (though Jaconi might have misread him in this regard) but kept his composure under every circumstance with which I saw him confronted over the season. In this respect, as well as in his light coloring, blond hair, blue eyes, and large stature, he seemed almost more Nordic than Italian.

On our ride back he was as calm as if he'd spent the day in a hammock (not in Genoa, obviously) listening to music and reading a book. He was pleased, of course, both with his own performance and with the team's historic win, but other than sharing a six-ounce split of sparkling wine bought at a roadside market, he displayed few signs of exultation.

Our conversation drifted idly, amid periods of comfortable silence. How does a goalkeeper, after all, describe a spectacular save, much less a dozen? Spectators can cheer, writers can write, bands can play as a result, but for the wizard the nature of the wizardry lies beyond the reach of words.

There was an Elton John tape in the cassette player and it played from start to finish once, then twice, and then again, so that eventually, as fatigue crept over us, it was the voice of the British singer that was heard with greatest frequency in the car.

> *I think it's gonna be a long, long time,*
> *Yes, I think it's gonna be a long, long time . . .*

I *knew* it would be a long, long time before I ever saw a match to equal Genoa–Castel di Sangro. And even longer, if ever, before I rode home from one alongside a goalkeeper of such ability and character.

I'd been hearing the word used all season long, in a variety of contexts, but it was not, I think, until after the triumph in Genoa that I fully appreciated how deep and widespread was the *carattere* and sense of dignity among our players.

At the Genoa airport we'd had a ninety-minute wait for the flight back to Rome. The team had just won the most stupendous victory in the history of the franchise, one that quite possibly would never be surpassed, yet they seated themselves calmly in the airport restaurant – interested in viewing the match highlights on television, of course, but with no one clamoring for strong drink or indulging himself in any sort of antics.

Wearing their gray suits, blue shirts, and neckties, they took a quiet pride in appearing as dignified professional men, even at a moment of such jubilation. Tired but elated, most sipped a glass of wine with their preflight meal but attracted no attention to themselves. When the flight was called, they took their places with ordinary folk on the line at the gate.

They responded warmly to any words of praise from departing *genovesi,* and there were a surprising number of such congratulations. They willingly signed autographs for anyone who asked (still a novelty for most of them), and only Claudio took the liberty of leaving his necktie untied, but then only Claudio wore his leather baseball cap with his suit. This was simply Claudio's sense of style.

On the flight to Rome, Antonello and a team trainer each ordered a split of spumante, which yielded three half-full plastic glasses apiece. These were distributed to those within easiest reach, but there were no toasts, no victory yelps, no demanding free liquor from or even any flirting with the flight attendants. Each man carried his joy privately, not because it lacked intensity, but because each was aware that others aboard might know nothing about them, might care nothing for them, and might be annoyed by any group celebration that intruded upon individual privacy.

Such decorum, to the best of my knowledge, did not come naturally to American sports teams, nor certainly – from much that I'd read – to English footballers returning from a stunning win.

But while the players of Castel di Sangro were not saints – they were at times coarse and crude and rough – the sense of good manners in public came naturally. It was simply the way of the *giocatore,* a part of the professional culture in Italy, and were one to deviate from it, as young Luca Albieri had done by misusing his cell phone on the flight back from Reggio Calabria, he wouldn't have to wait for a chewing out by Jaconi. He would be stamped, and not gently, by his teammates as a man lacking not only in maturity but in that trait each of them valued most highly – *carattere.*

We had six teams beneath us now in the standings, with only seven matches remaining, and we were as close to eleventh-place Venezia as the closest of our pursuers was to us. And it was Venezia we would play – *in casa* – the following Sunday. How different this promised to be from our first meeting, on that raw December Sunday only two days before Danilo and Pippo were killed.

If we won, in fact, we would move into a tie for eleventh place! Talk about heights heretofore undreamed of. Because Venezia had won only once away from home all season and because we were coming off the highest emotional high we would ever achieve, victory seemed quite within our grasp.

But not, apparently, to Osvaldo. *"La strada è ancora lunga,"* he must have said a hundred times that week. The road is still long. And he so frequently mumbled, *"Il Venezia è molto difficile, molto difficile Venezia,"* that Luca D'Angelo asked if this had become his new mantra. Osvaldo responded that he did not like jokes about communism. Luca replied that this had been a joke about Buddhism. *"E' la stessa cosa,"* Osvaldo grumbled in reply. The same thing.

Once again he seemed frozen by *la paura,* but this time it was fear of success. And once again he emphasized that he was approaching the upcoming match with the hope of gaining one point and one point only.

I was baffled, frankly, and told him so, which caused him to grow extremely irritated. Three of our next four matches would be *fuori casa,* I argued: three points here might well prove indispensable. But the bulldozer knew only one way, and that was to consider our glory in Genoa simply as more good luck rolled into a single afternoon than any man had a right to hope for in a season, and now instead of building on it, he seemed to be reacting feverishly against it.

The result was a lackluster, dispiriting 1–1 draw. Osvaldo had his point but, to my mind, at the cost of our far more precious momentum. Spinesi scored a clever goal when the match was only seven minutes old, but after Venezia tied in the thirty-ninth minute, all the fight seemed to go out of us. As *Tuttosport* wrote the next day, we were *senza sprint* – without pop, drive, or energy – and also *mancano idee,* or missing the element of imagination or inventiveness. Well, whose fault was that, Osvaldo?

In the days that followed, I walked around saying this aloud perhaps more often than I should have.

To be frank, communal life had gone from bad to worse at Via Peschiera 10. While Signor Rezza's Vito, who managed the building, remained on good terms with all, Osvaldo's annoyance at what he considered my unseemly offering of unasked-for advice and my even more inappropriate second-guessing after it was not taken paled beside the rage he'd built up in his heart against Antonello.

Already, for reasons known only to himself, he had dismissed from his mind and future planning both Franceschini and Russo – such promising newcomers, with such attractive styles of play, and with so much to offer a team *senza sprint* and *mancano idee*. Albieri, despite his crucial goal at Padova, had become almost as invisible.

Although sitting at the same lunch and dinner table with them five or six days a week, Osvaldo managed to entirely ignore them. Now on the training field, too, he acted, insofar as was possible, as if they were not even there. Occasionally, he would fire a brief, profane verbal burst at one of them for some error that only he had perceived, but after his one extended excoriation of Franceschini weeks earlier, he'd behaved for the most part as if they were simply unnecessary pieces of equipment cluttering the field.

It was obvious that he had soured badly on Antonello as well, again for reasons obscure. At Genoa only when D'Angelo had been carried off on a stretcher had Antonello been sent into the match. Against Venezia, when Osvaldo had taken his final step in the direction of preserving a draw instead of trying for a win by removing Martino with thirty minutes left and sending on a defender, the defender had been not Antonello but Rimedio.

Now, at the start of a morning training session in preparation for the Sunday match at Lucchese, he erupted in Antonello's direction for what would prove to be the final time. Antonello had no sooner set foot on the field than the screaming began.

"It's all your fault!" he shouted. "It's all your fault that De Juliis cannot be our goalkeeper anymore! It's all because of your stupid and lazy playing against Ravenna!" He was harking back now eight weeks in time, to Ravenna's goal that De Juliis should have saved but that Osvaldo had immediately blamed on Antonello, but it was apparent that bulldozers never forget.

"Always you were and always you will be a *C1* player at best! Maybe no better than *C2*. You have done more to hurt the defense this year than if Sabrina had played in your position! And you grow only slower and more stupid with time, always worse and never better. You should be ashamed to even lace up your cleats. You are not

a *giocatore,* but a *giocattolo!*" This was a child's toy, a simple object designed for the amusement of infants. It was also a terrible insult to
hurl at a professional.

The tirade continued for at least another ten minutes, until the
hideous notion entered Osvaldo's mind that the only proper thing to
do would be to have De Juliis step forward and for Antonello to issue
an apology to him in front of the whole squad.

Fortunately – although it came as a shock to Osvaldo because *no*
player was *ever* late for training – De Juliis was nowhere to be found.
I knew why but I wasn't saying.

Across the alleyway from Marcella's was a bar called Il Pub, fre-
quented by what Jaconi often derided as "the wrong sort," apparently
unaware of how much time the wives and children of certain *Società*
officers spent there, often in the company of such Castel di Sangro
players as Gigi, Galli, and De Juliis.

De Juliis had been at Il Pub the night before. He had still been
there early this morning. I knew because I had been with him and
some friends until about 3 A.M. listening to a performance by an
honest-to-God American blues singer who had grown up in Chicago.
I left at about three, feeling my services as interpreter were no longer
necessary since by then no one was making sense in any language,
but De Juliis and his party showed no signs of flagging. Thus, it had
not come as a total surprise when I did not see him at the 8 A.M. start
of training.

It was almost nine when Jaconi first sought him out to assist in the
humiliation of Altamura. De Juliis, a man whose decency never
wavered though his fortunes rose and fell, was an especially close
friend of Antonello's, at whose apartment he and his girlfriend had
spent many a long winter evening. No doubt he would have balked at
the scheme in any event, but he was nowhere within balking distance.

He finally turned up, red-eyed, at 10 A.M. But even this serious
breach of regulations was quickly rerouted by Osvaldo in the direction of Antonello. "There!" he shouted, pointing to De Juliis, who
was doubled over with apparent stomach cramps. "See him there?
That's your fault. Your fault! It's been all your fault since Ravenna!"

At that, Antonello simply walked off the field and went home.

Toward the end of the week, as I walked into Marcella's for dinner,
she told me I'd received Express Mail from America.

"From America?" I said. "Vanessa has escaped to America?"

Marcella glared at me, as she did at anyone who might make a less than reverent comment about Vanessa.

My package, in any event, was from Nancy. I knew immediately what it contained. One evening about two weeks earlier, the team's *massaggiatore,* a short and rather devious man named Angelo, who seemed to have irons in many fires, had knocked softly at my apartment door. He'd knocked so softly, in fact, that it was only on his third or fourth repetition that I was sure I'd heard knocking at all.

As soon as I opened the door, he put his finger to his lips and ducked inside, from where he immediately pointed to Jaconi's apartment next door. *"Non è affar suo,"* Angelo said. Whatever the purpose of his visit, he did not want Jaconi to know.

I asked him to take off his coat, to sit down, but no, no, he could stay for only a moment. Then he put his finger to his lips again and looked at me, nodding. He continued until I nodded back.

Only then did he remove from a pocket a neatly folded square of white paper. On it were printed four letters: DHEA. He sounded them out in a whisper, the *H* pronounced "acca" in Italian. Then he looked up at me.

"You can get? From America?"

"Angelo, what the hell are you talking about?"

"Two bottle, okay? *Due.*" He held up two fingers.

"Your English is very good, Angelo. But *non ho capito.* I do not know what you mean."

A look of exasperation crossed his face. More than two hundred million people in America and Castel di Sangro had to draw one so stupid.

"Is peel," he whispered. *"Una medicina."*

"DHEA?" I said. "I've never heard of it."

"Sh-sh-shhhhhhhh!" He looked back over his shoulder as if expecting Jaconi to barge through momentarily and seize his incriminating piece of paper.

Well, eventually he had to sit down, though he still refused to remove his coat. And then slowly, and with considerable confusion on my part, he explained that DHEA was some sort of vitamin-like substance or dietary supplement, which while not yet approved for sale by Italian pharmacies, was apparently dispensed like Tums tablets over the counter in America.

In Italy, *era vietato* – it was prohibited – but in free and easy America this mysterious substance could be sold *senza ricetta!* Angelo said. Even without a doctor's prescription!

"Okay?" he said. "You wife send? Two bottle? I pays. I pays. You no pay. I pays."

"Slow down, Angelo. I still don't even know what this is."

"Peels," he repeated. "I tell you: peels."

"Yes, but what kind of pills? What do they do?"

At this, Angelo blushed, lowered his head, and actually began to paw at my floor with the toe of one shoe.

Finally, he looked back up and said, *"Privato."*

"Angelo," I said, "you cannot come knocking on my door with a piece of paper with letters on it and tell me these are the name of pills that are illegal in Italy but you want me to have sent from America, and then refuse to tell me what they *are!*"

"Okay, okay," he said, but putting a finger to his lips again as if Jaconi were standing next door with his ear pressed to the living room wall. "Peels for *il sesso,*" he said, and pointed toward his crotch.

"Sex pills?"

"Sì, sì, sì, esatto." The man was perspiring, and it had to be from nervousness because even with a coat on, he could not have found my apartment overly warm.

"But how do they work?" I asked. "What do they do?"

Angelo took a deep breath and then apparently decided to tell all. "No peels," he said, "you fucks, you stop. *Ciao, buona notte.* Wit' peels, you fucks, you fucks again, you fucks again. All the night. All the day. You fucks like the fucker machine. Every lady is 'appy."

I got the point. (Although whatever he meant by "the fucker machine," I didn't want to know.) And how such a wonder drug as DHEA had escaped my notice (this being before the age of Viagra) puzzled me.

I was puzzled also by the fact that this request was coming from Angelo. He had a beautiful wife and three of the loveliest, most charming children in the town, and I would not have guessed that in some other life he cut such a wide swath through the ranks of Abruzzan women that he now was in need of pharmacological reinforcement.

And I said so. "It's not my business, Angelo. Private life is private life. But you? I am surprised."

Ehi! Mamma mia! I thought he would have a heart attack right there. *"No, no, no, no, no, no, no, no, Joe!* Peels not *per me!"*

"For who, then?"

He shook his head, held up his hands in a gesture of helplessness, and repeated again, *"È privato."*

I handed him back the paper. "I'm sorry," I said. "But if you want me to smuggle into Italy some medicine that is prohibited by the government here – and to risk going to jail like Vanessa and Gigi – then you at least have to tell me who it's for."

He took back the paper and shook his head sadly. "No jail. *Non è come la cocaina. È solo una medicina."*

"For who?" But as soon as I asked, I realized what the answer must be. Yes, yes, just as I'd always heard: They did you favors, and then they came seeking favors in return. And they did not expect to be turned down. "For Signor Rezza," I said. "Okay."

Angelo's denial of this intended recipient was even more emphatic than when I'd thought the pills were for himself. *"Non per il signor Rezza! Mai! Mai!"* Never. Never.

"Okay." I shrugged. *"Mi dispiace, Angelo."* I'm sorry. "You no tell me, I no get pills."

He looked at me, pursing his lips. Then he reached into his pocket for a pencil. On the same small square that contained the initials DHEA, he printed a name. He flashed the paper before my eyes without ever once uttering the name, then tore the paper into minuscule scraps, all of which he placed carefully within a pocket.

"Okay?" he asked.

"Okay, Angelo. Okay."

"Grazie, Joe. Però acqua in bocca, capito?" Keep it secret, understand?

I nodded. I understood. The name on the paper had been Gravina.

And now the pills had arrived, along with a note from Nancy saying that a doctor friend had assured her they had no effect whatever on either sexual desire or stamina but that they were among the current handful of such products being marketed to the particularly gullible.

The express mailing had cost more than the pills themselves, which had been less than five dollars per bottle. I passed them along to Angelo the next time I saw him, saying they were a gift from me to "Mister X."

Angelo seemed to like that concept. "Meester X," he said, grinning. "Okay, Joe. Like we be spies, no? Like in movie."

"Sì, Angelo. Come in un film. Come a Genoa."

Lucca is one of the Italian cities most favored by American tourists, primarily for its ancient and preserved inner city, shielded from the worst of modern encroachment by the highest, widest, and most functional wall still standing around any of the beguiling towns of Tuscany. The top of the wall is like a park circling the perimeter of the inner city, with grass underfoot and a wide assortment of tall shade trees overhead.

A sunny May Sunday in such a spot? Do Tuscan reveries come any sweeter?

Well, yes, if you have arrived instead in the congested and charmless sprawl that lies outside the wall (amid which the Lucchese stadium is located) and if the sole reason for your journey is to try to win at least one crucial point against a team four points beneath you in the *classifica*. And especially if Lotti has been left behind in order to recover from the flu.

Just as I was taking my seat, I suddenly encountered Pippo Biondi's mother and sister, who'd come to the match to show their continuing support for Pippo's team. I'd had no contact with them after having responded to the letter sent by Pippo's sister, and this unexpected meeting quickly reduced all three of us to tears again.

Only as the match began did they move to their own seats, which were about twenty yards to the right of me and three rows back, adjacent to those occupied by the parents of Rimedio, who had been such a friend to Pippo in life. I'd met Rimedio's parents on two or three occasions, and having done so, I had no doubts about the source of Rimedio's extraordinary class as a person. Pleased that Pippo's folk were in such compatible company, I turned my attention to the match, which had not begun well.

Lucchese, in fact, scored after only two minutes. Before Genoa I would have thought it was already over, despite the eighty-eight minutes remaining. But Genoa had showed that all things were possible and that some might even be achieved.

And only ten minutes later, a corner kick from Di Fabio was inadvertently headed into the Lucchese goal by one of their own players, who had been trying to clear it. This was by far the least glamorous of the ways in which it is possible to score in a football match, but it did tie the score at 1–1.

Little else of interest happened on the field during the half, but several minutes before it ended, I heard the sudden low rumble of male voices that in any language means trouble nearby. I stood to see the source of it.

To my amazement, I saw Rimedio's father – this genteel Roman with impeccable manners, stylish clothing, a beautiful wife, and the most honorable of sons – purple in the face, shouting vile curses, and then lunging, arms swinging and fists clenched tight, toward a small group of Lucchese supporters.

I could not imagine what they had done to anger him so. I started down my row to offer assistance but before I got there, both stadium stewards and police officers arrived and proceeded to eject a handful of nasty-looking Lucchese fans from the stadium.

At halftime I found Signor Rimedio standing on the lower level, near a refreshment stand, with one arm each around Pippo's mother and his sister, both of whom had been crying fresh tears.

While still quite flushed, Signor Rimedio was again in control of himself and explained in a very few words what had happened. The small group of Lucchese supporters, somehow having learned that the two women side by side at our end of the *tribuna* were the mother and sister of one of our players who'd been killed, had decided to amuse themselves by taunting them in ways more cruel and sadistic than the normal human mind could conjure.

As soon as this had begun, Signor Rimedio, a man of almost my own age, I assumed, threw himself into their midst, giving no thought whatever to his personal well-being, intent only on crushing these loathsome insects who'd somehow been allowed to roam free within the stadium.

The prompt arrival of security forces and the equally prompt ejection of the offenders had prevented any physical harm from being done to anyone, but Pippo's mother and sister now expressed their concern to me about the continuing purple tint to Signor Rimedio's cheeks and about the fact that perspiration continued to pour down his forehead.

He assured us that he was not about to have a heart attack and apologized for having made a scene. But it was clear that he'd earned the eternal gratitude of the two Biondi *donne.* My own respect counted for little compared to the feelings of Pippo's mother and sister, but for whatever it was worth, I told Signor Rimedio that he had that, too.

Then the second half began. Seven minutes later we watched De Juliis sprawl helplessly on his belly as Lucchese scored another goal to win the match, 2-1, and thereby climb within one point of us in the *classifica.*

As matters stood by Sunday night, May 11, the relevant portion of *la classifica* looked like this:

Reggina	38
Salernitana	37
CASTEL DI SANGRO	37
Cesena	36
Lucchese	36
Cosenza	34
Cremonese	31
Palermo	31

Four of the eight would survive. Four would not.

Only five matches remained.

For us, three of them would be *fuori casa,* and two of those against Lecce and Bari, two southern giants that now ranked third and fourth in *Serie B.*

The two home matches would pit us against Torino and Pescara, which along with Genoa, were at present locked with Bari in a terrific fight for the fourth and last promotion spot.

Thus, of the last five matches, four would be against teams ranked among the top seven in the division, while we were presently ranked sixth from the bottom. It would take more than a belief in *la potenza della speranza* to find glimmers of encouragement in that prospect.

One thing I made sure to do as soon as possible was to tell Rimedio of his father's courage and honor.

"I'm very proud of him," I said.

Rimedio gave me his biggest grin yet. *"Naturalmente,"* he said. *"Non potevamo che aspettarcelo."* It was only to be expected.

As breeders of thoroughbred racehorses have known for centuries, class really is in the genes.

35

Summer seemed to arrive overnight. It was only mid-May but the lower hills had suddenly grown so lush with green that they reminded me of the Caribbean or Southeast Asia. All over town, bare-chested men were mowing lawns I had not known existed. The smell of burning charcoal was in the air.

Yet however much the seasonal shift cheered the townspeople, it filled my heart with dread. We would face Torino at home in a rare Thursday night match. The very next morning we would depart on the interminable journey south to Lecce for a Sunday match that, in all probability, would be played in the heat and humidity of near-African intensity.

After that, only three matches would remain. We were in the end-game now, and it would be quick and merciless.

To me, even worse than the fear that it would not end well was the knowledge that as soon as it did end, I would have to leave Castel di Sangro. Upon the conclusion of the season, *salvezza* or not, would come the conclusion of my brief career in *calcio*.

For the others, at whatever level they found themselves, a new season would start in September, or even with training in August. But I would return to America, leaving behind all the passion and camaraderie that had given me life since September. My own identity had merged so totally with that of the town and the team that I could not imagine a future without either. The "I" who had been "we" for nine glorious if turbulent months would become "I" again, alone and forlorn.

It must be said, however, that in some ways my position in Castel di Sangro was becoming increasingly precarious. The more I'd learned the language, the more indiscreet I'd been in using it.

As my obsession with *la salvezza* had grown – and by now it was as if my own immortal soul hung in the balance – the more loudly and frequently I carped at Osvaldo about his lineup choices and tactics. During the entire second half of the Venezia match I'd cupped my hands around my mouth and shouted, "*Roo*-so . . . *Roo*-so," urging Osvaldo to send on Russo to bolster our flagging attack. Instead, he'd chosen the defender Rimedio, and I'd earned only dark glares from both Gravina and Signor Rezza.

Then at our hotel outside Lucca I'd come upon Jaconi sitting alone in the dining room, obsessively wiping the inside of an unused ashtray with his napkin. *"Nervoso?"* I'd asked, pointing.

For the briefest moment there had been pure fury in his eyes. Then he'd clenched his jaw and had muttered at me, *"Scrittore americano? Assolutamente no! Piuttosto folle americano!"* American writer? Certainly not! Insane American instead. It did not seem the time to point out that the two were not mutually exclusive.

Nor was it the moment to suggest to Osvaldo that even the crazy are sometimes correct. But *Il Tempo* termed our loss to Lucchese "a technical and tactical disaster," and even one of Jaconi's favorite players, Roberto Alberti, blamed Jaconi.

"Non è possibile che la squadra sia peggiorata così tanto solo in due settimane," he had said to me after the match. It just wasn't possible for us to have fallen apart so completely in only two weeks. Much of the blame for the post-Genoa collapse had to rest with our ham-handed, grudge-holding, fear-stricken *allenatore*.

Just as I felt that as long as Spinosa respected me, I could continue to respect myself, I believed that if Alberti agreed with me about lineup and tactics, I could not be completely in the wrong.

On the larger scale, however, right and wrong were irrelevant. Jaconi was and would continue to be the manager. I was a visitor from a land where people knew nothing about soccer. That I'd come to care so much might have seemed charming for a while, but my fanaticism was now clearly a considerable irritant.

Likewise with *La Società*. My relations with Gravina had begun to deteriorate at the time of the Raku Ponnick folly and now were simply nonexistent, my gift of DHEA notwithstanding. (Of course, for that he could not thank me, because I'd not supposed to know it was for him.) Whenever I came within his range of vision, he simply refused to look at me. He would not even say *ciao* if he came upon me in a group.

Also, Signor Rezza had begun to act differently toward me. No more would he grunt *"Salve"* and raise his cigar in greeting when he happened upon me at the training field. No more did his bodyguards nod and smile.

To be fair, both men had their reasons. In the weeks since Gigi's arrest, I'd speculated openly about the extent of Gravina's involvement in the entire drug-smuggling operation. Following Gigi's sudden release, I'd even more insistently expressed the view that a bribe must have been been paid by Signor Rezza and that its real intent had not been the prompt return of Gigi to the squad but the quashing of any further actions against Gravina.

I had logic on my side, I felt, but no hard facts to support it. All over Italy, of course – and especially in matters related to *calcio* – people expressed opinions every day that had no basis whatsoever in fact, and a fair percentage of these weren't even logical.

Nonetheless, in Castel di Sangro I was not one more anonymous voice. I was the *scrittore americano,* and because I was different I got noticed. Also, what others only whispered, I said aloud with what I liked to think was admirable candor but which some might have viewed as only a crass lack of sophistication.

I don't know what my motivation was. I don't know why I didn't just shut up – if not about tactics, at least about bribes. Did I think that by saying long enough and loud enough that both Signor Rezza and Gravina were crooks, I would prompt them to one day invite me back up to the mountaintop so they could confess all and beg my forgiveness?

I was not that unmoored from reality. But I was frustrated by how much remained intangible and elusive. I must also have felt (this whole period is somewhat hazy to me now, so buckled was I by stress as the *salvezza* squeeze grew ever tighter) that if I just kept banging away with American directness and persistence, I would somehow break through the wall of silence and evasiveness and then find spread out before me all the truths, sordid and otherwise, that Signor Rezza had spent half a century concealing.

Instead, I fear that I only made a pain in the ass of myself. Foolishly so, because much unpleasantness could have been avoided if I'd only borne in mind what had been the very first lesson I'd learned upon arrival: that indirection, which was a far different thing from insincerity, was a way of life here, having been practiced in these mountains since well before the birth of Christ.

All season long I'd made the mistake of inferring that openness and warmth somehow implied a lack of subtlety. Now I compounded the error by convincing myself that I'd learned things in my eight months here that had eluded these townspeople and their forebears for centuries.

In my defense, I can cite only *calcio*. Bathed in a nervous sweat day and night, I became aware that the game *was* my life. I could no longer imagine an existence without it. Yet hanging above me like the sword of Damocles was my awareness that in only a month I would have to leave it all behind.

This conflict led to certain inner tensions, an unfortunately large number of which resolved themselves only through outbursts of bizarre behavior on my part. "The fanatic is a fan in a madhouse," Galeano writes. But even he had never spent a full season as intimately connected with a particular team as I had.

Torino was like Genoa squared. True, the club had not been founded until 1906, but in *Serie A* competition over the years it had ranked even higher than its neighbor to the west. Behind Juventus, Inter Milan, and A.C. Milan, it was the fourth most successful club in Italian history and had won the *Serie A* championship seven times. Since the formation of *Serie A* in 1929, the current season was only Torino's fourth in a lower division. Their home stadium (shared with Juventus) seated more than 70,000 people. Only four years earlier they'd sold a single player to A.C. Milan for almost $20 million. On every imaginable scale, including the talent possessed by this year's squad, they dwarfed us. Never had we felt more Lilliputian than on the Thursday when Torino came to town.

By now, three of the four promotion positions were all but spoken for. Brescia was certainly going up, and probably Lecce and Empoli as well. Empoli was the surprise of the season, given that they'd been in *C1* the previous year and had reached *Serie A* only twice before in their history.

The fourth and last spot was still open, with Bari (fifty-one), Genoa (fifty), and Torino (forty-nine) the contenders. Bari would be our last opponent of the season. Genoa had provided us with our greatest glory. But Torino was here now, full of big-city, northern arrogance, demanding three points on a silver platter.

Fusco and Cristiano were both *squalificati* for us. Cristiano probably would not have played anyway, but Fusco's absence would be keenly felt. Just how keenly became apparent to me only at the pre-match meal, when Rimedio confided that he was starting.

This was not possible! Rimedio starting against *Torino? Mannaggia,* talk about feeding Christians to the lions, talk about a boy among men! Rimedio was barely twenty-one, and in only five matches all season had he even played enough to warrant a rating. Yes, yes, the boy had all the class, courage, and *carattere* in the world, and a father who'd showed those same qualities; but, please, Torino would eat him alive. Rimedio had started only one match all season, against Cremonese, which was now last among the twenty teams of *Serie B.* Even there he'd received a 5.5 *voto* and we'd lost. To start him tonight wasn't fair to him, or to the team, or to our thousands of *tifosi.*

I walked out of Marcella's halfway through the meal, and it had nothing to do with the fish. *Rimedio!* In two or three years, given good coaching and strong players to work with, it was likely that Rimedio would grow into a defender capable of playing against Torino. But this kid had been signed – *on my recommendation!* – after a tryout with a team of amateurs only last fall. Good God, this was Osvaldo's most damaging decision yet. I didn't care how much he hated Antonello, we needed the experience, the combativeness, and not least the physical strength of Altamura on the field from the start.

I was standing outside Osvaldo's office beneath the stadium, waiting for him when he arrived. I would be direct, but polite. He nodded at me, glaring, but did not say hello as he unlocked his office door. I stepped inside along with him.

"*Osvald'*," I said, "*Preferisco se tu non usi Rimedio.*" I'd prefer it if you didn't use Rimedio.

"*Puppami la fava,*" he replied. Suck my dick.

"*Scusa, Osvald'. Non mi piace affatto parlare cosi, ma –*" I don't at all like speaking like this, but –

"*Ciucciami il cazzo.*" Suck my dick.

"*Non puoi usare Rimedio!*" You cannot use Rimedio!

"*Fammi un pompino.*" Give me a blowjob.

We appeared to have reached an impasse.

"*Mi dispiace, ma non sono d'accordo con la tua scelta,*" I said. I'm sorry, but I don't agree with your choice.

"*Vaffanculo.*" Fuck off.

At that point, Spinosa entered the office, which he and Jaconi shared. Rather than drag a friend like him into this mess, I simply left, remembering at least to say, "*In bocca al lupo,*" the prematch idiom for "good luck."

Spinosa responded properly with "*Crepi il lupo.*" Death to the wolf. Fortunately, I was not able to hear Jaconi's reply.

For the first time since its construction, every seat in the new stadium was filled. More than 8,000 spectators – a crowd larger than the town's population by more than 50 percent – had crammed inside the gates to watch the match. It was, by a wide margin, the largest audience ever to watch anything that had happened in Castel di Sangro.

It was also the noisiest. With one voice, the crowd was chanting, "*Ca-stell-O! Ca-stell-O!*" even before the players took the field. And five minutes after the match began I was subjected to – and participated in creating – what I think was the loudest noise I'd ever heard in my life.

Torino had fouled us about twenty yards from their goal. This provided us with a free kick. Normally, free kicks from a distance of twenty yards or less provide teams with good scoring opportunities. Yet we'd failed to score a single goal on such a kick all season. Jaconi's theory was that we were simply unlucky. Mine was that Jaconi devoted no training time to practicing the various set plays that could be executed when such opportunities arose.

In any event, Claudio took this kick and drilled it hard. To our immense good fortune, it bounced off the head of a Torino defender who'd been unable to get out of the way. The angle at which it was deflected left the Torino keeper helpless to stop it, and we were ahead, 1–0.

Less than half an hour later, the situation was reversed. Torino was much the stronger team and demonstrated this convincingly in the minutes that followed our goal. Only a new array of impressive saves by Lotti kept them from evening the score.

Rimedio was a problem, being outrun and outmaneuvered time and again by Torino midfielders and attackers who simply had too much skill and experience for him. This put extra pressure on our other defenders, and as a result, Luca D'Angelo eventually committed a foul at the very edge of our penalty area.

From a distance of only twelve yards, the dangerous Scarchilli drove a shot that was even harder than Claudio's. It deflected slightly off Alberti and into our goal. The score was tied, 1–1.

Only two minutes later we were awarded another free kick, this one, as Torino's had been, from only twelve yards out, at the edge of the penalty area. For some reason, Jaconi wanted Spinesi rather than Bonomi to take the kick, and Spinesi did. It was on target, but the Torino goalkeeper blocked it with a dive. The ball bounced off his body, however, and directly onto the foot of the waiting Rimedio, who had been overlooked by the Torino defense. From a distance of five yards, he had the whole net open in front of him. Yet somehow he contrived to kick the ball wide. *Ah, madonna,* panic under pressure, the inevitable consequence of inexperience. This was yet one more reason why Altamura should have been on the field.

The half ended with the score still tied. Fifteen minutes into the second half, however, Rimedio was the victim of the worst refereeing decision I had seen since the excrementitious display by Rossi of Ciampino. This *arbitro* was one Ceccarini of Livorno, unknown to me at the time but a man whose name would come to live in infamy the following season after he refused to award a penalty to Ronaldo of Inter in a crucial match against Juventus. Not only was that decision clearly erroneous, it seemed so obviously the result of favoritism toward Juventus and the powerful Agnelli family that it became the basis for an entire book, published by one of the leading houses in Italy.

No one was going to write a book about an injustice done to Rimedio or to Castel di Sangro, but the red card that suddenly materialized in Ceccarini's hand seemed the result of dementia rather than anything that had occurred on the field.

As opposed to the choice of Rimedio as I had been, my heart went out to him now. For possibly the first time all night, he'd made a successful tackle, stripping the ball from a Torino attacker while making no contact at all with the man. There was no possible justification for even calling a foul, much less for an immediate expulsion!

Playing with a man advantage, Torino moved in for the kill. There were, however, two factors they could not control: One was the effect of 8,000 Castel di Sangro fans packed into a grandstand that pressed close against the edges of the field. It was not just the amount of noise we made that lifted our players, it was the quality of the sound.

La salvezza lay on the line. There was not one among us who did not believe that he or she could win it for us if only the intensity of our cry was sufficient. *God would hear!* And he or she or it would grant us not a miracle in this case, but simple justice.

Never before had I been so aware of the *tifosi* as being, collectively, the mythical "extra man" on the field. There had been cacophony from the start, but now it was as if each of us felt that *he* must replace Rimedio and could do so through sheer force of will, or at least volume. "The fan knows," Galeano writes, "who stirs up the winds of fervor that propel the ball when it sleeps." And so we did.

But it takes more than winds of fervor to block the ball when the other team shoots it with power and accuracy at the goal. And here was the other unforeseeable element: Super-Lotti.

For the final half hour it was as if the Genoa match had never stopped. If anything, Lotti was even more immense than he had been three weeks earlier. Certainly, the sheer relentlessness of the Torino attack was more than he'd had to cope with in Genoa. Torino was one of only half a dozen *Serie B* teams to have scored more than forty goals by that point in the season. They could let fly from anywhere and everywhere, and they did.

But Lotti coped. With a brilliance, intelligence, and degree of fortitude never before witnessed by the people of Castel di Sangro (who, after all, had seen the Genoa match only on television), he repelled every Torino shot, even as they fell upon him like hailstones. *La*

Gazzetta dello Sport said the next day, "They should build a monument to this man in the central square of this town, and all who love *calcio* should come and bow before it every day." Yes, he was that good.

In the midst of his unforgettable display there occurred another event that would have to be counted among the least likely of the season. As Torino pressed forward with seven men on attack, Claudio Bonomi captured the ball and immediately lofted a high and exquisitely placed pass far downfield to Spinesi.

Only one Torino defender had stayed back, and as he charged toward Spinesi, the young northerner coolly and precisely slid a pass across to, of all people, Guido Di Fabio. Immediately, "as with a lion's paw" in one account, Di Fabio kicked it past the Torino keeper for a goal – his first in *Serie B* in five years but, far more important, our second of the night.

The final score: Castel di Sangro 2, Torino 1.

At the end no one wanted to leave, so no one did. We stood there for the better part of an hour after the match – 8,000 exultant Castel di Sangro fans trying to sing "We Are the Champions" in English, as we had seen trimphant national teams from such countries as Germany do on television.

Di Fabio dedicated his winning goal to Pippo and Danilo, saying to the assembled television crews that "they would be crazy with joy tonight, to know that their determination and commitment was the inspiration for all that occurred."

Lotti said, "Tonight we all deserve *pagelle* of eight" (although he alone received that extraordinary rating the next day). He also said the fervor of the crowd had made him feel that he was playing with an extra pair of hands.

Outside the stadium fans had already produced bedsheets and paints, and immediately created huge posters portraying Superman in some instances and Batman in others. In either case, over the near life-size figures they printed, *SuperLotti,* or, rather quaintly, *Batman-Lotti.* It was as if Dylan Dog and Diabolik had suddenly become a single force provided by Providence to defend our goal, as just one more aspect of the miracle.

Joy reigned through the night. Only Jaconi failed to rise to the occasion. "What happened tonight," he told the press, "it was not normal." He reminded everyone, "Lotti and Di Fabio – these are players of *C2*. Torino is rightfully a team of *Serie A.*" Then he frowned and shook his head. *"No, non è normale."*

But *il calcio* is about joy as much as it is about anything. It is especially about the joy of the unexpected, even the unimaginable. Genoa had produced such a feeling, but that match had taken place far from home, and by 2:30 A.M., when the team bus had finally rolled down the deserted and chilly Via Settembre, the dancing in the streets had long since subsided.

But this happened right here, in our town. It happened in the stadium that for so many months had seemed only a figment of a futile imagination. A man down for the last half hour, we'd won the greatest victory ever won in Castel di Sangro.

And so, despite Osvaldo, joy reigned through the night.

36

All week, reversing a habit that had developed over months, I'd been walking to the stadium on the shady, not the sunny, side of the street. But it was only on Friday, May 16, the morning after the win over Torino, that for the first time since I'd arrived in Castel di Sangro eight months earlier, I felt uncomfortably hot.

If it was like this here, at 8:30 A.M., what would it be like in Lecce, not only at sea level but 400 kilometers farther south? The answer arrived promptly and without ambiguity, the heat swelling up to meet us before we'd descended even 1,000 feet.

The bus could not go faster than 100 kilometers per hour. Its "air-conditioning" was so feeble that at least half a dozen players walked to the front to check for themselves before the rest of us accepted that it was turned on at full power. The sound system, however, remained robust. This was our longest bus ride of the season, but even had we been going only as far as Villa Scontrone, it would have been the most uncomfortable as well.

For the first few hours nothing mattered. We were still on our Torino high. Strung out from sleeplessness, pumped up from the wondrous win, the players neither knew nor cared what the temperature was: The only numbers that mattered were those of *la classifica*.

Among the eight teams still fighting for *salvezza*, only Salernitana had lost the night before. Cesena and Cosenza had each played draws, while Reggina and Lucchese had kept pace with us by winning.

And so what faced us was this:

CASTEL DI SANGRO	40
Salernitana	40
Reggina	39
Lucchese	37
Cesena	37
Cosenza	35
Palermo	32
Cremonese	32

Four would make it, four would not. Palermo and Cremonese looked to be all but out of the running, if not yet mathematically eliminated. So at least there was that: Whatever happened, we had not been humiliated in *Serie B*. We had not been put to season-long rout, as it had appeared before the season and in December that we might be. Whether we were still standing at the end, three weeks from now, at least we would not have been first to fall.

Oh my God, I thought – I was starting to think like Jaconi!

Who, by the way, had greeted me cordially in the parking lot before we'd boarded. If he did not actually apologize for his rudeness the night before, he at least made an extended point of explaining that the pressure was eating him alive and that in the hour before such a match he did not think he could have behaved in civil fashion no matter whom he was talking to, or about what.

And if I did not actually apologize, I at least expressed regret over the poor timing of my objection to his lineup – and did not even hint that I now knew for certain I'd been right. Thus, we were back on what passed for good terms this late in such a stressful season.

The combination of heat, the anticipated duration of the trip, and exhaustion in the wake of the night before kept the players unusually subdued. Despite the win, Rimedio was downright inconsolable. He'd received a *voto* of 4 for the match, the worst mark given to any Castel di Sangro player all season. He had the character to come back from such an awful showing, but Jaconi, having been proved wrong, was not the sort to give him the chance to do so anytime soon. For Rimedio, the long ride to Lecce was a form of penance, nothing more.

Alberti sat beside me for a while. He did not speak of Gigi, of course, but of Jaconi. He wanted me to have no doubt that if the squad were to achieve *la salvezza,* it would be in spite of – *malgrado* – Jaconi, not because of him – *a causa di* – in any way. And he looked at me as he spoke, to make sure I wrote this in my notebook. *("Non a causa di Jaconi – malgrado!")* The man credited with being the team's master of *mentalità,* of whom Jaconi spoke so often with such respect, wanted there to be no mistake regarding his feelings on that point.

The bus stopped every two hours. The driver explained that this protected the engine against overheating, but nobody minded because it gave us all a chance to dash into whatever sort of convenience store was located nearest the gas pumps and grab all the chilled bottled water in stock.

Often, on the field, I'd seen players using water not only to drink but to pour over their heads in an attempt to cool themselves, and in the days of my more strenuous activity I'd frequently done it myself. But this was the first time I'd ever seen grown men take full bottles of water and pour the contents all over themselves before reboarding a bus. Even so, it was not until we were about eight hours into the trip that anyone first used a rest room.

This heat was not normal for mid-May. Everyone told me that, as if it would make me feel cooler. But I could watch the Italian weather channel, too. It was clear what had happened: a hot, dry out-of-season wind – if not quite a full-fledged sirocco – had suddenly blown up from North Africa, parching southern Italy and leaving the countryside seeming as sere as in August.

Given our direction, as well as the length of the trip, it seemed to me that our destination might as well be Tangiers. But that simply showed how badly skewed my sense of Italian geography remained. The North Africa syndrome was a trick played by the weather and terrain. Lecce has nothing to do with Africa. In fact, if one wanted to find a major city to which Lecce lay close, it would not be Rome but rather Athens or even Sofia. And from Milan? Lecce was almost as close to Beirut as it was to Milan. Small wonder that Christ stopped at Eboli.

As we rolled slowly toward the very bottom of the heel of Italy's boot, most of us dozed fitfully, expending no more energy than was required to will the journey to be over. Half asleep, I listened to two of the exceptions, Cristiano and Spinesi, engage in a spirited debate over the relative merits of Dylan Dog and Diabolik. Mimmo was with Dylan Dog, the original Italian superhero, all the way. But Spinesi said this only proved that people from Rome, unlike northerners, lacked the intellectual capacity to appreciate the cleverness of Diabolik, who was far less quick than Dylan Dog to resort to violence to get himself out of a scrape.

I awoke just enough to tell them that after six months of careful comparative study, I would have to cast my vote with Dylan Dog. This brought applause from Cristiano, but only scorn from Spinesi, who said he'd never realized until now that Americans were even dumber than Romans. Then he looked at my shoes, which admittedly were not the latest in high Italian fashion, and said he could have no respect for the opinion of anyone who would place his feet into such objects.

What *voto* did they deserve? he asked.

"My shoes? Oh, maybe five point five."

"Neanche per sogno!" he said. No way! Not even in your dreams. Only a 4 for my shoes, nothing higher. *"Come Rimedio,"* he added, leaning forward and rubbing Rimedio's hair.

Poor Fabio. Sleep had finally brought him respite from his misery, and now he was suddenly awakened by this! Well, life on the road was not easy. Especially not toward the end of a season in *Serie B.*

Cei was so heat-struck that he was attempting an English-language crossword puzzle. He took advantage of my semiwakefulness to ask for a twelve-letter nickname for Babe Ruth.

"Sultan of Swat," I murmured, but then had to sit up and spell it for him. And then, as with *Gatsby,* he was troubled. "Sultan" gave him no problem because the Italian word *sultano* means the same thing. But Davide had watched far too many American movies, and to him "swat" meant only a SWAT team – trained police killers, whose commanding officer could not possibly have been Babe Ruth because Babe Ruth had lived and died long before SWAT teams were developed.

In another context, it might have been amusing, but the temperature inside the bus was now pushing as close to ninety-five degrees Fahrenheit, as was the temperature outside.

"Swat! Davide," I said, and slapped myself on the arm, as if killing a mosquito. Then I dragged my Italian dictionary out of my traveling bag. There was a verb: *schiacciare.* I pointed to it, hoping he might somehow understand the use of this word in non-verb form as part of an American nickname from more than half a century before.

But Cei was nobody's fool. *"No,"* he said promptly. *"Non è possibile."* Then he took his thumb and pressed down hard on the armrest between us, as if squashing a bug. *"Schiaccio,"* he said. I crush. I squash. The Sultan of Squash? No, that would not work. Cei, however, knew how to pursue a literary scent, as he'd proved with East Egg and West Egg.

"Capisco, Joe!" he said after a few moments of thought. *"Schiaccio un avversario."* I crush an oppenent. Now, he could see. "Sultan of Swat" meant "a king who crushes the opponents."

"Sì, Davide, sì. Esatto," I said, relieved that we'd even come that close.

But after staring for a moment at the letters he'd filled in, Cei closed the crossword puzzle book.

"Come me," he said, grinning. *"Io sono il capitano – come il sultano. E domenica schiaccio il Lecce!"* He was the captain, a role he was delighted to equate with that of sultan. And on Sunday he would crush Lecce.

"Come Babe Ruth!" he said, clenching a fist and raising it in the air. *"Sono il sultano di SWAT!"*

I'd been told that Lecce was the Florence of the south, and in a sense this was true, although it was the architecture more than the art that amazed. "One of the most beautiful cities in Italy, hidden in the south of Puglia, and rarely visited by foreigners," one guide said. Certainly, at least within the range of my experience, Lecce was "Italy's most extravagant variation on the baroque," as described by the Internet guide *In Italy Online.* "Waiting to stupefy, with its little-known magnificence."

Our problem was that we already had been driven to a state of stupefaction – if not catatonia – by the length of the journey and the heat. By the time we arrived, we didn't care if the Greeks had been there before the Romans, we cared only about the air-conditioning in our hotel.

"The best air-conditioning system in all the south of Italy," the assistant manager assured us as we checked in. "Unfortunately, it does not come on until the first of June." *Porca miseria!* I had not realized the Coradetti was part of a chain!

There was weeping, there was gnashing of teeth, and the traveling *segretaria* of *La Società,* who had booked us into this hotel, faced the players' wrath, scorn, and ridicule.

But then Jaconi took command. And standing right there in the lobby, where the temperature was close to 100 degrees Fahrenheit at 8 P.M., and speaking to a team that had just endured a twelve-hour ride on a bus *not* equipped with air-conditioning (no matter who claimed what to the contrary) on the very day after its greatest *in casa* triumph of all time, he proclaimed air-conditioning to be unhealthy – *non sano* – just like garlic, and said that even if it had been available, he would have ordered the hotel to turn it off.

Later, he claimed that the lack of protest showed the force of his personality, but speaking only for myself, it was purely the result of exhaustion.

I fear that I did not do justice to Lecce, although even a one-hour walk through the center of the city left me feeling that this truly was the Kingdom of Oz. On Saturday we rode the bus to a training field quite far from the city and came away most impressed by the size and variety of the insects that made their home there – bugs not seen in any other part of Italy, and so fearsome that Cei recoiled even from crushing one with his foot.

The heat remained intolerable but was worse in the hotel than on the streets, so on Saturday night I walked the boulevards, lined with such extraordinary examples of architectural joie de vivre, marveling at the existence of what seemed a center of its own civilization in what I'd always thought was the middle of nowhere.

When I finally returned to the hotel, I spotted Gigi in a far corner of the lobby, bent over a writing desk. He and I had maintained a level of superficial banter since our first impulsive hug on the day of his return to Castel di Sangro. But I now accepted that there were many things he could not tell me, as well as many that he had told me which were false, so the relationship was not what it had been.

Nonetheless, as I approached, he quickly waved me to an adjacent seat. He told me he was writing a letter to Vanessa, but that there were many feelings for which he did not have the words.

I told him I knew how he felt. I said that even as a writer, I often found myself confronted with feelings for which I could not find adequate words. This seemed to surprise him. He had assumed, I suppose, that writers could write as naturally as *calciatori* could play football. Some would be better than others, but the very fact of being a professional imputed a not-inconsiderable degree of skill.

Yes and no, I said. Yes and no. He nodded. Then from under a notebook he brought forth a volume and displayed it to me almost shyly. It was a collection of the poetry of Pablo Neruda, who was, he said, Vanessa's favorite.

He said he'd spent the past hour and a half poring through the book, looking for the one phrase or verse that would best express what he felt. And he was convinced he'd found it, only moments earlier. But he wanted to know what I, as a writer, might think.

I tried to explain that in a matter of the heart such as this, he would be a far better judge than I. But Gigi insisted. Was this right? Was this good? Was this what he should send to Vanessa?

He handed me the book. The relevant passage was underlined. In English, it was

> *From each crime are born bullets*
> *that will seek out in you*
> *where the heart lies.*

There was so much, of course, I did not know. But if, after more than an hour of searching, Gigi felt that these words best represented the feelings he wished to express to Vanessa, then they must have.

"*Perfetto*," I assured him. And with that he gathered up his writing materials and together we rode the elevator up to our steaming rooms in which, somehow, we would try to get a few hours' sleep.

Maybe it was the heat on Sunday, which was even worse than on the two preceding days. Maybe it was still a process of recovery from the ecstasy induced by our win over Torino. Maybe it was that Lecce already knew their promotion to *Serie A* was secure, and so had little to play for. In any event, the match was dull enough to make anyone feel he'd suffered sunstroke even if he'd been sitting in the shade.

For his usual obscure reasons, Osvaldo had opted to play with

Spinesi as our lone forward and to use Michelini in midfield instead of either Russo or Franceschini. Before the match began, I knew we could not score with such a formation, especially when the Lecce goal was guarded by Fabrizio Lorieri, who'd played for six years in *Serie A* with both Torino and Roma and had been the bulwark of Lecce's recent rise from *C1* to the point where now they were assured of promotion to the top division. Even more than Ielpo of Genoa, the thirty-three-year-old Lorieri was the one *Serie B portiere* who could stand as at least Lotti's equal.

Half an hour into the match, Cei pulled a muscle. Making a face as if he'd just swallowed a garlic bulb whole, Osvaldo sent Antonello into the match. It was clear he expected the worst.

And the worst promptly arrived, though through no fault of Antonello's. Instead, it was Michelini who committed a needless foul inside our penalty area two minutes before the end of the half.

The kick was taken by Francioso, a veteran *attaccante* who already this season had scored fourteen goals. Lotti dove to his right – which proved to be the correct direction – as soon as Francioso's foot touched the ball. Even so, fully outstretched, he could not reach it. The ball, however, bounced off the goalpost that was just beyond Lotti's grasp. No goal. And no score at the half.

The second half consisted mostly of Castel di Sangro standing around, gasping for breath, while Lecce missed chance after chance to score. This time, it was not so much Lotti's heroics as their own inaccuracy that prevented them from getting on the board.

Afterward, a beaming Osvaldo proclaimed the 0–0 draw "a point of gold" and explained to the press how his tactics had made it possible. Given that Francioso alone had had *two* shots off the post, it seemed to me more a "point of luck," but at this stage a point was a point was a point.

Despite their dehydration and exhaustion, the players raced through their showers and sped from the dressing room and back to the bus in record time. They didn't want to miss the radio broadcast of the results of the day's other matches.

Reggina and Lucchese had won, Cosenza had tied, and both Salernitana and two others had lost.

Thus, we began the long trip home with some comfort from *la classifica,* even if none from air-conditioning.

With only three matches remaining, our little corner of the world looked like this:

Reggina	42
CASTEL DI SANGRO	41
Salernitana	40
Lucchese	40
Cesena	37
Cosenza	36
Palermo	32
Cremonese	32

We did not reach Castel di Sangro until 3:20 on Monday morning. Both physically and emotionally these had been the four most exhausting days of the season (excepting only the grief and emotional drain caused by the deaths of Pippo and Danilo), but we had emerged from them with four points, when, going in, zero had seemed more likely.

Was it possible? Could it happen? No one knew the answer, but with only three matches remaining and thirty-five already behind us, it seemed enough for the moment that the question could still be asked.

37

If only . . .

If only the match against Salernitana had been two minutes shorter . . .

If only Osvaldo had not insisted on starting Pistella as our only attacker . . .

If only Lotti had just said to hell with it at the end . . .

Most of all – if only the airplane carrying Philemon Masinga back to Italy from his Saturday night match in England with the national team of South Africa had been grounded just a little longer by fog . . .

If only any of these, we might have managed a draw against Salernitana instead of losing, 1–0, and losing Lotti for the rest of the season in the process.

A *Serie B* season consists of fifty-seven hours of playing time, not counting the bits and pieces added on by the referee every week, yet for us now it seemed that four minutes at the end of our gallantly fought match in Salerno might be remembered as having determined our fate.

Back in October, when we spent the night before our match with Empoli at the Italian national team headquarters at Coverciano, a number of the players and I had watched the *Serie B anticipo* match on television. Masinga had come on for Salernitana in the last twenty minutes, and I had touted him highly on the basis of having seen him play in England. But Fusco, in particular, had been skeptical, saying, "Not for *Serie B,* Joe. Too egotistical."

Masinga had played in about a dozen matches since, and had even scored a couple of goals, but he'd attracted little attention and I'd paid him little mind. At twenty-seven, he was a smart and energetic African player who'd gained experience not only in his home country but in England and Switzerland before arriving in Italy.

As we faced a rabidly hostile Salernitana crowd of almost 40,000 – the largest we'd played before all season – on the afternoon of Sunday, May 25, Masinga was still far from my mind. We were one point ahead of Salernitana and Lucchese and four and five in front of Cesena and Cosenza, respectively, with only three matches remaining. A win would give us nearly mathematical certainty of *salvezza,* but even a draw would have us knocking hard on heaven's door.

And Salernitana seemed more susceptible than most opponents to whatever lineup and tactical surprises we might spring. On attack they were scarcely better than we were, having scored only twenty-eight goals all year to our worst-in-division twenty-six. They'd given up forty, just as we had. We'd already beaten them, 1–0, and that had been with De Juliis in goal. Granted, they'd never been beaten *in casa,* but in seventeen home matches they'd been held to a draw eight times.

To me, the approach seemed obvious: Go after them aggressively from the start, shaking their *in casa* confidence by throwing at them Spinesi and Russo and Franceschini, none of whom they'd seen in January. With Lotti in goal, we could afford the risk.

Va da sè – it goes without saying – Jaconi did not see it my way. He began with a 4-5-1 formation, which, for reasons I could not begin to fathom, did not include Spinesi, who had scored two goals within the past month, who was growing in skill by the hour, and whose cocky temperament was made to order for a difficult away match such as this. Instead, our lone attacker was the slow and predictable Pistella, who'd scored only two goals all season, whose composite *pagelle* of 5.68 was by far the lowest among any of our regular players, and whom Jaconi had been loudly scorning since September.

I had no wish to precipitate another ugly incident by raising a last-minute objection, but I had to at least ask: Why not Russo, Franceschini, or Albieri, but most of all why not Spinesi?

"Non vale la pena di correre il rischio," he said. It's not worth the risk.

"What risk?" I asked.

"Della ferita. Avrò bisogno di lui contro il Pescara." The risk of injury. I'll need him against Pescara.

Ammazza! Was this possible? Spinesi would not be used in such a crucial match as this because Jaconi was afraid he might be injured, and therefore not able to play in the next possibly crucial match against Pescara? But what if he should be injured against Pescara, and thereby unable to play in the last match of the season against Bari, which might prove the most crucial of all? This was *la paura* carried to a degree of irrationality that simply staggered me.

"Capito?" Jaconi asked when I looked dazed. *"Non segneremo in ogni caso, così perchè lo rischierei?"* We're not going to score in any event, so why would I risk it? This seemed at the least a close cousin to Catch-22 – *why use the player most likely to score since we're unlikely to score?* – but at the same time it was the essence of "bulldozer logic," and I no longer had the will to resist.

"Capito, Osvald'," I said. *"E grazie."*

Still, thanks again largely to Lotti, we survived a scoreless first half. And ten minutes into the second, Jaconi threw caution to the winds and removed an ineffective Di Fabio in favor of Spinesi. But with the score still 0-0 and only twenty minutes remaining, he panicked and took off Cristiano, who had been playing superbly, in favor of the lead-footed veteran Michelini. This was the same time at which Masinga entered the match.

Masinga was not even supposed to be here. He'd played the night before at the famed Old Trafford stadium in Manchester, England, and had scored South Africa's only goal in a 2-1 loss to the national team of England. After such a performance, most players would not have even tried to get themselves from northern England to southern Italy within twelve hours simply to be available to a *Serie B* team whose manager might not even use him.

But Phil Masinga was not most players. He was the leading goal scorer in the history of South Africa and a man whose pride was as strong as his talent. After traveling by every means available short of hot-air balloon, he had arrived at the Salernitana stadium at halftime.

He spent fifteen minutes just limbering up as he gradually absorbed the situation, coolly assessing the strengths and weaknesses of each side this late into the match. Then, with only two minutes remaining, he struck. Dashing through a large hole in our back defensive line, Masinga took a perfectly placed pass and headed it into the upper corner of our goal. The ball actually bounced off the intersection of post and crossbar, but had such velocity and spin on it that from there it careened into the net.

Well, that would be the end of it: Salernitana 1, Castel di Sangro 0, despite still another performance by Lotti that *La Gazzetta dello Sport* described as *"bravissimo per tutta la partita."* Outstanding throughout the whole match.

But then the *arbitro* decreed that four extra minutes would be played. It was as if we'd been granted a new life – a last desperate chance to salvage a draw. If only we could score a goal!

Unfortunately, it went the other way. Pressing everyone forward, we were highly vulnerable to a swift counterattack, which was exactly what Masinga mounted, bearing down upon the solitary Lotti with two minutes of the extra time remaining.

Lotti did the only thing he could do, charging forward to knock Masinga off his feet before the attacker could get off his shot. For this – as he knew he would – Lotti received a red card. His desperate gamble, however, saved a certain second goal against us and preserved at least the theoretical chance for a draw.

But, no. Thoroughly rattled, we never even threatened after that, and walked off the field not only beaten by a man whom we'd never expected to see on it but knowing that our most valuable player, Massimo Lotti, would surely receive a two-match suspension (the automatic consequence of a red card) and therefore would not play for us again. We would have to face Pescara with De Juliis as our goalkeeper instead.

And so it would all come down to the Abruzzo Derby, part two. Castel di Sangro vs. Pescara, but this time with the entire season on the line for both teams, because just as we needed a win for *la salvezza,* so did Pescara to keep alive their long-shot chance of promotion to *Serie A.*

From our point of view, the results of the other Sunday matches could not have been worse. Lucchese had managed a draw at Torino to pull even with us, and both Cesena and Cosenza had won.

As June arrived, our situation was as follows:

Lucchese	41
CASTEL DI SANGRO	41
Cesena	40
Cosenza	39
Palermo	32
Cremonese	32

The endgame *was* merciless. Two already were out. Of the others, two would make it, two would not.

The green finally had climbed all the way back up the mountainside. The view from my window, therefore, was just what it would have been in September, if I'd been here instead of at the Coradetti. In that sense, nothing had changed. Yet I knew acutely that much had, and that the changes were inalterable. I knew also that in less than two weeks what had been in many ways the most intense period of my life would become just a poignant memory.

For the moment, however, my strongest feeling was a renewal of anger directed toward *La Società*. In a desperate effort to squeeze the last lire out of what might be our only season ever in *Serie B,* Gravina had ordered the immediate addition of 2,000 seats to the stadium, increasing its capacity by 25 percent, with, of course, a commensurate increase in revenue.

These men – Gravina and Signor Rezza – who had permitted their team to play the first three months of the season without any home field, as they weighed risk-benefit ratios, were now tacking on an extra 2,000 seats within a week, using construction techniques and materials that looked as if they'd come directly from a 1950s Erector set.

But worse – far worse – Signor Rezza had personally ordered that 25 percent of the seats in the stadium be sold to Pescara supporters.

Visitors customarily received a token amount – usually between 2 and 5 percent of tickets sold – but never more than that, for to allow in more of the opponent's *tifosi* not only created security problems but deprived the home team of its "twelfth man" advantage, which had proved so vital for us against Torino.

In this case, however, Signor Rezza had sold as a block to Pescara management (at a far higher price than he would have dared charge the people of Castel di Sangro) more than 2,000 tickets, all for seats in the south *curva,* directly behind one of the goals. Another five hundred, for the *tribuna,* would be retailed for even higher prices in Pescara.

Thus, instead of 10,000 voices cheering, chanting, and singing as one, there would be these despicable creatures from the sea – or seaside, anyway – cramming into *our* seats in order to hurl taunts, epithets, and quite probably bottles and hard metal objects at our players.

My reaction, which I see in retrospect might not have been the most prudent, was to stop on the street anyone I knew even vaguely and denounce Signor Rezza in the vilest terms that I was capable of, also repeating a rumor I'd recently heard: that the real reason the old man did not travel to away matches was that he was afraid of being killed by enemies.

At the same time, Gravina issued a statement through Giuseppe in which he said that the extraordinary sale of tickets to our opponent had been done "for reasons of the higher sportsmanship in which I so deeply believe." It was *not,* he stressed, as some *cinici* were saying, for base motives of profit and greed.

I also found myself with new worries about Jaconi. Since the loss at Salernitana, he'd taken to carrying a Bible with him everywhere and was apt to quote from it at the slightest provocation, or none at all.

"Osvald'," I asked him, *"perchè la Bibbia proprio ora?"* Why now, all of a sudden, the Bible?

He tapped the embossed gold letters on the cover and said, "In here, Joe, God has already written the result. It has been determined. By the reading, I simply try to peek over the shoulder of God in order to see what he has written."

I drew no comfort from the Scriptures myself, but I did buy a computer game called PC Calcio 5.0. It boasted almost up-to-the-minute statistics for every team and player in *Serie A* and *Serie B.* I immediately loaded it into my laptop and – using the formations and tactical options I thought each manager most likely to employ (*not* those I might have preferred myself), putting De Juliis in goal, and excluding D'Angelo, who was *squalificato* because of an excess of yellow cards – let the computer play out the Castel di Sangro–Pescara match.

Evviva! Urrà! We won, 2-1, on goals by Pistella and Bonomi! I stored the match on a file, which would allow me to replay it as often as I wanted. It was not only eerily realistic in its representation of the play, it also had a *telecronista* who announced the action in an appropriately excited tone of voice.

I brought the laptop to dinner at Marcella's on Wednesday night and, without revealing the result but explaining that I had "programmed" it realistically, I turned up the volume and let it run.

Osvaldo even put down his Bible and joined the crowd of players staring at the tiny laptop screen.

"Oooooh!" A groan went up as offsides was called against us. Then a cheer when Gigi made a hard tackle on a Pescara forward without receiving a yellow card. And then a rafter-raising roar as the "announcer" shouted excitedly, *"Il pallone a Pistella . . . tira – Goooooooll! . . . Castel di Sangro uno, Pescara zero."*

A pause for halftime was built in. The players shouted at me to override this somehow and get on with it. After all, *la salvezza* was at stake!

Pescara tied soon into the second half, and Fusco began arguing with Martino about who should have had responsibility for the Pescara midfielder coming down the right side who eventually made a perfect cross to a forward for the goal. De Juliis uttered a string of curses at his fate.

But with twenty minutes remaining, the virtual Bonomi unleashed a shot from about thirty yards out and it sailed swiftly and cleanly into the Pescara goal. I was sure the cheering in Marcella's could be heard all over town.

The players turned to their food with a spirit and enthusiasm I'd not seen in weeks. And even Osvaldo deferred for a night the reading he'd planned from Ecclesiastes.

The plain truth was, we were all going mad. The season had been too long and too hard, and now the pressure was simply too great.

Anything relating to the Pescara match was treated as a major news story that week. Thus, my computer game *risultato* was published under absurdly large headlines and, in the process, was transformed from a score generated by a $29 piece of software into the *"analisi esperte dello scrittore americano."* Flattered as I was to be considered, even whimsically, as a *calcio* expert by Italians, it still surprised me to read what I was presumed to be thinking or feeling and what I supposedly had said.

"We will win," I had confidently told *Il Messaggero*. "It will be hard fought, but the victory will go to Castel di Sangro. I have no doubt. This squad has overcome a thousand adversities. And you will see that on Sunday Pippo and Danilo will give their teammates a helping hand. The final score will be two to one. Our goals will come from Pistella and Bonomi. We will win. We *must* win!"

I had presumably grown so emphatic that my closing words could be rendered appropriately only by being translated into English. " 'We must win!' *lo scrittore ha detto.*" *We must win!* the writer said.

Actually, maybe I had said it. I didn't know anymore. I could scarcely separate my dream life from the waking moments of my day. For weeks I'd been clinging by my fingernails to the edge of a cliff that represented self-control and rationality, but now my grip was finally giving way.

Il Messaggero wrote of me: "He suffers, he is among the most ardent of *tifosi* even if his tone of voice is always calm." I went straight to Osvaldo with that one. "So you see?" I said. "It could be worse. Imagine if I ever got excited!"

I had intended this to be a joke. A brief, lighthearted respite from the intolerable pressures that mounted by the hour. But I was already too late. No further respites for Osvaldo.

He grabbed the paper from me and tore it in half. *"Bugie! Bugie!"* he shouted. Lies. Lies. "The newspapers are always printing lies!" Then he pushed a finger against my chest. "And do not say any more about the match. *È una sfortuna parlare in anticipo.*" It's bad luck to talk in advance. "Also," he said, "you are crazy to say Pistella will score a goal. Pistella is shit! I tell you this in October, but you don't listen. You say Pistella, Pistella, Pistella, and so I play him until the whole world sees he is shit. So no more talk of Pistella."

"But he is playing on Sunday, isn't he?"

"Of course. But only because the others are also shit!"

"Russo and Franceschini are not shit," I said.

"Fammi una sega!" he shouted. Jerk me off!

I guess that was as clear an indication as any that neither Russo nor Franceschini would be starting. It was also a clear indication that there was no point in my asking, If Pistella was such shit, how come he had started against Salernitana?

How different was this atmosphere from the sunny, festive ambience that had surrounded the first derby match in Pescara. Not only I but all Castel di Sangro was outraged by the *Società*'s decision to sell 25 percent of the match tickets to our opponent. It was unheard of. Literally. I asked and I asked, and everyone's answer was the same: no *società*, at any level, had ever before tried to milk extra profit from such a crucial match by permitting one-quarter of the home seats to be filled by supporters of the visitors.

Each player – and this included almost all of them – who'd been telling me throughout the season that *La Società* was greedy, insincere, and inept made a point of approaching me again to say, Now didn't I see what they'd meant? As if I had not already agreed, long ago.

And every one stressed that I should be sure to put *this* into my book. That was striking because no one even talked anymore about my book. For months it had been as if there wouldn't be any book: I was there simply because I was there, just a part of the fabric of the season.

Meanwhile, in Pescara, the large number of tickets made available only stirred an appetite for more. So widespread, apparently, was talk of *pescaresi* coming to Castel di Sangro without tickets and expecting to simply storm the gates that local police cars with loudspeakers on top cruised the streets for forty-eight hours, repeating the same message over and over again: "If you do not have a ticket, do not go to Castel di Sangro." There would be many *carabinieri* on hand, with instructions to arrest first and let magistrates ask questions later.

It was a point of more than academic interest, of course, that Pescara had as much at stake in this match as we did. Their fifty-four points put them within range of the two teams tied for the fourth and last promotion spot – Lecce and Genoa, each with fifty-seven. If those two lost while Pescara beat us, Pescara would go into the season's final match with a very real chance at *Serie A*. The one thing that seemed certain was that a draw would destroy the hopes of both sides. For the first and only time all season, therefore – however strongly his conservative instincts rebelled against it – Osvaldo would be forced to go all out for a win.

. . .

The *Società* announced on Thursday night that only six hundred tickets remained available, even for the Erector set additions. They would go on sale at the branch office (which was only half a block removed from *Società* headquarters, but which one could enter without first climbing three flights of stairs) at 9 A.M. the next day, limit: two to a customer, and cash only, please.

People began to gather at the door even before midnight, and their ranks swelled through the night even as a steady rain began to fall. These were the truest of the true *tifosi:* maybe too poor to buy a season ticket, but believers in the miracle and willing to undergo hardship in order to be present at this match. And they could all have been accommodated, of course, had it not been for Signor Rezza and Gravina.

It no longer bothered me that the old man didn't say *salve* when he saw me. I'd been proud in the past of enemies I had made, and by now I'd placed both Signor Rezza and Gravina in this category.

Not Osvaldo, however, despite our many tiffs. I might not have thought him the brightest or most daring *allenatore* in Italy, and I found repellent his abusive unfairness to his players, but I respected what I believed to be his sense of personal integrity, and I was deeply grateful to him for having been an exceptionally good neighbor all season long. No other *allenatore* in the country, after all, had been forced to put up with a stranger from America who might have arrived humbly enough but who'd wound up believing himself to be an expert.

The scene at the makeshift ticket office Friday morning was the ungodliest mess I'd ever seen. All I can say is that it's a good thing it happened in Castel di Sangro. Here, at least, people had enough decency and respect for others so as not to grow violent while trying to jump ahead in line.

In truth, it was not a line, but a heaving, surging throng, which, except for the gentility and unselfishness of those who composed it, would have threatened the well-being and even life of anyone caught up in it – trampling and suffocation being the most obvious dangers.

By noon the last of the tickets was sold. At least a thousand people from the town itself and from a host of nearby villages who'd been loyally supporting the team for years were turned away. Television trucks had arrived to film and broadcast the riot that many thought would ensue. But in the end the people of Castel di Sangro maintained their dignity and simply dispersed – badly disappointed but not about to turn into savages simply to provide a spectacle for television.

As much as the players themselves, I felt, these townspeople deserved *la salvezza*.

38

Saturday dawned perfectly. I walked to the stadium for what would be our last training session before we learned our fate.

Mathematically, if given a favorable confluence of other results, a win at Bari on June 15 might still earn us the necessary points, but to a man the players agreed that if we could not beat Pescara at home, we would have no chance against a far stronger Bari team, which would be playing in front of *their* home crowd of 60,000 and still fighting to return to *Serie A*.

So for practical purposes, our season would end the next day. By the time the team next gathered here, the hope that had sustained us all year would have been replaced by either joy or despair.

The stadium itself had never looked better. The clean, clear air so typical of Castel di Sangro had returned. The grass of the field was finally green again, a healthy green, and as the sun glinted off the freshly painted metallic surfaces of the grandstand, the whole place looked like a jewel. So tranquil today, but tomorrow the scene of such tumult. Aware that this was the last Saturday morning I'd ever spend here, I felt a sense of pain so sharp, it made me take in a quick breath.

In late afternoon I took a long walk through the town. I saw many people I knew. The hands of most of them were shaking from nervousness. An old man I did not know approached me. In a mixture of Italian and dialect, enhanced by many gestures, he told me he had not felt such fear for half a century. Not since the war, he said, when he could hear the American planes coming and knew that this meant that within minutes the killing bombs would fall again and that there was nowhere to hide.

That night Christian arrived for work at Marcella's bearing about 500 five-milligram Valium pills. "A friendly doctor" had been the source, he said. They were, of course, for spectators only.

The doctor's instructions, at least as interpreted by Christian, were to take two tonight at bedtime, two upon first awakening to-morrow morning, two more before lunch, then *three* at 3 P.M., one hour before kickoff, one more as the match began, and the final two, regardless of the score, at halftime.

This would be sixty milligrams of Valium within a twenty-four-hour period, consumed by people who by and large had no experience with tranquilizers. I told Christian that I thought the dosage might be a bit on the high side, but he scoffed.

"You don' know, Joe," he said. "We be *tranquillo* from the pill or else we must die from the explosion of the heart."

He handed me the dozen-pill dose he'd been passing out to other friends.

"You no look good, Joe. I think you need."

In looking at photographs taken of me the day of the match, I find that Christian was right: I did not look well. Nor did I feel well. Even after taking two Valium at bedtime and two more upon waking up – not that I slept for more than twenty minutes at a stretch – I still felt uncontrollably nervous and fearful.

With D'Angelo *squalificato* as well as Lotti, Osvaldo already had told me that he intended to start Rimedio instead of Antonello in his place. Shades of Torino! This was so insane, I could not even start to wrap my mind around it. De Juliis in goal with Rimedio protecting his right flank against the Pescara attacker Giampaolo, who had scored sixteen goals already this season, putting him fourth in the division. And with us trying to score against Morgan De Sanctis, now twenty, who already had been offered a contract for the following season by Juventus!

I considered these factors at lunch and then swallowed two more of the Valium. Everyone in Marcella's was doing the same, washing the pills down with large glasses of wine. This behavior was most un-characteristic, but so was the state of hysteria that provoked it. Mar-cella herself would not permit anyone to leave for the ten-minute walk to the stadium unfortified by at least one glass of grappa.

Luca D'Angelo, *squalificato* and eating his heart out over it, was standing with me at Marcella's. As a communist, he said, he could not drink alcohol, but he urged me to have a second grappa, which I did. "One for each goal we score," he said. It made sense.

By 3 P.M. I was among thousands already pressing through the gates. I remembered that there was something important about 3 P.M. Of course! Time for the three prematch Valium.

In the corridor that led to the locker room there was, in addition to Jaconi's office, a private suite within which *La Società* could enter-tain special guests. Attractively furnished and with a carpeted floor, this was the equal of any *calcio* hospitality suite I'd ever seen. Today, fresh trays of antipasti lay on tables covered by immaculate white linen cloths. Between them was a table containing some of the finest wines, liquors, and liqueurs available in Italy.

Needing to use a bathroom, I opened the door to the suite at 3:05 P.M. It was occupied by about a dozen people. I recognized the president of the Pescara *Società* from his picture in the papers. I also recognized Gravina and Maria Teresa, who'd chosen to hold this pri-vate party without me.

"Il bagno," I said, pointing to the men's room on the far side of the suite and walking toward it. I came out of the men's room and, need-ing something to wash down the three Valium, went straight for the table with the bottles. Neither Gabriele nor Maria Teresa, apparently, had any desire to introduce me to their guests. An Italian liqueur or aperitif or *digestif* – frankly, I didn't know what its intended use might be – called Fernet Branca caught my eye. I'd had a glass once, in the company of our team physician, at one of the hotels where we'd stayed. He had recommended it highly.

Still, what better than a glass of Fernet Branca with which to take the three Valium? Well, maybe water for one thing. The Fernet Branca stung and burned, made my eyes water, and caused me to cough. Only later I learned it was 80 proof.

"Scusi," I muttered in the direction of Gravina and Maria Teresa. Then, nodding toward them with what I hoped was at least a mod-

icum of graciousness, I left the suite, saying, *"In bocca al lupo,"* and climbed to my seat in the *tribuna d'onore.*

As the teams took the field, the 2,000 morons from Pescara who had been permitted entrance to the stadium – to *our* stadium – began sending up flares that produced blue smoke. *Blue! Their* color! That greedy bastard Rezza.

I thought briefly of walking over – he was seated only about twenty yards to my right – and telling him what I thought of him and his *Camorra* connections and his rotten-to-the-core *Società* and his drug-smuggling nephew-in-law and maybe a few things about Jaconi's lineup selection and tactics as well.

Before I could, however, the Pescara fans in the south *curva* began to act as badly as I'd known they would. Even before the match they started to smash with bottles the clear Plexiglas screen in front of their section, though by doing so they impaired their own view. But what could be expected from such fish heads? All they wanted was to destroy. To destroy as much of our stadium as they could, while their wretched, faltering team tried to destroy our last hope for *salvezza.*

La salvezza! The concept cut through my Valium haze in the manner of a lighthouse beacon penetrating a thick marine fog. Forget Rezza. Forget Gravina. Forget the scaly cretins from Pescara. This match was for *la salvezza,* and however it turned out, I would never experience another like it as long as I lived.

Remarkably, we took command from the start. Pescara looked sluggish and dull, not at all as if *Serie A* were beckoning. After fifteen tentative minutes we began to trust ourselves a bit and moved forward. At sixteen minutes Tonino Martino took one of his best shots of the season and only a Juventus-quality save from young De Sanctis prevented a goal. Two minutes later Tonino blasted another shot goalward. This one had De Sanctis beaten but – perhaps only a centimeter too high – bounced off the crossbar and back into play.

Already, however, an even more powerful presence was threatening the match. This was the *arbitro,* Trentalange of Torino. No bias for or against either team was evident, but Trentalange was a man who all through the 1990s had worked primarily *Serie A* matches. Recognizing the importance of this one, the Federation had assigned him to it.

From the start he seemed chiefly intent on proving that as an *arbitro* accustomed to *Serie A,* he was going to judge harshly any perceived deviations from the letter of the law by players he considered made of lesser stuff.

He gave Gigi a yellow card within five minutes. This seemed more a general warning than punishment for a specific infraction, as did the yellow shown five minutes later to Giampaolo. When a Pescara midfielder protested, however, Trentalange showed him the yellow card, too.

Just short of the half-hour mark came the first memorable moment of the match. Spinesi took a long pass with his head and redirected it to Pistella, who had run unmolested through the heart of a Pescara defense that actually seemed to create for him what one paper the next day described as "a spectacularly wide hole." From less than ten yards, Pistella drove the ball straight and true into the net, past a helpless De Sanctis.

We were ahead, 1–0, on a goal by "shit" Pistella. I liked the man so much – he was *prima classe* and had remained so even as he'd suffered through an absolutely nightmarish season – that I was even happier for him than I was for myself. But I was pretty happy for myself – for all of us – as well.

Only two minutes later Giampaolo lost the ball in the midst of a counterattack and committed a foul by immediately making a tackle from behind. Trentalange ran toward him even before he'd regained his feet, waving the yellow card and then, because it was Giampaolo's second, the red. *Giampaolo had been ejected from the match!*

With fifteen minutes of the first half and all of the second remaining, Pescara was deprived of their top goal scorer and would have to play the rest of the match with only ten men. Their immediate reaction was to begin quarreling among themselves and to play with a recklessness that Trentalange soon punished with two more yellow cards within a five-minute span.

Still bickering, Pescara defenders allowed Bonomi to unleash a shot described the next day as "a missile," and only another spectacular save by De Sanctis prevented us from leaving the field at halftime with a 2–0 lead.

Forty-five minutes gone, only forty-five still separating us from *salvezza.* Yet at halftime a surge of fear penetrated straight to my heart.

Our two weakest links, Rimedio and De Juliis, had not yet been tested. And even being a man down, Pescara was bound to attack more aggressively than they had, for they needed two goals, not just one, to keep alive any hope for promotion.

I feared for our ability to prevent them from scoring. Equally, I feared for our ability to score again. These fears worsened as, at the start of the second half, the Pescara manager replaced his most passive defender with a far more aggressive player named Colonnello, who had actually played for Castel di Sangro during their last two seasons in *C2*.

At the same time – and this absolutely defied explanation, for the far more experienced Martino had been perhaps our best player throughout the first half – Jaconi told Tonino his day was finished and sent on the talented but jittery Cristiano in his stead.

Thus began a phase of the match that *Il Messaggero* would describe as Pescara's "dancing gracefully while attacking with scalpels." De Juliis was proving adequate, as was Rimedio, but how long could they last? Meanwhile, our midfield missed Martino desperately.

Time was passing, however, and around me more and more people were looking at their watches to see how many minutes remained – our stadium not being equipped with a clock. Amazingly, we were into the last fifteen minutes. It was beginning to seem possible!

Unfortunately, at about this time Jaconi ordered the whole squad into *il bunker,* the most extreme of defensive formations, which meant we did not even mount the occasional counterattack that might have briefly taken the pressure off our defense.

All season long I'd seen this approach fail, and not only when applied by Jaconi. The American basketball truism that the best defense is a good offense is by no means inapplicable to *calcio,* but in the school for *allenatori* at Coverciano such doctrine apparently was considered heretical.

As more and more of our players clustered ever closer to our goal, Pescara began to shoot with frequency, velocity, and accuracy. At seventy-seven minutes, a journeyman forward named Di Giannatale took a rebound inadequately cleared by Cei and flicked it past De Juliis for the goal that made it 1–1, a score that spelled death for us but gave Pescara a fifteen-minute chance for new life.

"Fear crashed down again," wrote *Il Corriere dello Sport.* "In this moment, the nightmare of returning to *C1* was great."

But three minutes later – with only ten minutes remaining in the match and tension so strong that it threatened to trigger a mass cardiac arrythmia – Claudio dribbled the ball to a spot twenty yards from the Pescara goal and from that point unleashed as savage a shot as he'd ever taken in his life.

Morgan De Sanctis might as well have been a mannequin. The ball rocketed past him as if fired from a missile launcher.

A goal for Claudio – later described as a *eurogol,* meaning it would have been worthy of a Champions Cup match played between any of the strongest teams on the continent – and for all the rest of us, the "*Second* Miracle of Castel di Sangro."

Claudio was called a "godsend" by *Il Messaggero,* and though his name might not have appeared in Jaconi's Bible, no one in Castel di Sangro would have disagreed, not then and not ever.

Despairing of scoring two *more* goals in the remaining ten minutes, Pescara simply allowed the match to play out without incident.

Their *tifosi* in the south *curva,* however, went berserk. No longer content with shattering the Plexiglas in front of them, now hundreds tried to dislodge it, all the while hurling debris onto the field. Club-swinging police charged from both sides, and a melee ensued as the final moments of the match ticked away.

To us, this was of absolutely no interest. Once Trentalange blew his whistle, after three minutes of extra time, we cared only about the scores of other matches. These were announced even before our players left the field and were all we could have hoped for. Cesena had lost at Empoli, and Cosenza had managed only a draw in Padova.

Everyone understood the vital importance of these results immediately.

We had forty-four points.

Both Cosenza and Cesena had only forty.

No matter what might happen to us in Bari, they could not catch us.

It was over. The Gates of Eden had opened and we had danced in, with Claudio Bonomi leading the way.

It was over. And *come in un film* – like in a very, very long film, the ending brought tears of joy and of relief to all who had been privileged to see it from the beginning.

It was over. The players immediately and unanimously dedicated *la salvezza* to Pippo and Danilo, who in all probability had reached it before the rest of them, and in an even more lasting way.

"Next week, Joe, after we return from Bari," Roberto Alberti said to me amid the raucous jubilation of the locker room, "a few of us, a very few, will make a special trip to the graves of Pippo and Danilo to say a final good-bye. And we would like you to come with us."

I don't think I'd ever felt more honored in my life.

39

To awaken free from fear, free from nagging uncertainty, free from the need to live on hope – this was an experience I'd not before had in Castel di Sangro. I thought that after a period of adjustment, I might learn to like it. Maybe this was how normal people lived.

Well, maybe not. Normal people did not live suffused with such bliss. Nor did they live in a town festooned from end to end, top to bottom, inside and out, in red and gold. Nor did they spend the whole day – as did the residents of Castel di Sangro on Monday, and as did I – walking from one end of the town to the other and back again, under a clear blue sky and bright sun, with no purpose beyond the desire to greet one another and hug joyously. And it could not be normal for grown men to still be weeping openly at high noon.

"Not even in a film of Hitchcock could one have imagined such an ending," wrote *Il Corriere dello Sport.*

"It was a film filled with joy, with fear, with exultation," wrote *Il Tempo,* "and experienced with the heart in the throat."

"It was," said *Il Messaggero,* "after tragedy, pathos, scandal and despair, a film with a miracle ending, a film truly deserving the title of 'The Greatest Story Ever Told.'"

While they were at it, they might as well have nominated Claudio "the Godsend" Bonomi for an Oscar.

I saw Claudio briefly on Monday. He was downtown with his very pregnant wife, who was due to give birth to their first child within a week.

"I am amazed you did not have the baby yesterday," I said to her.

She blushed and mumbled something to Claudio. "She say," he told me, "yesterday in the match she has *un orgasmo* when I score, *non un bambino.*"

Then Claudio spoke seriously for a moment. Gesturing to the throngs still milling about the central square, he said, "You must always remember, Joe, these people. Not only on this day but how they are on all the days. So very special. If we win, if we lose, it changes nothing. They love us the same, for trying so hard.

"You do not know, but believe me: No other town in Italy is this way. I will be leaving. I have played my last match for Castel di Sangro. Next season I will be with Torino. But my heart will always rest here, with these people.

"*Il carattere?* Yes, the team has possessed it, but even more it is demonstrated on every day by the town. The *real* miracle of Castel di Sangro, Joe, is Castel di Sangro."

It was not until late in the day, when I finally got around to a more careful reading of the newspapers, that I realized we had won exactly as I (or, more accurately, as my PC Calcio 5.0) had predicted. The score had been 2-1 and our goals had come from Pistella and Bonomi.

That night, in response to public demand, I brought my laptop back to Marcella's and replayed the match for hours. *Come in un film,* we won, 2-1, every time.

On Tuesday morning, *come in* real life, Pescara fired their manager.

Among the strangest sensations of the new week was that of observing the annual shifting of tectonic plates from a secure vantage point. The four teams to be relegated to *C1* would be Cesena and Cremonese in the north, and Cosenza and Palermo in the south. Already assured of promotion to *Serie B* were *C1* teams Treviso from the north and Fidelis Andria from the south, with the other two to be determined by the same playoff system that had enabled the original *miracolo* to occur.

Coming down from *Serie A* would be Hellas Verona, Perugia, and Reggiana, as well as the loser of a playoff between Piacenza and Cagliari. The most open question remained which clubs from *Serie B* would go up to take their place. Only Brescia was certain of promotion. Empoli, Lecce, Bari, and Genoa were ranked second through fifth, in that order, separated by only one point each. Bari therefore would need to beat us in order to ensure their own return. A draw would leave them at the mercy of the result from Genoa.

To say it was our good fortune that we would not be traveling to Bari still in need of a point for our *salvezza* would be the understatement of the season. Quick shudders went down my spine at the thought.

Thanks to Claudio, and to Pistella – and to Empoli for beating Cesena, and to Padova for getting the draw against Cosenza – we were spared the need to contemplate any such nightmarish ending to the season. We had scored only twenty-nine goals, the lowest total in all of *Serie B,* but we had won the right to try to do better next year.

At that point, I could just as easily have gone home. The Bari match would be meaningless to us, and the prospect of another long bus ride south was not appealing. On the other hand, to spend a few totally relaxed days in the company of these extraordinary men who made up our team, and whom, once I left, I might never see again for the rest of my life, would be a joy.

Besides, on the day after the Bari match there would be the trip to the graves of Pippo and Danilo.

Having been given an extra day off, the players drifted back into town on Wednesday, many sporting a startling new "dress for success" look. Cristiano – little Mimmo – who had alternated betweeen two pairs of blue jeans all season long, was suddenly Calvin Klein from head to toe. Even Luca Albieri returned clad in as much Ralph Lauren as his bankbook would tolerate.

All, of course, would be receiving significant bonuses from *La Società* as part of their contractual reward for having earned *la salvezza.* And this time there was reason to hope that Signor Rezza might pay the money when due, because he and Gabriele had just made the biggest score of their lives in *il calcio.*

Gravina announced on Wednesday night that Claudio had been sold to Torino, effective June 30, for $3 million. This was, by at least a factor of ten, the highest price ever paid for a Castel di Sangro player. It seemed that despite Rezza's misgivings, this *Serie B* business was not turning out so badly after all.

Gravina announced also that Jaconi had signed a two-year contract extension. While this news was greeted with gladness by the townspeople, a number of the players were markedly less enthusiastic.

There also were those, such as Guido Di Fabio, for whom any further news of Castel di Sangro was irrelevant. He told me at dinner Wednesday night that his own contract was not being renewed and that Gravina had found no takers for him among the other clubs of *Serie B*. Thus, at thirty-two, despite the significant role he'd played in our attainment of *salvezza* (thirty-one appearances, fourth on the squad in number of minutes played, scorer of the match-winner against Torino, and with a composite *pagelle* of 6.05), he'd been deemed immediately expendable and would be returning to *C1*.

I expressed surprise and genuine regret, for Guido as much as anyone had embodied the much-touted element of *carattere* throughout even the season's bleakest months.

"Ah, Joe," he said, "it is all right. I receive a nice bonus, which I did not expect; I have the privilege to be a member of this group, composed of the finest men I've ever known in *calcio;* and next year I will be in *C1* with Fermana, where I played happily the year before I came here and which is only fifty kilometers from my home."

"Well, maybe it's not so bad," I said. "But still I feel very sad to think of you no longer being here."

"Joe! *Please* do not waste even one minute with such a thought. Do you not realize how much happiness I have just in knowing I no longer must play for Jaconi?" And with that he broke into a booming peal of laughter, and I had no doubt that he meant what he'd said.

Despite the news of departures and of contract renewals – which maintained the normal ratio of ten rumors for every fact – and notwithstanding my own sense that the story of Gigi and *la cocaina* had not yet reached its final chapter, the week was remarkably free of stress.

Training was not only casual but optional. Not even Osvaldo was always there. One day, in fact, he and I – once again the best of friends and neighbors – drove to a town in the Molise where Cei and Michelini were taking their first steps on the long, bureaucratic road to becoming licensed *allenatori*.

On the way, I apologized for all of my criticism, for any comments that may have seemed disrespectful, and for all my unsolicited advice.

"It is no problem," he said. "Often it was useful because I made myself think about each thing you said, and I asked myself, 'Could he be correct?' "

"And was I?"

"Not once. But it was good because in the end I felt even more sure about myself."

For Cei and Michelini, the exercise for the day had been to prepare a variety of offensive tactics, which would then be tested in a five-on-five formation. The whole business was taken very seriously, with frowning men in neckties carrying around stacks of elaborate charts and forms attached to clipboards. Realizing that Osvaldo long ago not only had cleared this hurdle but had made it safely across the far more extensive minefield at Federation headquarters at Coverciano, I wondered just how bad a candidate's tactical plans would have to be for him not to receive a passing grade. Nonetheless, I was told that approximately one in three hopefuls was weeded out at this level.

Soon I had my own role to play in the process. No arrangements had been made for a goalkeeper, and so, dreaming my last dreams of glory, I volunteered. And, God, did I ever love it!

Each save I made produced a moment of unbounded glee. Not that I didn't give up the odd goal as well, but for a fifty-four-year-old American who'd never played the game, I think I could have done worse. At the end of the day, when, covered with dirt and with one leg scraped raw, I dived almost horizontally to my left to punch away a short-range rebound just before the final whistle blew, I think I might have experienced the last spontaneously perfect physical moment of my life. In any event, I was damned sorry to return the borrowed gloves when it was over.

Osvaldo had left early because he was receiving an award in Sulmona before joining a large party for the team later on. I rode back with Michelini and Cei, both of whom had received passing grades.

"This life," I said in the car. "I never want to leave it. And you know, I think I might have a future."

"As an *allenatore?*" Michelini asked, only slightly incredulous.

"No, as a *portiere.* Maybe next season I can be number two in Castel di Sangro."

They both laughed and wished me luck. But Cei added that after my hectic season as *vice allenatore* to Jaconi, accepting a demotion to the role of a substitute player, who was not allowed to criticize tactics every week, might be hard on my ego.

"Per questa squadra," I said, *"farò il sacrificio."* For this squad, I will make the sacrifice.

That night an enormous party was given for the team by the lakeside village of Barrea, located within the boundaries of the Abruzzo National Park. Held outdoors, under kerosene lanterns, on a large, sloping lawn that led to the edge of the water, it prompted me to say to Cei, *"This* is like a party of Gatsby."

He looked around carefully, then winked at me and shook his head. "No, Joe. Too many children asking for autographs and not enough beautiful women."

It differed also in that during the course of it, various speeches were made. By Gravina, by Jaconi, by Claudio, by De Juliis (who remained far more a crowd favorite than did Lotti), and finally by *lo scrittore americano.*

I had never made a speech in Italian before, much less at a lectern equipped with a microphone and to a live audience numbering close to a thousand. But what I said came straight from the heart.

I told the audience that this had been the most special year of my life. Over the course of it, I had come to love the Abruzzo and to feel that Castel di Sangro was the true home of my soul. I had also come to know and to love each and every member of the Castel di Sangro team.

Now, I said, *"per me, è arrivata l'ora di partire."* The time had come for me to leave. Much as I longed to return to my wife and children in America, leaving was going to break my heart, because I knew that never again would I be so closely associated with such a magnificent group of men as the players who composed this Castel di Sangro *calcio* team.

I said I hoped very much that in years to come, the people of the area would remain loyal *tifosi* of Castel di Sangro *"in tempi buoni e cattivi"* – in good times and bad. And that if they ever felt their support starting to waver, they should simply remember the American, who had arrived in September and who had *mantenuta fiducia* – kept the faith – all season long.

Perhaps it was that mood – my guard down, my emotions drained, my thinking only of the happy ending – that caused me to be less than fully attentive half an hour or so later when a player walked up to me and began a quiet conversation. His identity matters much less than what he had to say.

"Thank you, Joe. That was kind."

"You're welcome. It was also well deserved."

"Yes, but someday you really should learn how to speak Italian."

"Vaffa . . . ," I began, in mock anger, but he quickly put his hand on my arm.

"Joe," he said. "Do the team and yourself one more favor."

"What is that?"

"Do not come with us to Bari."

"What?!"

"Stay here. Relax. Watch the match on television if you must. But simply rejoin us when we return. Do not come."

"Why do you joke with me like this? Of course I am coming to Bari. Why do you tell me I should not?"

"Only to make your life a little simpler. And ours, too. There is no more I can say. But please think very hard about it."

Then he walked on, leaving me alone in the darkness, a half-full wineglass in my hand, and not the slightest idea of what he'd been talking about.

It had been hot, truly hot, in the days preceding our departure for Lecce. But that had been early spring compared with the heat that blasted Castel di Sangro on Friday. A scorching, dry wind blew straight up from Africa, across the hundreds of miles of flat peninsula that lay to our south, and whacked us with the force of a hard slap across a sunburned cheek. This was the true sirocco, well known and much dreaded in Sicily and along the southern coast of Italy, but virtually unknown as far north as the Abruzzo.

When it did blow, however, the older and wiser residents of the town were known to say that it brought evil to where evil had not been before. It was truly an ill wind, which in the Abruzzo might rise only once or twice in a generation, but when it did, there was no escaping its ill effects.

And it was blowing full force as we boarded the bus for Bari on Saturday morning. The player who had spoken to me on Thursday night simply looked at me and shook his head. Then we were off, into the mouth of the dragon.

40

We'd been traveling south for about an hour – the temperature outside already well above ninety degrees Fahrenheit and the sirocco headwind so strong, it actually slowed the speed of the bus – when a player took the empty seat next to me and asked if he could look at my copy of that morning's *Il Corriere dello Sport*.

I handed it to him, already open to the section on *Serie B*. The lead story was about the extraordinary squeeze near the top of this year's *classifica*. While Brescia had already clinched promotion, the next four were Empoli (61), Lecce (60), Bari (59), Genoa (58). Only one of the four would not make it to to *Serie A*, but going into the last match of the season, it still could be any one of the four.

Empoli and Lecce, which would be playing teams already relegated to *C1*, looked like sure winners. So did Genoa, at home against relegated Palermo. Only Bari might face trouble, if we were in the mood to give it to them. If we even drew at Bari while Genoa won, it would be Bari, not Genoa, condemned to another year in *Serie B*.

The situation was, as *Il Corriere* said, *"molta delicata"* – very delicate, especially given that promotion to *Serie A* was worth more than $10 million to a team when all the corollary benefits were factored in.

After studying the page for a moment, the player said to me, *"Povero il Genoa."* Poor Genoa.

"Perchè?" Why?

"Because they will win but lose anyway."

"What do you mean?"

"They lose. They do not go to *Serie A*."

"But not if Empoli or Lecce or Bari should lose?"

"That will not happen."

"E' poco probabile, ma –" It is hardly probable, but –

"Scusa, Joe. È impossibile."

"Ah, but the ball is round," I said. "In *calcio* nothing is impossible."

"Joe, è vero? Tu non capisci? È tutto a posto." Is it true? You don't understand? Everything is arranged.

"Di cosa stai parlando?" What are you talking about?

He suddenly looked troubled and did not answer right away. Then he said, *"Scusami, Joe. Sarebbe meglio dimenticare tutto."* It might be better to forget everything.

He stood quickly, handed me back my newspaper, and returned to the rear of the bus.

I was getting some strange vibrations here, and they were not all coming from the laboring engine. As the sun beat down, however, I found myself dozing off even as a movie called *Cage II: The Arena of Death* blared its way through my nervous system. The plot consisted of a series of fights to the death, engaged in by men locked in cages with one another. As I dozed, the cage transmuted itself into a soccer goal and I found myself as a goalkeeper once more, with the bloodthirsty cries of the crowd in the movie transformed into cheers for each save I made.

I woke up after one especially jarring confrontation to find that I'd been joined by Lotti.

"Non ti piace?" he said, smiling, and gesturing toward the small screen. You don't like it?

"Massimo," I said, *"questo è solo per gli schemi."* This is only for the brain-dead.

"Infatti," he laughed, meaning, Yes, in this case that's true.

But then he turned serious and spoke to me in a very low voice.

"Joe," he said, *"è importante. Mi ascolti?"* This is important. Are you listening to me? I nodded and rubbed my eyes.

"Ho sempre voluto poter giocare contro il Pescara, ma domani, grazie a Dio, io non gioco." I will always wish that I could have played in the match against Pescara. But I thank God that I will not play tomorrow.

By now I was fully awake.

"*Perchè?*" I asked. "*Per paura?*" Why? Because of your fear? By now he knew me well enough to understand when I was teasing.

Still, he answered with the utmost seriousness. "*Non per paura, Joe. Per onore.*" Not fear, but honor.

And then he, too, walked to the back of the bus before I could ask any more questions.

We did not go all the way into Bari, but stopped at a beachfront hotel with a grand swimming pool in a resort town forty-five minutes up the coast.

"*Tranquillo,*" Jaconi told me as I checked in. He was smiling and seemed utterly relaxed. "*Molto tranquillo.*" His wife had come with him for this final match, so he'd driven down a day in advance instead of taking the bus.

By now, I was far from *tranquillo* myself. But maybe I was only a victim of my own overheated imagination. I found Jaconi's presence and manner reassuring. Surely, I reasoned, he would not bring his wife all the way from Civitanova to Bari unless it was to watch his team play with maximum effort in its final match, and perhaps even produce one last incredible feat of magic in front of 60,000 furious and disbelieving fanatics, and in the face of overpowering odds.

The heat was, if possible, even worse than in Lecce. By now it was June, but my naive hope for air-conditioning was quickly dashed by a desk clerk who said, "Of course we will not make air condition. We are cool by ocean breezings."

"*Lo scirocco?*" I asked.

He shrugged. "Mister," he said, "we will not make air condition because one time in ten year we have *lo scirocco*. Anyway, this be Puglia. Here we no waste the money like America."

"*Grazie,*" I said, and walked away. I'd begun my stay in Italy by trying to argue with a man behind the desk of a hotel, and I was not going to end it the same way. In fact, I'd come to consider it a rule of thumb: When in Italy do not *ever* try to argue with a man behind a desk. Because he is behind the desk and not in front it, he knows he is right. If he were not right, he would not be behind the desk. Bulldozer logic.

Almost physically disabled by the heat, the players shoved their dinners aside and made directly for the *piscina* (swimming pool) located in front of the hotel. Uncharacteristically, they directed that large quantities of beer and wine be brought to them. This was not behavior I thought Jaconi would have tolerated, especially not on the night before a match, but Jaconi had retired elsewhere with his wife.

It was not more than an hour before the players decided that anyone who walked out the front door of the hotel in search of a whisper of fresh air should be thrown immediately into the pool. This was not quite as provocative as it sounded because we were the only guests staying there and, other than me, the only prospective victims would be officials of *La Società* (not including Gravina, who would be driving down and back the next day).

To save anyone the task of deciding whether or not I should be spared, I came out the front door fully dressed and jumped into the pool unassisted.

This provoked widespread cries of *"Bravo!"* and *"Grande Joe!"* – cries that I realized I was not going to hear again and that I would miss.

I was treading water and thinking that it might be more bearable to spend the night in the pool instead of my room when I realized I had brought only a clean shirt for the next day and no other change of clothes. So I climbed out, went to my room, hung my clothes on the balcony, where the sirocco would dry them within an hour, and returned to poolside swathed in towels.

I took a beer and a poolside chair in that order and simply sat back and absorbed the ambience. Leaves of tall palm trees slapped together in the wind, but closer to poolside snatches of conversation could be heard.

"Three goals at most," a player said.

"Yes," another answered, "but not three to nothing."

"No," said a third, "we must score one."

"But not too early," said another, "or it looks like a *minaccia*" – a threat.

I sat very still and began to listen with intensity. Perhaps my new garb had rendered me unrecognizable, or else, at this point, the players simply did not care what I heard.

"But three at the most, that is agreed." There was a murmur of concurrence. I could not be sure how many players were actively involved in this discussion, but it was at least half a dozen.

"Maybe Bari gets greedy and tries for more."

"Don't worry. They have been instructed also."

"How do we score? And when?"

"That has been arranged. A *rigore*."

"A *rigore?*" one player protested. "That means one more fucking easy goal for Claudio, who does not need it."

"So what? He deserves it. Look what he did for us last week."

"Suppose he misses?"

"He won't miss."

"Suppose it is saved?"

"It will not be saved. Fontana is not an idiot." Fontana was the Bari goalkeeper.

The conversation lapsed for a few minutes. I could hear the sounds of cigarettes being lit, of wine being poured, of fresh cans of beer being opened.

Then a player said, "The first must come immediately. Even before the people take their seats. That way it is not noticed so much. And then two more, as they develop, but all in the first half."

"And in the second?"

A player laughed. "In the second we all lie down and take a nap."

"But this will not look bad?" a younger player asked, sounding worried.

Another laughed. "Look bad to whom? To the Bari *pubblico* that is already hysterical with the joy of returning to *Serie A?* To Matarrese, their president? On the highlight films of tonight, which no one will watch? Do not worry. No one pays attention at these times. Everyone looks the other way. Only be careful never to shoot at the Bari goal tomorrow. That would be a mistake."

Then someone stood and walked past the chair where I was sitting. He looked down. "Joe?" he said. "Is that you?"

"Yes."

"And you have been listening?"

"I have been sitting here. It was not possible not to hear."

"No problem, Joe. But this is *privato*. This is not for *il pubblico*."

"Fuck you," I said in English.

Another player immediately stepped forward. *"Quest' informazione deve rimanere strettamente confidenziale."* This information must be kept strictly confidential.

"Bullshit," I said in English.

"Joe," said a third player. "All year we trust you, and now you must not betray us."

"Betray?" I said. *"Scusa ma voi siete i traditori."* Excuse me, but you are the betrayers.

"Perchè siamo costretti. Non abbiamo un' altra scelta." We are forced. We have no choice. *"Non siamo felici."* We are not happy.

"Mi fate schifo!" You make me sick!

Then a player stepped forward and actually sat at the end of my pool chair. *"Mi dispiace dovertelo dire ma gli affari sono affari e questo non è affare tuo."* I'm sorry to say this to you, but business is business, and this business is none of yours.

"Everything," I said, "is the business of my book."

The player took a deep breath and looked back over at the others. Then he said, *"Sarebbe meglio se ci pensi di nuovo."* It might be better if you thought it over again.

"Mi dispiace ma devo rifiutare," I said in a tone of artificial formality. I am afraid I must refuse.

The player grew suddenly angry. *"In ogni modo non lo devi scrivere!"* On no account must you write this! Never before had a player spoken to me in such a voice.

I stood, clutching as many of my towels as I could grab.

"Mi spiace moltissimo," I said. *"Comunque senza dubbio voi tutti siete truffatori, proprio come Rezza e Gravina."* I feel awful. However, without doubt, you are all crooks, just like Rezza and Gravina.

No one said a word in response.

"Merdacce!" I added. Scum. *"Buona notte, merdacce! Spero che domani avrete quel che meritate."* I hope tomorrow you get what you deserve.

Having delivered myself of that sentiment, I walked back into the hotel and directly to my room and closed and locked the door behind me and wondered then how I was going to get through one of the most miserable nights of my life.

My *ragazzi*. These players I'd come to care about as I'd cared about no other group of men in all my life. In front of 60,000 people the next day, they were going to betray values far more important than my opinion of them, but I felt personally and deeply betrayed nonetheless.

It was one of the few nights of my life about which I can say with certainty I did not sleep for even a minute. I never even came close. I felt sick enough because of what I'd just heard and said, but beyond that the air, or lack of it, in my room seemed as if it might literally suffocate me.

Eventually, I dragged my mattress off my bed and out onto a concrete balcony, where the temperature might have been two or three degrees cooler but where the noise from an all-night disco located next to our hotel was as loud as the sound tracks on the bus. The sirocco had blown itself out, leaving behind a mass of still and hot air that weighed on me as heavily as my thoughts.

In the morning I put on my dry but sandy clothes and walked directly to poolside, where I made a great show of taking out my largest notebook and writing in it, although mostly all I wrote was, "I can't fucking believe this," on every page.

Eventually, Lotti came and took the empty chair next to mine. For a long time, we each sat still, saying nothing.

"Massimo," I finally asked, "would you do it?"

"Would I let in a goal deliberately?"

"Yes."

"Joe, I would like to say no with certainty. That would be simple and it would make you less troubled and would ensure that I would be treated as a man of honor in your book."

"You will be anyway, Massimo. Just please tell me the truth about this."

"Joe, the truth is, I do not know. I have never been confronted with such a situation, although I know they exist. Some teams that badly need points pay for them. Others to whom the points mean nothing accept. And it is not always only a matter of money. It can be a favor requested or a favor repaid between the presidents of the *Società*. It can be many things. In Italy it is called *il sistema,* and for someone who has not grown up with it, I am sure it can seem very complex."

"It doesn't seem complex. It just seems crooked."

He actually reached over and patted my arm. "Joe, speaking as your friend, and with the greatest of respect, I must tell you that I fear this is the price you pay for being *americano.* There are some aspects to our way of life that you simply cannot understand. And this one, because you care about it with such passion, when you cannot understand it, you curse it. And you curse also the players, who have come to care for you as you have for them. It would be a great pity for the season to end with such a painful misunderstanding."

"The players talk of my betrayal," I said. "But it is they who betray themselves."

"No, Joe, it is not so easy. This was not a choice the players made. Imagine if the Bari *Società* says to Castel di Sangro, 'Here are two *miliardi* for your help, plus we will not forget the favor you have done.' Joe: I know nothing of this, understand. I am only speak *per ipotesi*." Hypothetically. "Just so you might learn *la realtà*. But one thing, Joe, *non è ipotetica*. If Signor Rezza has said yes, every player must obey."

Then Lotti went elsewhere, and again I was alone for a while.

The next person to join me was Spinosa.

"Ti piace che il miracolo si sta transformando in merda?" I asked. Do you like to see the miracle turning to shit?

"Calma, Joe. Nessuno è contento. Ma nessuno può scegliere." No one is happy. But no one has a choice.

"Sì, sì, è il sistema," I said, waving a hand in disgust.

"Joe, I did not come to quarrel with you. I hope you understand that certain things must happen even though all players wish they would not. With great respect, you are an American who comes only to watch us for one season. Now you go home, but we must stay. For all our careers, all our lives, we must stay here.

"In Italy to have a career means many times you are unhappy. You must close your eyes and hold your nose and, most important, hold your tongue. I think this is not good, but also I know this is life. I hope that you understand this, at least in a small way. But if you do not, I ask anyway that you do not use *parole dure* – harsh words. Truly, there is enough misery over this without your curses to ring in our ears."

"But, Piero, I just cannot accept that a team which all year has fought so hard to win will now go out and play to lose!"

"Joe, it is only our bad luck that it is us. For any team that would play Bari today is the same. It is demanded by *il sistema*. You know that the president of Bari is Signor Matarrese. Do you know that it is his brother who has been the president of the *Federazione*? And a third brother is a cardinal in the Vatican?

"Anyway, today the team is tired. You know that. Tired in the legs, tired in the mind, tired in the heart. So they are told, 'You will lose.' If no one said nothing, we could not win against Bari."

"Then why is this necessary?"

"Well, Bari is very tired, too. Maybe they make a mistake. Maybe Claudio scores, or Spinesi. Maybe Bari hits the pole many times, as Lecce did. And a one-to-one draw would be for Bari a bigger calamity than the *terremoto*," than an earthquake. "For a matter of such importance, not one *granello*" – not one speck –"can be left up to chance."

"Piero, I will always have the greatest respect for you. But you will never convince me that this is right."

"Well, think also of this: Our job from the first week of the season was to win *la salvezza*. And we do. So we do our job: for ourselves, for the people of the town, even for you, to give a happy ending in your book. What happens after is not important."

"But it's wrong."

Spinosa smiled. "Joe, are you suddenly become the priest? I do not sit here for *confessarmi*," to make my confession. "I only wish to help you understand. Okay, I cannot do that. But I can tell you these things to remember: We are not the only one.

"Every season, at the end, is like this. One year ago, in the last week, Brescia must win at Cesena or else they face the relegation. *Pagano per i punti*. They pay for points. For three points. And they score two goals easily and win the match, two to one.

"And this year, Joe. I know of Lucchese, and Salernitana. *Pagano per i punti*. In the end they need to make forty-four points, just as we do. But they do not wait to the end. They take care of their business last Sunday, when they play Cremonese, from last place. You say *senza dubbio* they will win. But again there must be no *incertezza*," no uncertainty. "So they pay and they score four goals. You look in your statistics, Joe: Not one time all year, except last Sunday, does Lucchese score four goals in a match.

"And who also needs to be sure of forty-four points, not forty-three? La Salernitana. You look again in your statistic. In all the season, not one time does Salernitana win *fuori casa*. And also not on Sunday, but they make a draw at Venezia, one to one. For Venezia the result has no importance. For Salernitana it mean everything. Salernitana scores in fifteen minutes. Two minutes later Venezia scores. For the rest of the match it is *ballare il valzer* – to dance the waltz."

We fell silent, as Lotti and I had done earlier, and as the heat built and as the sun moved closer to the position it would occupy at noon.

"*È molto complicato,* Joe," Spinosa said. "I cannot explain. Probably, no one can. Probably, you must be born here and grow up here and only in that way you understand. It is like speaking our language. You have made much progression, but even you would not say you understand as much as you would like."

"Of course not. I still feel like an idiot in Italian."

"You are not an idiot in any language. But maybe think of *il sistema* like our language. It would be many years before you understood enough. And even then, if you study and practice for twenty years, still an Italian could say in half a minute, 'This is a *straniero* who never can truly be one of us.'

"I am sorry if this make you sad. I am sorry if this make you angry. But I must tell you as a friend that I am sorry also that last night you believe it was necessary for you to curse and to shout at these players. When one does not understand, Joe, that is the time for the soft voice. Or, maybe better, for no voice at all."

And then Spinosa, too, went away.

Yet all the rationalizations seemed abstract. Only the fact of *la bustarella* – the bribe paid or debt incurred or old debt canceled – the details of which would be known only to Matarrese and to Rezza (and probably also to Gravina), seemed real to me.

And so it remained, even on the bus ride to the stadium. None of the players made any reference to my outburst or to any of the things they'd said that triggered it. Only Cei, who was not playing because he'd received a red card in the final minutes of the Pescara match, stopped by my seat and said, "Remember. We are the land of Dante, but also of Machiavelli."

Then the bus pulled through a narrow metal gate and went down a sheltered ramp that led directly to the back door of the visitors' locker room. I'd never seen such tight security at any stadium. No one who did not belong here could possibly penetrate its many layers. And yet, as I stepped off the bus, I found myself looking directly into the eyes of Signor Rezza.

He was standing less than five feet from the exit. Every player who stepped down to enter the locker room would have to undergo his close scrutiny.

His usual two bodyguards were with him. But he was flanked also by four additional men I'd not seen before.

Suddenly, nothing was abstract. Signor Rezza had come to an away match. To a meaningless match, after his team already had won *la salvezza*. Clearly, he not come for the sport.

He did not speak a word to any player or to me. He did not have to. His stare, cold and pitiless, caught the eye of everyone who came off the bus. If a last-minute reminder had been needed, Signor Rezza was it, in all the corruption and menace his sagging face and blunt cigar exuded.

As for the match? At the opening whistle Tonino kicked the ball directly to a Bari midfielder who passed to an undefended Bari forward who shot from fifteen yards out and scored as De Juliis, waiting until the ball was safely past him, dove in its direction. That procedure had required less than twenty seconds.

For the next half hour the teams took turns kicking the ball out of bounds. Then a Bari player sent a long pass downfield to a teammate who was standing in front of the goal, with Luca D'Angelo behind him. Luca, who had blocked a hundred such passes during the season, jumped, but at the same time twisted his head out of the way to ensure that it would not make contact with the ball. The Bari player, unimpeded, headed it directly into the net.

Two minutes before the half ended, as a coterie of Castel di Sangro players stood by watching, a Bari midfielder launched a shot from twenty yards. De Juliis gave it a friendly wave as it went by. That made three, so De Juliis knew that his work, such as it might have been, was now finished for the season.

Just seconds before the half ended, Claudio ran into the Bari penalty area and tripped over himself and fell down as a Bari defender stood next to him, watching. The *arbitro,* one Treossi of Forli, another man who primarily worked *Serie A* matches and wanted to continue doing so, signaled for a penalty kick.

Claudio always shot penalties with his right foot. This meant that the ball had a tendency to go into what would be the left side of the net as he faced it. Apparently having been made aware of this, the Bari *portiere* lined up not in the center of the goal but two strides to *his* left, farther from where the ball could be expected to go.

And that was exactly where the ball went, as the Bari *portiere* dived toward it but from too far away. It was Claudio's tenth and last goal of the year (his fourth on a penalty kick) and it made the score – *che sorpresa!* – 3–1 at halftime.

The old men who took the sun while leaning against the facade of the Bank of Napoli building in the Castel di Sangro central square each morning displayed more energy on their most lethargic of days than did either team throughout the second half.

But just to remove any *granello* of doubt that might remain, Osvaldo removed Claudio after only ten minutes had passed and sent on Michelini. Trailing by two goals with thirty-five minutes remaining, the Castel di Sangro manager removes his one offensive star in favor of an aged midfielder who had never scored a goal in *Serie B* and who had managed just two in *C1* in a career that had spanned sixteen seasons.

The final score – *che sorpresa!* – was Bari 3, Castel di Sangro 1.

Genoa had won, 4–1, but Bari would be going up to *Serie A*. And Signor Rezza went back to Castel di Sangro, having apparently been granted safe passage for the day.

41

I must admit I was not good company on the bus ride. I tried as hard as I could to rationalize what I had seen, to remind myself of the powers of *il sistema,* of which obviously I had only the dimmest understanding, but the anger and disgust would not leave me.

Of them all, Rimedio had been the only one to play an honest match, in my opinion. He sat directly across the aisle from me, but immediately turned his face to the window and neither looked to nor spoke to anyone for hours. Perhaps this had been just as ugly a part of his education as it had been of mine, but I did not want to force him into deception by asking.

At one point Spinesi asked me if something was wrong.

"Two things, Gionatha," I said. "One, you are too young to be so corrupt, and, two, you are not even a good actor." Many players heard my remark. Not one, not even Spinesi, responded.

The only player with whom I initiated a conversation was Luca D'Angelo.

"So in the end, Luca," I said, "you do not have the courage of your politics."

"Tu non sei costretto a parlare," he said. You don't have to speak.

"No, but I choose to. You speak of the *Brigate Rosse"* – the Red Brigades – "of the 1970s as your heroes. But maybe they were only cowards, too. Killing the unsuspecting and defenseless for the sake of their own *sistema."*

"Ti consiglio di non dire stupidaggine!" I advise you not to talk nonsense.

"Luca," I said, *"penso che Che Guevara si vergognerebbe di te."* I think Che Guevara would be ashamed of you.

If I had called his mother a whore, the insult would not have been worse. He looked at me as balefully as anyone ever had in all my life. This was one man who would never be a friend again.

"ArrivederLa!" he said. This was the highly formal way to say goodbye, containing none of the warmth of *arrivederci.* And it was the last word Luca ever spoke to me.

After that, I slumped in my seat, turned my head to the window, and feigned sleep.

But at 2:10 A.M. when the bus finally arrived back at the parking lot outside our stadium and Roberto Alberti approached me to say, "We will leave from here at nine to go to the graves," I looked at him and my eyes filled with tears.

"I cannot go with you," I said. "Because after today I think you bring no honor to those graves. I think Pippo and Danilo would be ashamed of you, and of all the others. But thank you very much for inviting me."

"Suit yourself, Joe," he said, with no change of expression on his face. "Suit yourself."

I turned away and walked back through the night to my apartment.

On Monday morning I made arrangements to fly home Tuesday. Marcella's son Giovanni would drive me to Rome. I spent the rest of the day in my apartment, packing. In early afternoon I ducked out to the market across the street to buy some cheese and bread and wine. I didn't want to talk to anyone. I could not bear to go to Marcella's. I did not want to see the players who would have returned from their visit to Pippo's and Danilo's graves. My phone rang repeatedly but I did not answer.

In the evening, I wrote a note and pinned it to Osvaldo's door.

> If I may be permitted to express my opinion,
> I would like to say that you have disgraced
> both your profession and all of *calcio.*
> Sunday was shameful and repugnant and
> a betrayal of all in which I believe.

Well, in my book I will write the truth.
Notwithstanding your involvement
in this ugly fraud, I am extremely grateful
to you for having helped me so much
this season.
Best wishes for the season to follow,
and please give my warm regards to your wife.
And please show this also to Gravina, *il patron*
of this criminal *sistema*.

Later that night my living room light was on and my shade was not down because of the heat, and as I looked out my window, I saw Spinosa and his wife and son walking across the parking lot, which was a shortcut to the outdoor ice cream and coffee parlor where the players had enjoyed passing time.

He could see me clearly and he waved, then held up his cell phone. A moment later my telephone rang. He asked me to meet them for a final cup of coffee, which I did. On my way out, I noticed that my note had been removed from Osvaldo's door, which was strange, because Osvaldo was not expected back in town until Wednesday.

As soon as I reached the terrace outside the coffee shop, I saw that not only were the Spinosas at one table but that Gravina and Signor Rezza were at another.

"When is the last time Signor Rezza has come here to eat ice cream?" I asked Spinosa.

"Mai," he said. Never.

Then I waited for whatever would happen next. I did not have to wait long. In less than five minutes Gravina was standing over me, clearly wishing to say more than just good-bye.

I stood and turned to face him. I'd never seen him so close to losing control. He was so agitated that not only his hands but his voice shook, and his whole head trembled on his neck when he spoke, which he did, fast and loudly.

He told me my note to Jaconi was an insult not only to Jaconi but to *La Società*.

I said, "Good. That was what I intended."

He said it was also an insult to both him and to Signor Rezza personally, and that such personal insults could not be tolerated. Something would have to be done.

"Well, I'm leaving tomorrow, so whatever it is, do it fast."

"If you put into your book one word about *una bustarella,* about any problem with the Bari match, you will be so sorry that you will never wish to write again. Do you understand me?" And he looked in Signor Rezza's direction, as if to scare me, which, in fact, he did.

But I was more angry than afraid. *"Perchè guardi?!"* I shouted. *"Lui non sa nemmeno leggere."* Why do you look at him? He cannot even read.

Gravina put his finger on my chest. I pushed it away, but slowly. By now, quite a crowd had gathered.

He started shouting about how sorry he would make me that I had ever come to Italy, that he would see to it I never returned, and that he would be sure not a single copy of my book would ever be printed in Italian.

With that I lost any trace of dignity I might have had, as well as any remaining self-control.

"Chiudi il becco, cretino! Me ne fotto di te!" Shut your mouth, you moron! I don't give a fuck about you! Then I laughed and pointed at him. *"Tu credi che il DHEA servirà a tenere il tuo cazzo duro. Che coglionate!"* You believe DHEA will help your cock to stay hard. What fucking stupidity! *"Stronzo! Terrone!"* You shit! You *southerner!*

"Joe!" I heard Spinosa call.

At the same time, Signor Rezza made a noise. Gravina turned immediately toward him. A quick nonverbal communication passed between them. After this, Gravina said only that I would be facing big, big trouble from his *avvocati.* Fine. I'd had troubles with lawyers before. It was the *guardie del corpo,* the bodyguards, who worried me.

But that was the end of the scene. I don't think Gravina had been pleased to have between fifty and a hundred people overhear my comment that he was taking DHEA in an attempt to enhance his sexual performance.

Signor Rezza and Gravina then left, and Spinosa and I finished our coffees. I had no idea what Spinosa's young son had made of all this, and it was not a point I wanted to pursue.

Spinosa shook his head in what appeared to be genuine sorrow. "Now it is ruined," he said. "Now it is ruined forever between Castel di Sangro and you. Oh, Joe, you do not listen. The time for the soft voice! The time for no voice at all!"

"Piero, I was too angry."

"Always, Joe, that is the most important time for no voice."

Calming down a bit, I sighed. "I know you are right. I know I was wrong to speak that way. And it breaks my heart to think that tomorrow I will leave here and that I will never see any of the players again."

"You may see them, Joe. But not here. You will not be welcome again in Castel di Sangro."

"But my book was supposed to have a happy ending."

"And it could have, Joe. If you had permitted it to be so. But now you leave enemies and much bad feeling behind. And for what? Do you think you have changed *il sistema?*"

"Not by *un granello*," I admitted.

"Che peccato," he said. What a pity.

"Che fare?" I asked. What's to be done?

He shook his head. *"Niente. Joe, quello che è fatto è fatto."* Nothing. What's done cannot be undone.

Then he stood, saying it was time to go home and put his son to bed. I hugged the boy and then I hugged Fabrizia and then I hugged Spinosa with extra strength.

"I hope at least that you will be my friend," I said.

"Sempre," he said. *"Buon viaggio."*

And then he walked away with his family. Back toward the parking lot that led to the stone steps up to their lovely home across from the church that had not been bombed in the war. Spinosa, the man who had made the miracle happen. Possibly the best of a very good bunch.

Bari or no Bari, I knew I would miss them all for the rest of my life.

Yes, I would have had a happy ending if only I'd left a week sooner. But now it was too late for that. *Quello che è fatto è fatto.* What's done is done.

Va bè, not all fairy tales have happy endings. Just like not all miracles are forever.

For the Record

Within six weeks of the Bari match, Gravina sold fourteen of the twenty players who had made up the squad at season's end. Only Lotti, D'Angelo, Alberti, Cristiano, Rimedio, and Spinesi played for the team the following year. Even Marcella was "fired," as Gravina awarded the team's business to a restaurant in which he held an interest.

In March of the 1997–98 season, following Castel di Sangro's fifth scoreless defeat in a six-match span, Jaconi, too, was dismissed. Winning only five matches all season, the team finished at the bottom and was relegated to *Serie C1*.

As the 1998–99 season began, only Rimedio remained of the squad that had won *la salvezza*. Alberti and Michelini had retired. Di Fabio, De Juliis, Cei, Prete, Galli, Pistella, and Albieri had gone to other *C1* teams, as did Jaconi, who was hired by Savoia, a club located on the outskirts of Napoli. Altamura joined a *C2* squad.

Remaining in *Serie B* were only Lotti, Cristiano, Martino, Russo, and Franceschini. Fusco and Bonomi, however, had advanced to *Serie A,* both with Empoli (to whom Bonomi was sold by Torino). More recently, Spinesi, too, reached *Serie A* – ironically, with Bari, the team against which he had been so afraid to score. (Bonomi, incidentally, became the first ex–Castel di Sangro player ever to score a goal in S*erie A*.)

All criminal charges against Prete were eventually dropped, while none were ever filed against Gravina. Prete's wife, however, remained in custody, even into 1999.

A monument was built at the north end of the stadium to honor Pippo and Danilo. As for the others, their memories and the memory of that most special season of *salvezza* live on the hearts of the people.

LA CLASSIFICA SERIE B, 1996–97

Team	PTS.	W	D	L	Goals For	Goals Against
Brescia	66	18	12	8	49	34
Empoli	64	17	13	8	45	34
Lecce	63	16	15	7	52	39
Bari	62	15	17	6	52	35
Genoa	61	15	16	7	58	31
Pescara	54	14	12	12	50	38
Chievo Verona	54	12	18	8	44	40
Ravenna	52	14	13	11	43	35
Torino	50	13	11	14	45	48
Reggina	49	12	13	13	40	43
Foggia	48	11	15	12	40	40
Padova	48	11	15	12	41	43
Venezia	46	10	16	12	47	49
Lucchese	45	10	15	13	36	44
Salernitana	44	10	14	14	31	44
CASTEL DI SANGRO	44	12	8	18	29	45
Cosenza	41	9	14	15	44	55
Cesena	40	9	13	16	36	45
Palermo	35	6	17	15	40	55
Cremonese	32	7	11	20	30	55

STATISTICAL SUMMARY: CASTEL DI SANGRO, 1996–97

player	matches	min. played	goals	pagelle
ALBERTI, Roberto	32	2715	1	6.17
ALBIERI, Luca	15	313	1	6.33
ALTAMURA, Antonello	26	1751	1	6.05
BIONDI, Filippo	3	34	0	s.v.
BONOMI, Claudio	34	2921	10	6.31
CEI, Davide	27	2311	0	6.25
CRISTIANO, Domenico	20	1009	0	5.96
D'ANGELO, Luca	31	2517	1	6.05
DE JULIIS, Roberto	17	1521	n\a	6.18
DI FABIO, Guido	31	2572	1	6.05
DI VINCENZO, Danilo	9	656	2	5.78
FRANCESCHINI, Daniele	8	437	0	5.83
FUSCO, Pietro	30	2678	0	6.06
GALLI, Giacomo	17	1374	2	5.75
LOTTI, Massimo	19	1702	n\a	6.48
MARTINO, Tonino	34	2754	0	6.15
MICHELINI, Paolo	20	1258	0	5.88
PISTELLA, Andrea	34	1996	3	5.70
PRETE, Pierluigi	29	2356	0	5.98
RIMEDIO, Fabio	13	521	0	5.62
RUSSO, Daniele	11	462	1	5.92
SPINESI, Gionatha	20	1612	3	6.05
SPINOSA, Pietro	3	107	n\a	s.v.

Acknowledgments

I would like to thank the following people, who in one way or another contributed greatly to the quality of the time I have spent thus far following *il calcio* in Italy: Alexi Lalas and Jill McNeal, Michele Kreek, Vittorio Petrone, Roberto Baggio, Pietro Leonardi and Serena Nalesso, Renato and Carla Groppo, Massimo Pacifico, Bill and Edvige Coleman, Barbara Giannini, Corrado Miraldi, Mario Giaquinto, Italo Cucci, Leopoldo Gasbarro, Andrea Schianchi, Leandro Leonardi, Vincenzo Frascone, Maurizio D'Angelo Petrarca, Glauco Balzano, the officers of the Little Club of Genoa, "the Major," wherever he might be, the *fortissimi e troppo gentile* people of Castel di Sangro – all of them – and most of all, of course, the Castel di Sangro *ragazzi* and their families, who generously permitted me, for a time, the illusion that I was one of them.

To Marcella and her family, and to the finest next-door neighbor a man could ever have, Osvaldo Jaconi, I extend my deepest and most sincere gratitude.

And don't we all wish it had ended differently.

JOE MCGINNISS
Williamstown, Massachusetts
January 15, 1999